I0816811

The Soul of the Mishna

Yakov Nagen

The Soul of the Mishna

נשמת המשנה

Translated by Elie Leshem

Yeshivat Otniel
Maggid Books

The Soul of the Mishna

First Edition, 2021

Maggid Books
An imprint of Koren Publishers Jerusalem Ltd.

POB 8531, New Milford, CT 06776-8531, USA
& POB 4044, Jerusalem 9104001, Israel
www.maggidbooks.com

Cover design: Yehudit Cohen

The publication of this book was made possible
through the generous support of *The Jewish Book Trust*.

ISBN 978-1-59264-582-4, *hardcover*

A CIP catalogue record for this title is
available from the British Library

Printed and bound in the United States

Lovingly dedicated to my parents

Azriel and Ahuva Genack

*From you I have learned
love of God, Torah, and the Jewish people.*

Dedicated in honor of our children,
With gratitude to those who have been
and continue to be instrumental in their Jewish education,
And in memory of Dr. Saul G. Agus z"l

Nicole and Raanan Agus

In memory of our grandparents,
whose lives exemplified to us
the Nishmat HaMishna

Anny and Kalman Singer z"l
Yvonne and Julius Kuhl z"l
Rose and Benjamin Berger z"l
Frida and Shimon Laufer z"l and Aryeh Leib David z"l

Rachel and Shimon Laufer and family

Contents

"The blessed Holy One said, 'It is not good that the man should be alone; I will make him a helpmeet for him' – that is the Mishna"

(Zohar, Bereshit 1:27b)

Dvir's Final Mishna

In Ḥanukka of 2008, after years of exercising restraint, Israel launched Operation Cast Lead in the Gaza Strip, to defend residents of the south from unrelenting terror attacks. On January 4, 2009, the eighth of Tevet, the second day of the ground operation, the sad tidings arrived that the war had claimed its first victim among Israeli fighters. That was the day I first heard the name Dvir Emanuelof.

I, along with the rest of the people of Israel, was moved by Dvir's story. Having lost his father, he could have forgone combat service; yet he insisted on serving as a commander in an infantry unit. I did not imagine that in the ensuing months I would learn much more about the short, rich, meaningful life of Dvir, of blessed memory, or that everywhere I would go I would run into people who knew and loved him. And I certainly did not anticipate finding out that I, too, had a connection, albeit indirect, with him. I had touched his life through my book *The Soul of the Mishna*, and he touched my life deeply after his death.

It emerged that Dvir had identified to a large extent with the study method and approaches presented in *The Soul of the Mishna*. He studied the book alone often, and also studied it together with his mother, Dalia, in a regular *ḥavruta* study date. During a memorial event for Dvir thirty days after his death, the family asked me to explain what was behind my decision to write *The Soul of the Mishna*. The truth of my pre-prepared answer was reinforced by the life story of Dvir and the rest of his dear family.

Although I teach in a yeshiva, I believe the main arena for the revelation of the Torah is outside the walls of the *beit midrash*, in the broader circles of the Jewish people. The source for the commandment to study the Torah is the verse in *Shema* that enjoins us to "talk of them," to speak about the mitzvot. However, the verse does not tell us to do so in the *beit midrash* or the synagogue, but rather "when you sit in your house, and when you walk by the way" (Deuteronomy 6:7). The Torah's place is in the home, within the family, in the conversation between parents and children; its place is on the road, where one encounters the outside world.

But what aspect of Torah is most suited for the house and the road? I believe that the Mishna has an important role to play there. That is because the Mishna is easy to study; it is written in accessible, succinct Hebrew, summarizing the conclusions while omitting the lengthy discussions that underlie them. However, these qualities are a mixed blessing – by the same token, they can make studying Mishna a banal, technical exercise in reading and recitation. We must therefore learn to see the Mishna as a rich, astonishing document, a book holding the promise of profound discoveries regarding Torah, God, and life. It was in order to expose that dimension of the Mishna that I wrote this book.

When Dvir, of blessed memory, and Dalia set a regular study date, they opted to study the Mishna as a text, to truly encounter it. Their study was a fulfillment of the commandment and of the Torah's vision as expressed in the verse "and you shall teach them diligently to your children, and shall talk of them when you sit in your house" – to put the Torah front and center in the home, at the heart of the relationship between parents and children. To me, the story of the Emanuelofs gives special meaning to any reading of *The Soul of the Mishna*.

Following is a brief description of Dvir, as written by his mother, whose words attest to a life filled with love and sacrifice – for his family, for his people, and for God.

Yakov Nagen

Dvir

Dvir was born and educated in Jerusalem.

Upon graduating from high school, he chose to attend the Ahavat Yisrael *hesder* yeshiva in Netivot, whose name [meaning "love of the Jewish people"] is a testament to its mission as well as to Dvir's character. He would study in that small, modest yeshiva for two years.

During Dvir's second year of yeshiva, his father, Netanel, of blessed memory, died of a serious illness.

While studying at yeshiva, Dvir volunteered in various frameworks: mentoring youth, patrolling with the Civil Guard, and delivering food to underprivileged families.

Despite the fact that, as an orphan, Dvir was exempted from combat service, he decided to join the Golani Brigade, where he excelled and was sent to a commanders' course. After graduation he stayed on as an instructor in the course and was marked for officers' training. However, Dvir refused to begin the training without first serving in the field, so he was assigned as a sergeant in an infantry squad, which he commanded in the war.

At home, too, Dvir never stopped studying. After discovering *The Soul of the Mishna* and studying it on his own, he was so excited he initiated a regular study date with me. Every Shabbat afternoon that he was home from the army we would study together after the meal. Despite the heaviness and sleepiness of Shabbat afternoon, we never slacked off: we would sit together and study, with our conversation always wandering to current affairs, in the home and in general.

The final mishna we studied together dealt with the significance of commandments within the family. It emphasized the importance of the father-son relationship and mutuality within family relations: "All obligations of the son upon the father… [and] all obligations of the father upon the son" (Kiddushin 1:7).

It was not coincidence. Netanel and Dvir, father and son, both of blessed memory, were very close, and it was as though this mishna was written about them. Netanel fulfilled his obligations toward Dvir, to the full extent that the Mishna implies, and Dvir did the same for his father – in life, in illness, and in death (Dvir was privileged to recite

Shema at the moment of Netanel's passing). After losing his father, Dvir continued to fulfill his obligations toward me and toward the entire family. It seems Netanel and Dvir wanted to carry on their mutual relationship into eternity.

The chapter we studied concludes with a vision of intimacy between fathers and sons, the perpetuation of tradition through the line of succession. Dvir knew that he was safeguarding tradition; he was aware of his responsibility toward God, his parents, and his homeland.

He was a link in the chain.

Now, with Dvir gone, it is our responsibility to carry on our tradition in the light of his path: the path of faith, Torah, and service.

Dalia Emanuelof

Introduction

Marcel Proust taught us that life's biggest challenge is not to discover new lands, but to see the old ones with new eyes. This book attempts to realize that idea by studying the Mishna, which was redacted by Rabbi Yehuda HaNasi some 1800 years ago.

The Mishna's six orders and sixty-three tractates compile sayings attributed to Sages spanning the period from the destruction of the Second Temple in 70 CE through the second century. The Mishna is the "iron pillar" of the Oral Torah (Leviticus Rabba 21), and the Talmud is largely an elaboration and commentary on it.

The body of the Mishna is the halakha, the law; in this book I intend to uncover its inner spirit. I wish to reveal the ideas that underpin the Mishna's laws, and, where possible, to elucidate their existential implications. Through contemplating the minutiae of the law, we can unearth important principles relating to God's presence in the world, the connection between halakha and life, the relationships between parents and children and between husbands and wives, social justice, the Temple, the Land of Israel, and more.

But if we are to discover the soul of the Mishna, we must first adopt the right attitude in our study. One can uncover only what one is looking for. People tend to study Mishna in preparation for studying Talmud, or as a means of rounding out their general knowledge of Oral Torah. Though they may achieve these ends, the soul of the Mishna will remain hidden from these students. But when we approach the Mishna with an understanding of its inherent importance and with an awareness of halakha's spiritual implications, we can encounter its soul.

The Literary Method

In his research on the literary editing of the Mishna, my teacher Rabbi Dr. Avraham Walfish established a new method for studying it. Walfish proved that the editors of the Mishna consciously employed literary devices such as inclusio (envelope structures) and wordplay.[1] He also showed that the editors used literary devices to convey meaning.[2] It follows that studying the literary structure of the Mishna can reveal the stances of its editors on the laws that appear within it.

A few of those literary devices follow:

Wordplay: When the editors of the Mishna choose to employ terms that have multiple connotations and associations, they can hint at additional meanings. Thus, for example, in Tractate Rosh HaShana, the Mishna relates the story of a father and son who came to the Temple to testify to having spotted the crescent moon, heralding the advent of a new month. According to the Mishna, the priests accepted his evidence and that of his son. The overt meaning is that the priests allowed the father and the son to testify together. But the expression used, "*oto ve'et beno*," "him and his son," also alludes to another, negative connotation that implies criticism of the priests' conduct, by recalling a Torah prohibition: "And whether it be cow or ewe, you shall not kill it and its young (*oto ve'et beno*) both in one day" (Leviticus 22:28).

Parallels: We often find in the Bible that phrases are repeated in multiple stories in order to draw parallels between them, so that one story serves as the subtext for the other.[3] The Mishna, too, features parallels, often linking different tractates,[4] and sometimes, as we will see in the next chapters, linking the Mishna and the Bible. The Bible's influence

1. Avraham Walfish, *Literary Phenomena in Mishna and their Redactorial and Conceptual Meaning* (master's thesis, Hebrew University of Jerusalem, 1994) [Hebrew], 33–60; "Wordplays in the Mishna," *Netuim* 2 (1995) [Hebrew]: 75–95.
2. Ibid.
3. Yair Zakovitch, *Through the Looking Glass: Reflection Stories in the Bible* (Tel Aviv: Hakibbutz Hameuchad, 1995) [Hebrew].
4. Walfish, "Literary Considerations in the Redaction of the Mishnah and Their Meanings," *Netuim* 1 (1994) [Hebrew]: 51; Motti Perry, "Parallels Converge: Notes on the Literary Structure of Mishna Yoma," *Netuim* 13 (2005) [Hebrew]: 40–45.

on the structure and content of the Mishna is not only an expression of the fact that the Written Torah is the foundation for the Oral Torah; it is also due to the fact that the Bible was the main book available to the Sages and students of the Mishna, and thus was a source of many motifs, ideas, and associations. Inspiration from the Torah is evident not only from the fact that the Mishna quotes directly from Torah verses and elaborates on its laws; biblical figures such as Elijah the Prophet, Moses, King David, and the lovers in the Song of Songs also inform the shaping of many mishnayot. These parallels suggest additional meanings with which the Sages sought to infuse the Mishna.

Structure: The structure of an individual mishna or a chapter serves as a vehicle for drawing parallels between various elements, and can be expressive of a common idea. For example, the first and third chapters of Tractate Sanhedrin discuss judges, while the second chapter addresses the laws of kings. The Mishna thereby links two types of leaders, the judge and the king. Another example can be seen in the first chapter of Kiddushin, which addresses two issues: property law and mitzvot. The fact that each topic includes ten items hints at a connection between the two areas.

An additional method of uncovering the Sages' intentions is to pay attention to the overall approach of an individual Sage. For example, Rabbi Akiva's statements regarding the sanctity of the connection between husband and wife, and the importance of their love, can shed light on why he opines that a couple can divorce when one partner no longer finds the other attractive.

Implications of the Laws

In the Mishna – more so than in the Talmud and halakhic Midrash – most laws pertaining to a topic are concentrated in one place. The Mishna thus makes it easier for scholars to examine groups of laws and analyze their implications. For example, the final chapter of Berakhot includes a lengthy list of situations in which one is required to bless God. Each of these blessings expresses appreciation for the role of God in a specific circumstance; therefore, analyzing all the blessings as a whole can shed light on the general question of His place in the world. Similarly, analysis of the details of the laws in Tractate Pe'ah reveals the conception that *pe'ah*, the corner of the field left unharvested for the poor, is not considered a gift. Rather, it is seen as a property right of the poor – similar to the right of the field's owner. It is reasonable to infer the Mishna's underlying ideas in this way, because the Mishna, an ancient work, was compiled closer to the time when the foundations of halakha were coalescing. Back then, the connections between laws and the ideas that shaped them were more overt than in subsequent periods.

In several places throughout this book I diverge from the principles elucidated above, and adopt a more personal tone; for example, in the discussion of Tractate Yoma I relate two painful stories about life and death. I take this license because my goal with this book is to increase the Jewish people's love for the Mishna and to reveal its riches, which can be found in the full range of possible interpretations.

The Title of the Book

The book's chapters, addressing hundreds of mishnayot, are organized according to the order of the Mishna itself. The name of the book, "The Soul of the Mishna," is inspired by the words of the "Maggid Mesharim" (preacher of righteousness), the celestial entity that revealed itself to Rabbi Yosef Karo, the author of the *Shulḥan Arukh*. This maggid identifies itself as "the soul of the Mishna," and explains that Rabbi Yosef merited the revelation in part because of his study of the Mishna:

> "It is I, the Mishna, speaking through your mouth. I am the soul of the Mishna. For I, and the Mishna, and you unite as one. Therefore, you must revisit my mishnayot often, and you must not let your mind wander from them even for a single moment."[5]
>
> I began to recite mishnayot, and went on to read five chapters. Then, as I was reading the mishnayot, the voice of my beloved knocked within my mouth, lilting. And it said,

5. Maggid Mesharim on *Parashat Tazria*, cited in Dov Zlotnick, *The Iron Pillar Mishnah: Redaction, Form and Intent* (Jerusalem: Bialik Institute, 1988), 60.

> "The Lord is with you wherever you go.... But you must always cleave to me, and to the fear of me, and to my Torah and mishnayot.... By virtue of these six orders of Mishna that you know by heart, and by virtue of your practice of mortifications and asceticism ... the heavenly host has permitted me to speak with you as before."[6]

I hope to enable the reader to encounter many parts of this masterful work by studying a wide range of mishnayot. And I pray that by loving the Mishna and cleaving to it, we will come to cleave with our hearts and souls to the root of the Mishna – God Himself.

6. Maggid Mesharim on *Parashat Bamidbar*.

A Jew in the Street and a Jew in the Home

ברכות א, א

מֵאֵימָתַי קוֹרִין אֶת שְׁמַע בְּעַרְבִית? מִשָּׁעָה שֶׁהַכֹּהֲנִים נִכְנָסִים לֶאֱכֹל בִּתְרוּמָתָן עַד סוֹף הָאַשְׁמוּרָה הָרִאשׁוֹנָה, דִּבְרֵי רַבִּי אֱלִיעֶזֶר. וַחֲכָמִים אוֹמְרִים, עַד חֲצוֹת. רַבָּן גַּמְלִיאֵל אוֹמֵר, עַד שֶׁיַּעֲלֶה עַמּוּד הַשַּׁחַר מַעֲשֶׂה שֶׁבָּאוּ בָנָיו מִבֵּית הַמִּשְׁתֶּה, אָמְרוּ לוֹ, לֹא קָרִינוּ אֶת שְׁמַע. אָמַר לָהֶם, אִם לֹא עָלָה עַמּוּד הַשַּׁחַר, חַיָּבִין אַתֶּם לִקְרוֹת. וְלֹא זוֹ בִּלְבַד, אֶלָּא כָּל מַה שֶּׁאָמְרוּ חֲכָמִים עַד חֲצוֹת, מִצְוָתָן עַד שֶׁיַּעֲלֶה עַמּוּד הַשָּׁחַר. הֶקְטֵר חֲלָבִים וְאֵבָרִים, מִצְוָתָן עַד שֶׁיַּעֲלֶה עַמּוּד הַשָּׁחַר. וְכָל הַנֶּאֱכָלִין לְיוֹם אֶחָד, מִצְוָתָן עַד שֶׁיַּעֲלֶה עַמּוּד הַשָּׁחַר. אִם כֵּן, לָמָּה אָמְרוּ חֲכָמִים עַד חֲצוֹת, כְּדֵי לְהַרְחִיק אֶת הָאָדָם מִן הָעֲבֵירָה:

Berakhot 1:1

From when may one recite *Shema* in the evening? From the time when the priests go in to eat their *teruma* [produce consecrated for priestly consumption], until the end of the first watch – so says Rabbi Eliezer. And the Sages say: Until midnight. Rabban Gamliel says: Until the break of dawn. It once happened that [Rabban Gamliel's] sons came from a house of feasting. They said to him: We have not recited *Shema*. He said to them: If dawn has not broken, you are obligated to recite it. And [this is true] not only in this case; rather, in all cases where the Sages said that [some precept can be performed only] until midnight, their precepts are [still in force] until the break of dawn. [For example:] Burning the fats and limbs [of the sacrifices, on the Temple altar] – their precepts [can be performed] until the break of dawn. And [another example:] all [sacrifices] that may be eaten for one day – their precepts [of eating them can be performed] until the break of dawn. If that is so, why did the Sages say, "until midnight"? To distance a person from transgression.

What Does the Priests' Feasting Have to Do with *Keriat Shema*?

> From when may one recite *Shema* in the evening? From the time when the priests go in to eat their *teruma*.

While the opening of the Mishna is widely known, the connection between the question it poses and the answer is not. The solution to this mystery will reveal the Mishna's attitude not only toward the meaning of *Keriat Shema,* but also toward fundamental questions regarding life and the essence of humanity.

One would understand if the time for *Keriat Shema* in the evening would have been based on the definition of the beginning of the evening – say sundown or nightfall. Alternatively, since the source for the timing of the mitzva seems to be the term "when you lie down" (Berakhot 2a; see also Mishna Berakhot 1:3), it could have been defined as bedtime. Why, then, does the Mishna choose to define it as the time when the priests go in to eat their *teruma*? The beginning of the priests' meal is not merely a sign that it is time to recite *Shema*; rather, there is a substantive connection, for the Tosefta says: "From the time when the priests are able to eat their *teruma* [heave offering]. A sign for this is the coming out of the stars."[1] Thus, it is stated explicitly that the priests' meal is not a sign that night has fallen, but rather the reverse – the stars coming out constitutes a sign that it is time for the priests to eat. This is the reason that the timing of the priests' meal determines when we recite *Shema.*

The Talmud provides further perspectives on the Mishna that can help us solve the puzzle:

> From what time may one recite *Shema* in the evening? From the time that the poor man comes [home] to eat his bread with salt till he rises from his meal… From what time may one begin to recite *Shema* in the evening? From the time that the people come [home] to eat their meal

1. Berakhot 1:1; appears also in the Bavli, Berakhot 2b.

> on a Sabbath eve... From the time that most people come [home] to sit down to their meal. (Berakhot 2b)

The various opinions cited by the Talmud have a common thread: They all discuss the time when people come home in the evening to eat. We will thus rephrase the question: Why does the time when people come home in the evening to eat determine the time when they are required to recite *Shema*?

Why Do We Recite *Shema* Twice Every Day?

We can deduce the answer to our question by examining a second question. The essence of the mitzva of *Keriat Shema* is to accept the yoke of heaven (Berakhot 2:2, 2:5). But why must we declare our acceptance of the kingdom of heaven twice a day? Why is once not enough?

One possibility is that the declarations are meant to create a framework, bookending the day and defining everything that occurs in between as dedicated to heaven. In this model, *Keriat Shema* corresponds to the *tamid*, the daily burnt offering, which is brought at sunup and sundown and signals the opening and closing of each day's sacrificial rites in the Temple (Pesaḥim 58b).[2]

It turns out that this outlook informs the opinion of Rabbi Yehoshua ben Levi, who states that in the evening one should say the *Amida* before *Shema*, which should be recited just before sleep: "Rabbi Yehoshua ben Levi argues [differently]: Here there is an analogy between lying down and rising. Just as [at the time of] rising, the recital of *Shema* is adjacent to [rising from] bed, so also [at the time of] lying down, recital of *Shema* must be adjacent to [getting into] bed" (Berakhot 4b). It thus is not surprising that Rabbi Yehoshua also opines that "Though a person has recited *Shema* in the synagogue, it is a mitzva to recite it again upon his bed" (ibid).[3]

---

2. See midrashim below that compare *Keriat Shema* to the *tamid* sacrifice.
3. The problem with this approach is that if it were correct, the Torah should have stated, "when you rise and when you lie down," instead of the reverse.

When You Sit in Your House, and When You Walk by the Way

There is, however, another possible reason for the requirement to recite *Shema* twice. Naturally, our day-to-day life is divided in two: the part that takes place outside the house, usually during the day, and the part that takes place within our homes, generally during the night.

Yehuda Leib Gordon coined one of the mottos of the Jewish Enlightenment, or *Haskala,* movement: "Be a man in the street and a Jew in the home."[4] According to Gordon and other proponents of the Enlightenment, one's Judaism is a personal matter that, as such, should be confined to the privacy of one's home. This conduct is in contrast to the diametrically opposed behavior of others: Outwardly, they behave as Jews, but in their homes, away from others and the pressures of society, they set their Judaism aside and do as they please. The requirement to recite *Shema* twice daily signals to us that one must accept the yoke of heaven in both spaces – the home and the street. I see this insight as already embedded in the verse that teaches the requirement to recite *Shema*: "And shall speak of them when you sit in your house, and when you walk by the way" (Deuteronomy 6:7). The verse teaches us that we must "speak of them," the mitzvot, and accept the yoke of heaven wherever we go, whether "in your house" or when leaving it to "walk by the way." The rest of the verse, "and when you lie down, and when you rise up," merely sharpens and reinforces the first distinction between the home and the street.[5] Here lies the solution to the puzzle that opens

---

4. From his poem "Awaken, My People," published 1863.

5. One can raise several possible explanations as to the relation between the two sets of states. Perhaps one is a continuation of the other; lying down would thus be an extension of sitting in the house, and walking would extend the act of rising. Indeed, the time for the evening *Shema* begins based on "when you sit" and ends based on "when you lie down."

   It is also possible that each set reinforces the definition of the other. For example, "when you lie down" teaches us that sitting in the home is also associated with nighttime, while "when you sit in your house" shows that the obligation extends not only to the time when one is lying down, but rather to all of one's nocturnal time in the home. See the *Sifrei*: "When you rise" – I might think, even if one rose in the middle of the night. It is therefore written, "When you sit in your house and when

the mishna: The definition of the requirement rests on the time when one enters one's home to eat, which symbolizes the passage from the public to the private. The two spaces vary greatly in terms of the types of challenges that we face in them, and we must invest our effort in each one separately, so as to find the path that is unique to it.

In the following chapter, we will turn to the second part of the puzzle: Why, of all people, it is the high priest, who, in eating the *teruma* offering, is emblematic of the state of "when you sit in the house"?

---

you walk by the way." Scripture speaks of the common instance. This means that if the Torah had written only, "when you rise," we would have thought that even one who rises in the middle of the night should recite *Shema*. "When you sit in your house and when you walk by the way" teaches us that only in that context does rising necessitate *Keriat Shema*.

A Kingdom of Priests

ברכות א, א

מֵאֵימָתַי קוֹרִין אֶת שְׁמַע בְּעַרְבִית? מִשָּׁעָה שֶׁהַכֹּהֲנִים נִכְנָסִים לֶאֱכֹל בִּתְרוּמָתָן עַד סוֹף הָאַשְׁמוּרָה הָרִאשׁוֹנָה, דִּבְרֵי רַבִּי אֱלִיעֶזֶר. וַחֲכָמִים אוֹמְרִים, עַד חֲצוֹת. רַבָּן גַּמְלִיאֵל אוֹמֵר, עַד שֶׁיַּעֲלֶה עַמּוּד הַשַּׁחַר. מַעֲשֶׂה שֶׁבָּאוּ בָנָיו מִבֵּית הַמִּשְׁתֶּה, אָמְרוּ לוֹ, לֹא קָרִינוּ אֶת שְׁמַע. אָמַר לָהֶם, אִם לֹא עָלָה עַמּוּד הַשַּׁחַר, חַיָּבִין אַתֶּם לִקְרוֹת. וְלֹא זוֹ בִּלְבַד, אֶלָּא כָּל מַה שֶּׁאָמְרוּ חֲכָמִים עַד חֲצוֹת, מִצְוָתָן עַד שֶׁיַּעֲלֶה עַמּוּד הַשַּׁחַר. הֶקְטֵר חֲלָבִים וְאֵבָרִים, מִצְוָתָן עַד שֶׁיַּעֲלֶה עַמּוּד הַשַּׁחַר. וְכָל הַנֶּאֱכָלִין לְיוֹם אֶחָד, מִצְוָתָן עַד שֶׁיַּעֲלֶה עַמּוּד הַשַּׁחַר. אִם כֵּן, לָמָּה אָמְרוּ חֲכָמִים עַד חֲצוֹת, כְּדֵי לְהַרְחִיק אֶת הָאָדָם מִן הָעֲבֵירָה:

Berakhot 1:1

From when may one recite *Shema* in the evening? From the time when the priests go in to eat their *teruma* [produce consecrated for priestly consumption], until the end of the first watch – so says Rabbi Eliezer. And the Sages say: Until midnight. Rabban Gamliel says: Until the break of dawn. It once happened that [Rabban Gamliel's] sons came from a house of feasting. They said to him: We have not recited *Shema*. He said to them: If dawn has not broken, you are obligated to recite it. And [this is true] not only in this case; rather, in all cases where the Sages said that [some precept can be performed only] until midnight, their precepts are [still in force] until the break of dawn. [For example:] Burning the fats and limbs [of the sacrifices, on the Temple altar] – their precepts [can be performed] until the break of dawn. And [another example:] all [sacrifices] that may be eaten for one day – their precepts [of eating them can be performed] until the break of dawn. If that is so, why did the Sages say, "until midnight"? To distance a person from transgression.

We have explained why the hour at which people enter their home defines the beginning of the time when one can say *Keriat Shema*. Now, we must examine why the Mishna defines this hour based on a very particular event – the priests eating their *teruma* – and not a more normative one, such as the one cited by the Talmud: "From the time that most people come [home] to sit down to their meal" (Berakhot 2b).

It seems that the Mishna is addressed directly to the priest partaking of the *teruma*, establishing the priest as the archetype of Jewish religious life. To my mind, one of the Torah's most important messages is, "and you shall be unto Me a kingdom of priests, and a holy nation" (Exodus 19:6). The identity of each and every Jew contains a priestly layer, which also underlies many commandments that are derived from Temple rituals. For example, the morning handwashing is based on the purification of the priests in the Temple, and the tzitzit correspond to the priestly vestments.[1] It is thus fitting that submission to the yoke of heaven, which defines one's relationship with God, will emerge from the priestly stratum of one's identity.

Based on this insight, my teacher Rabbi Walfish suggests that since the *teruma* is consumed as a substitution for the burnt offerings,[2] then to derive the time for reciting *Shema* from the time for *teruma* is to hint that *Keriat Shema*, too, is a stand-in for the Temple rituals. Walfish supports his claim by pointing out that the other times listed by the Mishna are also taken from the world of the Temple: The end of the time for reciting *Shema* is, according to Rabbi Eliezer, "the end of the first watch," meaning the end of the first shift in the Temple.[3] The other opinions as to the end of the time for reciting *Shema* – midnight, according to the Sages, and the break of dawn, according to Rabban Gamliel – also correspond, respectively, to the end of the period of burning the fats and limbs of the daily sacrifice and the end of the time when a day's sacrifices may be consumed.[4]

1. See the following chapter.
2. See Hanoch Albeck, *Mishna* (Tel Aviv: Dvir, 1952) [Hebrew] 325–26.
3. Yoma 1:8.
4. Walfish, "Literary Considerations," 38–39. This point is further driven home by Rashi, which states that the Mishna's question "If that is so, why did the Sages say, 'until midnight'?" refers to both *Keriat Shema* and the consumption of offerings.

Walfish finds another parallel between *Keriat Shema* and the sacrifices, in the envelope structure of the tractate. The first mishna in Berakhot says, "From the time when the priests go in [*nikhnasim*] to eat their *teruma*," while the final mishna states, "One may not enter [*yikanes*] the Temple Mount" (Berakhot 9:5).[5]

I also see an envelope structure in the section of the Mishna that discusses *Keriat Shema* (chapters 1–3). The final topic there in relation to *Shema* is ritual impurity, specifically, that a man who has a seminal emission is required to immerse before he may recite *Shema* (Berakhot 3:4). The following mishna states: "If he went down to immerse [himself], if he is able to go up and to cover himself and to recite [*Shema*] before sunrise, he should go up and cover himself and recite. And if not, he should cover himself in water and recite" (3:5). There is a parallel between the beginning of the section, which mentions priests who immerse before eating *teruma*, thus defining the time for the evening *Shema*, and the ending of the section, which concerns itself with a layperson who immerses before *Keriat Shema*, establishing the end time for the morning *Shema*.

The parallel alluded to in the Mishna, between the Temple rites and *Keriat Shema*, is elucidated explicitly in the midrash:

> This can be likened to a sage whose son would serve him two meals every day – one in the morning and one in the evening. There came a time when the sage saw that his son had fallen into poverty and could no longer afford to carry on as before. He called his son to him and said, "My son, I know that you no longer have the strength to bring me two meals as you once did. Instead, all I ask is that you listen to me give sermons in synagogue twice a day; that will be as delightful to me as the two meals that you used to serve me." Similarly, the Holy One, blessed be He, said to the Jewish people, "In the past you would sacrifice to me twice daily – 'The one lamb you shall offer in the morning, etc.' (Numbers 28:4). I know that the Temple is destined

5. Ibid.

to be destroyed and that thenceforth you will no longer be able to bring sacrifices. Instead of the sacrifices, I ask [that you recite] *Keriat Shema* in the morning and *Keriat Shema* in the evening.[6] These I will receive more favorably than all the sacrifices." (*Yalkut Shimoni, Va'etḥanan* 810)[7]

As If They Ate from the Table of the Omnipresent

I wish to propose another dimension to the link between *Keriat Shema* and the sacrifices. The Mishna in our tractate notes that every day, after the limbs of the *tamid* were brought up the ramp of the altar, but before they were sacrificed, the priests would assemble in the Hall of Hewn Stones and recite the three passages of *Shema*.[8] The combination of reciting the verses and bringing the sacrifice enables the priests' verbal acceptance of the yoke of heaven to be an expression of the sacrifice's nonverbal meaning.

The combination also imbues with fresh meaning the order of the prayers, where *Keriat Shema* precedes the *Amida*, as well as the order of the Mishna, in which the laws of *Shema* (chapters 1–3) precede the laws of the *Amida* (chapters 4–5). The *Amida* stands in for the *tamid*

6. In the allegory, the son listens to his father's sermons, which are likened to *Keriat Shema*. This raises a fascinating point: The most important aspect of *Shema* is not one's recitation, but rather listening to it. In stating the words "Hear, O Israel," one addresses oneself, first and foremost, with an entreaty to listen to the voice of God. This idea is apparent in the opinion of Rabbi Yosei in the following Gemara: "One who recites *Shema* but does not make it audible to his ear has fulfilled his obligation; Rabbi Yosei says: Has not fulfilled his obligation. One who recites but does not articulate each letter – Rabbi Yosei says: Has fulfilled his obligation; Rabbi Yehuda says: Has not fulfilled his obligation" (Berakhot 2:3).
7. An additional example: "Reish Lakish said: One must be conscientious with *Keriat Shema*, for it is tantamount to all of the sacrifices. Just as the sacrifices were brought both in the morning and in the evening, so too *Keriat Shema* is recited in the morning and in the evening, as it is stated, 'when you lie down, and when you rise up'" (Deuteronomy Rabba [Lieberman], *Va'etḥanan*).
8. Tamid 4:3–5:1. See also Maimonides, *Mishneh Torah, Hilkhot Temidin UMusafin* 6:3–4.

(Berakhot 26b), so that the order – *Shema* before *Amida* – reconstructs the original model in the Temple.

The connection between *Keriat Shema* and the *tamid* casts our mishna in a new light. If the *teruma* is eaten in lieu of the sacrificial rites, then to recite *Shema* during the time allotted to eating *teruma* is to reconstruct the Temple model. The Mishna's choice to define the layman's obligation based on the time when the *teruma* was eaten shows us that when each and every one of us eats – if we are under the yoke of heaven, that meal is holy. This is an actualization of the vision inherent in the verse, "when you walk by the way and when you lie down, and when you rise up" – a vision that bounds all of our day-to-day existence in holiness.

The Sages say that the simple act of eating can be sanctified so that it is tantamount to a sacrificial offering: "At the time when the Temple stood, the altar used to make atonement for a person; now a person's table makes atonement for him" (Ḥagiga 27a). We find a similar idea in Tractate Avot (3:3):

> Rabbi Shimon says: Three who ate at one table and did not say upon it words of Torah – it is as if they ate from the offerings of the dead, as it is said, "For all of the tables are full of vomit and feces without the Omnipresent" (Isaiah 28:8). However, three who ate at one table and said upon it words of Torah – it is as if they ate from the table of the Omnipresent, blessed be He, as it is said, "And he said to me, this is the table that is before the Lord" (Ezekiel 41:22).

In Tractate Avot, the words of Torah elevate the act of eating. In our mishna, *Keriat Shema* fulfills the same role.[9]

---

9. The *Tanna* quoted in Avot, Rabbi Shimon, holds that the mitzva of *Keriat Shema* is fundamentally about Torah study: "It has been taught: R. Shimon b. Yoḥai says, 'It is right that "Hear" (*Shema*) should come before "And it shall 'come to pass," because the former prescribes learning and the latter teaching'" (Berakhot 14b); "[Rabbi Shimon's] reasoning [in stating that one must not interrupt one's Torah study in order to recite *Shema*] is that both constitute study. And one does not interrupt one's study for the sake of study" (Y. Berakhot 1:2).

Rabbi Abraham Isaac Kook poetically elucidated the vision of elevating the act of eating:

> When the idea of raising the sparks manifests in the soul as an inner realization, it impels the adept to always follow this holy path, which is the foundation of "in all your ways acknowledge Him".... Thus, all the actions of such a holy lover of Israel are exalted, to the extent that his eating becomes a true sacrificial offering and his drinking a libation. (*Shemoneh Kevatzim* 2:259)

Both aspects of the connection between *Keriat Shema* and the sacrificial rites are established. They can be seen as two dimensions of *Shema*, like the study of Torah, which is on the one hand a substitute for the sacrificial rites (Menaḥot 110a) and, on the other hand, the thing that can elevate eating to the level of sacrifice when it is included in the meal, as we saw in Avot.

The acceptance of the yoke of heaven can sanctify life itself. The Mishna teaches us that every individual is a priest of sorts – our consumption of food is likened to a sacrifice and our homes are temples.

A Prayer of the Poor

In contrast with the Mishna, which defined the time when one enters the house based on the priests' schedule, the Talmud (Berakhot 2a) features an opinion that derives the time for *Keriat Shema* based on the time when the poor come home. That opinion, too, seems to stem from an idea of the correct approach to God, in which meekness is the proper posture, as in the verse, "A prayer of the poor, when he faints, and pours out his complaint before the Lord" (Psalms 102:1).

The difference between a priest and a poor person corresponds to the difference between the two amoraic approaches to prayer, as described in the Talmud:

> Rabba son of R. Huna put on [expensive cloth] stockings and prayed, quoting, "Prepare to meet [your God, Israel]"

> (Amos 4:12). Rabba [son of Rav Yosef] removed his cloak, clasped his hands, and prayed, saying, "[I pray] like a servant before his master." (Shabbat 10a)

Even the poor person, whose diet consists of a salted crust, is capable of sublimity, the Mishna tells us:

> This is the way [to toil in] Torah: Eat bread with salt, and drink a small amount of water, and sleep on the ground, and live a life [whose conditions will cause you] pain, and in Torah you toil; if you do so, "happy shall you be, and it shall be well with you" (Psalms 128:2) – happy shall you be in this world, and it shall be well with you in the World to Come. (Avot 6:4)

Our Father, Our King

ברכות א, ב	**Berakhot 1:2**
מֵאֵימָתַי קוֹרִין אֶת שְׁמַע בְּשַׁחֲרִית. מִשֶּׁיַּכִּיר בֵּין תְּכֵלֶת לְלָבָן. רַבִּי אֱלִיעֶזֶר אוֹמֵר, בֵּין תְּכֵלֶת לְכַרְתִּי. וְגוֹמְרָהּ עַד הָנֵץ הַחַמָּה. רַבִּי יְהוֹשֻׁעַ אוֹמֵר, עַד שָׁלֹשׁ שָׁעוֹת, שֶׁכֵּן דֶּרֶךְ בְּנֵי מְלָכִים לַעֲמוֹד בְּשָׁלֹשׁ שָׁעוֹת. הַקּוֹרֵא מִכָּאן וְאֵילָךְ לֹא הִפְסִיד, כְּאָדָם הַקּוֹרֵא בַּתּוֹרָה:	From when may one recite *Shema* in the morning? From when one can distinguish between *tekhelet* (purple-blue wool) and white. Rabbi Eliezer says: [From when one can distinguish] between *tekhelet* and the color of leek, and one must finish reciting it by sunrise. Rabbi Yehoshua says: [One may recite *Shema*] until three hours [of the day], for such is the way of the sons of kings, to arise at the third hour. If one recites [*Shema*] later than this, he has not lost out, [but rather is] like one who reads the Torah.

Hearing and Seeing

The first opinion cited by the Mishna states that the time for the morning *Shema* begins as soon as one can distinguish between the color *tekhelet* (a shade of blue) and white. Since *tekhelet* and white are the colors of the tzitzit, the implication is that the time for the morning's *Keriat Shema* is derived from the time of the mitzva of wearing tzitzit. This sharpens the question as to the nature of the link between tzitzit and *Keriat Shema*, a link which is also apparent in the fact that tzitzit is the subject of the third passage of *Shema*. On the basic level, the connection lies in the idea that both *Keriat Shema* and tzitzit are signs that we are God's servants. In ancient times, a master would affix his seal to the clothing of his slaves to mark them as his property. The Talmud compares tzitzit to those seals.[1] The implication is that tzitzit is an expression of accepting the yoke of heaven through our clothing, while *Keriat Shema* signifies the same thing by way of speech.

Rabbi Re'em Hacohen puts forth a deep explanation for the link between *Keriat Shema* and tzitzit, as well as the uniqueness of each mitzva. The structure of *Shema* combines the two basic modes for the human encounter with the divine: listening and seeing. In the first and second passages, "*Shema*," "**Hear**" and "*Vehaya Im Shamoa*," "And it shall come to pass, if you shall **hearken**," acceptance of the yoke of heaven is effected through the experience of hearing, through listening for the voice of God echoing through the world. The third passage deals with tzitzit and the Exodus from Egypt, which symbolize submission to God through the experience of sight: "so that you may look upon it, and remember all the commandments of the Lord" (Numbers 15:39). Twice every day we accept the yoke of heaven; at night, when it is dark, the emphasis is on hearing,[2] while during daytime, when there is light, sight takes precedence. This is why the time for the morning *Keriat Shema* is based on the time for tzitzit.[3]

Our mishna features an additional opinion, that of Rabbi Eliezer, who links the beginning of the time for *Keriat Shema* to the capacity to distinguish between the colors *tekhelet* and leek green. What is the significance of green when it comes to *Keriat Shema*? While he too apparently holds that tzitzit determines the time for *Shema*,[4] he concludes that when one can first distinguish between *tekhelet* and white, one does not see the color *tekhelet*, but rather notices only that it is darker than white. Only when one can distinguish between *tekhelet* and leek green, which are similar hues, is it possible to truly see the color *tekhelet*.

---

1. Menaḥot 43b. See also *Tosafot* there, on the words "a seal of clay."
2. See Berakhot 3a, which states in the context of the nighttime *Shema* that the various parts of the night are defined based on the sounds that one hears.
3. Rabbi Hacohen expressed this idea during a class he delivered at the Otniel yeshiva in 5769.
4. Ezer Avraham posited another explanation for Rabbi Eliezer's opinion: that one can accept the yoke of heaven only at a time when one can distinguish between heaven (*tekhelet*) and earth (leek).

It seems that this is the gist of the Yerushalmi's explanation: "And what is Rabbi Eliezer's reasoning? 'That you may look upon it (*oto*)' (Numbers 15:39) – meaning, that it can be distinguished from among the dyed" (Y. Berakhot 1:1). The significance of discerning the *tekhelet* itself, rather than just distinguishing between it and white, emerges in the continuation of the talmudic text:

> It is stated in the name of Rabbi Meir: "That you may look upon [Him (*oto*)]" – this teaches us that when one fulfills the mitzva of tzitzit it is as if one receives the Divine Presence. This teaches us that the *tekhelet* is similar to the sea, and the sea is similar to the grass, and the grass is similar to the sky, and the sky is similar to the throne of glory, and the throne is similar to sapphire. As it is written: "Then I looked, and, behold, upon the firmament that was over the head of the cherubim, there appeared above them as it were a sapphire stone, as the appearance of the likeness of a throne" (Ezekiel 10:1).

The color *tekhelet* is reminiscent and evocative of the throne of glory. If one is to receive the Divine Presence, so to speak, by contemplating the color of one's clothes, one must be able to truly see and experience their color. God is crowned our King not through a sense of distance, but rather through a sense of intimacy: The *tekhelet* affixes God's seal to our clothing, and through it we can connect to Him and feel His presence.

Tzitzit and the Priestly Vestments

In linking the beginning of the time for the evening *Shema* to the priests,[5] the Mishna gives voice to the idea that every Jew is a priest of sorts. Setting the time for the morning *Shema* based on the time for tzitzit complements this idea, because there are also parallels between tzitzit and the Temple. For one, the color *tekhelet* characterizes the priestly

5. See the chapters on Berakhot 1:1.

vestments.[6] Like the vestments, and in contrast to regular clothes, tzitzit can be *shaatnez*, made with a mixture of wool and linen. A Jew who wears tzitzit is a priest of sorts, and dedicated to God's service.[7] The Jewish people, who wear tzitzit and recite *Shema*, are all "a kingdom of priests, and a holy nation" (Exodus 19:6).

The Children of Kings

The issue of the end of the time for the morning *Keriat Shema* raises another angle to the question of our identity. We saw above that this time is linked to when people rise, as the verse says, "and when you rise up" (Deuteronomy 6:7). The *Tanna'im* in the Mishna disagree as to when the time for rising ends. The opinion that was accepted in practice, that of Rabbi Yehoshua, states that *Shema* can be recited throughout the first three hours of the day, "for such is the way of the sons of kings, to arise at the third hour." But why would the habits of the select, elitist few, "the sons of kings," be relevant to the rising time of an ordinary person? As the *Kesef Mishneh* asked rhetorically, "Are the majority of people in the world sons of kings?"

It seems that the solution lies in an idea expressed explicitly in another mishna:

> [If] one has pains in his loins he may not anoint with wine or with vinegar; he may anoint with oil, but not rose oil. Children of kings may anoint their wounds with rose oil, since they are in the habit of so anointing on weekdays. Rabbi Shimon says: All of Israel are [considered] children of kings (Shabbat 14:4).

Halakha forbids the use of medicine on Shabbat. Although rose oil was generally in use as a medicine, the sons of kings would make regular use of it for other purposes. The first *Tanna* in the mishna concludes that only the sons of kings are allowed to use rose oil on Shabbat. But according

6. See Exodus, chap. 28.
7. Jacob Milgrom, *Leviticus 1–16* (New York: Doubleday, 1991), 412.

to Rabbi Shimon, everyone can use rose oil on Shabbat, because every Jew is inherently considered the child of a king. Rabbi Shimon's outlook has its philosophical roots in the ideas of his teacher, Rabbi Akiva:

> Beloved are Israel, since they are called children of the Omnipresent. Especially beloved are they, as it is revealed to them that they are called children of the Omnipresent, as it says, "You are children of the Lord, your God" (Deuteronomy 14:1). (Avot 3:14)

It appears, then, that our mishna defines the time for rising based on the habits of the sons of kings, based on the conception that every Jew is the child of a king.[8] From here we learn that even though, in reciting *Shema*, we declare God's kingship, His lofty status does not remove and isolate Him from us, for we are His children. This relationship is also underscored in the words of the *Avinu Malkeinu* (Our Father, Our King) prayer.

Rabbi Israel Besancon tells the following story: There was once a young boy who stood on the shore and waved at a large ship sailing out at sea.

A passerby asked the boy, "Whom are you waving to?"

"The captain," the boy replied.

"Do you think he is looking at you?" the passerby asked.

"Yes," the boy said.

The passerby challenged the boy: "Why would you think that the captain of such a ship would look at a young boy on the shore?"

---

8. The idea that every Jew is royalty is congruent with the character of Rabbi Yehoshua. On the one hand, Rabbi Yehoshua lived in poverty (Berakhot 28a); on the other, he had a relationship with the crown, which had great appreciation for him (Shabbat 127b, 152a). According to the Talmud, kings, too, rise at the third hour: "All the kings of the East and the West sleep to the third hour [of the day]" (Berakhot 4a), which highlights the Mishna's choice to speak of the sons of kings. This stems from an idea of the Jewish people's intrinsic status in the eyes of God, as sons of the King. It is interesting to note that the previous mishna, which sets the time by which the evening *Keriat Shema* must be recited, contains a story about actual "sons of kings" – the sons of Rabban Gamliel the prince.

"Because," the boy replied, "the captain is my father."

A Crown of Priesthood and a Crown of Kingship

The time for reciting *Shema* in the morning is defined based on the mitzva of tzitzit for the beginning, and on the rising habits of the sons of kings for the end. These seemingly disparate elements appear in the Zohar in the context of a discussion of tzitzit:

> The people of Israel are recognized as being sons of the Holy King, since they are all marked by Him: marked in their bodies with the holy insignia (circumcision), marked in their clothes with a wrap of mitzva (tzitzit)...in all ways marked as sons of the supernal King. Happy is their portion! (Zohar, *Va'etḥanan* 266a)

According to the Zohar, the tzitzit we wear is a sign not only of our role as a "kingdom of priests," but also of our royalty – that we are children of the King. It follows that not only the ending of the time for *Keriat Shema* is determined in a manner emphasizing that we encounter God as His children – but also the beginning, which is tied to tzitzit.[9]

9. Milgrom (*Leviticus*, 412) arrived at the same conclusion by examining the meaning ascribed to *tekhelet* in antiquity. The dye was expensive and rare in those days, and was considered a sign of royalty. Thus, Milgrom concluded that clothing the Jewish people in tzitzit adorned with *tekhelet* symbolized that they were "princes of God."

Wolf and Dog, Donkey and Wild Ass: *Keriat Shema* and Aesop's Fables

ברכות א, ב	**Berakhot 1:2**
מאימתי קורין את שמע בשחרית?	From when may one recite *Shema* in the morning?

The Talmud (Berakhot 9b) cites a *baraita* that adds two answers to the Mishna's question above: "It has been taught: R. Meir says: [The morning *Shema* is recited] from the time that one can distinguish between a wolf and a dog. R. Akiva says: Between a [donkey] and a wild ass."

Rabbi Meir and Rabbi Akiva determine the earliest time *Shema* can be recited in the morning based on a person's capacity to distinguish various species of animals from one another. But why would they choose this criterion for arriving at the time for *Keriat Shema*? It turns out that there is special significance to these two pairs of animals, which are also mentioned alongside each other elsewhere in the Mishna, in Tractate Kilayim (1:6):

> The wolf and the dog, the village dog [bred by villagers] and the fox, goats and deer, mountain goats and ewes, the horse and the mule, the mule and the donkey, the donkey and the wild ass – although they are similar to each other, they are forbidden to be crossbred (*kilayim*) one with another.

That mishna lists five pairs of species that should not be crossbred. We can gather from this mishna that the Sages considered these pairs of animals similar to one another, which can explain why in Berakhot, Rabbi Meir and Rabbi Akiva use them as signs for defining the amount of light needed to tell similar things apart: When there is sufficient light to distinguish between these similar animals, the time for the morning *Keriat Shema* begins.

But still, there is a problem. If the Sages indeed wanted to find a relevant example of the ability to tell similar things apart, would it not have made more sense to choose pairs of animals that a person would be more likely to encounter in the morning, such as a horse and a mule or a mule and a donkey? After all, wolves and wild asses are not exactly commonplace in areas settled by humans.

The question takes on even greater weight when we consider the Yerushalmi's opinion (Y. Berakhot 1:1), which determines the time for *Keriat Shema* based on the capacity to distinguish between two similar colors, *tekhelet* and leek green. What is the basis for defining the time based on the differences between animals rather than between colors, which are seemingly more accessible and recognizable?

It seems that the Sages were not out to find a practical definition of the time for *Keriat Shema,* but rather one that relates to the meaning of the mitzva. The essence of *Keriat Shema* is accepting the yoke of heaven. Rabbi Meir and Rabbi Akiva chose to reference only pairs of species that consist of one wild animal and one domesticated animal. Symbolically speaking, this means that the time for the mitzva whose import is accepting the yoke of heaven is based on the time when one can distinguish between animals that appear similar but have an essential difference: One has a master and the other does not.

The use of domesticated animals as an analogy for the relationship between humanity and God goes back as far as the prophets: "The ox knows his owner, and the donkey his master's crib; but Israel does not know, My people do not consider" (Isaiah 1:3). The donkey, a domesticated animal, appears here as a symbol of knowing its master. In the book of Daniel, by contrast, the wild ass is a symbol of rebellion against heaven. Daniel explains to King Nebuchadnezzar the meaning of his dream: "And he was driven from the sons of men, and his heart was made like the beasts, and his dwelling was with the wild asses ... until he knew that God Most High rules in the kingdom of men" (Daniel 5:21).

Still, it appears that there is further significance to the specific pairs of dog-wolf and donkey-wild ass. Perhaps unconsciously, the words of Rabbi Meir and Rabbi Akiva are a response to Aesop's Fables, where we also find stories that note the differences between the dog and the wolf and between the donkey and the wild ass:

> Once upon a time the Wolves said to the Dogs, "Why should we continue to be enemies any longer? You are very like us in most ways; the main difference between us is one of training only. We live a life of freedom, but you are enslaved to mankind." (Aesop's Fables, 139)

Both the mishna in Kilayim and the above fable deal with the similarity between dogs and wolves. According to the fable, the source of the difference is not external appearance but rather internal essence, or "training": the dogs are enslaved while the wolves are free. The fable implies that the wolves are superior, because freedom is preferable to bondage. This idea also appears in another fable, about a pack ass (a donkey) and a wild ass:

> A wild ass, who was wandering idly about, one day came upon a pack ass lying at full length in a sunny spot and thoroughly enjoying himself. Going up to him, he said, "What a lucky beast you are! Your sleek coat shows how well you live; how I envy you!" Not long after, the wild ass saw his acquaintance again, but this time he was carrying a heavy load, and his driver was following behind and beating him with a thick stick. "Ah, my friend," said the wild ass, "I do not envy you anymore, for I see you pay dear for your comforts." (Aesop's Fables, 148)

According to this fable, too, it is better to forgo comfort than to live in bondage.

Love and Commitment

Modern society identifies more with the wolf and the wild ass, who are free, than with the enslaved animals. Most Western people find the notion of "accepting a yoke" abhorrent.

In his song "My Freedom," the singer and songwriter Georges Moustaki, a French Jew, sings of a man who mourns the loss of his freedom. Only toward the end of the song does it emerge that the power that binds him is "love."

In *Keriat Shema* as well, in which we accept the yoke of heaven, the key word is "love." The verse that immediately follows "Hear, O Israel: The Lord our God, the Lord is one" (Deuteronomy 6:4) is "And you shall love the Lord your God with all your heart" (v. 5). It is a mutual love, as we can see in the ending of the blessing that precedes *Shema*, "who chooses His people Israel in love."

True love requires commitment – to fulfill our promises even when we do not feel like it or it is inconvenient. A woman once told me that she did not understand the significance of commitment to halakha. She maintained that no matter what she did, God would love her. I replied that I too believed that God's love for us is unconditional. The real question, I said, was not the extent of His love for us, but of our love for Him.

One can look at commitment as a loss of personal freedom. Or, one can see the absence of commitment as alienation, not liberty. As the Israeli singer and songwriter Berry Sakharof says in his song "Avadim" (Slaves), "Everybody wants to be free, but from what, God, from what? We're all slaves."

According to Rabbi Yehuda Halevi, by contrast, freedom is attained by accepting the yoke of heaven. Submission to that which lies beyond reality sets one free from enslavement to forces within reality:

> The slaves of time are slaves of slaves;
> The slave of God alone is free.
> And so when others seek their lot,
> God is lot enough for me

Each Person May Recite It in His Usual Way

ברכות א, ג

בֵּית שַׁמַּאי אוֹמְרִים, בָּעֶרֶב כָּל אָדָם יַטּוּ וְיִקְרְאוּ, וּבַבֹּקֶר יַעַמְדוּ, שֶׁנֶּאֱמַר (דברים ו) וּבְשָׁכְבְּךָ וּבְקוּמֶךָ. וּבֵית הִלֵּל אוֹמְרִים, כָּל אָדָם קוֹרֵא כְדַרְכּוֹ, שֶׁנֶּאֱמַר (שם) וּבְלֶכְתְּךָ בַדֶּרֶךְ. אִם כֵּן, לָמָּה נֶאֱמַר וּבְשָׁכְבְּךָ וּבְקוּמֶךָ, בְּשָׁעָה שֶׁבְּנֵי אָדָם שׁוֹכְבִים, וּבְשָׁעָה שֶׁבְּנֵי אָדָם עוֹמְדִים. אָמַר רַבִּי טַרְפוֹן, אֲנִי הָיִיתִי בָא בַדֶּרֶךְ, וְהִטֵּתִי לִקְרוֹת, כְּדִבְרֵי בֵית שַׁמַּאי, וְסִכַּנְתִּי בְעַצְמִי מִפְּנֵי הַלִּסְטִים. אָמְרוּ לוֹ, כְּדַי הָיִיתָ לָחוּב בְּעַצְמְךָ, שֶׁעָבַרְתָּ עַל דִּבְרֵי בֵית הִלֵּל:

Berakhot 1:3

The school of Shammai says: In the evening all people should recline and recite [*Shema*], and in the morning they should stand, since it says: "and when you lie down, and when you rise up" (Deuteronomy 6:7). But the school of Hillel says: Each person may recite it in his usual way [posture], since it says, "and when you walk by the way" (v. 7). If so, why does it say: "and when you lie down, and when you rise up"? [It means:] at the time when people are lying down, and at the time when people are arising. Said Rabbi Tarfon: "I was once traveling on the road, and I reclined to recite [*Shema*] in accordance with the view of the school of Shammai, and [by doing so] I put myself in danger of [attack by] bandits." They [the other Sages] said to him: "You would have deserved to be guilty for your own fate, since you went against the view of the school of Hillel."

The school of Shammai concludes, based on the verse "and you shall talk of them … when you lie down, and when you rise up" (Deuteronomy

6:7), that the evening *Shema* should be recited while reclining, while the morning *Shema* should be recited while standing. What is behind this demand, according to the school of Shammai? The verse beginning with "Hear, O Israel" (v. 4) contains two elements: the acceptance of the yoke of heaven ("the Lord our God") and the unity of the divine ("the Lord is one"). The first section of *Keriat Shema* deals with the various ways in which these ideas can be instilled and embedded in all areas of life. One must internalize the word of God in thought ("upon your heart" – v. 6), speech ("and you shall talk of them"), and deed ("And you shall bind them.... And you shall write them" – vv. 8–9). One must be aware in speech of God's unity and His kingship everywhere and at every time: "when you sit in your house, and when you walk by the way, and when you lie down, and when you rise up" (v. 7). Similarly, one should manifest physical actions that express God's unity and kingship, so that they surround one's body and home: "And you shall bind them for a sign upon your hand, and they shall be for frontlets between your eyes. And you shall write them upon the doorposts of your house, and upon your gates" (vv. 8–9). Thanks to a variety of expressions in a range of areas, one's entire existence is enveloped in Torah and mitzvot, and one's day-to-day life shelters under the wings of the Divine Presence.

Our day is divided into two periods, daytime and nighttime. *Keriat Shema* must apply to both periods, and is thus recited twice daily – in the morning and in the evening – and imbues the entire day with spiritual content. In light of this insight, the conclusion of the school of Shammai is clear: If one is to realize the essence of *Keriat Shema* not only on the temporal level, by reciting it in the two periods of the day, but also through the specific content that characterizes each period – lying down in the evening and rising in the morning – then one should recite it in a manner that is typical of the time when it is being recited.

In All Your Ways Acknowledge Him

Although the school of Hillel does not require a specific style of recitation, and rules that "each person may recite it in his usual way," it is not because it is more lenient or does not want to impose. Rather, their ruling stems from a different worldview than that of the school of

Sh'ammai: They conclude that there is another way to inject life with spiritual content.

The school of Hillel relies on the words, "and when you walk by the way," and concludes that "each person may recite it in his usual way." In other words, the culmination of accepting the yoke of heaven is a state in which that yoke becomes a natural part of one's life, a part of one's way. This, the school of Hillel says, is the overarching purpose of the first section of *Keriat Shema*, which deals with imbuing all of life and all of existence with spiritual content. Indeed, having a single prescribed manner for reciting *Shema* would remove it from the natural flow of life. This is why the Talmud states that those who follow the opinion of the school of Shammai are taking "worthless" action (Berakhot 11a). Although it seems at first that the opinion of the school of Hillel, which is not particular about how *Shema* is to be recited, does not contradict the opinion of the school of Shammai, which prescribes the manner for reciting *Shema*, this is not the case. According to the school of Hillel, there is an explicit commandment to recite *Shema* in one's individual "way," as an organic aspect of one's life.[1] Furthermore, according to the school of Hillel, one can recite *Shema* even while one is walking or working (11a), without interrupting the natural flow of life.

This approach, which embeds the yoke of heaven in one's everyday life, is also apparent in a law cited by the Yerushalmi, according to which one can interrupt one's recitation of *Shema* even mid-verse: "'and you shall talk of them' – implying that one is permitted to speak while reciting them" (Y. Berakhot 2:1).[2] *Keriat Shema* blends into life so naturally that one is permitted to interrupt it with extraneous speech.

---

1. See the siddur of Rabbi Amram Gaon (*Keriat Shema* and its blessings, written by Rabbi Amram in the ninth century), which asserts that the school of Hillel requires that each person recite *Shema*, each in their usual way: "Those people who are seated and rise when the time for *Keriat Shema* arrives adhere to the opinion of the school of Shammai and transgress the opinion of the school of Hillel... Shall we say that the school of Hillel permits [to recite *Shema*] standing up?... Did we learn, 'The school of Hillel says: Each person may recite it whether seated, standing, or lying down'? Rather, we learned, 'They stand and recite, they sit and recite.' It follows that if one is standing, one need not sit down, and if one is sitting one need not sit up; rather, each reads in his usual way."
2. My thanks to my friend Rabbi Yehudah Glick for pointing this out.

To sum up, at first glance it appears that following the opinion of the school of Shammai can elevate us to a state in which all of life is imbued with spiritual content. However, when we examine the issue in depth, we learn that the opinion of the school of Hillel can raise one to an even more exalted state, in which spirituality permeates not merely a formal representation of life, but natural life itself.

Disputes for the Sake of Heaven

Sefer Yetzira (*The Book of Creation*), an ancient kabbalistic tome, describes Creation as having three dimensions: world, year, and soul, which can be thought of as place, time, and the human. The dispute between the two schools as to the proper way to accept the yoke of heaven echoes other differences between them regarding the correct approach to those three dimensions:[3]

> The school of Shammai says: Flame, and [then] Grace after Meals, and [then] spices, and [then] Havdala. The school of Hillel says: Flame, and [then] spices, and [then] Grace after Meals, and [then] Havdala. The school of Shammai says [the blessing ends with]: "Who created the light of fire." The school of Hillel says: "Creator of the lights of fire." (Berakhot 8:5)

The school of Shammai's formulation of Havdala blesses God in the past tense, "who created." As they see it, fire was created in the distant past, and the human being blesses the Creator for a historic event. For the school of Hillel, on the other hand, Creation is constantly renewing itself, so that God's presence is still active in every moment within reality and should be blessed. Hence another difference between the two schools'

---

3. Israel Knohl ("A Parasha Concerned with Accepting the Kingdom of Heaven," *Tarbiz* 53 (1984) [Hebrew]: 26) has already highlighted the connection between this dispute between the schools of Hillel and Shammai and their broader conceptions of holiness. Two of the sources cited later in this chapter are quoted by him: the Talmud in Tractate Beitza and the quote from *Avot DeRabbi Natan*.

versions of the blessing: The school of Shammai blesses the creation of the original fire, and thus uses the singular – "the *light* of fire" – while the school of Hillel blesses the present, where there is a profusion of fire, and thus hails the "Creator of the *lights* of fire." Here, too, we see how the school of Hillel acknowledges God's presence in the material world, in day-to-day life, while the school of Shammai gives primacy to that which is inaccessible to humanity: the moment of creation.

Perhaps this is what underpins the famous dispute between the schools of Shammai and Hillel regarding Ḥanukka candles (Shabbat 21b). The school of Hillel rules that on the first night one should light a single candle and add another one every evening, reaching a total of eight candles on the eighth night. The school of Shammai concludes that one starts with eight candles and removes one every evening, finally remaining with a single candle. The school of Hillel explains that "we promote in [matters of] sanctity but do not reduce." The school of Shammai might agree that holiness should be increased, but from their perspective, a multiplicity of lights would not indicate a greater connection to holiness; rather, the movement toward holiness would be inverted – culminating in the single light that symbolizes the source.

The same pattern occurs in a story about the differences in the approaches of Shammai and Hillel themselves, demonstrating that the dispute between the two schools was not incidental or particular to one issue but reflected an ancient, fundamental difference in worldview:

> They related concerning Shammai the Elder [that] all his life he ate in honor of Shabbat. [Thus] if he found a well-favored animal he said, "Let this be for Shabbat." [If afterwards] he found one better favored, he set aside the second [for Shabbat] and ate the first. But Hillel the Elder had a different trait, for all his actions were for the sake of Heaven, as it is said: "Blessed be the Lord, day by day" (Psalms 68). It was likewise taught: The school of Shammai says: From the first day of the week [prepare] for Shabbat; but the school of Hillel says: Blessed be the Lord, day by day. (Beitza 16a)

Shabbat is the holy day that disrupts the routine of the workweek. That is why, according to the school of Shammai, one should direct one's attention and deeds toward it. By contrast, the school of Hillel says that one can, and should, also serve God through "profane" actions, such as eating on a weekday, because people can also encounter their creator in the natural life of the present, not only in the moments when it is transcended.

Further evidence of Hillel's outlook, that "all your actions should be for the sake of Heaven," can be found in *Avot DeRabbi Natan* (2:30):

> All your actions should be for the sake of Heaven, like Hillel. When Hillel would go somewhere, people would ask him, "Where are you going?" [He would reply,] "I'm going to perform a mitzva." "What mitzva, Hillel?" "I'm going to the bathroom." "But is that a mitzva?" "Yes," he replied, "to keep the body from deteriorating." [Another time they asked,] "Where are you going, Hillel?" "I'm going to perform a mitzva." "What mitzva, Hillel?" "I'm going to the bathhouse." "But is that a mitzva?" He said, "Yes, to cleanse the body. Know that this is indeed the case, for even the caretaker charged with scrubbing and polishing the statues in the courtyards of kings receives an annual salary. How much more so for us, who are created in the image and likeness [of God], as it is written, 'for in the image of God He made man' (Genesis. 9:6)."

According to Hillel's outlook, ascribing concrete significance to the fact that humanity was created in God's image plays up the immanence of holiness. Just as God permeates all of time and all of reality, so too, He is present in each and every human being. If every person, body and soul, is holy, then even our basic – and base – bodily functions can become mitzvot. The following source also assigns religious significance to the consumption of food:

> The school of Shammai says: The appearance offering is two silver [*ma'a*], and the festival offering is a silver *ma'a*.

> The school of Hillel says: The appearance offering is a silver *ma'a,* and the festival offering is two silver [*ma'a*]. (Ḥagiga 1:2)

The disagreement is over the minimal value of offerings that can be brought to the Temple during the festival pilgrimages. The appearance offering is a burnt offering that is fully consumed on the altar, whereas one who brings a festival offering eats part of it and sacrifices the rest. According to the school of Shammai, the appearance offering is the more important of the two, because it requires a greater investment than the festival offering, which the believer shares with God. The school of Hillel, on the other hand, holds that the offering that one partakes of is the more important of the two, based on the idea that people can be elevated even through simple acts, such as eating meat.

The final dispute that we will present is more philosophical in tone, but it too boils down to the same fundamental difference between the schools of Shammai and Hillel. Its subject is the order of Creation:

> The school of Shammai says: Heaven was created first and afterwards the earth was created…The school of Hillel says: Earth was created first and afterwards heaven…The school of Hillel said to the school of Shammai: According to your view, a man builds the upper story [first] and afterwards builds the house!…The school of Shammai said to the school of Hillel: According to your view, a man makes the footstool [first], and afterwards he makes the throne! (Ḥagiga 12a)

The Talmud's reasoning makes clear that whatever is created first is also of primary importance. According to the school of Shammai, the earth, meaning physical reality, is of secondary importance to heaven. It compares the earth to a footstool, which is secondary to the throne. The school of Hillel, on the other hand, says the earth is the house itself, the essence and purpose of creation, while considering heaven a second (and secondary) story.

Both Are the Words of the Living God

Rabbi Aviya Hacohen recently published a book whose title may be translated as: *Appearing before the Lord: Essays on Tractate Ḥagiga*. Among other topics, he writes about the dispute between the schools of Shammai and Hillel, and proposes an approach similar to the one I outline above. Hacohen makes a fascinating claim: The dispute between the schools of Shammai and Hillel reflects two competing outlooks in the Torah – one that is espoused in the book of Deuteronomy and another that emerges from the other books of the Torah. In his treatment of the mishna in Tractate Ḥagiga that asks whether the main offering is the appearance offering, which is fully consumed on the altar, or the festival offering, which is eaten by the believer, Hacohen writes: "The root of the journey to the House of the Lord in the book of Exodus is the journey of the slave to his master, who must be appeased with gifts. The book of Deuteronomy, despite stating that "they shall not appear before the Lord empty[-handed]," does not emphasize the offerings. The journey is not that of a slave to his master, but rather a pilgrimage of joy that is shared with all of the needy – stranger, orphan, and widow."

After analyzing the verses, he concludes: "The school of Hillel…emphasizes the individual's happiness and preserves the spiritual outlook of the book of Deuteronomy, while the school of Shammai… preserves the spiritual outlook that underlies the rest of the portions of the Torah that deal with the festivals."[4] To my mind, Hacohen's idea injects new meaning into the talmudic tale (Eiruvin 13b) of the *bat kol* that declares that both sides in the disputes between the schools of Hillel and Shammai are "the words of the living God" – both have their roots in the words of God as revealed by the Bible.

Hacohen takes his discussion of the disputes between the schools of Shammai and Hillel even further, linking it to aspects of modern Jewish thought. He cites Rabbi Jacob Joseph of Polonne, a student of the Baal Shem Tov who often comments, in his book *Toledot Yaakov Yosef*, on the connection between Hasidism and Hillel's Torah, and between

---

4. Aviya Hacohen, *Appearing Before the Lord: Essays on Tractate Ḥagiga* (Ein Tzurim: Mishlavim, 2016) [Hebrew], 42.

the *mitnagdim* (the opponents of Hasidism) and Shammai's Torah. He writes in summation:

> The novelty of Hasidism lies in its revelation of the divinity of the human soul, which is why the works of the Baal Shem Tov and Hasidism apply the *sefirot* to the human soul. Thus, the focus of the Baal Shem Tov's divine service is the human being, who is created in [God's] image – an element that also underlies Hillel's Torah. The focus of Hillel's divine service is the revelation of God in man, as we see time and again in the Mishna in Tractate Ḥagiga and elsewhere.[5]

The Torah of the Land of Israel

There is no doubt that the Judaism associated with the school of Hillel has been resurgent in recent years. The individual experience, and especially joy and love, has taken on an increasingly central role in religious life. The well-known talmudic dictum that "Since the day that the Temple was destroyed, the Holy One, blessed be He, has nothing in this world but the four cubits of halakha alone" (Berakhot 8a) was evident of an exilic religiosity, which hews to the worldview of the school of Shammai. The return to the Land of Israel allows us to recognize God's place in all of life's expressions, and especially in humankind – its inner world and experience.

Here is Rabbi Abraham Isaac Kook, the great poet of the school of Hillel's take on life:

> God's radiant light, which permeates all of the worlds, animating them and saturating them with the sustenance of supernal bliss from the source of life, infuses all souls and angels, all creatures, with the strength to discern the inner aspect of the sense of life.... so that there is no need to say that one eats in order to learn [Torah], pray, and perform mitzvot, for that is but a middling trait; rather, that eating

5. Ibid., 63–64.

> itself, as well as speaking, and all of the processes and feelings of life are suffused with holiness and light. (*Shemoneh Kevatzim* 2:62, 65)

Elsewhere, Rabbi Kook writes:

> The condition in which God can be apprehended only through religion relegated the world to the depths of baseness. God should be discernible in all of life, in all of Creation, and thus in any case be known throughout life and Creation. Religion is a tool, a means to refine actions, attributes, feelings, society's internal and external conventions, in a manner that prepares life and Creation for the knowledge of God. God is revealed through religion only to the extent that religion itself is hewn from that which lies above religion.... Our living Torah is not a discrete religion; our living Torah is a revelation of God, who is revealed through it as He is revealed through the rest of Creation. The Torah and Creation, as they become one, reveal God in life...God is revealed in everything, both holy and profane.[6]

Fear God, and Keep His Commandments; for This Is the Whole Person

The realization that the opinions of the school of Shammai are also "the words of the living God," and that the roots of both schools have been present in the Jewish people's religious life from the outset, lead me to believe that it is important in our generation that the emphasis on the school of Hillel not erase the school of Shammai. Alongside the great need to call attention to humanity and its divine nature, it is an approach to Torah that comes with risks. It may lead people to think that their

---

6. Abraham Isaac Kook, Manuscripts, vol. 2, "*Pinkas HaDapim*" 1:20 [Hebrew], available at he.wikisource.org/.

personal experience is the only legitimate criterion, and that they are not obligated to do anything that doesn't "speak to them." A focus on the self can inflate the ego to the point of solipsism: "I am, and there is none else beside me" (Zephaniah 2:15). The solution, to my mind, is to continue tempering the approach of the school of Hillel with that of the school of Shammai.

For years I have been starting every day of study with my students by noting the date and reciting the verse, "This is the day which the Lord has made; we will rejoice and be glad in it" (Psalms 118:24). But before reciting the verse about rejoicing, and having acknowledged that experience must be wedded to awe and a strict observance of halakha, we recite this verse from Ecclesiastes (12:13): "The end of the matter, all having been heard: fear God, and keep His commandments; for this is the whole person."

Halakha: Law and Life

Berakhot 2:5

A groom is exempt from reciting *Shema* on the first night, until Saturday night if he has not done the deed. A story about Rabban Gamliel who recited [*Shema*] on the first night that he got married: His students said to him, "Didn't you teach us, our teacher, that a groom is exempt from reciting *Shema* on the first night?" He said to them, "I will not listen to you, to remove the kingdom of heaven from me for even one hour."

ברכות ב, ה

חָתָן פָּטוּר מִקְּרִיאַת שְׁמַע בְּלַיְלָה הָרִאשׁוֹן עַד מוֹצָאֵי שַׁבָּת, אִם לֹא עָשָׂה מַעֲשֶׂה. מַעֲשֶׂה בְּרַבָּן גַּמְלִיאֵל שֶׁקָּרָא בְלַיְלָה הָרִאשׁוֹן שֶׁנָּשָׂא. אָמְרוּ לוֹ תַּלְמִידָיו, לֹא לִמַּדְתָּנוּ, רַבֵּנוּ, שֶׁחָתָן פָּטוּר מִקְּרִיאַת שְׁמַע בְּלַיְלָה הָרִאשׁוֹן. אָמַר לָהֶם, אֵינִי שׁוֹמֵעַ לָכֶם לְבַטֵּל מִמֶּנִּי מַלְכוּת שָׁמַיִם אֲפִלּוּ שָׁעָה אֶחָת:

Rabban Gamliel's students learned from him that a groom is exempt from reciting *Shema* on his wedding night, so they assumed that he would conduct himself in keeping with that rule. Much to their surprise, however, he did recite *Shema* on his wedding night. Rabban Gamliel defies his students' expectations in similar ways in the next two mishnayot:

> [Rabban Gamliel] washed on the first night after his wife died. His students said to him, "Didn't you teach us, our teacher, that a mourner is forbidden to wash?" He said to them, "I am not like other people. I am delicate." (Berakhot 2:6)
>
> And when [Rabban Gamliel's] slave Tavi died, he received words of comfort for him. His students said to

> him, "Didn't you teach us, our teacher, that one does not receive words of comfort for slaves?" He said to them, "My slave Tavi was not like other slaves. He was acceptable (*kasher*)." (Berakhot 2:7)

These three stories are concerned with lifecycle events, and convey an important lesson regarding the relationship between halakha and life, and between the words spoken in the *beit midrash* and the actualization of Torah through action. The law is generalized by definition, and relates to an uncomplicated theoretical reality. Life, on the other hand, is complicated and multifaceted, and one cannot issue a halakhic ruling without applying judgment. One must examine each and every scenario and weigh its unique facets, and ultimately arrive at a ruling that takes into account all aspects of the question.

According to the letter of the law, a mourner is forbidden to wash. The purpose of this law is to deprive the mourner of a special pleasure, but not to make the mourner suffer. Rabban Gamliel thus concludes that a delicate man is permitted to wash, because otherwise he would experience considerable suffering. In a similar vein, according to halakha one must not mourn for a slave, but that applies only to an ordinary slave, not one as upstanding as Tavi.

As for reciting *Shema* on one's wedding night – the halakha is that the groom is not obligated. But if the groom chooses to recite it anyway, especially if he is someone like Rabban Gamliel, he can perform the mitzva without having to rely on explicit permission.[1]

Rabban Gamliel's sharp response to his students – "I will not listen to you, to remove the kingdom of heaven from me for even one hour" – shows us that his departures from the letter of the law are acts not of rebellion, but of deference to the yoke of heaven and the will of God. Hence the wordplay: When his students claim that he is exempt from *Shema*, Rabban Gamliel replies, "I will not listen (*shome'a*) to you," where listening is identified with obedience. Thus he emphasizes his total submission to God – he does not obey (*shome'a*) anyone who calls for

---

1. See Berakhot 2:8.

him to skip the Lord's *Shema*.[2] The Mishna contrasts the naiveté of the students, who do not grasp the spirit of the law and its flexibility, with the profundity of Rabban Gamliel, who listens to the Torah, understands it deeply, and can thus adapt its precepts to any situation.

Rabbi Eliezer's Maidservant

A fascinating comparison can be drawn between Rabban Gamliel's reaction to the death of his slave Tavi and Rabbi Eliezer's conduct after the death of his maidservant. The Talmud cites the story of Rabbi Eliezer in the context of discussing our mishna:

> When the maidservant of Rabbi Eliezer died, his disciples went in to condole with him. When he saw them, he went up to an upper chamber, but they went up after him. He then went into an anteroom and they followed him there. He then went into the dining hall and they followed him there. He said to them: I thought that you would be scalded with warm water; I see you are not scalded even with boiling hot water [Rashi: Meaning that I expected you to understand based on my more subtle hint]. Have I not taught you that a row of comforters is not made for male and female slaves, and that a blessing of mourners is not said for them, nor is condolence offered for them? What then do they say for them? The same as they say to a man for his ox and his ass: "May the Almighty replenish your loss." So for his male and female slave they say to him: "May the Almighty replenish your loss." (Berakhot 16b)

2. The relation between the three stories in the first chapter of Berakhot and the three stories in the second chapter drives home the Mishna's message that Rabban Gamliel's behavior stems from adherence to halakha, rather than rebellion. The theme of the three stories in Chapter 1 is deference to halakha (see Yisrael Rosenson, "Aggadic Elements in Mishnayot Tractate Berakhot," *Netuim* 2 (1994) [Hebrew]: 52–57). The first of the three stories, like the first of the stories in our chapter, is about Rabban Gamliel – but whereas in our chapter Rabban Gamliel diverges from his own teachings, there he submits to the majority opinion.

In contrast to Rabban Gamliel, Rabbi Eliezer conducts himself in accordance with the law as he taught it in the *beit midrash*. What is peculiar in the story is that despite the fact that Rabbi Eliezer's stance is well-known, his students insist on trying to console him – even when he attempts to evade them. Another question is why, if the students forgot what he taught them, he does not correct them immediately, but rather attempts to evade them until there is nowhere else to go?

I suggest that Rabbi Eliezer is deeply pained by the death of his maidservant, so that he is torn between the halakhic principle and his feelings. His students' actions stem from their recognition of his distress and his need for consolation. But Rabbi Eliezer the Great, considered a successor of the school of Shammai,[3] chooses to set his feelings aside and adhere to the letter of the law, refusing consolation.[4]

The Halakha Follows the School of Hillel

The Mishna chooses to relate the story of Rabban Gamliel and his slave, not the one about Rabbi Eliezer and his maidservant. As we have seen, when it comes to accepting the yoke of heaven, Rabban Gamliel's approach upholds the ideas of the Sages of the school of Hillel. To them, accepting the yoke of heaven is not about adhering to the literal interpretation of "when you lie down, and when you rise up," but rather about reciting *Shema* in one's "usual way," as a natural part of one's life, in keeping with the verse, "and when you walk by the way." According

3. Shabbat 130b. See Rashi there on the words "was [a follower] of Beit Shammai." Rabbi Aviya Hacohen, in his book *Appearing Before the Lord*, cites many examples supporting the claim that there is a fundamental disagreement between the schools of Hillel and Shammai regarding the correct approach to interpreting Scripture – whether or not to adhere to the words and their connotations (56–57).
4. Further evidence of this interpretation can be found in a story in Tractate Sukka (27b) that describes Rabbi Eliezer engaging in similar behavior. There, he is asked a halakhic questions and responds by "evading." The first two times he is asked the question, he attempts to change the subject, but the third time he literally runs away. The Talmud explains that he did this not because he did not know the law, but rather "because he never said anything which he had not heard from his master." As in the story in Tractate Berakhot, Rabbi Eliezer is torn due to his formalistic approach to halakha.

to Rabban Gamliel, true commitment to halakha must take into account the singularity of the situation one is facing; otherwise, the law will not necessarily give expression to halakha's deeper content.

The Hebrew word "halakha" is nearly identical to the word *halikha,* "walking." The Torah employs the metaphor of "when you walk by the way" to describe the individual's divine service in every time and place.

The Unanswered Prayer

ברכות ג, א

מִי שֶׁמֵּתוֹ מוּטָל לְפָנָיו, פָּטוּר מִקְּרִיאַת שְׁמַע וּמִן הַתְּפִלָּה וּמִן הַתְּפִלִּין. נוֹשְׂאֵי הַמִּטָּה וְחִלּוּפֵיהֶן וְחִלּוּפֵי חִלּוּפֵיהֶן, אֶת שֶׁלִּפְנֵי הַמִּטָּה וְאֶת שֶׁלְּאַחַר הַמִּטָּה, אֶת שֶׁלַּמִּטָּה צֹרֶךְ בָּהֶן פְּטוּרִים, וְאֶת שֶׁאֵין לַמִּטָּה צֹרֶךְ בָּהֶן חַיָּבִין. אֵלּוּ וָאֵלּוּ פְּטוּרִין מִן הַתְּפִלָּה:

Berakhot 3:1

One whose dead lies before him [not yet buried] is exempt from reciting *Shema*, from saying *Shemoneh Esreh* and from wearing tefillin. The pall bearers and their replacements and the replacements of the replacements, regardless of whether they are in the front or in the back of the casket: those who are needed to carry the casket are exempt, and those who are not needed to carry the casket are obligated [to recite *Shema*]. These and those are exempt from reciting *Shemoneh Esreh*.

On Friday, June 24, 2005, there was a shooting attack near Beit Hagai. Aviad Yehuda – the son of my friends Rabbi Neria Masour, a colleague at the Otniel yeshiva, and his wife Eva – was wounded. Throughout Shabbat and Saturday night, we prayed and cried, beseeching God to have mercy on Aviad. But the answer was no. On Sunday morning, Aviad's loving and beloved soul ascended to heaven.

After the funeral, we at the yeshiva felt that we could not continue with our usual course of studies. We decided instead to focus on the case of the mourner, through the prism of the third chapter of Berakhot. Our studies sparked a fascinating debate among the students as to the mourner's exemption from *Keriat Shema, Amida,* and tefillin when the dead has yet to be buried. Some saw that exemption as a way of honoring the deceased by showing that the mourner is devoted exclusively to them. Others suggested that when a person is grappling on a personal level with the most difficult questions regarding faith, evil, and the existence of death in the world, they should not be forced to make declarations and recite prayers that they might not fully identify with, as the Mishna states elsewhere: "Do not console [your friend] at the time when his deceased lies before him" (Avot 4:18). But there were those who had the opposite thought. One student, Aharon Zeff, put forward a novel interpretation of the mourner's exemption. The purpose of praying and accepting the yoke of heaven, he said, was to connect us to God. But when our dead lies before us, we do not need those means for connecting to God, for He is right there in front of us. This Torah insight came to Aharon at Aviad's funeral, during which all of the participants felt, alongside terrible pain, God's tangible presence.

After the Shiva mourning period, the yeshiva resumed its usual course of studies. I opened my notes and saw the final lesson we learned on Thursday, the day before the terror attack:

> "Moreover concerning the stranger.... Hear in heaven, Your dwelling place, **and do according to all that the stranger calls to You for; that all the peoples of the earth may know Your name, to fear You**, as do Your people Israel, and that they may know that Your name is called upon this house which I have built" (I Kings 8:41–43). However, when an Israelite prays before You in this Temple, "**grant him all that his heart seeks**, for You alone know what is in the heart of every man" (v. 39). (*Midrash Tanḥuma, Teruma* 9).

The Midrash explains that when non-Jews pray, He grants their requests, because He wishes to make His name known. But the Jewish people, who are closer to Him, do not require this approach. God is more genuine with them and, rather than granting their overt requests, responds to their deeper needs. In my notebook I found the following comment on the midrash: "The fact that God can say 'no' to us is evidence of the depth of the connection between us, the intimacy – not distance."

Tannaitic Prayer: Routine and Flow

ברכות ד, ג-ד

רַבָּן גַּמְלִיאֵל אוֹמֵר, בְּכָל יוֹם מִתְפַּלֵּל אָדָם שְׁמוֹנֶה עֶשְׂרֵה. רַבִּי יְהוֹשֻׁעַ אוֹמֵר, מֵעֵין שְׁמוֹנֶה עֶשְׂרֵה. רַבִּי עֲקִיבָא אוֹמֵר, אִם שְׁגוּרָה תְפִלָּתוֹ בְּפִיו יִתְפַּלֵּל שְׁמוֹנֶה עֶשְׂרֵה, וְאִם לָאו מֵעֵין שְׁמוֹנֶה עֶשְׂרֵה:

רַבִּי אֱלִיעֶזֶר אוֹמֵר, הָעוֹשֶׂה תְפִלָּתוֹ קֶבַע, אֵין תְּפִלָּתוֹ תַּחֲנוּנִים. רַבִּי יְהוֹשֻׁעַ אוֹמֵר, הַמְהַלֵּךְ בִּמְקוֹם סַכָּנָה, מִתְפַּלֵּל תְּפִלָּה קְצָרָה. אוֹמֵר, הוֹשַׁע הַשֵּׁם אֶת עַמְּךָ אֶת שְׁאֵרִית יִשְׂרָאֵל, בְּכָל פָּרָשַׁת הָעִבּוּר יִהְיוּ צָרְכֵיהֶם לְפָנֶיךָ. בָּרוּךְ אַתָּה ה' שׁוֹמֵעַ תְּפִלָּה:

Berakhot 4:3–4

Rabban Gamliel says: Every day a person must pray eighteen [blessings of *Shemoneh Esreh*]. Rabbi Yehoshua says: [One may say] an abbreviated [form of the] eighteen [blessings]. Rabbi Akiva says: If his prayer is fluent in his mouth, he must say eighteen; and if it is not – an abbreviated eighteen.

Rabbi Eliezer says: One who makes his prayer "set," his prayer does not constitute pleading [for Divine mercy]. Rabbi Yehoshua says: One who is traveling in a dangerous place should offer a brief prayer [and] say: Save, God, Your people, the remnant of Israel; at every period of transition let their needs be before You. You are the Source of all blessing, God, who heeds prayer.

Rabban Gamliel's Edict

In the beginning of our mishna, Rabban Gamliel rules that one must recite the same prayer every day, the *Shemoneh Esreh*. There are those who opine that during the Second Temple period prayer was not considered an obligation, so that Rabban Gamliel's statement here does not only formalize the words of the prayer, it enshrines the very obligation to pray.[1]

Rabban Gamliel, the president of the Sanhedrin, was grappling with the dangers faced by his people in the wake of the destruction of the Temple, which was both a national and spiritual focal point. His edict on prayer posits a single religious act to unite his divided people and pose an alternative to the spiritual connection to God that was once provided by the Temple service.

But there is also a price to standardizing prayer and making it an obligation – loss of spontaneity and individuality. Indeed, some of Rabban Gamliel's contemporaries opposed his edict, led by Rabbi Eliezer the Great.

Still, it is important to note that the formalization of prayer was not only a matter of expediency due to the reality post Destruction, but a spiritual value in its own right. Faced with the assertion of Rabbi Eliezer the Great that "One who makes his prayer set (*keva*), his prayer does not constitute pleading," one can reply that "One who makes his prayer pleading, his prayer is not set." The capacity to commit and persevere – not only when prayer is convenient or when one feels like praying – is an important element of divine service. The Talmud cites the idea that the *Amida* "prayers were instituted to replace the [*tamid*] daily sacrifices" (Berakhot 26b). *Tamid* means constant in Hebrew; the power of the *tamid* sacrifice derives from its regularity. That is why, according to Rabban Gamliel's outlook, regularity is one of the defining characteristics of the prayers that are instituted to replace the daily sacrifices.

The Bible includes a prayer that can be seen as an antecedent of the type of prayer formalized by Rabban Gamliel. According to Daniel, prayer is a religious rite that is deeply tied to the temporal dimension. This is why he persists in praying three times a day, even when the king decrees death to one who prays to anyone other than the king:

1. Ezra Fleischer, "On the Beginnings of Obligatory Jewish Prayer," *Tarbiz* 59 (1990) [Hebrew]: 397–441.

> And when Daniel knew that the writing was signed, he went into his house – now his windows were open in his upper chamber toward Jerusalem – and he kneeled upon his knees three times a day, and prayed, and gave thanks before his God, as he did aforetime. (Daniel 6:11)

Daniel knows that his prayers contravene the king's decree, and he is punished for it. The king throws him into the lions' den, but believes that God will come to his aid in recognition of his habitual divine service:

> Then the king commanded, and they brought Daniel, and cast him into the den of lions. Now the king spoke and said to Daniel: "Your God whom you serve continually, He will deliver you." (Daniel 6:17)

The king reminds Daniel of the true reason God intervenes to rescue him: the regularity of his prayers.

One Who Makes His Prayer Set, His Prayer Does Not Constitute Pleading

It is no surprise that the person who comes out in opposition to Rabban Gamliel, his brother-in-law Rabbi Eliezer the Great, is emblematic of the individual who remains steadfast in his position even if that means paying a heavy price. We also see this characteristic in the famous story about the oven of Akhnai, when Rabbi Eliezer chooses excommunication over capitulation to the opinion of the rabbi whose ruling he disagrees with.[2]

Here, Rabbi Eliezer follows an approach that derives prayer from the Patriarchs rather than from the *tamid* sacrifices.[3] This outlook, which plays up the individual aspect of prayer, informs his position in the mishna. Indeed, both Talmuds describe Rabbi Eliezer's unique expression in prayer. According to the Yerushalmi, Rabbi Eliezer would "utter a

---

2. Bava Metzia 59b.
3. See the *baraitot* that oppose one another on this issue in Berakhot 26b.

new prayer every day" (Y. Berakhot 4:3). Naturally, such renewal would spring from the daily revitalization of the worshipper's subjective experience. The Bavli relates that Rabbi Eliezer would apply his approach that no two prayers should be alike, to others as well:

> Our Rabbis taught: Once a certain disciple went down before the ark in the presence of Rabbi Eliezer, and he drew out the prayer to a great length. His disciples said to him: Master, how longwinded this fellow is! He replied to them: Is he drawing it out any more than our Master Moses, of whom it is written: "The forty days and the forty nights [that I fell down]"? Another time it happened that a certain disciple went down before the ark in the presence of Rabbi Eliezer, and he cut the prayer very short. His disciples said to him: How concise this fellow is! He replied to them: Is he any more concise than our Master Moses, who prayed, as it is written: "Heal her now, O God, I beseech You"? (Berakhot 34a)

According to Rabbi Eliezer, how long the *ḥazan* spends leading prayers is not a matter of concern for the congregation; on the contrary, prayers with elements that are unique to the time and the worshipper are considered *more* exalted – comparable, even, to the prayers of Moses himself.

Formalized Pleading

When it comes to the dispute between Rabban Gamliel and Rabbi Eliezer, we can conclude that "both [opinions] are the words of the living God." The roots of prayer can be found in both the Patriarchs and the sacrifices. It is true that "one who makes his prayer set, his prayer does not constitute pleading," but it is also true that "one who makes his prayer pleading, his prayer is not set." The challenge is to find a way to synthesize these two truths.

Apparently, Rabbi Eliezer the Great was originally opposed to Rabban Gamliel's edict standardizing prayer, but the editors of the Mishna choose to cite him as an independent opinion in mishna 4, rather than place the opinion next to Rabban Gamliel's opinion in mishna 3. Consequently, Rabbi Eliezer's words are taken not as a challenge to Rabban Gamliel on the question of when one should pray or what one should say, but rather as guidance on how one should pray. This is reinforced by the Talmud's presentation of Rabbi Eliezer's opinion:

> Rabbi Eliezer says: [One who makes his prayer set, his prayer does not constitute pleading]. What is meant by set? Rabbi Yaakov b. Idi said in the name of Rabbi Oshaya: Anyone whose prayer is like a heavy burden on him. The Rabbis say: Whoever does not say it in the manner of supplication. Rabba and R. Yosef both say: Whoever is not able to insert something fresh in it[4] ... Abaye bar Avin and Rabbi Ḥanina bar Avin both said: Whoever does not pray at the first and last appearance of the sun. (Berakhot 29b)

All the amoraic approaches cited by the Talmud are concerned with various aspects of the manner of prayer: the worshippers' feelings and style, their private additions, and the surroundings in which they pray. There is no dispute with the standardization of prayer.

Although Rabbi Eliezer's original opinion is not accepted halakhically, and the formula and times of prayer remain standard, the spirit of his opinion and his warning about the dangers of rote prayer have a large, enduring impact:

> One must pray in a supplicatory manner, like a beggar entreating at the gate, and calmly, and [one's prayer] must not appear as a burden that one is eager to be rid of. (*Shulḥan Arukh, Oraḥ Ḥayim* 98:3)

4. In contrast with the Yerushalmi, here the implication is that one should add words to the standard prayer rather than replace it with something entirely new.

Between Two Mountains: An Abbreviated *Shemoneh Esreh*

As we have seen, two towering giants, Rabban Gamliel, who was the president of the Sanhedrin, and Rabbi Eliezer the Great, represent two opposing paradigms of prayer: prayer as obligation, with a standard text; and flowing, spontaneous prayer.

Each of these approaches to prayer poses its own difficulties. When the phrasing is standardized, it takes massive effort to focus one's consciousness and feelings on words written by another, especially when one has recited those same words countless times in the past. But the other approach is not simple either. Not everyone is blessed with the originality and creativity of Rabbi Eliezer, who would compose a new prayer every day. If one can say that the challenge with Rabban Gamliel's prayer is that it is too set, Rabbi Eliezer's prayer can be said to be "too loose."

Bridging the gap between the two is the opinion of Rabbi Yehoshua, who, as we will see, posits three methods for striking a balance between the opinions of his colleagues.

In Berakhot 4:3, Rabbi Yehoshua and Rabbi Akiva raise the possibility of an abbreviated *Shemoneh Esreh*. Rabbi Akiva clearly favors the full *Shemoneh Esreh* over the abbreviated form, which he says is only for those who cannot recite the full version. Rabbi Yehoshua, on the other hand, favors the abbreviated (*me'ein*) *Shemoneh Esreh* for everyone.

What is an "abbreviated *Shemoneh Esreh*"? *Me'ein* connotes something that contains another thing, as we see elsewhere in the Mishna: "Bless upon the bad which contains (*me'ein*) good, and upon the good which contains (*me'ein*) bad" (Berakhot 9:3); "[If] one performed many labors, all of which stem from (*me'ein*) the same principal labor" (Shabbat 7:1). We can thus say that "*me'ein Shemoneh Esreh*" is something of a middle ground in the dispute about prayer: on the one hand, it retains the framework of eighteen blessings that guide us regarding what to pray for; on the other, it releases us from the need to recite a standard phrasing and frees each of us to express every issue in our own way.[5] In doing

5. It seems that this is indeed how Rav interpreted Rabbi Yehoshua's statement: "What

so, Rabbi Yehoshua finds the golden mean, shaping a prayer that is both "set" (in its themes) and "pleading" (in its unique content and style).

While ultimately the halakhic ruling is that one should recite the full *Shemoneh Esreh*, the spirit of Rabbi Yehoshua's rejected opinion – like that of Rabbi Eliezer – lives on. The worshipper is given the option to append to each blessing an abbreviated form of that blessing:

> Said Rav Yehuda the son of Shmuel bar Shilat in the name of Rav: Even though it was said that one should pray for his private needs only at "Who hears prayer," nevertheless, if he is disposed to say **at the end of any blessing something** [personal supplications] **like** (*me'ein*) [the subject of] **that blessing**, he may do so. (Avoda Zara 8a)
>
> **If he wanted to add in each of the middle blessings something like that blessing, he may add.** How so? If he had a sick person, he asks for mercy in the blessing "Heal us." If he needed a livelihood, he would ask in the Blessing of the Years. (*Shulḥan Arukh, Oraḥ Ḥayim* 119:1)

Personal Prayer

Rabbi Yehoshua suggests another compromise between the two facets of prayer, the set and the spontaneous:

> Rabbi Yehoshua says: One who is traveling in a dangerous place should offer a brief prayer [and] say: Save, God, Your people, the remnant of Israel; at every period of transition let their needs be before You. You are the Source of all blessing, God, who heeds prayer. (Berakhot 4:4)

---

is meant by 'an abbreviated eighteen'? Rav said: An abbreviated form of each blessing" (Berakhot 29a). There, Shmuel posits that an abbreviated *Shemoneh Esreh* is a prayer called "Give Us Discernment" (*Havinenu*). Shmuel's approach is consonant with that of Rabbi Akiva, who prescribes the abbreviated form only in special cases, when one cannot recite the full version. It is hard to see his opinion as an interpretation of Rabbi Yehoshua's outlook or to consider "*Havinenu*" an alternative with status equal to that of *Shemoneh Esreh*.

On one hand, the words of the prayer are prescribed, but on the other, it is uttered only in the appropriate circumstances, when one "is traveling in a dangerous place." It is noteworthy that our chapter, which deals with the relation between personal prayer and standardized prayer, describes a special prayer tailored to a specific person:

> Rabbi Neḥunya ben HaKana would offer a brief prayer when he entered the study hall and when he left. They said to him: What is the place [nature] of this prayer? He told them: "Upon my entrance, I pray that no mishaps should occur because of me; and upon my departure, I offer thanksgiving for my portion." (Berakhot 4:2)

The prayer of Rabbi Neḥunya ben HaKana, which deals with the study hall and Torah study, emerges from his worldview, which considers Torah the key to everything, as in his statement in Tractate Avot (3:5):[6]

> Rabbi Neḥunya ben HaKana says: Anyone who accepts the yoke of Torah upon himself, they lift from him the yoke of government and the yoke of the way of the world. And anyone who casts from himself the yoke of Torah, they place upon him the yoke of government and the yoke of the way of the world.

The question conveyed to Rabbi Neḥunya by his colleague – "What is the place of this prayer?" – can also be directed at the editor of our chapter, who interposed this mishna between 4:1, which prescribes the times for *Shemoneh Esreh*, and 4:3, which deals with the very obligation to pray *Shemoneh Esreh*. But the structure of the chapter raises the possibility that there is nothing incongruous about the positioning of the mishna about Rabbi Neḥunya ben HaKana. It seems to me that the editor of

---

6. The link between the mishna about Rabbi Neḥunya ben HaKana in Tractate Berakhot and the one about him in Avot is explicated by Yisrael Rosenson ("Aggadic Elements," 62–63), who also notes the Mishna's meaning as to the relationship between Torah and prayer.

the chapter sought, in a systematic way, to strike a balance between personal prayer and standardized prayer. Here is how that tension plays out:

	Type of Prayer	Topic of Mishna
Mishna 1	*Shemoneh Esreh*	Prescribes the times for prayer
Mishna 2	Personal prayer	Rabbi Neḥunya ben HaKana (a prayer for Torah study)
Mishna 3	*Shemoneh Esreh*	The obligation to pray daily
Mishna 4	Personal prayer	Rabbi Eliezer ("One who makes his prayer set, his prayer does not constitute pleading") and Rabbi Yehoshua (prayer in times of danger)

The editor of our chapter structures it so that it alternates personal prayer with standardized prayer. In this way, the chapter sheds light on the richness of the world of prayer, which features a set, standardized element alongside one that is individual and spontaneous.

The Time for Evening Prayer

In 4:3, Rabbi Yehoshua opposes Rabban Gamliel on the question of standardized prayer, offering an "abbreviated *Shemoneh Esreh.*" Rabbi Yehoshua also differs with Rabban Gamliel on the question of the requirement to pray three times daily. While he seems to agree that people should recite Shaḥarit (morning) and Minḥa (afternoon) prayers, he opines that there is also prayer that depends on a person's own initiative, and he considers the Maariv (evening) prayers optional.[7] Rabban Gamliel's harsh response to Rabbi Yehoshua's refusal to yield to the Sanhedrin's ruling, according to which Maariv is compulsory, ultimately led to

7. Berakhot 27b.

the former being ousted from the presidency.[8] According to the Talmud, the mishna that opens our chapter adopts Rabbi Yehoshua's approach:

> Shaḥarit [can be said] until midday. Rabbi Yehuda says until four hours into the day. Minḥa [can be said] until the evening. Rabbi Yehuda says until the middle of the afternoon. Maariv has no set time, and Musaf can be said all day. Rabbi Yehuda says until seven hours into the day. (Berakhot 4:1)
>
> Maariv has no set time. What is the meaning of "has no set time"? Shall I say it means that it could be said any time in the night? Then let it state: The time for the evening prayer is the whole night! But what in fact is the meaning of "has no set time"? It is equivalent to saying the evening prayer is optional. As Rav Yehuda said that Shmuel said: With regard to the evening prayer, Rabban Gamliel says it is compulsory, whereas Rabbi Yehoshua says it is optional. (Berakhot 27b)

The section of the mishna above that deals with Maariv differs from the sections that discuss the other prayers. Whereas for the other prayers Rabbi Yehuda disagrees with the times prescribed by the first *Tanna* in the mishna, for Maariv there is no mention of a dispute. Furthermore, other prayers have a defined time, while Maariv, as the Talmud notes, does not; the phrase "has no set time" suffices.

The word used here to denote a set time, *keva,* also appears elsewhere in our chapter. Rabbi Eliezer the Great uses it in a negative context, stating that "one who makes his prayer set (*keva*), his prayer does not constitute pleading." We can thus deduce that "has no set time (*keva*)" is not merely a lenient statement as to the correct time for Maariv; it also indicates that the absence of a fixed schedule reflects a positive spiritual value, as it facilitates prayer that is imbued with pleading.[9] According to

8. Ibid.
9. I recently discovered that Rabbi Walfish has already offered this explanation. See "Teaching the Mishnah as a Literary Text," in *Teaching Classical Rabbinic Texts: Studies in Jewish Education,* vol. 8 (Jerusalem: Magnes Press, 2003), 41–45.

the Vilna Gaon,[10] the phrase "has no set time" means "it does not have its own time," implying that one can recite Maariv so long as one is not obligated to say another prayer. The time for Maariv is thus between the end of the time for Minḥa and the beginning of the time for Shaḥarit.

The first mishna in our chapter teaches us, then, that there are two types of prayer. The regular prayers, Shaḥarit and Minḥa, are modeled after the *tamid* sacrifices in the destroyed Temple, and one recites them based on a sense of commitment and at regular times: "The one lamb you shall offer in the morning, and the other lamb you shall offer at dusk" (Numbers 28:4). The second, spontaneous type of prayer is Maariv. It issues forth from an inner inclination, does not have a set time, and, according to Rabbi Yehoshua, is optional.

10. In *Shenot Eliyahu* on the Mishna.

The Secret of the Early Pious People's Prayer

ברכות ה, א

אֵין עוֹמְדִין לְהִתְפַּלֵּל אֶלָּא מִתּוֹךְ כֹּבֶד רֹאשׁ. חֲסִידִים הָרִאשׁוֹנִים הָיוּ שׁוֹהִים שָׁעָה אַחַת וּמִתְפַּלְּלִים, כְּדֵי שֶׁיְּכַוְּנוּ אֶת לִבָּם לַמָּקוֹם. אֲפִלּוּ הַמֶּלֶךְ שׁוֹאֵל בִּשְׁלוֹמוֹ, לֹא יְשִׁיבֶנּוּ. וַאֲפִלּוּ נָחָשׁ כָּרוּךְ עַל עֲקֵבוֹ, לֹא יַפְסִיק:

Berakhot 5:1

[One] should not stand up to pray unless he is in a serious frame of mind (*rosh*). The early pious people used to wait one hour and then pray, in order to direct their hearts toward the Omnipresent [lit. the place]. [While one is reciting *Shemoneh Esreh*,] even if the king greets him, he should not respond to him, and even if a snake wraps around his heel, he should not interrupt.

The devotion that we aspire to in prayer requires the cooperation of the worshipper's entire body. This idea emerges clearly from the structure of the mishna: the first sentence discusses the **head** (*rosh*), the second mentions the direction of the **heart**, and the third describes an unusual situation involving the worshipper's **heel**.[1] Thus, from head to foot, the verse "All my bones shall say" (Psalms 35:10) is fulfilled.[2]

1. My thanks to Shlomo and Shira Sadeh, who elucidated this point for me.
2. It seems that both the king and the snake that threaten the worshipper carry symbolic meaning. The prohibition against responding even to a king teaches us to put our loyalty to the King of kings before our loyalty to a flesh-and-blood monarch (see the aggada in Berakhot 32b). The prohibition against stopping even when a snake wraps around one's heel hints at Adam and Eve's sin in the Garden of Eden (see the aggada in Berakhot 33a: "It is not the [snake] that kills, it is sin that kills").

The heart of the mishna lauds the prayer of the "early pious people" (*ḥasidim rishonim*), but does not elaborate on their internal process as they wait and "direct their hearts toward the Omnipresent." It also does not say what directing one's heart consists of. The kabbalists ascribed to the early pious people techniques for attaining the Holy Spirit,[3] and linked the wait to "meditative techniques for entering into a suitable frame of mind."[4] It seems to me that we can corroborate this idea by comparing our mishna to a passage in *Sefer Yetzira* (*The Book of Creation*), one of the most ancient kabbalistic works:

> Ten *sefirot* of Nothingness / Bridle your mouth from speaking / And your heart from thinking / And if your heart runs/ return to the place. It is therefore written, / "The *ḥayot* running and returning." (Ezekiel 1:24) / Regarding this a covenant was made. (*Sefer Yetzira* 1:8)

Sefer Yetzira enjoins us to "bridle" our speech and thought. If, inadvertently, one's mouth speaks or one's heart thinks, he must "return to the place," linking the place in the prayers to the Omnipresent. This demand draws a parallel between the worshipper and the *ḥayot* described as "running and returning" in the vision of the divine chariot in Ezekiel.

Rabbi Aryeh Kaplan interprets the instructions in *Sefer Yetzira* as a meditative technique. The object of meditation is to clear the mind of thought and attain a higher consciousness that usually eludes us due to the constant flow of thoughts. There are techniques for doing so that involve concentrating on mantras, but the meditation prescribed in *Sefer Yetzira* is among the most difficult and meaningful. Its purpose is to enable one to experience the divine *sefirot*, and it aims to silence all thought. Rabbi Kaplan refers to this practice as meditation on "nothingness." He says that the state of consciousness at which one arrives after

3. For sources, see Aryeh Kaplan, *Meditation and Kabbalah* (Boston: Weiser Books, 1986), 20, n. 9.
4. Ibid.

such a clearing of the mind is the key to the mystical experience, and is in fact the beginning of the training to become a prophet.[5]

But the passage in *Sefer Yetzira* leaves a matter unexplained – what is "the place" that one is to return to if one's "heart runs"? Rabbi Kaplan understands it as the physical plane, which one should withdraw to so as not to be swept away by the mystical experience.[6] But to my mind, the opposite interpretation is true: The "place" is the very thing that the early pious people strove to attain – the divine. When the mouth and the heart run, in speech and in thought, it removes one from the higher consciousness to which *Sefer Yetzira* enjoins one to return – to the lofty place, to the place of divinity.[7]

This interpretation is supported by the fact that in tannaitic literature, God is often referred to as "the Place" (*HaMakom*), usually translated as "the Omnipresent."[8] Furthermore, some versions of *Sefer Yetzira* include a passage that states explicitly that God is "the place":

> ...with the Holy Palace in the center. Blessed be the glory of the Lord from His place. **He is the place** of the cosmos, and the cosmos is not His place. (*Sefer Yetzira* 4:2)

There is another connection between this passage and the one advising to "return to the place": The enjoinment is linked to the *ḥayot* of the vision of the divine chariot ("It is therefore written, 'The *ḥayot* running

---

5. See Kaplan, *Sefer Yetzirah: The Book of Creation* (Boston: Weiser Books, 1997), 64. Rabbi Aryeh Kaplan opines that this type of meditation was "one of the ways of prophecy," and cites the kabbalists as saying that this is the essence of Ezekiel's vision; see Kaplan, *Jewish Meditation: A Practical Guide* (New York: Schocken Books, 1985), 78–79.
6. Kaplan, *Yetzirah*, 67.
7. In the Gruenwald edition of *Sefer Yetzira*, the text reads "return to the place whence you came." I propose that this refers to the place that one left due to one's heart "running."
8. See Ephraim E. Urbach, *The Sages: Their Concepts and Beliefs* (Jerusalem: Magnes Press 1975), 66–79.

and returning'"), the very same *ḥayot* that proclaim "Blessed be the glory of the Lord from **His place**." We thus learn that the "place" that one returns to is the place of the Lord. The bridling of the mouth and heart bring one to "the place," while the "running" of speech and thought remove one from that place.

We saw above that the *Sefer Yetzira* compares a person's conduct to that of the *ḥayot* in the divine chariot. In a similar vein, the Talmud asserts that a worshipper should pray in the same posture as the *ḥayot*:

> Rabbi Yosei, son of Rabbi Ḥanina, also said in the name of Rabbi Eliezer b. Yaakov: When one prays, he should place his feet in proper position, as it says, "And the feet [of the *ḥayot*] were straight feet." (Berakhot 10b)

We learn that in prayer, one should strive to emulate the angels of the divine chariot – from one's inner world to one's position.

The possibility that the prayer practices of the early pious people should be understood in light of the passage on "nothingness" in *Sefer Yetzira* is bolstered by the choice of words in the two sources, both of which emphasize one's control of one's heart: "Bridle your mouth from speaking and your **heart** from thinking"; "in order to direct their hearts toward the Omnipresent." Both describe the object of cleaving in holiness as "the place": "And if your heart runs return to **the place**"; "in order to direct their hearts toward **the place**." Finally, the two sources use the same root, sh-v in order to connote concentration, once in a positive context: "return (*shuv*) to the place," and once in a negative context: "even if the king greets him, he should not respond to him (*yeshivenu*)."

The similarities between the two sources open up the possibility that contemplation before prayer can not only increase concentration and release one from the spell of one's thoughts, but also induce a true mystical experience via meditative awareness – the prayer of the early pious people. Such an outlook, that waiting before prayers means quieting one's speech and thoughts, can be found in Maimonides's commentary on our mishna: "Wait – pause before prayer for an hour, during which conversation and thought cease, and then begin praying."[9]

9. See also Maimonides's statement in the *Mishneh Torah*: "One should clear his mind from all thoughts and envision himself as standing before the Divine Presence" (*Hilkhot Tefilla* 4:16). There are two stages: first one must clear his mind of thoughts and only then envision himself standing before the Divine Presence. Rabbi Natan Ophir comments (in an unpublished essay titled "Maimonides as a Teacher of Cleaving to the Divine") on the meditative implications of these passages, and seeks to associate them with a larger, coherent system that Maimonides developed in relation to quieting the thoughts, meditating, and being in a constant state of cleaving to God. In his essay, Ophir explains the mechanism of quieting the thoughts by way of neuropsychology. The human brain has two hemispheres, he says, and the higher functions of consciousness have recently been identified with the right brain. The quieting of speech and thought, which are identified with the left hemisphere, enable the right hemisphere to come to the fore. We will revisit Ophir's ideas in our discussion of mishna 5:5 in the next chapter.

The Prayer of Rabbi Ḥanina ben Dosa: Intention and Prophecy

ברכות ה, ה

הַמִּתְפַּלֵּל וְטָעָה, סִימָן רַע לוֹ. וְאִם שְׁלִיחַ צִבּוּר הוּא, סִימָן רַע לְשׁוֹלְחָיו, מִפְּנֵי שֶׁשְּׁלוּחוֹ שֶׁל אָדָם כְּמוֹתוֹ. אָמְרוּ עָלָיו עַל רַבִּי חֲנִינָא בֶּן דּוֹסָא, שֶׁהָיָה מִתְפַּלֵּל עַל הַחוֹלִים וְאוֹמֵר, זֶה חַי וְזֶה מֵת. אָמְרוּ לוֹ, מִנַּיִן אַתָּה יוֹדֵעַ. אָמַר לָהֶם, אִם שְׁגוּרָה תְפִלָּתִי בְּפִי, יוֹדֵעַ אֲנִי שֶׁהוּא מְקֻבָּל וְאִם לָאו, יוֹדֵעַ אֲנִי שֶׁהוּא מְטֹרָף:

Berakhot 5:5

One who is praying, and makes a mistake, it is a bad omen for him; and if he was an agent of the congregation, it is a bad omen for those who have sent him [the congregation], because a person's agent is [considered] like himself. They used to say about him, about Rabbi Ḥanina ben Dosa: When he would pray for the sick, he would say: This one will live and that one will die. They said to him: How do you know? He replied to them: If the prayer is fluent in my mouth, I know that it has been accepted; and if not, then I know that it has been torn up.

Rabbi Ḥanina ben Dosa possessed the unique ability of knowing in advance which of his prayers would be accepted. This knowledge, he explained, had to do with the question of whether or not a certain prayer was "fluent" in his mouth. If "fluent" means the absence of mistakes, Rabbi Ḥanina's confidence is difficult to understand, as all prayers should be fluent. But Shlomo Naeh[1] shows that manuscripts

1. Shlomo Naeh, "'Creates the Fruit of Lips': A Phenomenological Study of Prayer According to Mishnah Berakhot 4:3, 5:5," *Tarbiz* 63 (1994) [Hebrew]: 185–218.

of the Mishna do not say "fluent" (*shegura*), but rather *shagra*, which connotes a strong flow. The choice of words highlights the passivity of Rabbi Ḥanina's prayer. According to Naeh, such prayer contravenes the idea of purposeful focus during prayer, in which prayer is guided by the worshipper's "intention (or direction) of the heart."[2] The description of prayer as flowing is an expression of God "creating the fruit of the lips" (Isaiah 57:19)[3] and guiding one's prayer. Such prayer is tantamount to a prophecy that rests upon the worshipper. Thus, we can understand how, when such prophetic prayer rested upon Rabbi Ḥanina ben Dosa, he knew that his payer had been accepted.

Walfish, based on the structure of Berakhot chapter 5, challenges the traditional notion that "the fruit of the lips" and "the intention of the heart" are mutually exclusive.[4] Clearly, the topic of our chapter is intention, and it is apparent that Rabbi Ḥanina ben Dosa's approach has much in common with the rest of the mishnayot in the chapter. Rabbi Ḥanina, as the Tosefta shows us, is among the early pious people mentioned in 5:1, whose prayer is infused with the intention of the heart. There are also terms from 5:2 that we recall in 5:5; "This one will live (*ḥai*) and that one will die (*met*)" (5:5) is reminiscent of "[We] mention the request for rain in [the blessing of] Resurrection of the Dead (*Teḥiyat Hametim*)," and the question, "How do you know?" brings to mind the blessing of Endower of Knowledge, which is at the center of 5:2. Mishna 5:3 is about mistakes made during prayer, and the mishna about Rabbi Ḥanina, significantly, begins with a question about the implication of just such a "mistake." In 5:5, a prayer that fails in that fashion is referred to as "*meturaf*" (a word translated above as "torn up" but that also has

2. Naeh cites the Tosefta, which he says presents both approaches. Rabbi Akiva states: "If a person is fluent with his prayer it is a good omen for him, and if he is not fluent with his prayer it is a bad omen for him." In contrast, Abba Shaul states: "[A person] who prays [*Shemoneh Esreh*] must pay attention [to the meaning of the words]. There is a reference for [the need of attention in] prayer [in the Bible]: 'Prepare their hearts, pay attention' (Psalms 10:17)."
3. This is indeed the verse that the Talmud (Berakhot 34b) cites as the source for Rabbi Ḥanina's approach.
4. Walfish, "Response: To S. Naeh, 'Creates the Fruit of Lips,'" *Tarbiz* 65 (1996) [Hebrew]: 301–314.

connotations of distraction and insanity), while 5:4 states that "One who leads the prayers should not respond after [the blessing of] the priests [by saying] 'Amen,' because of the lost concentration (*teruf*) [that might ensue]." Walfish, in light of the mishna's literary structure, claims that we should distinguish between ecstasy – in which the speech flows and prayer is no longer under one's control – and inspiration, which comes to one through active effort.

I believe that in light of my interpretation of the mishna about the early pious people, based on *Sefer Yetzira*,[5] we can come to understand "directing the heart toward the Omnipresent" and "fluent" prayer as two stages in the same process. We can accept Walfish's claim that Rabbi Ḥanina ben Dosa's prayer is founded on the intention of the heart, while also holding, like Naeh, that there is a prophetic element to it. By waiting an hour before prayer, the early pious people succeeded in "bridling their mouths from speaking and their hearts from thinking," i.e., in freeing themselves of the constant flow of thoughts. Thus these pious men arrived at a higher level of consciousness, a state in which a worshipper's heart is attuned to the Omnipresent and he can commune with the supernal realms.

The early pious people's process, including that of Rabbi Ḥanina, is explained nicely by Rabbi Natan Ophir,[6] in neuropsychological terms. The human brain has two hemispheres: the left, which specializes in language processing and analytical skills, and the right, which has to do with intuition, special awareness, and holism. By quieting one's speech and thoughts, one arrives at a state that enables right-brain awareness. This consciousness is conducive to mystical experiences, to contact with the Beyond, which requires these tools.

We will conclude with the words of the *Tur*, which describes the connection between divine service of the early pious people in terms of intention and their attainment of a state close to prophecy:

> How so "his thought"? The *Baraita* states that the worshipper should "direct his heart," meaning that one should focus

---

5. 5:1.
6. In an unpublished paper.

on the meaning of the words coming out of one's mouth, as if the Divine Presence were in front of him, as it is stated, "I have set the Lord always before me." Pious people and men of great deeds would seclude themselves and bring intention to their prayers, so that they would transcend their corporeal forms, and the growing influence of their spiritual faculty would bring them almost to the point of prophecy." (*Tur, Oraḥ Ḥayim* 98)

The Order of the Blessings

Berakhot, chapter 6

The Mishna opens with the mitzva of *Keriat Shema,* which is about accepting the yoke of heaven – the foundation of all of the mitzvot. Yet the tractate is not named for *Shema* (chapters 1–3), nor is it named for *Shemoneh Esreh* (chapters 4–5); rather, it is named for the topic that it ends with – blessings (chapters 6–9). Below I will suggest that the reason is the fact that Berakhot is the opening tractate in the Order of Zera'im (Seeds), which deals with laws that apply only in the Land of Israel. But first it is worth noting that other topics discussed in our tractate are fundamental to the mitzvot of the Order of Seeds. The laws that apply only in the Land of Israel have to do with agriculture, whose success, as we learn from *Keriat Shema,* depends on adhering to the word of God:

> And it shall come to pass, if you shall hearken diligently to My commandments which I command you this day, to love the Lord your God, and to serve Him with all your heart and with all your soul, that I will give the rain of your land in its season, the former rain and the latter rain, so that you may gather in your corn, and your wine, and your oil. And I will give grass in your fields for your cattle, and you shall eat and be satisfied. Take heed to yourselves, lest your heart be deceived, and you will turn aside, and serve other gods, and worship them; and the anger of the Lord will be kindled against you, and He will shut up the heaven, so

> that there shall be no rain, and the ground shall not yield its fruit; and you will perish quickly from off the good land that the Lord has given you. (Deuteronomy 11:13–17)

Furthermore, as the Mishna (5:2) notes, when we pray we praise God for the rain, which the crops depend on.

The Blessing of the Earth

> How does one recite blessings for fruits? On fruits growing on a tree, one says, "...Who created the fruit of the tree," except for wine; on wine, one says, "...Who created the fruit of the vine." On fruits growing from the earth, one says, "...Who created the fruit of the ground," except for bread; on bread, one says, "...Who brings forth bread from the earth." On vegetables, one says, "...Who created the fruit of the ground." Rabbi Yehuda says: [One should say instead,] "...Who created various types of herbs." (6:1)

The topic sentence for the section that deals with blessings is, "How does one recite blessings for fruits?" The first mishna is concerned with blessings we make over produce: fruits, wine, vegetables, and bread. Later in the chapter we find out that for foods that are not produced from the earth, such as milk, eggs, meat, and fish, a single, general blessing, "For Everything" (*Shehakol*), suffices. It is noteworthy that these foods, despite their importance in the human diet, are defined negatively, as foods that are not produced from the earth, or in the Mishna's words (6:3): "On a thing that does not grow from the earth, say: 'For everything.'"

The implication is that blessings are largely intended for items that grow from the earth. The connection to the earth in also evident in the blessings recited after eating. Grace after Meals (*Birkat HaMazon*) and *Berakha Me'ein Shalosh* are recited only after eating food derived from the seven species native to the Land of Israel (6:5). The Talmud (Berakhot 21a) derives the obligation to say Grace after Meals from the verse, "And you shall eat and be satisfied, and bless the Lord your God for the good land that He has given you" (Deuteronomy 8:10). That the blessing is for the land that God gave us is also apparent in the text of Grace and Meals: "We offer thanks to You ... for the good land."[1]

The Blessing of the Earth and the Curse of the Earth

The link between the blessing and the earth is what informs Rabbi Yehuda's opinion that also when it comes to blessings before eating, the seven species have priority:

> If one has before him many different species, Rabbi Yehuda says: If there is among them one of the seven species, bless on that one. But the Sages say: Bless on whichever he desires. (6:4)

When it comes to "cursed species," Rabbi Yehuda's opinion is that emphasis should be placed not on one's enjoyment of the food, but rather on its symbolic meaning. Thus, he concludes that one should not recite a blessing over such foods, even if they are tasty and a source of nourishment:

> On a thing which does not grow from the earth, say: "For everything." On vinegar, and on unripe fruits, and on the locusts, say: "For everything." On milk, and on cheese, and on eggs, say: "For everything." Rabbi Yehuda says: Anything which is a cursed species should not be blessed upon.

My friend Rabbi Amnon Dokov points out that the three examples of a "cursed species" in this chapter are taken from the curses that God threatens the Israelites with before they enter the land, in Deuteronomy. Locusts correspond to "You shall carry much seed out into the

1. Similarly, in bringing first fruits to the Temple, one gives thanks to God not only for the fruits, but mostly for the land. That is why first fruits must be of only the seven species (Bikkurim 1:3) and be produced on land owned by the one who brings them (Bikkurim 1:1–2).

field, and shall gather little in; for the **locust** shall consume it" (Deuteronomy 28:38). Vinegar corresponds to "You shall plant vineyards and dress them, **but you shall neither drink of the wine**, nor gather the grapes; for the worm shall eat them" (v. 39). Unripe fruits correspond to "You shall have olive trees throughout all your borders, but you shall not anoint yourself with the oil; for **your olives shall drop off**" (v. 40).

The blessings over food can be understood as part of a broader context of dialogue between humans and God. People must learn to distinguish between God's blessings and His curses.

Human Blessings and Divine Blessings

In reciting blessings, we express our awareness that the divine blessings have reached their intended target, meaning that the focus is not the blessings that we recite to God but rather the blessings that we receive from God.

In the Five Books of Moses, God's main blessing to humanity is the fruit of the land: "The Lord will command the blessing with you in your barns, and in all that you put your hand to; and He will bless you in the land that the Lord your God gives you" (Deuteronomy 28:8). Similarly, in *Shemoneh Esreh*, the Blessing of the Years (*HaShanim*) includes a request that God bless the crops ("Bless … all the varieties of its produce for good).

The Order of Seeds describes the human reaction to laws that apply only in the Land of Israel. The reaction can be verbal – recitation of a blessing (the subject of Tractate Berakhot) – or practical: mitzvot that reflect the awareness that the land and its blessings are a gift to humanity from God.

The link between the laws of the Land of Israel and God's blessings to the land is explicated in the *Vidui Maaser* (the confession of the tithe). Immediately after the Torah's description of the mitzva of first fruits (Deuteronomy 26:1–11), is the text that the pilgrim recites: he thanks God for the blessings of the land and declares that he has fulfilled the mitzvot that are linked to it. Then he asks God to continue to bless the land:

> When you have made an end of tithing all the tithe of your increase in the third year, which is the year of tithing, and have given it to the Levite, to the stranger, to the fatherless, and to the widow, so that they may eat within your gates, and be satisfied, then you shall say before the Lord your God: "I have put away the hallowed things out of my house, and also have given them to the Levite, and to the stranger, to the fatherless, and to the widow, according to all Your commandment which You have commanded me.... Look forth from Your holy habitation, from heaven, and bless Your people Israel, and the land that You have given us, as You did swear to our fathers, a land flowing with milk and honey." (Deuteronomy 26:12–15)

The Mishna explores the formulation of this confession, and finds allusions to the ten laws that apply only in the Land of Israel:

> How was the declaration made? "I have put away the hallowed things out of my house" (Deuteronomy 26:13) – this is second tithe (*maaser sheni*) and the fruit of plants in their fourth year (*neta revai*). "Have given them unto the Levite" – this is the Levite's tithe (*maaser Levi*). "And also have given them" – this is *teruma* and *terumat maaser*. "Unto the stranger, to the fatherless, and to the widow" – this is the poor man's tithe, *leket* [fallen gleanings given to the poor], *shikheḥa* [forgotten gleanings given to the poor], and *pe'ah* [corner of a field given to the poor]..."Out of my house" – this is *ḥalla* [dough that must be set aside for the priest]. (Maaser Sheni 5:10)

Regarding the verse, "Look forth from Your holy habitation, from heaven," the Mishna adds: "We have done what You decreed upon us, so too You, do what You promised us" (Maaser Sheni 5:13). The implication is that God's blessings to the land depend on our fulfillment of the laws that depend on the land.[2]

The content of Tractate Berakhot is thus linked to the Order of Seeds, for it describes an aspect of the relationship between God and humanity.

The Mishna employs literary devices to weave Berakhot into the rest of the Order of Seeds. The first mishna in the tractate opens with the text, "From when may one recite *Shema* in the evening? From the time when the priests go in to eat their *teruma*" (1:1), which defines the time for accepting the yoke of heaven based on the *teruma*.

Keriat Shema is a mitzva of recitation ("may one recite *Shema*"); Bikkurim, the final tractate in the Order of Seeds, also begins with a mitzva of recitation: "Some bring first fruits and recite" (Bikkurim 1:1). In *Keriat Shema,* we proclaim our fealty to the Lord; in the first fruits recitation we bear witness to God keeping His promise to us.

Tractate Berakhot concludes with a story from the Book of Ruth that links the blessings of the human realm to the laws that apply only in the Land of Israel: "And, behold, Boaz came from Bethlehem, and said unto the reapers: 'The Lord be with you.' And they answer him: 'The Lord bless you'" (Ruth 2:4). Boaz blesses the reapers while fulfilling the obligation to leave gifts for the poor (vv. 2–3, 15–23), which is the topic of the next tractate, Pe'ah.[3]

"Berakhot" (blessings) is not only the title of the first tractate in the Order of Seeds; it also hints at a theme of the entire order, which is devoted to how we relate to God's blessings.

---

2. See also the verse, "When you reap your harvest in your field, and forget a sheaf in the field, you shall not go back to fetch it; it shall be for the stranger, for the fatherless, and for the widow; so that the Lord your God may bless you in all the work of your hands" (Deuteronomy 24:19).
3. I thank to my brother Rabbi Dani Genack, who pointed this out to me.

Bread from Heaven and from the Earth

ברכות ו, א

כֵּיצַד מְבָרְכִין עַל הַפֵּרוֹת. עַל פֵּרוֹת הָאִילָן אוֹמֵר, בּוֹרֵא פְּרִי הָעֵץ חוּץ מִן הַיַּיִן, שֶׁעַל הַיַּיִן אוֹמֵר בּוֹרֵא פְּרִי הַגָּפֶן. וְעַל פֵּרוֹת הָאָרֶץ אוֹמֵר בּוֹרֵא פְּרִי הָאֲדָמָה, חוּץ מִן הַפַּת, שֶׁעַל הַפַּת הוּא אוֹמֵר הַמּוֹצִיא לֶחֶם מִן הָאָרֶץ. וְעַל הַיְרָקוֹת אוֹמֵר בּוֹרֵא פְּרִי הָאֲדָמָה. רַבִּי יְהוּדָה אוֹמֵר, בּוֹרֵא מִינֵי דְשָׁאִים:

Berakhot 6:1

How does one recite blessings for fruits? On fruits growing on a tree, one says, "...Who created the fruit of the tree," except for wine; on wine, one says, "...Who created the fruit of the vine." On fruits growing from the earth, one says, "...Who created the fruit of the ground," except for bread; on bread, one says, "...Who brings forth bread from the earth." On vegetables, one says, "...Who created the fruit of the ground." Rabbi Yehuda says: [One should say instead,] "...Who created various types of herbs."

In our discussion of Tractate Berakhot's inclusion in the Order of Seeds, we noted the link between blessings and the Land of Israel. But blessings have an even simpler, more ancient aspect – the link to Creation.

Four blessings cited in the mishna offer praise to God for His creation. This link to Creation explains why the special blessings are recited only over foods derived directly from the land, and for other foods there is only a general prayer: "For Everything" (*Shehakol*) (6:3). Adam was prohibited from consuming meat (Sanhedrin 59b), and the food that God gave him was entirely plant based: "And God said, 'Behold, I have given you every herb yielding seed, which is upon the face of all the earth, and every tree, in which is the fruit of a tree yielding seed – to you it shall be for food'" (Genesis 1:29).

Among the blessings in our mishna, the one recited for bread – "...Who brings forth bread from the earth" – seems incongruous. After all, is it God who brings forth bread from the earth? As the Tosefta notes, the production of bread requires significant human toil: "How much the first man toiled before he tasted [even] one mouthful? He planted [grain], plowed, reaped, bound sheaves, threshed, winnowed, selected, ground, sifted, kneaded, and baked, and [only] after that [he] ate [bread]" (Berakhot 6:5). Apparently the background for the blessing is the story of Creation. The formulation is based on a verse from the psalm beginning "*Barkhi nafshi et Hashem*," "Bless the Lord, O my soul," which extols the wonders of God's creation: "Who causes the grass to spring up for the cattle, and herb for the service of man; to bring forth bread out of the earth" (Psalms 104:14). After he eats from the fruit of the Tree of Knowledge, Adam is cursed: "In the sweat of your face you shall eat bread" (Genesis 3:19). The formulation of the blessing – "Who brings forth bread from the earth" – hints at the rectification of that sin and a return to a prelapsarian state, in which people relate to the bread they consume not only in relation to their toil, but also as God's gift.

Creation Here and Now

The blessing's motifs, which invoke the Land of Israel, Creation, and the Garden of Eden, reinforce one another. The world was created in an ideal, pristine state, in which humanity lived in the Garden, in God's presence. After he sinned, Adam was banished from Eden. The story of the Five Books of Moses is the story of the return to the Garden, with the Children of Israel playing the part of Adam and the Land of Israel and its blessings serving in the role of Eden. The blessing includes the words "Who brings," in the present tense; Creation is not an event of the deep past, but a constant process of divine presence within the world.

Who Brings Forth Bread from Heaven and from the Earth

The blessings are evocative of both Creation and the Land of Israel – two connotations that are brought together by a third: the manna that the Israelites ate in the desert. The Torah calls the manna, "bread from heaven" (Exodus 16:4). The book of Deuteronomy teaches the Israelites the lesson of the story of the manna on the eve of their entry into the Land of Israel:

> And He afflicted you, and suffered you to hunger, and fed you with manna, which you did not know, and neither did your fathers; so that He might make you know that man does not live by bread alone, but by everything that proceeds out of the mouth of the Lord does man live.... For the Lord your God brings you into a good land.... a land of wheat and barley, and vines and fig trees and pomegranates; a land of olive trees and honey; a land in which you shall eat bread without scarceness, in which you shall not lack anything.... And you shall eat and be satisfied, and bless the Lord your God for the good land that He has given you.... lest when you have eaten and are satisfied, and have built goodly houses, and dwelt therein.... then your heart be lifted up, and you forget the Lord your God, who brought you forth out of the land of Egypt, out of the house of bondage.... who fed you in the wilderness with manna, which your fathers knew not, so that He might afflict you, and so that He might prove you, to do you good at your latter end; and you say in your heart: "My power and the might of my hand has gotten me this wealth" (Deuteronomy 8:3–17)

The story of Creation was a lesson about the divine gifts to humankind. Yet, over the generations, the fact that God is the source of all bounty and blessing in the world was forgotten. The change to the natural order in the desert, which included bread from heaven, was meant to teach us anew that forgotten truth. Upon entering the land, we must recall this revelation, and know that the blessings of the land are also God's gift. This is the message that can be gleaned from the above verses as to the obligation to recite blessings after eating (Berakhot 21a): "And you shall eat and be satisfied, and bless the Lord your God for the good land that He has given you."

The connection to the manna imbues the blessing over the bread with another layer of significance – just as God produced bread from heaven, it is He "who brings forth bread from the earth."

Manna and the Omer

So as to ensure that we do not forget the lesson of the manna, God commands Moses to keep a jar of it in the Ark of the Covenant:

> And Moses said: "This is the thing that the Lord has commanded: Let an Omerful of it be kept throughout your generations, so that they may see the bread with which I fed you in the wilderness".... so Aaron laid it up before the Testimony, to be kept. (Exodus 16:32–34)

The memory of the manna is also kept actively. Erel Sharf considers the Omer offering, which is brought every year on Passover, as a reenactment of the story of the manna.[1] The Omer is a measure of a tenth of an ephah (Exodus 16:36). The word Omer appears six times in the context of the manna, and denotes the amount of manna that each individual received; the Omer offering is named after the measure of the manna. The manna stopped falling when the Israelites entered the Land of Israel, around Passover, which is the time for bringing the Omer offering.[2] The Mishna (Menaḥot 10:3) describes the reaping of the Omer as a massive, well-attended ceremony, reminiscent of the description of the people going out to collect the manna.

---

1. Erel Sharf, "An Omer is the Tenth Part of an Ephah," *Alon Shvut* 147 (1996) [Hebrew].
2. See sources ibid., 50.

The Omer is an offering from the year's new crops, which can be consumed only once the offering is brought. The reconstruction of the manna in the form of the Omer offering is a reminder that, just like the manna in the desert, the Omer and the rest of the crops in the Land of Israel are gifts from God to the Jewish people.

Where Is God?

Berakhot, chapter 9

Where is God in the world? Our intuitive answer to that question is, everywhere. But in truth, in our individual realities we mostly do not feel God's presence. Rabbi Menachem Mendel of Kotzk was once asked where God could be found. He replied that God can be found wherever He is allowed to enter. In the spirit of that statement, we can say that when a Jew utters, "Blessed are You, Lord," he is declaring that God is the root of the thing he is acknowledging in his blessing, thus revealing God's place in the world and focusing his consciousness on Him.

> The final chapter of Tractate Berakhot features a series of situations and scenarios in which one is expected to recite blessings that go beyond the usual blessings over food and mitzvot, implying that God is the originator of all of those situations.

Miracles

> He who sees a place where miracles were done for Israel should say, "Blessed [is He] who did miracles for our fathers in this place." (Berakhot 9:1)

One would think that God's presence and action are apparent in a place where a miracle was done. But the reality is different, and even miracles can be denied. According to the Talmud (Berakhot 9b), Elijah the prophet, when he stood on Mount Carmel, prayed for two things: first, that God would grant him a miracle, and second, that those who would witness it would not say, "It was the work of sorcery." But even when a miracle is acknowledged, it is not always easy to ascertain that it is a blessing rather than a curse:

> As they were returning from the burial of their father, they saw their brother go to the pit into which they had hurled him, in order to bless it. He blessed the pit with the benediction, "Blessed be the place where He performed a miracle for me," just as anyone is required to pronounce a blessing at the place where a miracle had been performed in his behalf. (*Midrash Tanḥuma, Vayeḥi*)

Joseph is unique not only in his understanding that God directed the events that led to his sale into slavery (as he says to his brothers, "it was not you that sent me here"), but in his capacity to acknowledge that the events that caused him such suffering were in fact a blessing.

Uprooting Idolatry

> [If he sees] a place that had idol worship uprooted from it, he says, "Blessed [is He] who uprooted idol worship from our land." (Berakhot 9:1)

Our mishna begins with a blessing for miracles and moves on to a blessing for the eradication of idol worship. The very attribution of the elimination of idolatry to God is a novelty. Clearly, it is human and natural processes that are behind the removal of idol worship. But since the outcome has religious significance – God's victory over idolatry – one must assume that He has a hand in these processes, and thus consider Him the cause.

Nature

> On comets, and on earthquakes, and on lightning and on thunder, and on storms say, "Blessed [be He] whose

> strength and might fill the world." On mountains, and on hills, and on seas, and on rivers, and on deserts say, "Blessed [is He] who makes the works of the beginning." Rabbi Yehuda says: One who sees the great sea says, "Blessed [is He] who made the great sea," only if he sees it occasionally. On rain and on good news say, "Blessed [is He] who is good and does good." And on bad news say, "Blessed [are You] the true judge." (Berakhot 9:2)

This mishna is exquisitely structured. It opens with two five-item lists, adding up to a typological number – ten natural phenomena. Five is also the number of blessings in the mishna. Additionally, in Hebrew, the mishna contains several examples of alliteration, assonance, and rhyme.

As we noted, the ten phenomena are of the natural world – unlike the previous mishna, there is no miraculous process or "religious" outcome. And yet, one who witnesses these phenomena is required to bless God. Thus one declares one's belief that the forces of nature are in fact the forces of God and His might. In other words, God does not only "oversee" Creation; He is active within it.

Just as the chapter is structured to place miracle (mishna 1) before nature (mishna 2), so too among the natural phenomena listed by our mishna, the rare (comets and earthquakes) precedes the relatively commonplace (lightning, thunder, and storms). Thus, the Mishna directs the reader's attention to see God in ever more aspects of life.[1]

Creation

The five components of the first list (comets, earthquakes, lightning, thunder, and storms) are dynamic, while the five components of the second list (mountains, hills, seas, rivers, and deserts) are static entities that exist from the dawn of Creation. In both, one must see the hand of God, the architect of the entire cosmos. The phrasing of the blessings refers to the present – "who makes the works of the beginning" – thus

---

1. Ehud Rosset, "On Mishnah Instruction Using the Method of In-Depth Analysis – Berakhot 9:2 and Megillah 4:2," *Netuim* 1 (1994) [Hebrew]: 87.

expressing the idea that Creation, and God's presence within it, is not a thing of the past, but rather is happening in every moment.

The Rashbatz offers another explanation for the reference to Creation in the present tense. He says that the continued existence of the world depends on an ongoing influx of God's light:

> After creating it, He maintains it, and if He were not to sustain it, it would devolve back into chaos. The Holy One, blessed be He, is unlike the builders who, after constructing a house, are no longer needed, for He, after creating the world, maintains and sustains it. Just like the form that sustains matter, He is the world's form and its end… this is the import of the formulation [in the morning prayer] Creator of Light (*Yotzer Or*): "Who in His goodness renews every day, continuously, the work of Creation." (*Magen Avot* on Mishna Avot 2:14)

Good and Evil

> On rain and on good news say, "Blessed [is He] who is good and does good." And on bad news say, "Blessed [are You], the true judge." (Berakhot 9:2)

We must bless the bad as well as the good. Thus, the mishna teaches us that God is the source of everything – the good and the bad. In the book of Isaiah, God attests to having created darkness and evil:

> I am the Lord, and there is none else; beside Me there is no God. I have girded you, though you have not known Me. So that they may know from the rising of the sun, and from the west, that there is none beside Me; I am the Lord; and there is none else. I form the light, and create darkness; I make peace, and create evil; I am the Lord, Who does all these things. (Isaiah 45:5–7)

The point of God's words is to emphasize that only He is the Lord and "there is none else beside Me.... none else." The time of the Sages, like other eras, saw widespread belief in the dualistic idea that God reigns only over the good, while evil is governed by an entirely different force. The Mishna, in response, rejects this idea by requiring us to acknowledge God's reign over all. Despite the discomfort that the question of evil generates in the believer, to relinquish faith in a single God who governs reality is no solution. Later in our chapter the Mishna provides an explicit response to the heretics in the form of another principle of Jewish faith, the belief in a World to Come:

> All the endings of blessings when they were in the Temple, they would say, "From the world." When the heretics corrupted [matters] and said, "There is no world but this one," [the Sages] instituted this so that they should say, "From the world and until the [next] world." (Berakhot 9:5)

Human Actions

> When one builds a new house, and acquires new vessels, he says, "Blessed [is He] who kept us alive, [and sustained us, and brought us to this time]." (Berakhot 9:3)

On the face of it, the construction of a house and the acquisition of vessels are human actions, justifying an approach along the lines of, "My power and the might of my hand has gotten me this wealth" (Deuteronomy 8:17). But in fact, it is God who sustains people's very lives, along with their actions, so that even human achievements require the blessing, "Blessed [is He] who kept us alive."[2]

2. See the verse that follows the one ascribing achievements to human power: "But you shall remember the Lord your God, for it is He who gives you power" (Deuteronomy 8:18).

Peace

The chapter, and the entire tractate, ends with a requirement to greet one's fellow with the name of God:

> And they instituted this, that a person shall inquire after the peace (*shalom*) of his fellow with the name [of God], as it says, "And behold, Boaz came from Bethlehem and said to the harvesters, 'May the Lord be with you,' and they said to him, 'May the Lord bless you.'" (Ruth 2:4). And it says, "The Lord is with you, great and valorous one." (Judges 6:12). And it says, "Do not scorn, because your mother is old" (Proverbs 23:22). And it says, "It is time to do for the Lord; they have broken Your Torah" (Psalms 119:126). Rabbi Natan says: They nullified Your Torah because it is time to do for the Lord. (Berakhot 9:5).

Shalom, or Peace, is a name of God[3] and a "vessel that retains blessing," given to the Jewish people by God.[4] Throughout the chapter we encountered many answers to the question of God's place in the world – whether He is above reality or within it, transcendent or immanent, in the miraculous or in nature, in good or in bad, in the past or in the present, in the actions of heaven or in the actions of humans. It is fitting, then, that a tractate that deals largely with the relationship between humanity and God concludes with yet another area in which God is present – peace among human beings. In the following chapters we will delve fully into the implications of this ending.

Having discussed the many contexts and situations in which the Mishna sees the hand of God acting in the world, we can relate to

3. "Rabbi Yudan, son of Rabbi Yosei, taught: Great is peace, for God's name is called Shalom, as it is written (Judges 6:24): '[He] called it Adonai-Shalom'" (Leviticus Rabba 9).
4. "Rabbi Shimon ben Ḥalafta said: The Holy One, blessed be He, found no vessel that can [sufficiently] hold the blessing for Israel, save for peace, as the verse states (Psalms 29:11): 'The Lord will give strength to His people; the Lord will bless His people with peace'" (Uktzin 3:12).

Rabbi Abraham Isaac Kook's beautiful words regarding the ubiquity of the Divine Presence:

> The divine is revealed in the world in all its beauty and splendor, in every spirit and soul, in every vertebrate and insect, in every plant and flower, in every nation and state, in the sea and its swells, in the canopies of the sky and the majesty of its heavenly bodies, in the talents of every speaker, in the visions of every writer, in the imagination of every poet, and the ideas of every thinker, in the feelings of every passionate being, and in every hero's courageous tempest. (*Orot HaKodesh* 119)

Love You to Death

ברכות ט, ה

חַיָּב אָדָם לְבָרֵךְ עַל הָרָעָה כְּשֵׁם שֶׁהוּא מְבָרֵךְ עַל הַטּוֹבָה, שֶׁנֶּאֱמַר (דברים ו) וְאָהַבְתָּ אֵת יְיָ אֱלֹהֶיךָ בְּכָל לְבָבְךָ וּבְכָל נַפְשְׁךָ וּבְכָל מְאֹדֶךָ. בְּכָל לְבָבְךָ, בִּשְׁנֵי יְצָרֶיךָ, בְּיֵצֶר טוֹב וּבְיֵצֶר רָע וּבְכָל נַפְשְׁךָ, אֲפִלּוּ הוּא נוֹטֵל אֶת נַפְשְׁךָ. וּבְכָל מְאֹדֶךָ, בְּכָל מָמוֹנֶךָ. דָּבָר אַחֵר בְּכָל מְאֹדֶךָ, בְּכָל מִדָּה וּמִדָּה שֶׁהוּא מוֹדֵד לְךָ הֱוֵי מוֹדֶה לוֹ בִּמְאֹד מְאֹד....

Berakhot 9:5

A person is obligated to bless upon the bad just as he blesses upon the good. As it says, "And you shall love the Lord your God with all your heart, and with all your soul, and with all that you have" (Deuteronomy 6:5). "With all your heart" – with your two inclinations, with the inclination of good and the inclination of evil. "And with all your soul" – even if He takes your soul. "And with all that you have" – with all your money. Alternatively, "With all that you have (*me'odekha*)" – with every measure that is measured for you, thank Him very much (*me'od me'od*).

This amazing mishna, which concludes Tractate Berakhot, will accompany us in the ensuing chapters as well. The opening comment on the verse "And you shall love" could be read as a purely aggadic commentary, waxing poetic on the importance of love for the divine. But it turns out that its most demanding element – "'with all your soul' – even if He takes your soul" – has practical halakhic significance. The Talmud (Berakhot 61b) cites the same commentary in the name of Rabbi Akiva, who gave his own life to sanctify God's name. In Tractate Sanhedrin, a similar commentary is quoted in the name of Rabbi Eliezer as evidence that one must die rather than participate in idolatry. Let us examine the text in Sanhedrin so as to better understand the import of the commentary in our mishna:

> Rabbi Yoḥanan said in the name of Rabbi Shimon ben Yehotzadak: By a majority vote, it was resolved in the upper chambers of the house of Nitza in Lod that for every law of the Torah, if a man is commanded, "Transgress and suffer not death," he may transgress and not suffer death – except idolatry, incest [including adultery], and murder. Now may not idolatry be practiced [in these circumstances]? Has it not been taught: Rabbi Yishmael said: How do we know that if a man was bidden, "Engage in idolatry and suffer not death," he should do so, and not be slain? From the verse, "[You shall therefore keep my statutes and my judgments, which if a man do] he shall live in them" (Leviticus 22:18) – but not die by them... They ruled as Rabbi Eliezer. For it has been taught, Rabbi Eliezer said: "And you shall love the Lord your God with all your heart, and with all your soul, and with all that you have" – since "with all your soul" is stated, why is "with all that you have" stated? And since "with all that you have" is written, why also write "with all your soul"? For the man to whom life is more precious than wealth, "with all your soul" is written, while to he who values his wealth more than his life, the Torah says, "with all that you have." (Sanhedrin 74a)

The full implications of this debate became apparent to me only in the wake of a very painful occurrence. On December 27, 2002, during a Friday night meal, terrorists stormed the kitchen at the Otniel yeshiva. Four students who were in the kitchen managed to lock the door to the dining room, where dozens of students were singing and dancing. Thus the four saved their friends, but they – Noam, Yehuda, Zvi and Gabriel – were murdered. After their funerals, we felt that we could not carry on with our previous curriculum, so the yeshiva began to study the question of martyrdom. I had previously studied that debate many times, and knew much of the classic talmudic commentary about it. But when we began to study martyrdom in light of the personal sacrifice of those four students, the issue took on a whole new aspect. Suddenly we realized that the focus is not death, but rather life. The Talmud, in explaining the demand that one "be killed and not transgress" by murdering another, asks rhetorically, "Perhaps his blood is redder?" We realized that the issue is not the severity of murder but rather the sanctity of the other's life. As for the demand that one prefer death over participation in idolatry, the source – "And you shall love" – shows us that the point is not the aversion from idol worship but rather love of God.

The dispute cited by the Talmud regarding idolatry sounds like a lovers' debate. According to Rabbi Yishmael, "he shall live in them but not die by them," meaning that God loves us so much that he is willing to forgo his own commandments to save our lives. Rabbi Akiva, on the other hand, opines that "with all your soul" means "even if He takes your soul." The loving worshipper is willing to give his life for God.

Ultimately, all three transgressions that one is enjoined to die rather than commit are about love: Idolatry undermines love of God, murder destroys the love of humanity, and adultery damages the love shared by husband and wife. According to Rabbi Akiva, the source of all three loves is holy. The Mishna in Tractate Avot (3:14) quotes him as saying, "Beloved is man, since he is created in the image [of God]." In addition, he is considered the source of the statement, "When husband and wife are worthy, the Divine Presence abides with them" (Sota 17a).

Rabbi Akiva's Death

> When Rabbi Akiva was taken out for execution, it was the hour for the recital of *Shema,* and while they combed his flesh with iron combs, he was accepting upon himself the kingship of heaven. His disciples said to him: Our teacher, even to this point? He replied: All my days I have been troubled by this verse, "with all your soul," [which I interpret to mean] "even if He takes your soul." I said: When shall I have the opportunity of fulfilling this? Now that I have the opportunity, shall I not fulfill it? He prolonged the word "*eḥad*" (one) until he expired while saying it. A *bat*

> *kol* went forth and proclaimed: Happy are you, Akiva, that your soul has departed with the word *eḥad!* (Berakhot 61b)

Rabbi Akiva experienced his martyrdom not as pain but rather as a release from pain. In dying, he reached the pinnacle of his life. Similarly, the Zohar (*Pekudei* 254b) explains that when the Talmud says Rabbi Akiva departed the Orchard in peace,[1] it means that he died of "love." In the Midrash, Rabbi Akiva himself explains the connection between martyrdom and love:

> Rabbi Akiva says: I shall speak of His beauty" – of the praise of the Holy One, who spoke and brought the world into being. The peoples of the world ask Israel, "How is your Beloved different from the beloved [of all the other nations] that you have thus sworn us?" (Song of Songs 5:9) – that you thus die for Him and are thus murdered for Him? For it is written, "therefore the maidens love You" (1:3) – they love You unto death, and it is written (Psalms 44:23), "for Your sake we are killed all the day." (Mekhilta of Rabbi Yishmael, *Masekhta DeShira* 3)

We will conclude with the words of Rabbi Shimon Gershon Rosenberg, or Shagar:

> To die for love, which was what Rabbi Akiva yearned for, is the ultimate gesture of love and its pinnacle. One becomes the quintessential servant of God. Rabbi Akiva's take on "they love You unto death"... is the yearning to return to the unity of love, through death.[2]

---

1. Ḥagiga 14a tells the story about the four Sages who delved the depths of Jewish mysticism ("the Orchard") and that only Rabbi Akiva came out unscathed ("in peace").
2. Shimon Gershon Rosenberg (Shagar), *They Love You Unto Death* (Efrat: Bina L'Itim, 2004) [Hebrew].

Laymen's Blessings

ברכות ט, ה

...כָּל חוֹתְמֵי בְרָכוֹת שֶׁהָיוּ בַמִּקְדָּשׁ, הָיוּ אוֹמְרִים מִן הָעוֹלָם. מִשֶּׁקִּלְקְלוּ הַמִּינִין, וְאָמְרוּ, אֵין עוֹלָם אֶלָּא אֶחָד, הִתְקִינוּ שֶׁיְּהוּ אוֹמְרִים, מִן הָעוֹלָם וְעַד הָעוֹלָם. וְהִתְקִינוּ, שֶׁיְּהֵא אָדָם שׁוֹאֵל אֶת שְׁלוֹם חֲבֵרוֹ בַּשֵּׁם, שֶׁנֶּאֱמַר (רות ב) וְהִנֵּה בֹעַז בָּא מִבֵּית לֶחֶם, וַיֹּאמֶר לַקּוֹצְרִים יְיָ עִמָּכֶם, וַיֹּאמְרוּ לוֹ, יְבָרֶכְךָ יְיָ. וְאוֹמֵר (שופטים ו) יְיָ עִמְּךָ גִּבּוֹר הֶחָיִל. וְאוֹמֵר (משלי כג) אַל תָּבוּז כִּי זָקְנָה אִמֶּךָ. וְאוֹמֵר (תהלים קיט) עֵת לַעֲשׂוֹת לַיְיָ הֵפֵרוּ תוֹרָתֶךָ. רַבִּי נָתָן אוֹמֵר, הֵפֵרוּ תוֹרָתֶךָ עֵת לַעֲשׂוֹת לַיְיָ:

Berakhot 9:5

All who ended the blessings when they were in the Temple would say, "From the world." When the heretics corrupted [matters] and said, "There is no world but this one," [the Sages] instituted this so that they should say, "From the world and until the [next] world." And they instituted this, that a person shall inquire after the peace of his fellow with the Name [of God], as it says, "And behold, Boaz came from Bethlehem and said to the harvesters, 'May the Lord be with you,' and they said to him, 'May the Lord bless you'" (Ruth 2:4). And it says, "The Lord is with you, great and valorous one" (Judges 6:12). And it says, "Do not scorn, because your mother is old" (Proverbs 23:22). And it says, "It is time to do for the Lord, they have broken your Torah" (Psalms 119:126). Rabbi Natan says: They nullified your Torah because it is time to do for the Lord.

The Mishna learns from the blessings of Boaz and the harvesters that when we inquire after the peace of our fellow, we should use God's name. One could perhaps think, in light of the extreme caution that is generally exercised when it comes to uttering God's name, that there was something wrong with the actions of Boaz and the harvesters. The

Mishna thus makes clear that the actions of the ancients are worthy of respect ("Do not scorn, because your mother is old"). The Mishna is aware of the problematic nature of the ordinance, and thus bases it on the verse, "They nullified your Torah because it is time to do for the Lord," which legitimizes, in extraordinary circumstances, the transgression of prohibitions.

The ordinance touting the importance of peace between people calls to mind the Talmud's comments on the ordeal of the *sota,* or suspected adulteress, in the Temple: "in order to make peace between husband and wife, the Torah commanded, let My Name, written in sanctity, be dissolved in water" (Nedarim 66b).[1] To my mind, the ordinance has another, hidden layer: The Mishna links together two ordinances related to blessings – one in the context of the Temple and one that is universal. In their blessing, the priests utter God's name: "So shall they put My name upon the children of Israel, and I will bless them" (Numbers 6:27). In addition, the ordinance is derived from the words of the harvesters, "God bless you" – the words that open the priestly blessing. The heading of the ordinance, "peace" (*shalom*), is the word with which the priestly blessing ends, and is the title of the final blessing of the *Shemoneh Esreh, "Sim Shalom."*

In seeking a source for the ordinance, the Mishna does not suffice with the story of Boaz and harvesters. It quotes another verse: "And the angel of the Lord appeared to him, and said to him: 'The Lord is with you, great and valorous one'" (Judges 6:12). On the face of it, the choice to cite this second source for the ordinance appears incongruous: In this verse it is an angel – rather than a human being – that blesses Gideon, who is subsequently also blessed by God. Yet, perhaps this is exactly what the Mishna is teaching us: In the priestly blessing, it is the priests who say the blessing, but the blessing itself comes from God – "and I will bless them." In the verse describing Boaz and the harvesters, a person does the blessing, while in the verse about Gideon it is an angel – but in

1. In the context of the importance of peace between husband and wife, it is noteworthy that the word "peace" appears in Tractate Gittin ten times – more than in any other tractate of the Talmud.

both cases we learn that the blessing comes from God.[2] The following verses are laden with allusions to the priestly blessing – peace and the shining of God's countenance:

> And Gideon said: "Alas, O Lord God! For as I have seen an angel of the Lord face to face." And the Lord said to him: "Peace be upon you..." So Gideon built an altar there to the Lord, and called it Adonai-Shalom. (Judges 6:22–24)

The link to the priestly blessings sanctifies the encounter between two people, turning it into a locus of divine presence, and transforming the person delivering the blessing to a priest of sorts. In the present day, even though this ordinance is no longer the established custom, each and every one of us can still choose to emulate God by shining our countenance at others, in peace.

Ending as Beginning

In our discussion of the first mishna in Berakhot, we mentioned that Rabbi Avraham Walfish sees a connection – via a literary device called inclusio, or envelope structure – between that mishna and the final mishna in the tractate. Noting that the topic of both mishnayot is *Keriat Shema*, Walfish writes: "The framing of the tractate links its topics together in a spiritual-philosophical sense: *Keriat Shema* is recited in the beginning and end of the day.... It is with good reason that the talmudic Sages included the story of the death of Rabbi Akiva in the debate that relates to our mishna, for 'when Rabbi Akiva was taken out for execution, it was the hour for the recital of *Shema*.'"[3] Walfish finds another, hidden link between the two mishnayot. In 1:1, the Mishna says, "From the time when the priests go in (*nikhnasim*) to eat their *teruma*," and in 9:5 it says,

2. An interesting link between the stories is the fact that Boaz, like Gideon, is referred to as a "great and valorous one" (Ruth 2:1).
3. Walfish, "Literary Considerations," 38–39.

"One may not enter (*yikanes*) the Temple Mount." Thus he points out a connection between *Keriat Shema* and the priests' Temple rituals.[4]

If we take the above idea a step further, it can help us understand the framing of the tractate. The third part of our mishna also includes an envelope structure: The tractate begins with defining the time for *Keriat Shema* based on the hour when the priests consume their *teruma*. It ends with the blessing that laymen offer to their fellows, which is based on the priestly blessing. The framing of the Mishna drives home the idea that we encountered throughout Tractate Berakhot: All of Israel are "a kingdom of priests, and a holy nation" (Exodus 19:6).

4. Ibid., 39.

Connections of Peace

Berakhot 9:5; Pe'ah 1:1

ברכות ט, ה, פאה א, א

חַיָּב אָדָם לְבָרֵךְ עַל הָרָעָה כְּשֵׁם שֶׁהוּא מְבָרֵךְ עַל הַטּוֹבָה, שֶׁנֶּאֱמַר (דברים ו) וְאָהַבְתָּ אֵת יְיָ אֱלֹהֶיךָ בְּכָל לְבָבְךָ וּבְכָל נַפְשְׁךָ וּבְכָל מְאֹדֶךָ. בְּכָל לְבָבְךָ, בִּשְׁנֵי יְצָרֶיךָ, בְּיֵצֶר טוֹב וּבְיֵצֶר רָע וּבְכָל נַפְשְׁךָ, אֲפִלּוּ הוּא נוֹטֵל אֶת נַפְשְׁךָ. וּבְכָל מְאֹדֶךָ, בְּכָל מָמוֹנֶךָ. דָּבָר אַחֵר בְּכָל מְאֹדֶךָ, בְּכָל מִדָּה וּמִדָּה שֶׁהוּא מוֹדֵד לְךָ הֱוֵי מוֹדֶה לוֹ בִּמְאֹד מְאֹד.

A person is obligated to bless upon the bad just as he blesses upon the good. As it says, "And you shall love the Lord your God with all your heart and with all your soul and with all that you have." (Deut. 6:5) "With all your heart" – with your two inclinations, with the inclination of good and the inclination of evil. "And with all your soul" – even if He takes your soul. "And with all that you have" – with all your money. Alternatively, "With all that you have (*me'odekha*)" – with every measure that is measured for you thank Him very much (*me'od me'od*).

לֹא יָקֵל אָדָם אֶת רֹאשׁוֹ כְּנֶגֶד שַׁעַר הַמִּזְרָח, שֶׁהוּא מְכֻוָּן כְּנֶגֶד בֵּית קָדְשֵׁי הַקֳּדָשִׁים. לֹא יִכָּנֵס לְהַר הַבַּיִת בְּמַקְלוֹ, וּבְמִנְעָלוֹ, וּבְפֻנְדָּתוֹ, וּבְאָבָק שֶׁעַל רַגְלָיו, וְלֹא יַעֲשֶׂנּוּ קַפַּנְדַּרְיָא, וּרְקִיקָה מִקַּל וָחֹמֶר. כָּל חוֹתְמֵי בְרָכוֹת שֶׁהָיוּ בַּמִּקְדָּשׁ, הָיוּ אוֹמְרִים מִן הָעוֹלָם. מִשֶּׁקִּלְקְלוּ הַמִּינִין, וְאָמְרוּ, אֵין עוֹלָם אֶלָּא אֶחָד, הִתְקִינוּ שֶׁיְּהוּ

One must not be frivolous near the eastern gate, for it is near the foundation of the house of the Holy of Holies. One may not enter the Temple Mount with his staff, or with his sandal, or with his belt-pouch, or with dust on his feet, and may not make it a shortcut, and spitting is forbidden, as deduced from [the principle of] lesser to greater. All who ended the blessings when they were in the Temple would say, "From the world." When the heretics corrupted [matters] and said, "There is no world but this one," [the Sages] instituted this so that they should say,

אוֹמְרִים, מִן הָעוֹלָם וְעַד הָעוֹלָם. וְהִתְקִינוּ, שֶׁיְּהֵא אָדָם שׁוֹאֵל אֶת שְׁלוֹם חֲבֵרוֹ בַּשֵּׁם, שֶׁנֶּאֱמַר (רות ב) וְהִנֵּה בֹעַז בָּא מִבֵּית לֶחֶם, וַיֹּאמֶר לַקּוֹצְרִים יְיָ עִמָּכֶם, וַיֹּאמְרוּ לוֹ, יְבָרֶכְךָ יְיָ. וְאוֹמֵר (שופטים ו) יְיָ עִמְּךָ גִּבּוֹר הֶחָיִל. וְאוֹמֵר (משלי כג) אַל תָּבוּז כִּי זָקְנָה אִמֶּךָ. וְאוֹמֵר (תהלים קיט) עֵת לַעֲשׂוֹת לַייָ הֵפֵרוּ תּוֹרָתֶךָ. רַבִּי נָתָן אוֹמֵר, הֵפֵרוּ תוֹרָתְךָ עֵת לַעֲשׂוֹת לַייָ:

"From the world and until the [next] world." And they instituted this, that a person shall inquire after the peace of his fellow with the Name [of God], as it says, "And behold, Boaz came from Bethlehem and said to the harvesters, 'May the Lord be with you,' and they said to him, 'May the Lord bless you'" (Ruth 2:4). And it says, "The Lord is with you, great and valorous one" (Judges 6:12). And it says, "Do not scorn, because your mother is old" (Proverbs 23:22). And it says, "It is time to do for the Lord, they have broken your Torah" (Psalms 119:126). Rabbi Natan says: They nullified your Torah because it is time to do for the Lord. (Berakhot 9:5)

The literary structure of the chapter's final mishna is no less than a masterpiece that sheds light on all of the concentric circles surrounding it: the chapter, the tractate, the order, and the entire Mishna.

Nesting Doll of Blessings

A nesting doll, or *matryoshka,* is a large doll containing a smaller but otherwise identical doll, which contains yet another doll, even smaller but also identical, etc. Tractate Berakhot is concerned with three topics, in this order: *Keriat Shema, Shemoneh Esreh,* and blessings. The final chapter of the tractate contains, in a chiastic structure, these three topics: blessings (9:1–3), *Shemoneh Esreh* (9:3–4), and *Keriat Shema* (9:5, which interprets the verse, "And you shall love" from *Shema* in order to define the meaning of accepting the kingdom of heaven).

But this is not the final nesting doll. The final mishna itself also contains all three of the topics, in order of their appearance earlier in the tractate, beginning with *Keriat Shema,* continuing with proper behavior on the Temple Mount, which informs many of the laws relating to prayer and synagogues,[1] and ending with two ordinances regarding blessings.

In the final mishna, as in the rest of the chapter, there is a dialogue with the preceding mishnayot. The beginning of the mishna defines the obligation to bless upon the bad as well as on the good, which is a response to 5:3: "One who says [in prayer]…'On the good shall Your Name be mentioned,' silence him." The middle of the mishna says, "One must not be frivolous near the eastern gate," which is parallel to "[One] should not stand up to pray unless he is in a serious frame of mind." The holiness of the eastern gate derives from its location, "near the foundation of the house of the Holy of Holies" – a formulation that appears twice in the fourth chapter (4:5–6) in relation to the place where one should direct one's heart in prayer. Finally the ordinance that the mishna ends with – that "a person shall inquire after the peace of his fellow with the Name [of God]" – sheds fresh light on the mishnayot that debate the possibility of greeting another and returning a greeting while reciting *Shema* (2:1: "at the breaks, one may greet out of honor and return a greeting to any person") or praying *Shemoneh Esreh* ("even if the king greets him, he should not respond"). As we saw in the previous chapter, all three parts of the mishna constitute an envelope structure in relation to the first mishna of the tractate.

From God to Humanity

Tractate Berakhot, in a general sense, is concerned with the encounter between the human and the divine. The decision to conclude it with a discussion of encounters between people, at the heart of which is also God's name, teaches us that interpersonal relationships are also part of the encounter with the numinous. This is far from self-evident: The students of Rabbi Akiva – though they certainly were exacting when it came

1. See below for the connection to prayer. As for synagogues, the prohibition against using the Temple Mount as a shortcut appears in the Mishna in Tractate Megilla as one that also applies to synagogues, based on the idea that places of worship are tantamount to the Temple: "Nor should it be used as a shortcut, as it is said, 'I will bring your sanctuaries into desolation' (Leviticus 26) – that is, they remain sanctuaries even in their desolation" (Megilla 3:3).

to prayer and blessings – all died because they did not show respect for one another (Yevamot 62b).

The connection between the human and the divine is evident in the literary structure of the closing words of the mishna. These link up to the mishna that follows – the one that opens Tractate Pe'ah:

> These are the things that have no measure: *Pe'ah* [the corner of the field that, while harvesting, must be left for the poor], first fruits [which must be brought to the Temple and given to the priest], the appearance offering [brought to the Temple on pilgrimage festivals], acts of kindness, and the study of the Torah. These are the things whose fruits one enjoys in this world, while the principal remains for one in the next world: Honoring one's father and mother, acts of kindness, and bringing peace between a person and his fellow. But the study of Torah is equal to them all. (Pe'ah 1:1)

The Mishna in Berakhot says, "they instituted this, that **a person** shall inquire after **the peace of his fellow** with the Name [of God]"; in Pe'ah we learn the implications of this corrective: "bringing **peace** between **a person and his fellow**."

In Berakhot, the blessing extends to two worlds: "When the heretics corrupted [matters] and said, 'There is no world but this one,' [the Sages] instituted this so that they should say, 'From the world and until the [next] world.'" In Pe'ah, the reward extends to both worlds: "These are the things whose fruits one enjoys in this world, while the principal remains for one in the next world."

Berakhot says, "Do not scorn, because your mother is old"; Pe'ah refers to "Honoring one's father and mother."

But more than anywhere else, the link between the human and divine is evident in the verse that the Mishna cites in Berakhot as a source for the requirement to utter God's name when greeting another person: "And behold, Boaz came from Bethlehem and said to the harvesters, 'May the Lord be with you,' and they said to him, 'May the Lord bless you'" (Ruth 2:4). My brother Rabbi Dani Genack pointed out to me that, in its biblical context, this verse appears at the heart of the story of Ruth collecting the gleanings of the harvesters (vv. 2–17), which is significant considering the fact that Tractate Pe'ah is all about agricultural gifts to the poor.

As we established, Berakhot is devoted to the relationship between the human and the divine, especially the acknowledgement of the blessing that God bestows upon us. Pe'ah is devoted to the interpersonal realm, and especially the sharing of God's bounty.

The linking of the two tractates by way of the edict regarding greetings in the name of God highlights the deep connection between the interpersonal realm and the relationship with the divine. Here is Rabbi Zvi Yehuda Kook on the meaning of that edict:

> Through this [edict], the true value of proper social relations among all people was established and determined… that they are a manifestation of the divine aspect whereby the entire Jewish people are named after God, as is every individual Jew and as are their proper interpersonal relationships.[2]

The edict regarding blessing one's fellow with the name of God teaches us that people not only receive God's blessings but are also required to pay those blessings forward. In the story of Boaz and the harvesters, Boaz passes on God's blessing by greeting others with God's name and leaving gleanings for the poor.

The link between the human and the divine can also be found in the impetus for the edict. In the Mishna's reading, the verse "It is time to do for the Lord, they have broken your Torah" teaches us that blessing another person is not only a human need, but rather something one does "for the Lord," meaning that a blessing for the other is a blessing for God. Every encounter with another human being is an encounter with God.

The internal structure of the mishna further sharpens this idea. It begins with love for God and ends with peace among people. The mishna derives the obligation to sanctify God's name from the obligation to love Him; peace among people must be made "in the name of

2. Rabbi Zvi Yehuda Kook, *Lenetivot Israel* (Beit El: Me'avnei Hamakom, 2002), 317.

God." This means that in both the human and the divine realms, God's name must be sanctified.

The opening of Tractate Pe'ah further reinforces the connection between the two realms. The list of things that have no measure, with which the mishna begins, includes both interpersonal commandments and obligations toward God. The reward that one earns for bringing peace between two people, as with the other interpersonal mitzvot mentioned in the Mishna (honoring one's parents and engaging in acts of kindness) is given in two worlds – this, the human, one; and the divine next world.

Tractate Avot states, "On three things the world stands: on the Torah, on [divine] service, and on acts of kindness" (1:2). Berakhot deals with service – *Keriat Shema, Shemoneh Esreh,* and blessings. Pe'ah concerns itself with acts of kindness, an element that is twice mentioned in our mishna. The third element – the Torah – is equal in importance to the rest (Pe'ah 1:1). It too is a motif linking the two mishnayot, appearing twice in each of them.[3]

Peace Is the Objective of the Torah

Berakhot, the first tractate of the Mishna, ends with peace in the name of God, and thus corresponds to the final mishna of the last tractate, Uktzin (3:12):

> Rabbi Shimon ben Ḥalafta said: The blessed Holy One found no vessel that can hold the blessing for Israel, save for peace, as the verse says, "The Lord will give strength

3. In addition to those ways in which the two mishnayot are linked that we have discussed, there are additional literary devices indicating that tractates Berakhot and Pe'ah may be considered a single unit. Thus, for example, the first chapter of Berakhot begins with, "From when" (*me'eimatai*) and relates to the question of the appropriate time for *Keriat Shema.* The word "*me'eimatai*" next appears in the Mishna in the beginning of the final chapter (8:1) of Pe'ah ("From when [*me'eimatai*] is everyone permitted in [taking] *leket*?"). Furthermore, there are parallels between the final mishna in Pe'ah and the final mishna in Berakhot – references to old age, trust in God, and the question of divine recompense.

> to His nation, the Lord will bless His nation with peace" (Psalms 29:11).[4]

The Mishna concludes with peace, as do the priestly blessing, the *Amida* prayer, *Kaddish,* and Grace after Meals. Peace is Judaism's ultimate goal; it is the pinnacle to which we aspire. In the Talmud (Gittin 59b), Abaye asks about a law that is explained as being "in the interests of peace":

> Abaye said to Rav Yosef: Is this rule only [a rabbinical one] in the interests of peace? Does it not derive from the Torah? [Rav Yosef] answered: It does derive from the Torah, but its objective is to maintain peace. For the purpose of the entire Torah is also to promote peace, as it is written, "Its ways are ways of pleasantness and all its paths are peace" (Proverbs 3:17).

The Torah in Prayer

In the preceding sections, I suggested that the edict at the end of Tractate Berakhot is based on the priestly blessing, and that the tractate's concluding mishna links up to the one that follows it, in the beginning of Tractate Pe'ah. And indeed, in the morning prayers, just after the blessings of the Torah, are two sections, one after the other: the priestly blessing, followed by an expanded version of the first mishna in Pe'ah. Let us examine this juxtaposition so as to better understand the connection between the two sections:

> May the Lord bless you and keep you. May the Lord shine His face upon you and be gracious to you. May the Lord lift His face to you and grant you peace.

4. This parallel is even more pronounced in the Talmud, where Tractate Berakhot ends with the same verse that concludes Tractate Uktzin: "The Lord will give strength to His nation, the Lord will bless His nation with peace." It is also noteworthy that Eduyot, an ancient tractate that was probably completed as a standalone book, also ends with peace.

> These are the things that have no measure: *Pe'ah*, first fruits, the appearance offering, acts of kindness, and the study of the Torah. These are the things whose fruits one enjoys in this world, while the principal remains for one in the next world: Honoring one's father and mother, acts of kindness, rising to go to the *beit midrash* in the morning and in the evening, hosting guests, visiting the sick, providing for the bride, escorting the dead, and bringing peace between a person and his fellow. But the study of Torah is equal to them all. (From the morning blessings)

The two sections diverge in their subject matter: The first is the priests' blessings for the shining of God's countenance – "May God shine His face upon you" – and the second is about the many obligations one has.

Yet, they have some things in common, in terms of both content and form. In the original Hebrew, the priestly blessing is fifteen words long, just like the numerical value of one of God's names – Yah. The verse that appears right after the blessing in the Torah is "So shall they put My name upon the children of Israel, and I will bless them" (Numbers 6:27). The content of the blessing too, features the idea of putting God's name upon the Jewish people, through the shining of the countenance, meaning the encounter with God: "May God shine His face upon you.... May God lift His face to you." Another shared element is the root s-y-m, which repeats both in the blessing – "and grant you" (*veyasem*) – and in the following verse – "So shall they put" (*vesamu*); this is noteworthy when we consider that Shalom is one of God's names (Shabbat 10b).

The second section refers to five items that "have no measure" along with ten precepts that are rewarded in both worlds. Thus, in all, there are fifteen items on the list, the same as the number of words in the priestly blessing. Some of the precepts exemplify the content of the priestly blessings – a shining countenance and peace. The third mitzva on the list is the appearance offering, the gist of which is the encounter between man and the divine countenance: "Three times in the year all your males shall appear before the face of the Lord God" (Exodus 23:17). The penultimate item is peace: "bringing peace between a person and his fellow." This, precisely, is the ending of the priestly blessing:

"and grant you peace." Furthermore, most of the items relate to interpersonal relationships and can thus be described as having the goal of "bringing peace."

The link between both the form and the content of the priestly blessing and the list beginning, "These are the things," hints that just as in the priestly blessing God's name is put upon the people of Israel, so too when the people of Israel abide by these precepts, God's name rests on us:

> The Lord will establish you as His holy people, as He has sworn to you, if you keep the commandments of the Lord your God, and walk in His ways. And all the peoples of the earth shall see that the name of the Lord is called upon you, and they shall be afraid of you. (Deuteronomy 28:9–10)

One way in which God's name rests upon us is "from above." The priests stand on the dais, bless the people and imbue them with bounty and light. But God tells us that there is another way, one that begins "from below," with the work that is within anyone's capacity to do. By keeping His commandments and walking in His ways, we can arrive at a state where "the name of the Lord is called upon you." It seems that these verses are not only a promise, but also a definition: A society that conducts itself according to the commandments and the values they stand for – which can be distilled from the fifteen (*Yah*) items on the list – is a society upon which the names of the Lord can be called.

Humble Charity

פאה ה, ו

הַמּוֹכֵר אֶת שָׂדֵהוּ, הַמּוֹכֵר מֻתָּר וְהַלּוֹקֵחַ אָסוּר. לֹא יִשְׂכֹּר אָדָם אֶת הַפּוֹעֲלִים עַל מְנָת שֶׁיְּלַקֵּט בְּנוֹ אַחֲרָיו. מִי שֶׁאֵינוֹ מַנִּיחַ אֶת הָעֲנִיִּים לִלְקֹט, אוֹ שֶׁהוּא מַנִּיחַ אֶת אֶחָד וְאֶחָד לֹא, אוֹ שֶׁהוּא מְסַיֵּעַ אֶת אֶחָד מֵהֶן, הֲרֵי זֶה גּוֹזֵל אֶת הָעֲנִיִּים. עַל זֶה נֶאֱמַר (משלי כב) אַל תַּסֵּג גְּבוּל עוֹלִים:

Pe'ah 5:6

If someone sells his field, the seller is permitted [in *leket*, *shikheḥa*, and *pe'ah*] and the buyer is forbidden. A person may not hire a worker on the condition that [the worker's] son may glean after him. One who does not allow the poor to glean, or who allows one and not another, or who helps one of them – he is stealing from the poor. Regarding this it is said, "Do not encroach upon the border of those who go up [to glean]" (Proverbs 22:28).

There is an element of social justice to charity, because giving it diminishes the gap between rich and poor. Yet, the very fact that the rich is the "giver" and the poor person the "receiver" could in fact reinforce the class difference between them. In contrast, a farmer does not "give" to the poor person; rather, his action is self-directed – he stops himself from reaping the corner (*pe'ah*) of his field, leaving it for the stranger and the poor:

> And when you reap the harvest of your land, you shall not wholly reap the corner of your field; neither shall you gather the gleaning of your harvest. And you shall not glean your vineyard; neither shall you gather the fallen fruit of your vineyard; you shall leave them for the poor and for the stranger: I am the Lord your God. (Leviticus 19:9–10)

Our mishna reflects the idea that the corner of the field is the property of the poor person rather than the owner of the field. With other tithes and offerings, the giver can decide which priest or Levite he will give to, but when it comes to gleanings, one who does so is considered a thief: According to the Mishna he is "encroaching upon" the gleaners, meaning trespassing. Why are the poor referred to as "those who go up"? The Yerushalmi (Pe'ah 5:5) suggest that it is a reference to the generation of Israelites who first ascended to the Land of Canaan. Thus, the Mishna hints that the rights of the poor to the fields, to glean from their corners, are vouchsafed by the original division of the land, and are no less valid than the rights of the landowner.[1] It follows that the owner of the field does not "give" to the poor, but rather the poor takes what is his by right.[2] This is also why a poor person is permitted to collect *leket* and *pe'ah* from the field of someone who forbade him to benefit from anything he owns (Nedarim 11:3).[3] Furthermore, a farmer who favors one poor person over another or prevents him from harvesting the *pe'ah* is considered a thief.

Pe'ah is at the top of the list of precepts that have "no measure," meaning that there is no prescribed size for the corner that the owner of the field must set aside. According to the Mishna, the size of the corner is determined in part by "the abundance of humility" (Pe'ah 1:2). The Mishna does not say, "the abundance of generosity," because *pe'ah* does not derive from generosity but rather from humility – from the understanding that I have no more rights to the field than do the poor.

---

1. One expression of the rights of the poor to the field lies in the following explanation: In contrast with tithes and offerings, where the obligation relates only to what has already been reaped and severed from the ground, with *pe'ah* the poor have rights to the field itself, and can thus harvest crops that are still connected to the ground.
2. Rabbi Meir's opinion, which we hold by, states that when there is doubt in *leket*, everything goes to the poor, "since doubtful *leket* is [nevertheless considered] *leket*" (Pe'ah 4:11). On the face of it, the halakha should have been the opposite – that when there is doubt, everything belongs to the owner, based on the principle that "the burden of proof is on the claimant." The idea that the poor person is not an outsider, but rather has rights to the field going back generations, explains why the burden of proof is not on him.
3. My thanks to Chanoch Wasserman for pointing this out.

The Mishna describes the ideal manner in which the mitzva of *pe'ah* is fulfilled:

> The people of Beit Namer would gather that which was on [marked by] the rope and give *pe'ah* from each and every row. (Pe'ah 4:5)

Usually, in order to harvest their corner, the poor would have to wait until the end of the harvest. The people of Beit Namer, however, would divide their fields into rows and set aside for the poor a part of each row, so that they could collect *pe'ah* while the owner was still working his part of field. The Mishna's terminology further drives home the extent of the partnership that the people of Beit Namer forged with the poor: It does not say that they "would harvest," but rather that they "would gather." The Mishna generally employs the word "gather" to describe the actions of the poor (see, e.g., Pe'ah 4:9: "He who collects *pe'ah*"). The people of Beit Namer were so humble that they related to themselves as though they were poor persons and related to the poor as though they were the owners of their fields. Furthermore, it seems that the word "rope" (*ḥevel*) in the mishna is a pun, because it is the same word for "region" in the sense of an inherited parcel of land (see, e.g., Joshua 17:14: "one lot and one part (*ḥevel*) for an inheritance"). The use of this word in the Mishna implies that the poor, too, have an inheritance in the land.

In recent years, social justice issues have taken center stage in Israeli public discourse. The government's economic policies created major problems among many members of the so-called "disadvantaged" classes of society. It is fitting for there to be professional discussion of the government's economic vision in light of the complex realities in the State of Israel. But beyond that, each of us must protest unethical treatment of the poor. The Jewish people, throughout the generations, saw helping the poor as part of society's natural responsibility, and did not question the right of the poor to rely on such aid. Maimonides defines charity thus:

> The word *tzedaka* is derived from *tzedek,* which means justice; justice being the granting to everyone who has a

> right to something, that which he has a right to and giving to every being that which corresponds to his merits. (*Guide for the Perplexed* III:53)

Even if there is a temporary situation wherein the poor cannot be helped, society must bemoan this situation and keep in mind its basic responsibility toward them. Instead, we hear more and more condescending statements – the complete opposite of an "abundance of humility" – and even accusations leveled at the poor.

In order to root out such condescension, when the Torah calls on us to give charity it reminds us that what we have, too, is a gift from heaven:

> If there be among you a needy man, one of your brethren, within any of your gates, in your land, which the Lord your God gives you, you shall not harden your heart, nor shut your hand from your needy brother. (Deuteronomy 15:7)

In contrast with the outlook that considers the poor as a burden and a drag on society, the Torah considers our engagement with them a blessing to the world:

> You shall surely give him, and your heart shall not be grieved when you give to him, because it is for this thing the Lord your God will bless you in all your work, and in all that you put your hand into. (Deuteronomy 15:10)

This is the place to note that the mitzva of *pe'ah* also contends with another category of concerns related to charity: that when we give directly to the poor, we perpetuate a passive outlook on their part, which in itself can sometimes cause poverty. *Pe'ah*, on contrast, impels the poor to act: They must come to the field themselves and reap their part of the harvest.[4]

4. Thank you to Carmel Weissman, who pointed this out to me.

The First-Fruits Experience

Bikkurim 3:1

The Five Books of Moses tell the story of deferred promises, of obstacles that prevent the realization of expectations. Our forefathers are ever on the way, and it seems they will never reach the Promised Land. But finally, near the end of Deuteronomy, in the description of the ritual of first fruits, the ending is divulged:

> And it shall be, when you come into the land that the Lord your God is giving you for an inheritance – and possess it, and dwell therein – that you shall take of the first of all the fruit of the ground.... "And the Lord brought us forth out of Egypt with a mighty hand.... And He has brought us into this place, and has given us this land, a land flowing with milk and honey. And now, behold, I have brought the first of the fruit of the land, which You, O Lord, have given me." And you shall set it down.... And you shall rejoice in all the good that the Lord your God has given you. (Deuteronomy 26:1–11)

The above verses are laden with future-tense verbs: possess, dwell, take, set down. The mitzva of bringing first fruits to the Temple is portrayed as a continuation of the conquest and settlement of the land. Thus, the tone is not imperative or legalistic, but rather fits into the description of future life in the Promised Land. Bringing first fruits is an inseparable part of the happy ending to the people's desert wanderings, a personal expression of rejoicing and thanks over the fulfillment of the divine promise, a state of fairytale bliss: "And they lived happily ever after."

Every year, those who bring first fruits recap the entire story – from the descent into Egypt until the Exodus and the salvation from bondage. The bringer tells it all in the first person, as a personal story, thus fulfilling the Mishna's imperative: "a person must see himself as though he [personally] had gone out of Egypt" (Pesaḥim 10:5). Every year, we experience the story anew.

The Mishna also emphasizes individual experience when it comes to bringing the fruits themselves:

> How does one designate the first fruits? One goes into one's field and sees a fruit-bearing fig tree, a fruit-bearing [grape]vine, or a fruit-bearing pomegranate tree, and ties it [the fruit] with a string and says, "Behold, these are first fruits." Rabbi Shimon says, even so, one reiterates and declares them first fruits once they have been picked from the ground. (Bikkurim 3:1)

Our mishna's style is reminiscent of the biblical verses, in that it relates a story rather than a halakhic imperative. Like the verses, it is organized around a series of actions – "goes into," "sees," "ties," and "says" – and like the verses, it is hard to distinguish between mere description and the halakhic imperative mood. "Behold, these are first fruits" can just as easily be a description of the reality of "a fruit-bearing fig tree" as it is a halakhic declaration. A naïve reader of our mishna would not conclude that the declaration, "Behold, these are first fruits," has halakhic implications.

The Mishna describes the special moment where a farmer first sees the fruits of his labor. According to the Mishna, the fruits that one dedicates for first fruits are determined not by external measures, but rather by one's personal outlook. As in the Bible, this emphasizes the commandment's personal and subjective side. Rabbi Shimon defines the fruit dedicated to first fruits based on two moments – when they are seen and when they are picked. The first *Tanna* in our mishna, in contrast, defines it solely based on the moving moment when the farmer first sees the fruits – unlike most agricultural commandments, there is no requirement to wait for the harvest.

The first year that first fruits were brought to the Temple in Jerusalem, everyone was immensely excited. The Mishna's emphasis on one's emotions in the moment when one finds the first fruits in one's field helps to maintain those feelings of discovery, freshness, and renewal every year. When one brings the first fruits to the Temple, one brings produce that is charged with emotion, and thus can express, simply and completely, his joy over the fulfillment of God's promise in his life.

First Fruits: Who Brings to Whom?

Bikkurim, chapter 3

With first fruits, on the face of it, it appears as though the person is the giver and God is the receiver. However, if we examine the verses regarding first fruits, we learn that although giving is mentioned many times, the roles are reversed, and it is God who gives to humans. The bringing of first fruits, in contrast, is not described as "giving"[1]:

> And it shall be, when you come into the land that the Lord Your God is giving you for an inheritance – and possess it, and dwell therein – that you shall take of the first of all the fruit of the ground.... "And the Lord brought us forth out of Egypt with a mighty hand.... And He has brought us into this place, and has given us this land, a land flowing with milk and honey. And now, behold, I have brought the first of the fruit of the land, which You, O Lord, have given me." And you shall set it down.... And you shall rejoice in

1. In this context, the description of the mitzva of first fruits can be contrasted with the description of the tithe: "When you have made an end of tithing all the tithe of your increase in the third year, which is the year of tithing, and have given it to the Levite, to the stranger, to the fatherless, and to the widow, so that they may eat within your gates, and be satisfied, then you shall say before the Lord your God: 'I have put away the hallowed things out of my house, and also have given them to the Levite, and to the stranger, to the fatherless, and to the widow'" (Deuteronomy 26:12–13).

> all the good that the Lord your God has given you. (Deuteronomy 26:1–11)

As we explained above, the bringing of first fruits to the Temple is meant to express the happiness and joy of one who has seen God's promises fulfilled. In other words, the focus of the commandment is God's giving to man, not vice versa. This point is put into starker relief when the Mishna describes the bringing of first fruits to the Temple:

> A bull would go before them, whose horns would be plated with gold, and it would have an olive wreath around its head. The flute would play before them until they neared Jerusalem. Once they neared Jerusalem, they would send [a messenger] ahead of them and adorn their first fruits. The overseers and the officers and the treasurers would go out to greet them; in accordance with the stature of those coming in would they go out. All the artisans of Jerusalem would stand before them and greet them, "Our brothers from such and such place, come in peace!" (Bikkurim 3:3)

First fruits are brought to the Temple in a picturesque procession, accompanied by musicians and gold-adorned animals. As soon as the procession arrives at the big city, it is greeted by dignitaries, and residents stand in its honor, as they would before an elder or a sage. There is of course no correlation between the monetary value of the first fruits and the honor that its bringers are accorded.

The key to understanding this procession lies in grasping the importance of first fruits, not as mere fruit, but as a symbol of life in which the divine promise has been actualized. The rejoicing of the people of Jerusalem upon seeing the bringers, and the honor that they heap on them, is the final detail in the scene described by the Mishna of the first-fruits procession:

> The flute would continue playing before them until they arrived at the Temple Mount. Once they arrived at the Temple Mount, even Agripas the king would carry his

> basket on his shoulder and enter until he reached the courtyard. Once they got to the courtyard, the Levites would speak in song (Psalms 30:2), "I will extol You, O Lord, because You have raised me and not allowed my enemies to rejoice over me." (Bikkurim 3:4)

Bringers of first fruits would have to enter the Temple with a basket on their shoulders. The importance of the positioning of the bringer as part of the ceremony implies that when one brings the fruits to the Temple, one is in fact showing oneself before God. Furthermore, when one would enter the courtyard, the Levites would not sing about the fruits but rather about the human realm: "I will extol You, O Lord, because You have raised me." The focus is the person, and the fruits are merely a means to express the joy in that person's life.

> How do they bring up the first fruits [to Jerusalem]? All the cities of a region would go into the [central] city of that region and sleep in the streets of that city without going into the houses. When they arose, the supervisor would say, "Arise! Let us go up to Zion, to the house of the Lord our God." (Bikkurim 3:2)

The mishna opens by asking how the people would "**bring up** the first fruits" and ends with the statement "Let us **go up** to Zion, to the house of the Lord our God." At first the fruits are brought up, and then the people are elevated ever higher.

Shabbat in Place

Shabbat 1:1

There are two [types of] transfers on Shabbat that amount to four inside, and two that amount to four outside. How so? [This is illustrated by] a poor person standing outside and a homeowner [standing] inside: [If] the poor person reaches his hand inside and puts [something] into the hand of the homeowner, or takes [something] from [the hand] and brings it outside, the poor person is liable and the homeowner is exempt. [If] the homeowner reaches his hand outside and puts [something] into the hand of the poor person, or takes [something] from [the hand] and brings it inside, the homeowner is liable and the poor person is exempt. [If] the poor person reaches his hand inside and the homeowner takes [something] from it, or puts [something] into it, and [the poor person] brings it outside, they are both exempt. [If] the homeowner reaches his hand outside and the poor person takes [something] from it, or puts [something] into it, and [the homeowner] brings it inside, they are both exempt.

שבת א, א

יְצִיאוֹת הַשַּׁבָּת שְׁתַּיִם שֶׁהֵן אַרְבַּע בִּפְנִים, וּשְׁתַּיִם שֶׁהֵן אַרְבַּע בַּחוּץ. כֵּיצַד. הֶעָנִי עוֹמֵד בַּחוּץ וּבַעַל הַבַּיִת בִּפְנִים, פָּשַׁט הֶעָנִי אֶת יָדוֹ לִפְנִים וְנָתַן לְתוֹךְ יָדוֹ שֶׁל בַּעַל הַבַּיִת, אוֹ שֶׁנָּטַל מִתּוֹכָהּ וְהוֹצִיא, הֶעָנִי חַיָּב וּבַעַל הַבַּיִת פָּטוּר. פָּשַׁט בַּעַל הַבַּיִת אֶת יָדוֹ לַחוּץ וְנָתַן לְתוֹךְ יָדוֹ שֶׁל עָנִי, אוֹ שֶׁנָּטַל מִתּוֹכָהּ וְהִכְנִיס, בַּעַל הַבַּיִת חַיָּב וְהֶעָנִי פָּטוּר. פָּשַׁט הֶעָנִי אֶת יָדוֹ לִפְנִים וְנָטַל בַּעַל הַבַּיִת מִתּוֹכָהּ, אוֹ שֶׁנָּתַן לְתוֹכָהּ וְהוֹצִיא, שְׁנֵיהֶם פְּטוּרִין. פָּשַׁט בַּעַל הַבַּיִת אֶת יָדוֹ לַחוּץ וְנָטַל הֶעָנִי מִתּוֹכָהּ, אוֹ שֶׁנָּתַן לְתוֹכָהּ וְהִכְנִיס, שְׁנֵיהֶם פְּטוּרִין:

The first chapters of Tractate Shabbat are organized chronologically. The first chapter begins with actions that are forbidden on Friday afternoon, continues with actions that are forbidden just before nightfall, and ends with actions that are permitted as night falls. The next chapters are concerned with preparations for Shabbat – candle lighting and the insulation of dishes that began to cook before Shabbat.[1]

Incongruent in this regard is the chapter's first mishna, which is concerned with the laws of transferring between domains, one of the thirty-nine labors that are prohibited on Shabbat and are elucidated in Chapter 7. Two questions arise from the choice to open the tractate with the laws of transferring: (1) Why did the editor of the Mishna diverge from the chronology; and (2) why doesn't this mishna appear in its natural place, after the thirty-nine prohibited labors that are detailed in Chapter 7?

Commentators have contended with these questions since the days of the *Rishonim*.[2] Maimonides suggests two solutions:

> The fact that they decided to begin with the laws of transferring between domains, even though it is enumerated at the end [of the list] of prohibited labors... is due to this labor being widespread and something that many err in, because it does not involve the use of tools. Additionally, it was prepended to reinforce the understanding that it is a prohibited labor even though it does not seem like work. (Maimonides's Commentary on the Mishna, Shabbat 1:1)

Maimonides explains that transferring objects between domains is a "widespread activity" and thus a stumbling block for many. Additionally, he says that on the face of it, transferring objects does not seem like labor, yet it is forbidden on Shabbat and people should be mindful of

1. Avraham Goldberg, *Commentary to the Mishna: Shabbat* (New York: Jewish Theological Seminary of America, 1976) [Hebrew], 14.
2. Rabbi Yehuda Shaviv summarizes a range of answers to these questions from the *Rishonim* and *Aḥaronim*, including Maimonides and the *Penei Yehoshua*, which are quoted here. See "Why Did Tractate Shabbat Open with the Laws of Transferring," in *Batzir Aviezer* (Alon Shvut: Zomet, 1990) [Hebrew], 233–43. Avraham Goldberg summarizes many more opinions and adds several new explanations; see Goldberg, *Commentary to the Mishna*, 2–3.

the fact. It is due to these two reasons, according to Maimonides, that Tractate Shabbat opens with the laws of transferring objects.

Other commentators say that the issue of transferring objects is placed in the beginning of the tractate because it includes information crucial to understanding the mishnayot further along in the chapter.[3] Yet others explained it as part of an attempt to play up Pharisee law in the face of Sadducee law.[4]

Among the various interpretations, I am drawn to the approach of the *Penei Yehoshua,* which is rooted in the particular language of the mishna:

> There are two transfers on Shabbat that amount to four. And *Tosafot* asked…why did the Mishna open with, etc. But with all humility, I do not know why they found this difficult; indeed, it makes sense that [the Mishna] opened with the laws of transferring (*yetziot*), for the law of transferring is gleaned from the verse, "let no man go out (*yetze*) of his place"…This is why [the Mishna] did not say "taking out" (*hotzaot*) – because it was quoting the verse…In the Torah, the verse that states "let no man go out" appears in *Parashat Beshallaḥ,* in the context of the manna, a commandment that they were given at Mara. The other [prohibited] labors, in contrast, are derived from the verse, "you shall not do any manner of work," which appears in [*Parashat*] *Yitro,* a commandment that they were given at Sinai. (*Penei Yehoshua* on Shabbat 2a)

There are two passages in the Torah that discuss the labors prohibited on Shabbat. The first, in the context of the manna in *Parashat Beshallaḥ* (Exodus 16:29), forbids transferring objects between domains; the second, in the Ten Commandments in *Parashat Yitro* (Exodus 20:9), forbids labor on Shabbat. The first relates only to transferring, while the second applies to all manner of activities deemed "work." The prohibition on

3. *Tosafot* on Shabbat 2a, on the words, "There are two transfers."
4. Goldberg, *Commentary to the Mishna,* 3.

transferring, the *Penei Yehoshua* writes, is the first commandment in the Torah regarding Shabbat, which is why the tractate opens with it. The *Penei Yehoshua* bolsters his assertion with a quote from the Mishna, which uses the word "*yetziot*" for "transfers" rather than the more obvious "*hotzaot*," echoing the Torah in *Beshallaḥ*: "let no man go out (*yetze*) of his place."

Abide on Shabbat

Being a standalone law, the prohibition against transferring between domains takes on a special quality that relates to a fundamental aspect of Shabbat, which is why the Mishna addresses it first: not only because of the order of the Torah text, but also due to the essential, philosophical primacy. The special status of the law regarding transfers also explains the fact that it takes up fully a third of Tractate Shabbat. Meanwhile, the debates in the ten-chapter Tractate Eiruvin are derived from the prohibition against exiting the Shabbat boundary, which is itself deduced from "let no man go out of his place." The laws of *muktze* – restrictions on touching or moving certain objects on Shabbat – are also connected to the laws of transferring. Furthermore, those who assert that *muktze* is a biblical prohibition derive it from the ban on exiting the Shabbat boundary, in *Parashat Beshallaḥ*,[5] while those who see it as a rabbinic prohibition link it to the prohibition on transferring among domains.[6] Either way, most of the halakhic deliberations in Tractate Shabbat have to do with transferring and its various ramifications.

Before we get to the essence of transferring between domains, let us look at the passage from which it is derived:[7]

> Six days you shall gather it; but on the seventh day is the Sabbath, in it there shall be none.... "See that the Lord has

---

5. Pesaḥim 47b.
6. Beitza 37a.
7. For more on "let no man go out of his place" as the source for the prohibition against transferring and its definitions, see *Tosafot* on Eiruvin 17b (on the words, "for any prohibition given"), Shabbat 2a (on the words, "There are two transfers"), and Shabbat 4a (on the words, "Surely removal and depositing").

> given you the Sabbath; therefore He has given you on the sixth day the bread of two days; every man must abide in his place, let no man go out of his place on the seventh day." So the people rested on the seventh day. (Exodus 16:26–30)

The first commandment regarding Shabbat enjoins one not to go out of his place. The Sages interpreted that to mean a prohibition on one exiting the private domain while holding an object,[8] as well as on exiting the Shabbat boundary even when one is not holding anything. The linguistic similarity between the word for the imperative "abide" (*shevu*) in the Torah and the word "Shabbat" shows us that it is a commandment that relates to one of the core aspects of Shabbat. First and foremost, it is a day of rest, in which we abide in our places. During the six weekdays we leave our places and act upon reality; on Shabbat we stop moving and "abide" in our places.

The Mishna's term "transfers (*yetziot*) on Shabbat" not only invokes the verse by using the word *yetziot* rather than *hotzaot* to denote transfers; it also recalls the contrast between "Shabbat" and "going out" ("*yetzia*"), as it appears in the verse: "the Lord has given you **the Sabbath**...let no man **go out** of his place."

Throughout the six days of the week, we change the face of reality. Our actions denote a conception of reality as lacking,[9] and humanity's inability to accept that lack. Action is forward-looking, toward a different reality that will appear as a result. The essence of Shabbat is the opposite: accepting reality as it is here and now, enabling one to be present in the moment.

The movement outward – which can be broken down into the various activities and prohibitions – is the basic movement of one who wishes to change the world. By avoiding such movement, we accept our place, accept reality, and accept and receive Shabbat.

---

8. See citations in previous note.
9. The Mishna lists the activities that are prohibited on Shabbat (Shabbat 7:2). Instead of noting the number of prohibitions as thirty-nine, it chooses to describe them as "forty minus one." Our weekday activities reflect a consciousness of lack.

Some Kabbala books draw an interesting parallel between these laws on the one hand – the prohibition against transferring and the requirement to abide in one place – and God's rest after creating the world, on the other hand. According to Kabbala, the process of Creation is first and foremost an emanation of divinity, from a primal state of total unity to the plurality characteristic of a created world. In this comparison, the divine realm is the "private domain," while plurality is the reality of the "public domain." On Shabbat, there is no movement between the domains.[10]

Going out on Shabbat and Going out of Egypt

> Six days you shall work, and do all your labor; but the seventh day is the Sabbath of the Lord your God, in it you shall not do any manner of labor.... And you shall remember that you were a slave in the land of Egypt, and the Lord your God brought you out. (Deuteronomy 5:12–14)

According to the biblical text, refraining from labor is evocative of the Exodus from bondage in Egypt. Accordingly, there is an opinion that states that the labors forbidden on Shabbat are the very same tasks that the Israelites were forced to carry out as slaves in Egypt.[11] This aspect of Shabbat, too, imbues the law of transferring with special significance. Bondage in Egypt is described as "a burden," and Exodus as the release from that burden:

> Therefore say to the children of Israel, I am the Lord, and I will bring you out from under the burdens of the Egyptians.... I am the Lord your God, who brought you out from under the burdens of the Egyptians. (Exodus 6:6–7)

---

10. See *Tolaat Yaakov*, "*Sod HaShabbat*" 4. I heard it said in the name of my friend Rabbi Dov Berkovitz that the Mishna's choice of characters can be taken as hinting at the kabbalistic idea: The homeowner stands for God, while the poor person, who is in the public domain, represents our world.
11. See *Tosafot* on Pesaḥim 117b, on the words "that you may remember," citing the Midrash.

The word used for "burden" here, "*sevel*" (which also connotes suffering), literally means something that is carried.[12] Thus, carrying out, i.e., shouldering a burden, is the archetype of the subjugation in Egypt.[13] This idea lends additional meaning to the unique language that opens Tractate Shabbat: The word "*yetzia*" is Hebrew for "going out." When we go out of Egypt, out of suffering, out from under our burdens, we can find release and rest.

---

12. See, for example, Genesis 49:15.
13. My brother Rabbi Dani Genack identifies another expression of the centrality of transferring, in the sense of carrying objects, in the context of slavery in Egypt. The conditions of the Israelites' slavery was worsened when Pharaoh compelled them to transport on their own the straw that they needed as raw material for making bricks.

The Source of the Shabbat Labors

שבת ז, ב

אֲבוֹת מְלָאכוֹת אַרְבָּעִים חָסֵר אֶחָת. הַזּוֹרֵעַ. וְהַחוֹרֵשׁ. וְהַקּוֹצֵר. וְהַמְעַמֵּר. הַדָּשׁ. וְהַזּוֹרֶה. הַבּוֹרֵר. הַטּוֹחֵן. וְהַמְרַקֵּד. וְהַלָּשׁ. וְהָאוֹפֶה. הַגּוֹזֵז אֶת הַצֶּמֶר. הַמְלַבְּנוֹ. וְהַמְנַפְּצוֹ. וְהַצּוֹבְעוֹ. וְהַטּוֹוֶה. וְהַמֵּסֵךְ. וְהָעוֹשֶׂה שְׁנֵי בָתֵּי נִירִין. וְהָאוֹרֵג שְׁנֵי חוּטִין. וְהַפּוֹצֵעַ שְׁנֵי חוּטִין. הַקּוֹשֵׁר. וְהַמַּתִּיר. וְהַתּוֹפֵר שְׁתֵּי תְפִירוֹת. הַקּוֹרֵעַ עַל מְנָת לִתְפֹּר שְׁתֵּי תְפִירוֹת. הַצָּד צְבִי. הַשּׁוֹחֲטוֹ. וְהַמַּפְשִׁיטוֹ. הַמּוֹלְחוֹ, וְהַמְעַבֵּד אֶת עוֹרוֹ. וְהַמּוֹחֲקוֹ. וְהַמְחַתְּכוֹ. הַכּוֹתֵב שְׁתֵּי אוֹתִיּוֹת. וְהַמּוֹחֵק עַל מְנָת לִכְתֹּב שְׁתֵּי אוֹתִיּוֹת. הַבּוֹנֶה. וְהַסּוֹתֵר הַמְכַבֶּה. וְהַמַּבְעִיר. הַמַּכֶּה בַפַּטִּישׁ. הַמּוֹצִיא מֵרְשׁוּת לִרְשׁוּת. הֲרֵי אֵלּוּ אֲבוֹת מְלָאכוֹת אַרְבָּעִים חָסֵר אֶחָת:

Shabbat 7:2

The primary [prohibited] labors are forty minus one: sowing, plowing, reaping, binding sheaves, threshing, winnowing, selecting, grinding, sifting, kneading, baking, shearing wool, bleaching, hackling, dyeing, spinning, weaving, the making of two loops, weaving two threads, dividing two threads, tying and untying, sewing two stitches, tearing in order to sew two stitches, capturing a deer, slaughtering, or flaying, or salting it, curing its hide, scraping it [of its hair], cutting it up, writing two letters, erasing in order to write two letters [over the erasure], building, tearing down, extinguishing, kindling, striking with a hammer, [and] transferring from one domain to another, These are the forty primary labors minus one.

> The laws concerning Shabbat... are like mountains hanging by a hair, for they have scant scriptural basis but many halakhot. (Ḥagiga 1:8)

The Oral Torah includes many laws relating to Shabbat, but the written Torah contains only a general warning: "you shall not do any manner of labor" (Exodus 20:9). How did the Sages derive such an intricate system of halakhot from a single verse? What is the source of those halakhot, and where did the Sages learn them from?

The Mishna in Tractate Shabbat counts thirty-nine labors that are prohibited on Shabbat. On the face of it, these are basic work activities that people toil at during the week, as the Torah states in the previous verse: "For six days you shall labor and do all your work" (Exodus 20:8). Indeed, the list corresponds with the basic weekday activities, as described by Ben Zoma in the Tosefta:

> How much did the first man toil before he tasted [even] one mouthful? He sowed [grain], plowed, reaped, bound sheaves, threshed, winnowed, selected, ground, sifted, kneaded, and baked, and [only] after that [he] ate [bread]... How much did the first man toil before he wore a shirt? He sheared [wool], bleached, hackled, dyed, spun, wove, and sewed, and [only] after that he wore [clothes]. (Tosefta Berakhot 6:5)

The Tosefta lists, in order, the first seventeen labors in our mishna, and says they are tasks that are crucial to the production of a person's basic needs: food and clothing. The rest of the labors listed in the Mishna in Tractate Shabbat also provide basic human needs: shelter, tools, and writing.[1]

In light of the above, it is surprising that both the Bavli and Yerushalmi say the source of the thirty-nine prohibited labors is the

1. See Goldberg, *Commentary to the Mishna*, 14.

labors of the Tabernacle.[2] Apparently, this is based on other mishnayot in our tractate that make that connection. For example, in Chapter 12:

> One who writes two letters, whether with his right [hand] or with his left, whether the same letter or two different letters, or in two pigments, in any language, is liable. Rabbi Yosei said: They made one liable for writing two letters only because [one makes] a mark, since this is how they would write on each board of the Tabernacle, to know which its companion was. (Shabbat 12:3)

Rabbi Yosei explains why one who writes on Shabbat with one's left hand is liable, even though it diverges from one's usual way of writing. His answer is that the source for the ban on writing is the Tabernacle: There, they would not use letters but rather marks, and whereas letters are written precisely, in making a mark there is no real difference between the right hand and the left hand; so too the resultant prohibition – against writing on Shabbat – does not draw that distinction.

The law of transferring also links between different kinds of actions relating to the prohibition and the rituals of the Tabernacle:

> How so? If there are two balconies facing each other in the public domain, one who reaches over or throws [an article] from one to the other is exempt. If both are on the same row, one who reaches over is liable, while one who throws is exempt, for thus was the service of the Levites. (Shabbat 11:2)

How do we bridge the gap between these activities in their usual, mundane sense, as it emerges from the Bible and Chapter Seven of our tractate – tasks whose purpose is to fulfill peoples' basic needs – and the many mentions of the Tabernacle in the context of the same actions? If we are to answer that question, we must first shed light on the connection between the Tabernacle and the labors that are forbidden on Shabbat.

2. See, for example, Shabbat 49b.

The Tabernacle Service and the Creation of the World

In the Talmud (Shabbat 49b), Rabbi Ḥanina b. Ḥama links the thirty-nine forbidden labors of the Tabernacle service. Rashi explains that the Torah in *Parashat Vayak'hel* juxtaposes the verses describing the labors required for the Tabernacle with the verses prohibiting labor on Shabbat. This proximity is no coincidence; rather, it points to an essential aspect of Shabbat.

God's rest at the end of Creation was a hiatus from creating the world. The Sages note many parallels in the Five Books of Moses between the construction of the Tabernacle by human beings and the creation of the world by God. Indeed, just as God rests on the seventh day after six days of work, so too the Israelites rest on Shabbat, after six days of toiling for the Tabernacle. For the people of Israel, rest is first and foremost a hiatus from the labors that went into the construction of the Tabernacle. This is the profound meaning of the juxtaposition of Shabbat and the Tabernacle.

This interpretation is in keeping with the talmudic outlook by which the Tabernacle is not only the source for the thirty-nine labors, but the basis of their character and essence. A *baraita* states:

> It was taught as the opinion that it corresponds to the forms of labor in the Tabernacle. For it was taught: Liability is incurred only for a labor that had a corresponding one in the Tabernacle. They sowed, hence you must not sow; they reaped, hence you must not reap. (Shabbat 49b)

The Rashba notes, based on the line "They sowed, hence you must not sow," that "the Torah warns us regarding the labors of the Tabernacle," meaning that the Tabernacle is the source for the labors that are prohibited on Shabbat. It is thus clear why, for the Talmud, the Tabernacle is the source not only of the general list of labors, but also of their details, including the requirement that the labors constitute "skillful workmanship," an expression that the Torah uses in the context of the service in the Tabernacle (Exodus 35:33), and many other elements.[3]

According to the Talmud, the heart of the prohibition against labor on Shabbat is not humanity toiling away for six days of the week, but rather the holy work of people emulating their creator.

Defining "Labor"

Still, there is a way in which we can rely on the mundane definition of labor as toiling for the fulfillment of basic human needs, while still retaining the connection to the labors of the Tabernacle.

When the Torah presents us with a word whose definition eludes us and cannot be precisely gleaned from the context, we must investigate the other instances in which it appears in the Torah. The word "*melakha*" (translated above as labor) appears sixty-five times in the Five Books of Moses. In thirty instances, the text does not define *melakha,* but rather warns against engaging in it on Shabbat and festivals. Six instances do not even refer to human labor. Of the twenty-nine remaining instances, five refer to labor in the general sense, and fully twenty-four come in the context of the Tabernacle. Thus, based on the biblical text, the word *melakha* should be defined in light of its connotations in the context of the Tabernacle.[4]

It seems to me that this was the intention of Maimonides in his commentary on our mishna. This hinges on the term "*avot melakhot,*" which we translated above as "primary labors," but whose literal meaning is "parent labors": "All of the parents (*avot*) that [the Mishna] lists are called parents because they were part of the construction of the Tabernacle, **which was called** *melakha.*"

It follows that, in contrast with the explanation we posited above, there is no essential connection between the Tabernacle and the labors forbidden on Shabbat; rather, the Tabernacle service is a means for

3. See, for example, Shabbat 74b–75a, 102b–103b.
4. See Exodus 35:31–35. The text even emphasizes four times that the builders of the Tabernacle were either engaged in, or were expert in, "all manner of workmanship (*kol melakha*)."

understanding the term "*melakha*" – what is defined as labor. While the focus is indeed human labor and toil in the six weekdays, it is an elusive category. The Tabernacle thus serves as a vantage from which we can comprehensively define the activities that constitute labor.

Elsewhere, I suggested that this is the approach in the Yerushalmi. This is evident in the Yerushalmi's treatment of the prohibition against transferring between domains:[5]

> From where do we learn that transferring is called labor (*melakha*)? Rabbi Shmuel said in the name of Rabbi Yoḥanan: "Moses commanded, and they caused it to be proclaimed throughout the camp, etc." (Exodus 36:6). The people refrained from taking [objects] out of their homes to give to the treasurers, and from taking them out of their hands to put into the chamber. Rabbi Ḥizkiya said in the name of Rabbi Aḥa: We learn it from this verse (Jeremiah 17:22): "Do not carry a burden out of your houses on the Sabbath day, and do not do any labor" (Y. Shevuot 1:1).

There was transferring of objects in the Tabernacle, but that in itself is not sufficient proof for the Yerushalmi that it is a forbidden labor on Shabbat. It seems that this is because, for the Yerushalmi, the Tabernacle does not define what constitutes labor, but only what is "called labor." The Tabernacle can indicate what things are referred to as *melakha,* but when an action that takes place in the Tabernacle does not look like labor, we need external evidence that it is indeed considered labor. In this case, the Yerushalmi relies on a verse from Jeremiah.

In light of this conception of the laws of Shabbat, by which the Tabernacle is only a means for understanding what falls under the category of *melakha,* the Yerushalmi refrains almost entirely from deriving the

5. Menachem Mendel Kasher also pointed this out in *Torah Shelemah* 7:1499.

details of the forbidden labors from the Tabernacle service.[6] Instead, the Yerushalmi draws these definitions from the human meaning of labor.[7]

Human Labor and Divine Labor

We explained the significance of the Tabernacle service in the context of comparing between it and Creation. But what is the significance of the human hiatus from weekday labor? Commenting on the verse, "For six

6. Among other things, the term "skillful workmanship," which is very significant in the Bavli, goes unmentioned in the Yerushalmi.
7. For example, according to the Yerushalmi (12:3 in the Raavya version; the print edition is missing the words "*bet-beta*," which deemphasizes the Greek, though it is still there), one is liable for writing on Shabbat only in the Assyrian or Greek alphabets: "What is intended by 'in every tongue'? Even *alef-alpha* and *bet-beta*." This limitation has nothing to do with the Tabernacle, where, as we saw above, there was no writing in letters. It seems that the Yerushalmi arrives at this definition based on a conception of human culture that ascribes value only to writing in Assyrian and Greek letters. Its definition also relies on the general sense of "writing," as it appears in other contexts in the Torah, such as the writ of divorce (ibid). In contrast, the Yerushalmi does not cite the *baraita* that appears in the Talmud (Shabbat 103b) in relation to the prohibition against writing, by which one is liable, based on the Tabernacle service, even if he merely scratches a surface on Shabbat.

   Furthermore, the Yerushalmi cites dozens of secondary prohibited activities (*toladot*) derived from the primary prohibitions against sowing and plowing (Shabbat 7b, 10a). These are tasks in which a person engages in the field – from sowing to reaping. These tasks appear in the Mishna and Tosefta Shevi'it, and define the agricultural activities prohibited during a Sabbatical year. In contrast, the Bavli prohibits only activities that are similar to sowing and plowing (Shabbat 73b), and would probably not forbid the long list of activities that appears in the Yerushalmi.

   The book *Eglei Tal* famously opens with the assertion that the Bavli and Yerushalmi differ on the question of whether the prohibited Shabbat activities are derived only from the construction of the Tabernacle (Bavli), or also from the Tabernacle service and rituals (Yerushalmi). Based on what we have established here, the explanation is straightforward: According to the Bavli, the connection is established by the juxtaposition in the biblical verses of Shabbat and the construction of the Tabernacle, and the construction of the Tabernacle corresponds to Creation. Accordingly, the Shabbat activities are derived only from the *construction* of the Tabernacle. The Yerushalmi, which, in contrast, considers the Tabernacle a means for discovering what falls under the category of labor (*melakha*), sees no reason to make the distinction.

days you shall work and do all your labor" (Exodus 20:8), the Mekhilta of Rabbi Shimon states:

> "For six days you shall work" – Rabbi says: This is another decree, for just as Israel were enjoined with the positive commandment of Shabbat, so too they were enjoined about work. Rabbi Elazar ben Azarya says: Great is Shabbat, for the Divine Presence did not dwell upon Israel until they labored, as it is written, "And let them make Me a Sanctuary, that I may dwell among them" (Exodus 25:8).

The Mekhilta's message is that weekday work is also a mitzva. This can be derived from a verse that appears further along in that chapter: "for in six days the Lord made heaven and earth, the sea, and all that is in them" (Exodus 20:10). A person's toil during the six days of the week is parallel to God's toil during the six days of Creation, with the corollary being that a person's home is parallel to God's home. It is fitting that in the Torah of the Land of Israel holiness is present within life itself as well.

Sowing or Plowing

Perhaps there is another dimension to the outlook that emphasizes human work. Our mishna, as it is quoted in the Bavli, opens its list of prohibited labors with sowing. In the Yerushalmi,[8] in contrast, the mishna is quoted as opening the list with the prohibition against plowing.

This can be related to the two aspects of Shabbat as it is presented in the Torah. In the Ten Commandments in *Parashat Yitro*, Shabbat is described as a reminder of Creation (Exodus 20:11), while the Ten Commandments in *Parashat Va'etḥanan* frame the day as a reminder of the Exodus (Deuteronomy 5:15).

The difference between these two versions of the Mishna mirrors the twin approaches to Shabbat that we elaborated above. If the focus is

8. This is also the case in manuscripts of the Mishna that represent the tradition of the Land of Israel, such as the Kaufmann Manuscript.

to remember Creation, the list of labors should begin with sowing. However, if the focus is human toil, sowing is secondary, and the list should rather open with the most-labor intensive part of farming – plowing.

Checking for *Ḥametz* and Eliminating the Evil Urge

פסחים א, א

אוֹר לְאַרְבָּעָה עָשָׂר, בּוֹדְקִין אֶת הֶחָמֵץ לְאוֹר הַנֵּר. כָּל מָקוֹם שֶׁאֵין מַכְנִיסִין בּוֹ חָמֵץ אֵין צָרִיךְ בְּדִיקָה. וְלָמָּה אָמְרוּ שְׁתֵּי שׁוּרוֹת בַּמַּרְתֵּף, מָקוֹם שֶׁמַּכְנִיסִין בּוֹ חָמֵץ. בֵּית שַׁמַּאי אוֹמְרִים, שְׁתֵּי שׁוּרוֹת עַל פְּנֵי כָל הַמַּרְתֵּף. וּבֵית הִלֵּל אוֹמְרִים, שְׁתֵּי שׁוּרוֹת הַחִיצוֹנוֹת שֶׁהֵן הָעֶלְיוֹנוֹת:

Pesaḥim 1:1

On the evening of the fourteenth [of Nisan] they search the house for *ḥametz* by the light of a candle. Every place into which *ḥametz* is not brought does not require searching. So why did they rule that two rows of the wine cellar [must be searched]? [This is actually] a place into which *ḥametz* might be taken. The school of Shammai says: two rows over the front of the whole cellar. The school of Hillel says: the two outer rows, which are the uppermost.

Rabbinic literature and the Zohar feature several sources that portray *ḥametz* as a symbol of the evil urge.[1] Thus, in the hasidic understanding of the mishna, the search for leaven, or *Bedikat Ḥametz*, symbolizes the search for evil in one's own self – and one's obligation to eliminate it. The candle represents the positive forces in the soul: the urge for good and the light of Torah. These are the tools with which *ḥametz* can be rooted out of the heart.

But is this merely a nice midrashic idea, or does it in fact reveal the soul of the Mishna? In referring to "the evening of the fourteenth," our mishna uses the expression, "*or l'arbaa asar*." The word *or*, which

1. For example, Berakhot 17a; Zohar, *Vayeḥi* 226b and *Tetzaveh* 182a; and more.

means light, recurs in the same sentence: "by the light of (*le'or*) a candle." Could these two connotations of "light" be alluding to a spiritual reality? Admittedly, the wording of our mishna alone is not enough to establish this idea. Still, I propose that this is the interpretation that the Bavli gives the mishna, and that from the heart of the Talmud we can arrive at the soul of the Mishna:

> On the evening of the fourteenth, they search the house for *ḥametz* by the light of a candle. They do not search by sunlight, nor by moonlight, but rather only by candlelight, for candlelight is greater. Even though there is no explicit proof for this, it is a remembrance for that which is discussed, "And in that time I will search through Jerusalem with candles [and I will punish the men who are settled on their lees]" (Zephaniah 1:12), and that which it says (Proverbs 20:27), "The candle of God is a human soul [searching the innermost parts of the belly]." (Tosefta Pesaḥim 1:1)

Commenting on the Mishna's requirement that the search be carried out by candlelight, the Tosefta cites two verses. The first describes the eradication of sinners from Jerusalem, and the second relates to an inner search, within humanity, in "the innermost parts of the belly." In both contexts, the search by candlelight symbolizes a spiritual search that is meant to uncover human evil, in order to eradicate it. These two verses, cited as context for the halakha stated in the mishna, hint at the connection between the physical and the spiritual searches.

While the Tosefta uses those verses as a reference, "even though there is no explicit proof," the Bavli below cites them as the source for the mishna, in answer to the question, "How do we know this?" In light of the Bavli's reliance on biblical verses, some of the *Rishonim* concluded that *Bedikat Ḥametz* is itself biblical law.[2] Unlike the Tosefta, for which citing the two verses suffices, Rav Ḥisda integrates them into a detailed inquiry into the source of the Mishna's ruling:

2. Rabbeinu Nissim on Alfas 1a.

> "By the light of a candle, etc." How do we know this? Rav Ḥisda said, By deriving [the meaning of] "finding" from "finding," and "finding" from "searching," and "searching" from "searching," and "searching" from "candles," and "candles" from "candle." "Finding" from "finding" – here it is written, "Seven days there shall be no leaven found in your houses" (Exodus 12:19), while elsewhere it is written, "And he searched, and began at the eldest, and left at the youngest, and the cup was found [in Benjamin's sack]" (Genesis 44:12). "Finding" [is learned] from "searching" [mentioned] in its own connection. And "searching" from "candles," as it is written, "And in that time I will search through Jerusalem with candles" (Zephaniah 1:12). And "candles" from "candle," as it is written (Proverbs 20:27), "The candle of God is a human soul searching the innermost parts of the belly." (Pesaḥim 7b)

Thus, the Bavli appears to portray an essential connection between the verses describing a spiritual search by candlelight and the Mishna's treatment of the physical search for *ḥametz*.

Light and Night

> And our *Tanna*, why does he not employ [the word] "*leilei*"? He employs a refined expression, in accordance with Rabbi Yehoshua ben Levy. For Rabbi Yehoshua ben Levy said: One should not utter a crude expression with one's mouth, for the Torah employs a circumlocution of eight letters rather than utter a crude expression, for it is said (Genesis 7:8), "of pure beasts and of beasts that are not pure." (Pesaḥim 3a)

The Talmud says that our mishna, in order to maintain purity of speech and refrain from mentioning negative phenomena, uses the euphemistic "*or l'arbaa asar*" (which, as noted above, contains the word *or*, or "light") rather than the more common "*leilei arbaa asar.*" We see that the very use of the "light" to indicate the proper time for *Bedikat Ḥametz* is itself evidence of a more refined spirituality and purity of speech. Thus, the Mishna conveys a lesson regarding both the physical action of removing *ḥametz* from the home and the internal process of purifying the mouth of negativity.

The Talmud then relates two stories that highlight the importance of maintaining purity of speech. A close reading reveals a deep connection to our mishna:

> There were three priests. One said, "I received as much as a bean [of the shewbread]"; the second said, "I received as much as an olive"; while the third said, "I received as much as a lizard's tail." They **investigated** his [the latter's] pedigree and found a blemish of unfitness in him. But did we not learn: One must not **investigate** from the altar and above? Do not say, a blemish of unfitness, but a baseness that made him unfit. [Rashi: He was himself coarse and would despise divine sacrifices, and was thus unworthy of service.]…
>
> A certain Syrian [i.e., non-Jew] used to go up and partake of the Passover sacrifices in Jerusalem, boasting: It is written, "No alien shall eat from it…no uncircumcised person shall eat from it," yet I eat from the very best. Rabbi Yehuda ben Beteira said to him: Did they supply you with the fat tail? No, he replied. [Then] when you journey up there say to them, "Supply me with the fat tail." When he went up he said to them, Supply me with the fat tail. They replied, "But the fat tail belongs to the Most High!" They inquired, "Who told you [to do] this?" He answered, "Rabbi Yehuda ben Beteira." They wondered, "What is this [matter] before us?" They **investigated** his pedigree, and discovered that he was a Syrian, and killed him. Then they sent [a message] to Rabbi Yehuda ben Beteira: "Peace be with you, Rabbi Yehuda ben Beteira, for you are in Netzivin, yet your net is spread in Jerusalem." (Pesaḥim 3b)

The key word in both stories is "investigate" (*bedika*). In the first story, the priests investigate a colleague who uses vulgar speech, and find that he is indeed unfit to serve in the Temple. In the second, the priests investigate a person who seeks to eat the fat tail of the Passover sacrifice, which is not to be consumed by anyone, and find that he is not Jewish and is forbidden from consuming any part of the sacrifice. The Talmud, which up to that point discusses proper speech, returns to the mishna's main topic: checking or searching (*bedika*) in the context of Passover. In both stories, the investigation relates to the nature of a human being and the discovery of a blemish that requires their "elimination" – in the first, the priest is defrocked, and in the second the man is killed.

The linguistic link between these two stories and our mishna is evidence of the broadening of *bedika* from the physical realm (the search for *ḥametz*) to the spiritual realm. Furthermore, a parallel can be drawn between the two stories and the two verses cited by the Tosefta and the Talmud: The verse from Zephaniah tells of a search for sinners in Jerusalem, while the second story in the Talmud is about an investigation that finds a non-Jew who has sinned. The verse in Proverbs says that God searches "the innermost parts of the belly" – just as an investigation of the priest in the second story uncovers his baseness.

What Is Light?

The discussion that opens Tractate Pesaḥim asks whether the word *or*, "light," refers to nighttime or daytime. The Talmud debates the question at length, citing many proofs in support of each side. On the face of it, it seems like a complex, tangled debate, but the *Beit Yaakov* highlights its deliberate, precise, artistic structure:

> The Talmud cites seven proofs showing that *or* (light) is day and seven proofs showing that *or* is evening. First it cites seven proofs from the Written Torah: Six of them demonstrate that light is day, while the middle one is about starlight, meaning that light is evening. Then it cites seven proofs from the Oral Torah: Six of them demonstrate that *or* is evening, and the middle one shows that *or* is day. This

> is because the Written Torah is called "day" and the Oral Torah is called "night." (Rabbi Yaakov Leiner, *Beit Yaakov* on the Torah, *Likkutim* on Pesaḥim, 152)

The realization that the talmudic debate is structured in a deliberate fashion requires us, the readers, to pay attention to the details. A closer reading reveals that during the discussion, another meaning arises from some of the sources: light as a symbol for the World to Come. Here, then, is another way in which the meaning of light extends from the physical into the spiritual realm.

The Story Ends Where the Tractate Ends

In the midrash introduced above by Rav Ḥisda, the link between the prohibition "there shall be no leaven found in your houses" and the candlelight search is a verse from the story of Joseph and his brothers: "And he searched, and began at the eldest, and left at the youngest" (Genesis 44:12), at which point the missing goblet is found in Benjamin's sack. The Talmud, in the beginning of the first debate in our tractate, cites a verse from the same story as the first of seven proofs from the Written Torah:

> What is *or*? Rav Huna said: Light, while Rav Yehuda said: Night (*leilei*)...An objection is raised: "As soon as the morning was light (*or*), the men were sent away" (Genesis 44:3), which proves that *or* is day. (Pesaḥim 2a)

The verse proves that the word "*or*" denotes daylight, and that is why the Talmud quotes it. But it seems that it was no coincidence that this verse was chosen as the opening of the tractate: The Israelites' bondage in Egypt began with the selling of Joseph into slavery, and it is thus fitting to mention the first stage of that story at the outset of the tractate that deals with the festival of the Exodus.

The ending of the tractate, fittingly, invokes the ending of the story:

> Rabbi Simlai was present at a *Pidyon HaBen*. He was asked: It is obvious that for the *Pidyon HaBen* it is the father who must recite the blessing, "…Who has sanctified us with Your commandments and commanded concerning *Pidyon HaBen*." But as for the blessing, "Blessed…who has kept us alive, and preserved us, and enabled us to reach this season" – does the priest recite it or the child's father? Does the priest recite the blessing, since the benefit redounds to him, or does the child's father recite it, since it is he who carries out a religious duty? [Rabbi Simlai] could not answer the question, so he went and asked it at the study hall, and he was told: The child's father recites both blessings. And the law is that the child's father recites both blessings. (Pesaḥim 121b)

Tractate Pesaḥim ends with a discussion of *Pidyon HaBen*, the redemption of the firstborn. On its face, the discussion has no relevance to Passover, but in fact it is deliberately placed. In the Torah, too, the commandment regarding *Pidyon HaBen* is part and parcel of the story of the Ten Plagues and the Exodus. In fact, the Exodus itself can be seen as a *Pidyon HaBen*: The Lord sends Moses to Pharaoh to say, "Israel is My son, My firstborn" (Exodus 4:22), and to demand, "Let My people go" (5:1). Indeed, the removal of the Israelites from Egypt is referred to as a *pidyon*, a redemption.[3] The story of the Exodus is thus the story of God's redemption of His firstborn.[4]

As we have seen, the tractate opens with the beginning of the story – when Joseph's brothers first experience bondage in Egypt – and ends where the story ends, with the blessing for *Pidyon HaBen*.

> Thus have our masters taught: A father is obligated to do five things for a son: to circumcise him, to teach him Torah, to redeem him (*Pidyon HaBen*), to teach him a trade, and

---

3. Deuteronomy 8:7, 15:15, 24:18.
4. Consequently, the significance of *Pidyon HaBen* lies in it being a reenactment on a small scale of the massive event of the Exodus from Egypt.

to take a wife for him. The father is the Holy One, blessed be He, and the son is Israel. Just as a [human] father is obligated to his son, so does the Holy One, blessed be He, do for Israel...The father is obligated to redeem his son; similarly the Holy One, blessed be He, did so for Israel: He redeemed them, as stated (I Chronicles 17:21), "And who is like Your people Israel, a unique nation on earth, whom God went to redeem as a people for Himself." (*Midrash Tanḥuma, Shelaḥ* 26)[5]

5. This idea can also be found in the Zohar (*Teruma* 174b), based on the verse, "and redeemed you...from the hand of Pharaoh king of Egypt" (Deuteronomy 7:8).

Redemption of the Past and Redemption of the Present

פסחים ג, א

אֵלּוּ עוֹבְרִין בַּפֶּסַח, כֻּתָּח הַבַּבְלִי, וְשֵׁכָר הַמָּדִי, וְחֹמֶץ הָאֲדוֹמִי, וְזִיתוֹם הַמִּצְרִי, וְזוֹמָן שֶׁל צַבָּעִים, וַעֲמִילָן שֶׁל טַבָּחִים, וְקוֹלָן שֶׁל סוֹפְרִים. רַבִּי אֱלִיעֶזֶר אוֹמֵר: אַף תַּכְשִׁיטֵי נָשִׁים. זֶה הַכְּלָל: כָּל שֶׁהוּא מִמִּין דָּגָן - הֲרֵי זֶה עוֹבֵר בַּפֶּסַח. הֲרֵי אֵלּוּ בְּאַזְהָרָה, וְאֵין בָּהֶן מִשּׁוּם כָּרֵת.

Pesaḥim 3:1

These must be removed on Passover: Babylonian *kutaḥ*, Median beer, Idumean vinegar, Egyptian *zitom*, the dyer's pulp, cooks' dough, and the scribes' paste. Rabbi Eliezer says: Women's ornaments too. This is the general rule: Whatever is of a species of grain must be removed on Passover. These are subject to a warning, but they do not involve *karet*.

The mishna opens with four foods and beverages that contain *ḥametz* and that thus, according to the commentary of Rabbi Ovadia of Bartenura, must be "eradicated from the world" on Passover.

As the Talmud (Pesaḥim 42b) notes, these four comestibles are related to four nations. One is named for Babylonia, another for Media, the third for Edom, and the fourth for Egypt. All four are empires that at one point subjugated Israel: bondage in Egypt, exile in Babylon and Media (Persia), and finally the exile imposed by Edom (Rome), which was still in force during the time of the Mishna. It seems that the Mishna chooses these foods and beverages as illustrations of *Biur Ḥametz* in order to hint that eradicating them from the world symbolizes our deliverance from the oppressions of the past, and our yearning to be redeemed from our present subjugation.[1]

1. See for example Y. Pesaḥim 10:2, which explains that the four cups of wine consumed during the Passover Seder are analogized to the four nations that subjugated Israel. The term "the four nations" is generally used to describe the subjugations that came after the Exodus from Egypt, and generally includes Greece (See Mekhilta, *Yitro* 9). My brother Rabbi Dani Genack pointed out to me that a prayer quoted in Tractate Berakhot (17a) juxtaposes *ḥametz* and the subjugation to the nations: "Sovereign of the Universe, it is known full well to You that our will is to perform Your will, and what prevents us? The yeast in the dough and the subjection to the foreign powers."

At the Seder We Are All Poor, We Are All Free

פסחים י, א

עַרְבֵי פְסָחִים סָמוּךְ לַמִּנְחָה, לֹא יֹאכַל אָדָם עַד שֶׁתֶּחְשַׁךְ. וַאֲפִלּוּ עָנִי שֶׁבְּיִשְׂרָאֵל לֹא יֹאכַל עַד שֶׁיָּסֵב. וְלֹא יִפְחֲתוּ לוֹ מֵאַרְבָּעָה כוֹסוֹת שֶׁל יַיִן, וַאֲפִלּוּ מִן הַתַּמְחוּי:

Pesaḥim 10:1

On the eve of Passover close to Minḥa one may not eat until nightfall. Even the poorest person in Israel must not eat [on the night of Passover] until he reclines. And they should give him not less than four cups [of wine], and even from the charity plate.

After the tractate discusses the laws of *ḥametz* and the Passover sacrifice, the final chapter turns to the laws of the Seder.

Our mishna discusses three obligations, including the obligations to recline and drink four cups. But the formulation is puzzling; the halakha discusses the poor person's obligation to perform mitzvot that have not been explicitly mentioned yet. Should the mishna not have begun with the requirements to recline and drink four cups, and only afterward note that the poor share these obligations? Instead, the mishna turns what seems like a "postscript" – the poor person's obligation – into the main topic.

But before we discuss the mishna's surprising structure, we must get to the bottom of the poor person's obligation to perform the mitzvot of the Seder. As Rashi points out, the Mishna refers to someone who can be "the poorest of the poor" – one who eats from the public charity plate and does not have enough food even for two meals. It seems incongruous that such a person would be obligated to take part in a large feast at which people recline like the rich and drink a large amount of wine. Furthermore, one could think it improper for a person who lives off others' generosity to throw an expensive banquet.

It seems to me that the reason for this unusual obligation is hinted at in the mishna. The Hebrew formulation for "the poorest person in Israel," (*ani shebeYisrael*) emphasizes the poor person's intrinsic status – he is not "merely" a poor person; he is a member of the Jewish people. This affiliation in itself lends one a lofty position, regardless of his socioeconomic standing. It is the source of the right and obligation of the poor person to conduct himself on the Festival of Freedom as if he were rich. "All of Israel are the sons of kings" (Shabbat 14:4).

This interpretation of our mishna is supported by another source that uses the phrase "the poorest person in Israel," but in the context of the obligation to compensate a person that one has humiliated:

> This is the general rule: All is in accordance with the person's honor. Rabbi Akiva said: Even the poor[est] people in Israel are regarded as free people who have lost their possessions, for they are the children of Abraham, Isaac, and Jacob. (Bava Kama 8:6)

Countering the opinion that the amount of the compensation is determined by "the honor" of the injured party, meaning their social status, Rabbi Akiva asserts that there can be no distinction between people on this score. He explains that "even the poor in Israel," who are ostensibly of low standing, should be treated like "free people who have lost their possessions." According to Rabbi Akiva, the poor too are "free people," and humiliating them is an egregious wrong.

Thus, noting that a poor person is "in Israel," which is to recognize their true innate value, explains not only the relevance of the Seder to them; it also expresses, more than anything else, the true joy of Passover eve. We do not glorify wealth and success as defined by external criteria, but rather celebrate our innate, internal honor and freedom.

The centrality of the poor person in the Mishna's discussion of the Seder has a deeper implication, which led the Mishna to open its treatment of the laws of Passover eve with the requirement that the poor, too, drink four cups of wine. During the Seder, one is required to relive the experience of the Exodus: "In every generation a person is obligated to regard himself as though he personally had gone forth from Egypt" (Pesaḥim 10:5).[2] One of the main aspects of the Exodus is the reversal, the deliverance from squalor and subjugation: "He brought us forth from slavery into freedom, from sorrow into joy, from mourning into festivity, from darkness into great light, and from servitude into redemption" (10:5). This is the reason that the Seder begins with, "This bread of poverty," and the declaration, "We were slaves to Pharaoh in Egypt," and that on that very night one becomes a free person. The first mishna emphasizes the poor person because, as the Seder begins, each and every Jew must feel as though they are themselves living in privation and slavery.[3] Only afterward can they go back to feeling the joy of the redemption every year anew.

---

2. See the discussion of the differences between the manuscript and print edition of the Mishna, below.
3. The Sages took a similar view of the opinion, raised by the Talmud, that only the two last cups of wine should be drunk while reclining: "The last two cups necessitate reclining, [because] it is precisely then that there is freedom; the first two cups do not necessitate reclining, [because] one is still reciting, 'We were slaves'" (Pesaḥim 108a).

The Four Acts of Seder Night

פסחים פרק י

Pesaḥim, chapter 10

...וְלֹא יִפְחֲתוּ לוֹ מֵאַרְבָּעָה כּוֹסוֹת שֶׁל יַיִן, וַאֲפִלּוּ מִן הַתַּמְחוּי: (פסחים י, א)

And they should give him not less than four cups [of wine], and even from the charity plate. (10:1)

מָזְגוּ לוֹ כּוֹס רִאשׁוֹן, בֵּית שַׁמַּאי אוֹמְרִים, מְבָרֵךְ עַל הַיּוֹם, וְאַחַר כָּךְ מְבָרֵךְ עַל הַיַּיִן. וּבֵית הִלֵּל אוֹמְרִים, מְבָרֵךְ עַל הַיַּיִן, וְאַחַר כָּךְ מְבָרֵךְ עַל הַיּוֹם: (שם י, ב)

They poured him the first cup. The school of Shammai says: First he blesses over the day and then over the wine. The school of Hillel says: First he blesses over the wine and then over the day. (10:2)

מָזְגוּ לוֹ כּוֹס שֵׁנִי, וְכָאן הַבֵּן שׁוֹאֵל אָבִיו... (שם י, ד)

They poured him a second cup, and here the son questions his father... (10:4)

מָזְגוּ לוֹ כּוֹס שְׁלִישִׁי, מְבָרֵךְ עַל מְזוֹנוֹ. רְבִיעִי, גּוֹמֵר עָלָיו אֶת הַהַלֵּל, וְאוֹמֵר עָלָיו בִּרְכַּת הַשִּׁיר. בֵּין הַכּוֹסוֹת הַלָּלוּ, אִם רוֹצֶה לִשְׁתּוֹת, יִשְׁתֶּה. בֵּין שְׁלִישִׁי לִרְבִיעִי, לֹא יִשְׁתֶּה: (שם י, ז)

They poured him a third cup, he blesses over his meal. A fourth [cup], he concludes the Hallel, and recites over it the blessing of song. Between these cups, if he wants he may drink; between the third and the fourth he may not drink. (10:7)

The four cups of wine that we drink during the Seder have a variety of meanings. The Bavli says that the multiple cups are a general symbol of the freedom that we celebrate with the Seder: "Our Rabbis instituted four cups as symbolizing freedom" (Pesaḥim 117b). The Yerushalmi,[1] however, sees symbolic meaning in the number of cups; four cups correspond to the four stages of redemption, or to the four "cups of calamity" that God is destined to serve the nations of the world. These explanations consider the four cups as a single unit, and give it meaning. In contrast, the Mishna in our chapter considers each cup individually, delineating its role and unique place. The four cups contribute to the shaping of both the ceremony and the text, and the detailed discussion of their roles reveals the chapter's literary structure.

The first night of Passover is called Seder night[2] (*seder* denotes an ordered sequence) because of the many actions and rituals that it includes. One role of the four cups is to lend structure to the banquet and its rituals. The cups frame the important stages of the Seder, divide it into well-defined units, and direct the attention of the participants to the beginning of each stage. In the beginning, the participants arrive at the place of the banquet and mark the start with a first cup, for Kiddush. During the meal,[3] the pouring of the second cup signals that the time has come to converse and fulfill the obligation to "tell your son" (Exodus 13:8): "They poured him a second cup, and here the son questions his father" (Pesaḥim 10:4). The words "and here" highlight the cup's role as a marker. The third cup, the cup for Grace after Meals, signals the end of the meal, and the fourth ushers in the last stage of the evening: thanksgiving and song. We can think of the four cups as four acts in the grand play that each Jewish family stages every year on Seder night.[4]

1. Y. Pesaḥim 10:1.
2. Though it does not appear in the Mishna or Talmud, the term "Seder night" (*Leil HaSeder*) expresses aptly the richness and variety of the feast of Passover eve, even as far back as the Mishnaic era.
3. The Mishna seems to show that *Maggid*, the stage of the Seder during which we relate the story of the Exodus, takes place after the meal, unlike today, when it comes before. See Joseph Tabory, *The Passover Ritual Throughout the Generations* (Tel Aviv: Hakibbutz Hameuchad, 2002) [Hebrew], 70–78. Some *Rishonim* explain that the change in custom is due to the destruction of the Temple (ibid).
4. My thanks to Yitzhak Kardus for suggesting this image. It is also worth noting that, in light of the idea that the role of the cups of wine is to divide the Seder into segments, it is clear why the Mishna emphasizes the pouring, rather than the drinking, of the cups – each stage begins with the preparation of the cup.

Another element that emerges from the description of the cups in the Mishna is their connection to speech. Each of the cups is juxtaposed with an utterance: the first is linked to Kiddush, the second to *Maggid*, the third to Grace after Meals, and the fourth to Hallel and song. The connection between the cups and the utterances is bidirectional: there is no cup without speech, and no speech without a cup.[5] The link is emphasized in the description of the final cup: "A fourth [cup], he concludes the Hallel, and recites over it the blessing of song." This cup is tied to both Hallel and the blessing of song, two elements that the Mishna apparently brings together in order to relate all of its topics to the four cups. There are versions of the Bavli that mention a fifth cup: "Our rabbis learned: We say the Great Hallel over a fifth cup – so said Rabbi Tarfon" (Pesaḥim 118a). The fifth cup, too, is linked to speech – in this case the Great Hallel.

But are the various spoken segments attached to the cups in order to imbue them with meaning, or could the cups merely be playing a supporting role alongside the important statements of the Seder? Both approaches have merit,[6] though it seems that the cups are mostly ancillary to speech, as *Tosafot* state: "Evidently, the four cups were only instated so that one could say Hallel and [words of] Aggada over them" (Sukka 38a). It is also true that in many ceremonies, a cup of wine serves to lend a certain status. When the mitzvot of the Seder night are recited over a cup of wine, they become more tangible, and the atmosphere becomes more solemn and dignified. In addition, imbibing wine contributes to speech, and, like the telling of the story of the Seder, is done through the mouth. Drinking can also generate a feeling of freedom, so that participants' words will come from the heart.[7]

---

5. The fifth mishna in the chapter, "Whoever does not make mention of these three things…" (Pesaḥim 10:5), is part of *Maggid*. In the next chapter, we will examine this mishna.

6. An example for when speech serves the object appears in 10:5, which requires one to explain the three mitzvot of the Seder: the *pesaḥ* sacrifice, matza, and bitter herbs.

7. The *Aḥaronim* deliberate as to whether the presence of the cup is more important than its consumption. The debate has many practical implications: If drinking takes primacy, then one must consume most or all of the cup, but if the cup's presence is what matters most, even a sip will suffice. See the Griz on Maimonides, *Hilkhot Ḥametz UMatza*.

The Haggada of Rabban Gamliel

פסחים י, ה

רַבָּן גַּמְלִיאֵל הָיָה אוֹמֵר, כָּל
שֶׁלֹּא אָמַר שְׁלֹשָׁה דְבָרִים אֵלּוּ
בַּפֶּסַח, לֹא יָצָא יְדֵי חוֹבָתוֹ,
וְאֵלּוּ הֵן, פֶּסַח, מַצָּה, וּמָרוֹר.
פֶּסַח, עַל שׁוּם שֶׁפָּסַח הַמָּקוֹם
עַל בָּתֵּי אֲבוֹתֵינוּ בְּמִצְרָיִם.
מַצָּה, עַל שׁוּם שֶׁנִּגְאֲלוּ
אֲבוֹתֵינוּ מִמִּצְרָיִם. מָרוֹר, עַל
שׁוּם שֶׁמֵּרְרוּ הַמִּצְרִים אֶת חַיֵּי
אֲבוֹתֵינוּ בְּמִצְרָיִם לְפִיכָךְ אֲנַחְנוּ
חַיָּבִין לְהוֹדוֹת...

Pesaḥim 10:5

Rabban Gamliel would say: Whoever does not make mention of these three things on Passover does not fulfill his duty. And these are they: the *pesaḥ* [sacrifice], matza, and bitter herb. The *pesaḥ* because the Omnipresent passed over the houses of our fathers in Egypt. The matza because our fathers were redeemed from Egypt. The bitter herb because the Egyptians embittered the lives of our fathers in Egypt... Therefore it is our duty to thank...

This mishna is considered especially complex,[1] and is the subject of many disagreements. One question has to do with the relationship between its two parts. Some suggest that "*pesaḥ*, matza, and bitter herb" is a recent addition that is meant to summarize the gist of Rabban Gamliel's words further along in the mishna. Then there are those who contend that the first part of the mishna constitutes Rabban Gamliel's original ruling, and the explanations that begin with "The *pesaḥ* because" were

1. Ephraim E. Urbach, "Review of 'Passover Haggadah,' by Daniel Goldschmidt," *Kiryat Sefer* 36, no. 2 (March 1961) [Hebrew]: 143–150.

additions from another literary source.[2] Furthermore, there is a question as to whether the obligation to mention *pesaḥ*, matza, and bitter herb stems from the requirement to tell the story of the Exodus, or instead from the commandments regarding those three elements. There are also differing approaches to Rabban Gamliel's motives. Some saw his statement as being directed "against the worldview of the Christians and the messianic cult, who ate the *pesaḥ* sacrifice or matza and bitter herbs to commemorate the Last Supper,"[3] while others saw it as a response to the destruction of the Temple. According to them, Rabban Gamliel feared that the abolishment of the *pesaḥ* sacrifice would also spell the end of the related mitzvot: the consumption of matza and bitter herbs.

We will attempt to propose a source and explanation for Rabban Gamliel's ruling by examining the manuscripts for our chapter in the Mishna. To my mind, Rabban Gamliel's approach is rooted in a reading of the verses describing the story of the Exodus. This reading is also apparent in the other mishnayot in our chapter, which together convey a coherent outlook on the commandment to retell the story of the Exodus.

We will begin with a comparison between the print edition of the Mishna and the Kaufman Manuscript, which aligns with the other manuscripts of the Mishna – the Parma manuscript, the Cambridge manuscript, and the version of the Mishna in the Leiden manuscript of the Yerushalmi.

2. Ibid., 148. A summary of the approaches on this question can be found in Tabory, *Passover*, 361.
3. Daniel Goldschmidt, *The Goldschmidt Passover Haggadah* (Jerusalem: Bialik Press, 1960) [Hebrew], 52.

Print edition	Kaufman Manuscript
Rabban Gamliel would say: Whoever does not make mention of these three things on Passover does not fulfill his duty. And these are they: the *pesaḥ* [sacrifice], matza, and bitter herb. The *pesaḥ* because the Omnipresent passed over the houses of our fathers in Egypt. The matza because our fathers were redeemed from Egypt. The bitter herb because the Egyptians embittered the lives of our fathers in Egypt.	Rabban Gamliel would say: Whoever does not make mention of these three things on Passover does not fulfill his duty: the *pesaḥ* [sacrifice], matza, and bitter herbs. The *pesaḥ* because the Omnipresent passed over the houses of our fathers in Egypt. The bitter herbs because the Egyptians embittered the lives of our fathers in Egypt. The matza [because] they were redeemed from Egypt.
In every generation a person is obligated to regard himself as though he personally had gone forth from Egypt, because it is said, "And you shall tell your son on that day, saying: 'It is because of that which the Lord did for me when I came forth out of Egypt'" (Exodus 13:8).	
Therefore it is our duty to thank, praise, laud, glorify, raise up, beautify, bless, extol, and adore Him who did all these miracles for our fathers and ourselves: He brought us forth from slavery into freedom, from sorrow into joy, from mourning into festivity, from darkness into great light, and from servitude into redemption. Let us say before Him, Hallelujah!	Therefore it is our duty to thank, praise, laud, glorify, raise up, [and] exalt Him who did all these miracles for ourselves and our fathers, and brought us forth from slavery into freedom. Let us say before Him, Hallelujah!

The print edition seems to indicate that we should divide the mishna into two units. The first includes Rabban Gamliel's ruling and explanations for the three mitzvot, while the second relates to the requirement to approach the Exodus as a personal experience, one that we should thank God for. But in the manuscripts of the Mishna, such a division is impossible. Since they do not include the paragraph that begins with "In every generation" and ends with "when I came forth out of Egypt," the word "therefore" relates to the explanations regarding the foods consumed during the Seder.

This fact can explain the discrepancy in the manuscripts. The order of the three items listed by Rabban Gamliel in the beginning of the mishna is "*pesaḥ,* matza, and bitter herb(s)," which is congruent with the order of the subsequent explanations in the print edition. In the manuscripts, however, the order of the explanations is different – *pesaḥ,* followed by bitter herbs and only then matza. Many explanations have been given for this discrepancy. Some see it as proof that the mishna stitches together two different sources: Rabban Gamliel's statement is one, and the explanations are the other.[4] Some even contend that the different sources were expressions of different historic realities: The explanations were from the Diaspora period, so they put the bitter herbs (the symbol of bondage) before the matza (the symbol of redemption).

I think there is another explanation. As we noted, the manuscripts show that the sentence starting with "Therefore" does not refer to "In every generation," but rather to the opening of the mishna. It seems that the order of the explanations for the three items is different because the editor of the mishna linked the obligation to thank and praise to redemption – "The matza [because] they were redeemed from Egypt." Retaining the order "*pesaḥ,* matza, and bitter herb(s)" would have incongruously juxtaposed "The bitter herbs because the Egyptians embittered…" with giving praise.

In contrast, the order of the items in the beginning of the mishna – "*pesaḥ,* matza, and bitter herb(s)" – aligns with the order in the biblical verse: "…roast with fire, and matzot; with bitter herbs they

4. Urbach, "Haggadah," 147–48.

shall eat it" (Exodus 12:8).[5] Rabban Gamliel's reliance on the verse is readily apparent in the manuscript version, which uses the plural "herbs," just like the verse (rather than "herb," as in the print edition). The difference between the order of the items in the opening of the mishna and in the explanations is deliberate, and Rabban Gamliel's statement and the subsequent section can be seen as a single unit.

Rabban Gamliel's Source

If Rabban Gamliel's opening declaration is indeed inspired by Exodus 12:8 then – in light of how the sentence beginning with "Therefore" ties into that statement – perhaps the Torah verses can also yield an explanation for the order of the various other elements in our chapter, thus revealing a deeper hermeneutical aspect to his comments.

Exodus 12:25–27 lays out the four stages of relating the story of the Exodus to one's children:

> And it shall come to pass, when you come to the land that the Lord will give you, as He has promised, (1) that you shall keep this service. (2) And it shall come to pass, when your children shall say to you: What do you mean by this service? (3) And you shall say: It is the sacrifice of the Lord's *pesaḥ,* for He passed over the houses of the children of Israel in Egypt, when He smote the Egyptians, and delivered our houses. (4) And the people bowed their heads and worshipped.

According to the Mekhilta, the words, "And the people bowed their heads and worshipped" teach us of one's obligation to thank God upon hearing of the miracles of the Exodus:

> "And the people bowed their heads" – to teach you that any who sees and hears of these miracles that the blessed Holy One performed for Israel in Egypt must offer praise.

5. Ibid., 148.

> Indeed, it is written, "And Moses told his father-in-law.... and Jethro rejoiced.... and Jethro said: 'Blessed be the Lord.'" (Mekhilta, *Masekhta DePesaḥ* 42)

Thus we learn that there are four stages to relating the story of the Exodus: the father performs "this service," the child asks about it, the father explains, and they conclude with thanks and rejoicing. These stages all appear in our chapter, and constitute the framework for mishnayot 3–7:[6]

1. Performing "this service" – Mishna 3:

> They bring [it] in front of him. He dips lettuce until he reaches the appetizer...They bring before him matza, lettuce, and *ḥaroset*...And in the Temple they bring the body of the *pesaḥ* before him.

2. The Child's Question – Mishna 4:

> They poured him a second cup, and here the son questions his father. If the son lacks the intelligence to ask, his father instructs him: Why is this night different from all other nights? On all other nights we dip once; on this night we dip twice. On all other nights we eat *ḥametz* or matza, on this night only matza. On all other nights we eat roasted, stewed, or boiled meat, on this night only roasted...

3. The Father's Explanation – Mishna 5:

> Rabban Gamliel would say: Whoever does not make mention (*amar*) of these three things on Passover does not fulfill his duty. And these are they: the *pesaḥ* [sacrifice], matza, and bitter herb. The *pesaḥ* because...

6. The quotes are based on the Kaufmann Manuscript.

> It is worth noting that Rabban Gamliel uses the word *amar,* just like the verse, "and you shall say (*va'amartem*): It is the sacrifice of the Lord's *pesaḥ*"

4. Praise and Thanksgiving – the end of Mishna 5:

> Therefore it is our duty to thank, praise, laud, glorify, raise up, [and] exalt Him who did all these miracles for ourselves and our fathers, and brought us forth from slavery into freedom. Let us say before Him, Hallelujah!

The main difference between the order in the biblical text and in the mishna is that the verses explain the *pesaḥ* sacrifice, while the mishna explains the reasons for matza and bitter herbs as well. It seems that this expansion originated with Rabban Gamliel. He interprets the phrase "this service" to refer not only to the *pesaḥ* sacrifice, as the verses in Exodus 12:20–27 imply ("and you shall say: It is the sacrifice of the Lord's *pesaḥ*"), but also to matza and bitter herbs, based on another verse: "roast with fire, and matzot; with bitter herbs they shall eat it" (Exodus 12:8). Indeed, we saw above Rabban Gamliel's association for that verse. The link between Rabban Gamliel's statement and Exodus 12:25–27 is especially evident in the Munich 95 manuscript of the Mishna: "The *pesaḥ* because the Omnipresent passed over the houses of our fathers in Egypt. As the Torah states, 'and you shall say: It is the sacrifice of the Lord's *pesaḥ*' (v. 27)."

It follows that when Rabban Gamliel asserts that one must say, "*pesaḥ,* matza, and bitter herbs" he is referring not only to reciting the words, but also to explaining them. Thus, his ruling is not just another detail in the laws of *pesaḥ,* matza, and bitter herbs, but rather the heart of the Exodus story. While the Torah's statement regarding the requirement to mention "this service" appears to apply only to "the sacrifice of the Lord's *pesaḥ,*" Rabban Gamliel teaches us that our explanations of the day's rituals must also cover the matza and bitter herbs, meaning all of the elements mentioned in Exodus 12:8.

Four That Are Fewer Than One

ראש השנה א, א

אַרְבָּעָה רָאשֵׁי שָׁנִים הֵם. בְּאֶחָד בְּנִיסָן רֹאשׁ הַשָּׁנָה לַמְּלָכִים וְלָרְגָלִים. בְּאֶחָד בֶּאֱלוּל רֹאשׁ הַשָּׁנָה לְמַעְשַׂר בְּהֵמָה. רַבִּי אֶלְעָזָר וְרַבִּי שִׁמְעוֹן אוֹמְרִים, בְּאֶחָד בְּתִשְׁרֵי. בְּאֶחָד בְּתִשְׁרֵי רֹאשׁ הַשָּׁנָה לַשָּׁנִים וְלַשְּׁמִטִּין וְלַיּוֹבְלוֹת, לַנְּטִיעָה וְלַיְרָקוֹת. בְּאֶחָד בִּשְׁבָט, רֹאשׁ הַשָּׁנָה לָאִילָן, כְּדִבְרֵי בֵית שַׁמַּאי. בֵּית הִלֵּל אוֹמְרִים, בַּחֲמִשָּׁה עָשָׂר בּוֹ:

Rosh HaShana 1:1

There are four New Years: The first of Nisan is the New Year for kings and for festivals. The first of Elul is the New Year for the tithe of beasts. Rabbi Elazar and Rabbi Shimon say: the first of Tishrei. The first of Tishrei is the New Year for years, for Sabbatical and Jubilee years, for planting and for [tithe of] vegetables. The first of Shevat is the New Year for trees, according to the words of the school of Shammai. The school of Hillel says: On the fifteenth of that month.

The four chapters of tractate Rosh HaShana feature two main themes. The first two are concerned mostly with the declaration of the new month, and the last two are about Rosh HaShana. It is thus surprising to find that the tractate begins with the various New Years – a topic that one would expect to come up in the second half of the tractate. There are many explanations for the seemingly incongruous placement of this first mishna, but to my mind the very question is fundamentally mistaken. It seems that the subject of the mishna is actually Rosh Ḥodesh, or the New Month, even though the term New Year appears five times and Rosh Ḥodesh is not even mentioned.

Four Cannot Be One

When four different dates mark a New Year, the individual value of each as the opening day of the year diminishes. Exclusivity is a prerequisite for the existence of the New Year, for only one day can be the first, the beginning. Our mishna turns the New Year into a relative term: a New Year is the beginning of the year for only certain issues, which are sometimes technical and specific. In all other respects, these days are ordinary days, without any special character or unique commandments to set them apart.

Our Rosh HaShana, the first of Tishrei, is the only date on the list that is mentioned in the Torah. But it too does not receive any special treatment in the mishna, and it is placed only third on the list. The second mishna in the chapter also ignores the uniqueness of Rosh HaShana, listing it among other days of judgment throughout the year:

> At four set times the world is judged: On Passover in respect to the produce; on Shavuot in respect to the fruit of the tree; on Rosh HaShana all the people of the world pass before Him like a division of soldiers [a numerus], as it says, "He who fashions the hearts of them all, who discerns all their doings" (Psalms 33:15). And on Sukkot they are judged in respect to rain. (Rosh HaShana 1:2)

All New Years Are Also New Months

We can better understand our mishna if we grasp that the main topic of the first two chapters is the sanctification of the new month, meaning Rosh Ḥodesh, not Rosh HaShana and the other New Years. The dates cited in the mishna begin with Nisan, which is "the beginning of months; it shall be the first month of the year to you" (Exodus 12:2), and not Rosh HaShana, which is "the New Year for years." Furthermore, all four New Years listed in the mishna fall on the first of a month – the first of Nisan, the first of Elul, the first of Tishrei, and the first of Shevat. Thus the mishna highlights the importance of Rosh Ḥodesh, and, by extension, the process of sanctifying and declaring the new month.

In actuality, however, the mishna's assertion that the four New Years fall on Rosh Ḥodesh does not represent a consensus, and all four dates are disputed. First, the Talmud notes that the first of Nisan is not the New Year for festivals, because the festival falls in the middle, not the beginning, of the month: "How can [the New Year] for the festivals be on the first of Nisan? It is surely on the fifteenth of Nisan!" (Rosh HaShana 4a). Furthermore, the Tosefta states that the New Year "for kings and for festivals" is the entirety of Nisan rather than a specific date in that month.

Second, according to Rabbi Elazar and Rabbi Shimon, the New Year for the tithe of beasts is the first of Tishrei rather than the first of Elul, meaning that there are at most three New Year dates. Third, most traditions mark the New Year for Jubilee years on the tenth of Tishrei. The Talmud claims that our mishna, which states that it falls on the first of Tishrei, represents a sole, dissenting opinion. Fourth, according to the opinion of the school of Hillel, the New Year for trees is not the first of Shevat, but rather the fifteenth of that month. It is noteworthy that, despite the fact that we rule according to the school of Hillel, the Mishna chooses to highlight the opinion of the school of Shammai by using the formulation "**according to** the words of the school of Shammai" rather than the more common "**these are** the words of the school of Shammai."

In my view, the fact that in each of the cases the editor of our mishna chooses to emphasize the opinions in which New Years fall on Rosh Ḥodesh indicates that it is meant as a preface to matters concerning the new month.

Rosh HaShana and Rosh Ḥodesh

We have established the significance of our mishna's placement at the beginning of the tractate, but the relevance of the laws of Rosh Ḥodesh to Rosh HaShana remains a question. Beyond that, as Rabbi Avraham Walfish notes, the structure of the tractate as a whole reinforces the connection between the two topics; the chapters that deal mostly with Rosh Ḥodesh also refer to Rosh HaShana, and vice versa.[1] What is the import

1. Walfish, *The Literary Method of Redaction in Mishnah based on Tractate Rosh HaShanah*

of this connection? I believe that the key to the answer can be found in the original biblical connotation of the first of Tishrei:

> Speak to the children of Israel, saying: In the seventh month, on the first day of the month, you shall have a solemn rest, a memorial proclaimed with the blast of horns, a holy convocation. You shall do no manner of servile work, and you shall bring an offering made by fire to the Lord. (Leviticus 23:24–25)

The Bible never calls the first of Tishrei "Rosh HaShana." In fact, it emphasizes that it is in the middle of the year – "In the seventh month, on the first day of the month" – meaning that its significance does not derive from its being the New Year. Indeed, it is hard to understand why this day is even holy. The Torah provides no explanation – only a date. Therefore, it seems that the answer is the date itself, meaning that its holiness derives from its being the first day of the seventh month. As we know, the seventh day is holy, as is the seventh year, the Sabbatical year; apparently, so is the seventh month, and especially its first day.[2] This idea is stated explicitly by Philo of Alexandria, who calls it "sacred-month-day."[3]

(PhD diss., Hebrew University of Jerusalem, 2001) [Hebrew], 293. In three of the chapters, the secondary topic is mentioned explicitly (1:1–2; 3:1; 4:4), while in Chapter 2 the discussion regarding the sanctification of the new month in 2:9 can be read as referring to Tishrei (ibid). This structure sheds light on the question that we started with regarding the placement of the first mishna (ibid., 295). Here is Rabbi Walfish's conclusion regarding the link between the two topics: "On one hand, the declaration of the new month owes its crucial halakhic importance to its implications on the holidays, and specifically Rosh HaShana. On the other hand, Rosh HaShana should be seen as an enhanced Rosh Ḥodesh of sorts" (ibid., 296).

2. See Leviticus Rabba (29): "'In the seventh month' – the seventh is always prized… among the years, the seventh is prized – 'But in the seventh year shall be a Sabbath of solemn rest for the land' (Leviticus 25:4). Among the days, the seventh is prized – 'And God blessed the seventh day' (Genesis 2:3). Among the months, the seventh is prized – 'In the seventh month.'"
3. Philo of Alexandria, *Exposition of the Law* 2:188, available at archive.org.

The special status of the seventh month is also apparent in its many holy days and festivals – four, one in every week. Altogether, the month includes ten holy days, a round, symbolic number. The link between the holiness of the seventh month and its festivals is also apparent in the recurrence of the word *shabbaton* (translated above as "solemn rest") in relation to them. It is a word that the Bible does not use in relation to Passover and Shavuot. In fact, elsewhere the Torah uses the word *shabbaton* only in relation to the seventh day (four times) and the seventh year (twice).[4]

But how is the seventh month like Shabbat and the Sabbatical year when the latter two are at the end of a cycle, while Tishrei is in the middle of a twelve-month year? I believe the answer lies in the fact that the year is cyclical, meaning that after its midpoint it comes progressively closer to its beginning. Thus, the point in the year that is farthest from the beginning is its middle day, the first day of the seventh month.

The main commandment associated with the holiday – "a day of blowing the horn" (Numbers 29:1) and "a memorial proclaimed with the blast of horns" – points at an additional connection between Rosh HaShana and Rosh Ḥodesh, as the latter is also associated with a commandment to blow horns:

> Also in the day of your gladness, and in your appointed seasons, and on your new moons, you shall blow with the trumpets over your burnt offerings, and over the sacrifices of your peace offerings; and they shall be to you a memorial before your God: I am the Lord your God. (Numbers 10:10)[5]

---

4. Another commonality of the Tishrei festivals is the number of offerings: Whereas there are two bullocks on Passover, Shavuot, and Rosh Ḥodesh, on most of the Tishrei festivals – Rosh HaShana, Yom Kippur, and Shemini Atzeret – one bullock is offered. Sukkot revolves around the number seven: A total of seventy bullocks are sacrificed over the course of the seven-day festival, including seven on its final day.
5. Our Sages derive the laws of blowing shofar from this verse. See Yitzhak Brand, "With Trumpets and Sound of the Horn Shout Before the King, the Lord," *Daf Kesher: A Newsletter for the Students of Har Etzion* 300 (1991) [Hebrew].

The idea that Rosh HaShana's holiness derives from the fact that it is a Rosh Ḥodesh can help us to explain the structure of our tractate, which opens with the sanctification of the new month and continues with the laws of blowing shofar. Furthermore, the structure and editing enable a flow from one topic to the next. For one, the chapter that deals with the Rosh HaShana shofar begins with a mishna about Rosh Ḥodesh.[6] In addition, the first law of blowing shofar does not state that it is referring to the Rosh HaShana shofar, but rather seems to be about *shofarot* in general:

> All *shofarot* may be used except for that of a cow, because it is a horn. Rabbi Yosei said: Are not all *shofarot* called horns, as it states (Joshua 6:5), "When they make a long blast with the ram's horn"? (Rosh HaShana 3:2)

The End Is the Beginning

So far we have been considering Rosh HaShana as the first day of the seventh month. But we cannot divorce the Mishna from its original context, and indeed, the term "Rosh HaShana" appears in our tractate nine times. These twin roles – the first of the seventh month and the New Year – represent two aspects of time and the yearly cycle, one cosmological and the other historical. Any examination of the first of Tishrei must consider the interplay between these two dimensions.

On the cosmological level, Tishrei is the time of the creation of the world, while, historically speaking, it is the seventh month from the formation of the people of Israel and its emergence from Egypt. It follows that the chronological end point of the historical process – the farthest date from the beginning of the story – coincides with the beginning of "cosmological time."

I see a profound idea implied by the convergence of these two timelines. The Torah's conception of end times is founded on a vision of the world returning to its original state, filled with living waters, an idealized conception of nature, and divine kingship and revelation. The

6. Walfish, *Rosh HaShanah*, 293.

fact that the end point of the historical process indicates a return to the dawn of Creation can teach us something about humanity's role in rectifying the world. The vision of a renewed Creation, which blends the beginning and ending of the world, differs from the original Creation in that it is not only God's handiwork – it gives humanity the right and responsibility to take part in Creation by rectifying and advancing it.

The Elitists and the Democrats

ראש השנה א, ז

אָב וּבְנוֹ שֶׁרָאוּ אֶת הַחֹדֶשׁ, יֵלְכוּ. לֹא שֶׁמִּצְטָרְפִין זֶה עִם זֶה, אֶלָּא שֶׁאִם יִפָּסֵל אֶחָד מֵהֶן, יִצְטָרֵף הַשֵּׁנִי עִם אַחֵר. רַבִּי שִׁמְעוֹן אוֹמֵר, אָב וּבְנוֹ וְכָל הַקְּרוֹבִין, כְּשֵׁרִין לְעֵדוּת הַחֹדֶשׁ. אָמַר רַבִּי יוֹסֵי, מַעֲשֶׂה בְטוֹבִיָּה הָרוֹפֵא, שֶׁרָאָה אֶת הַחֹדֶשׁ בִּירוּשָׁלַיִם, הוּא וּבְנוֹ וְעַבְדּוֹ מְשֻׁחְרָר, וְקִבְּלוּ הַכֹּהֲנִים אוֹתוֹ וְאֶת בְּנוֹ, וּפָסְלוּ אֶת עַבְדּוֹ. וּכְשֶׁבָּאוּ לִפְנֵי בֵית דִּין, קִבְּלוּ אוֹתוֹ וְאֶת עַבְדּוֹ, וּפָסְלוּ אֶת בְּנוֹ:

Rosh HaShana 1:7

If a father and a son have seen the new moon, they should both go [to Jerusalem], not that they can join together as witnesses but so that if one of them is disqualified the other may join with another witness. Rabbi Shimon says that a father and son and all relatives are eligible to testify to the appearance of the new moon. Rabbi Yosei said: It happened once that Tuvia the doctor saw the new moon in Jerusalem along with his son and his freed slave. The priests accepted his evidence and that of his son, and disqualified his slave. But when they appeared before the court they accepted his evidence and that of his slave, and disqualified his son.

The mishna describes two disputes between the court and the priests relating to the competency of witnesses who sanctify the new month with their own testimony: one regarding relatives and the other regarding a freed slave.

It seems that the two disputes are intertwined, and reflect an essential moral difference. The priests, the most exalted group in the nation, emphasize the importance of a person's lineage, and, accordingly, consider former slaves to be incompetent witnesses. The Sages of the court, in contrast, represent the people, and hold a more egalitarian view. They measure individuals based on their actions, not on the identity of their progenitors: "the scholar *mamzer* takes precedence over the ignorant high priest" (Horayot 3:8). A former slave is competent, for he is now a Jew, but relatives are not. The demand that witnesses to the new moon not be dependent on one another comes from the idea that they are representatives of the entire nation and not a specific group, a specific family.

A careful reading of our mishna reveals a play on words that implies criticism of the priests' outlook. The statement, "The priests accepted his evidence and that of his son" (*oto ve'et beno*) is reminiscent of a Torah prohibition: "And whether it be cow or ewe, you shall not kill it and its young (*oto ve'et beno*) both in one day" (Leviticus 22:28).[1]

The dispute between the court and the priests raises the question of hierarchy. The sanctification of the new month is of importance primarily to the Temple, which is seemingly the "domain" of the priesthood. And yet, it emerges from our mishna that the court, which is separate from the priests, has "veto power." As we saw in the beginning of Tractate Yoma, when it comes to the rituals of Yom Kippur, at the center of which is the high priest, the court and its elders are at the top of the hierarchy, and the priest is their agent:

> The elders of the court handed him over to the elders of the priesthood and they took him up to the upper chamber of the house of Avtinas. They adjured him and then left. And they said to him [when leaving]: "Sir, high priest, we are agents of the court, and you are our agent and the agent of the court. We adjure you by the One who caused His name to dwell in this house that you do not change anything of what we said to you." He turned aside and wept, and they turned aside and wept. (Yoma 1:5)

The court plays an even more central role in declaring the new month. There, unlike Yom Kippur, where the high priest is the one who performs

1. My thanks to my wife, Michal, who pointed this out to me.

the rituals, it is the court and the people who have the power to sanctify the month:

> The head of the court says, "Sanctified," and all the people answer after him, "Sanctified, sanctified." (Rosh HaShana 2:7)
>
> If the court and all of Israel saw it, if the witnesses were examined and there was no time left to say "Sanctified" before it grew dark, then the month is impregnated [it has thirty days]. (Rosh HaShana 3:1)

An act of speaking, by the court and the people, is what determines the start of the month. The crowd is called "all of Israel," signifying that it represents the entire nation – even those who are not present.[2] The power to manifest holiness is not restricted to any single group; rather, the entire Jewish people is "a kingdom of priests, and a holy nation" (Exodus 19:6).

2. For a discussion of the significance of the partnership between the court and the people in the process of sanctifying the new month, see Walfish's summary in *Rosh HaShanah*, 264.

The Journey of the Moonlight

Rosh HaShana 2:2–3

Originally they used to light torches [to signal that the new month had been decreed]. When the Samaritans disrupted this, they decreed that messengers should go out.

How did they light the torches? They used to bring long poles of cedar, and reeds, and olive wood, and flax fluff, and they tied them all together with a string. And someone used to go up to the top of a mountain and light them with fire and wave them back and forth, and up and down, until he saw the next one doing the same thing on the top of the second mountain; and so on the top of the third mountain.

ראש השנה ב, ב-ג

בָּרִאשׁוֹנָה הָיוּ מַשִּׂיאִין מַשּׂוּאוֹת. מִשֶּׁקִּלְקְלוּ הַכּוּתִים, הִתְקִינוּ שֶׁיְּהוּ שְׁלוּחִין יוֹצְאִין:

כֵּיצַד הָיוּ מַשִּׂיאִין מַשּׂוּאוֹת, מְבִיאִין כְּלֻנְסָאוֹת שֶׁל אֶרֶז אֲרֻכִּין וְקָנִים וַעֲצֵי שֶׁמֶן וּנְעֹרֶת שֶׁל פִּשְׁתָּן וְכוֹרֵךְ בִּמְשִׁיחָה, וְעוֹלֶה לְרֹאשׁ הָהָר וּמַצִּית בָּהֶן אֶת הָאוּר וּמוֹלִיךְ וּמֵבִיא וּמַעֲלֶה וּמוֹרִיד עַד שֶׁהוּא רוֹאֶה אֶת חֲבֵרוֹ שֶׁהוּא עוֹשֶׂה כֵן בְּרֹאשׁ הָהָר הַשֵּׁנִי, וְכֵן בְּרֹאשׁ הָהָר הַשְּׁלִישִׁי:

There was a time when the grand proclamation of the new month would reach the people by way of torches. That practice was phased out even before the mishnaic era, because of the Cutheans, also known as the Samaritans. But if the torches were no more than an efficient means for conveying information, the Mishna would not see fit to teach us about them. The fact that the Mishna chooses to linger on the story of the lighting of the torches teaches us that the act of lighting, and even just the preparation for it, is imbued with spiritual significance.[1]

The description of the preparation and lighting of the torches is laden with allusions to the Temple rituals: The torchbearer would "**go up to the top** of the mountain" to light the fire. This turn of phrase evokes the priests, whom the Mishna says would "[**go**] **up to the top** of the altar" (Tamid 2:1) in order to organize the pile of wood. The mishna details the manner in which the torches were waved – "back and forth, and up and down" – just as the priest would wave certain sacrifices: "back and forth, up and down" (Menaḥot 5:6). According to the Talmud, these motions are charged with symbolism: "Back and forth – to Him who has dominion over the [four] directions; up and down – to Him who has dominion over heaven and earth." (Menaḥot 62a). The chain of torches begins at the Mount of Anointing, also known as the Mount of Olives, which faces the entrance to the Temple. Several Temple rituals were performed on this mountain, including the burning of the red heifer.[2]

The effort to link the torches to the Temple is part of a theme by which the Mishna presents the process of sanctifying the month as one with independent significance. The journey of the witnesses, the sanctification in the court, and the spreading of the word – these are not just means for determining dates, but divine service in themselves, and thus holy.

The Witnesses of the New Moon as Pilgrims

The Mishna's rich, detailed description[3] of the voyage to Jerusalem by the witnesses to the new moon provides evidence of the importance of that voyage. The pilgrims who make the journey to Jerusalem to fulfill

---

1. It seems that this is why the first mishna of the second chapter notes the previous custom, under which the testimony of all people was accepted. This law reflects the democratic character of the sanctification of the new month, which is open to the entire nation.
2. "The priest who burned the red heifer would stand on the top of the Mount of Olives and direct his gaze carefully to see the opening of the Sanctuary at the time of the sprinkling of the blood." (Middot 2:4)
3. Rosh HaShana 1:6–9.

the commandment to be seen – "all your males shall appear before the face of the Lord God" (Exodus 23:17) – and the witnesses come to Jerusalem to attest to having seen.[4] In both instances, seeing is equated with an encounter with the Divine Presence: Of the pilgrim it is said, "As He comes to see, so he comes to be seen" (Ḥagiga 2a), and Rashi explains, "that the [pilgrim] sees the Divine Presence." When it comes to the sanctification of the new month, the Talmud says, "Rabbi Aha b. Ḥanina also said that Rabbi Asi said that Rabbi Yoḥanan said: Whoever pronounces the benediction over the new moon in its due time welcomes, as it were, the Divine Presence… In the school of Rabbi Yishmael it was taught: Had Israel inherited no other privilege than to greet the presence of their Heavenly Father once a month, it would have been sufficient" (Sanhedrin 42a).

The court's reliance on witnesses to sanctify the new month shows us that their testimony had a ritual aspect. Indeed, the court had the power to declare the new month even without witnesses, based solely on the same calculations that determine the Jewish calendar today. Thus, the many difficulties and complications that stem from having to wait for witnesses are by no means a necessity. And yet, the court prefers to declare the new month based on witness testimony, even when it requires Shabbat desecration: "On account of two months they desecrate Shabbat: on account of Nisan and Tishrei" (Rosh HaShana 1:4).

The Talmud explains this insistence by stating that "it is a religious duty (mitzva) to sanctify [the new month] via actual observation" (Rosh HaShana 20a). The fact that the sanctification of the month based on eyewitness testimony is a mitzva is what enables the desecration of Shabbat, even though Rosh Ḥodesh can be determined without it. The Yerushalmi adds to the same idea:

> Rabbi Elazar said: The [sacrificial] members and fat pieces that are not consumed by evening – [the priest] must make

---

4. The desire to lend the voyage the characterizes of a pilgrimage explains why the Mishna chose to include here some of the mishnayot that deal with the sanctification of the month in Jerusalem (2:5 and others), despite the fact that during the time of the Mishna, the court was in Yavne or the Galilee.

> a fire for them and burn them on their own, and they take precedence [over Shabbat]...Rabbi Ze'ira asked of him: Can something that is not a prerequisite [for the priest's continued work] take precedence [over Shabbat]? He replied: **Indeed, the witnesses of the [new] month are not a prerequisite [for declaring the new month] but do take precedence [over Shabbat].** (Y. Yoma 4:6)

The inherent value of sanctifying the month is even more apparent here: The witnesses are allowed to desecrate Shabbat even though Rosh Ḥodesh can be declared without their testimony, which is compared to the Temple offerings.

Betrothal and Sanctifying the New Month

In order to understand the spiritual significance that the Mishna ascribes to the sanctification and declaration of the new month, we must first note that the very term "sanctifying the month" (*kiddush haḥodesh*) implies holiness. The Mishna emphasizes the importance of the declaration, "Sanctified," regarding the month, a declaration without which the new month cannot be determined:

> The head of the court says, "Sanctified," and all the people answer after him, "Sanctified, sanctified." (Rosh HaShana 2:7)
>
> If the court and all of Israel saw it, if the witnesses were examined and there was no time left to say "Sanctified" before it grew dark, then the month is impregnated [it has thirty days]. (Rosh HaShana 3:1)

Just as a man betroths his wife by declaring "Behold, you are consecrated [sanctified] to me," the people of Israel sanctify the new month by declaring, "Sanctified." The sanctification of the new month is no mere legal formality determining whether or not a month has begun; it is an event that imbues the new time with holiness.

A Journey of Light

> At what places did they light the torches? From the Mount of Olives [in Jerusalem] to Sarteva, and from Sarteva to Grofina, and from Grofina to Ḥavran, and from Ḥavran to Beit Biltin. From Beit Biltin they did not move, but rather waved [the torch] back and forth and up and down until he saw the whole of the Diaspora before him lit up like one bonfire. (Rosh HaShana 2:4)

The story of the sanctification of the month begins with the crescent appearing anew and revealing its light. On the first day, it reveals only a small portion of itself, and only for a brief period. When a Jew sees that tiny light and brings news of his sighting to Jerusalem, he can testify to what he has seen and imbue it with holiness. It is then that the direction of the light changes – from Jerusalem outward. The light of the torches spreads from the Mount of Olives, which faces the Temple, and extends from mountaintop to mountaintop and from person to person, until it illuminates all places where the people of Israel reside, lighting up the entire nation and "the whole of the Diaspora before him lit up like one bonfire."

From Amalek to Jericho

ראש השנה ג, ב	Rosh HaShana 3:2
כל הַשּׁוֹפָרוֹת כְּשֵׁרִין חוּץ מִשֶּׁל פָּרָה, מִפְּנֵי שֶׁהוּא קֶרֶן. אָמַר רַבִּי יוֹסֵי, וַהֲלֹא כָּל הַשּׁוֹפָרוֹת נִקְרְאוּ קֶרֶן, שֶׁנֶּאֱמַר (יהושע ו), בִּמְשֹׁךְ בְּקֶרֶן הַיּוֹבֵל.	All *shofarot* may be used except for that of a cow, because it is a horn. Rabbi Yosei said: Are not all *shofarot* called horns, as it says, "When they make a long blast with the ram's horn"? (Joshua 6:5).

Our mishna, which opens the tractate's discussion of shofar blowing, quotes a verse from the book of Joshua. Rarely does the Mishna cite the sources for its rulings, so there is cause to ask if there is a deeper reason for its decision to quote this verse. In our case, we can glean an answer from the context of the verse and the structure of the tractate. First, let us examine the final mishna in our chapter:

> "And it came to pass, when Moses held up his hand Israel prevailed…" (Exodus 17:1). Did the hands of Moses wage war or break [Israel's ability] to wage war? Rather, this teaches that as long as Israel would look upward and subject their hearts to their Father in heaven they prevailed, and if not they fell. Similarly, "Make for yourself a fiery serpent and mount it on a pole. And if anyone who is bitten shall look at it, he shall live" (Numbers 21:8). Did the serpent kill, or did the serpent keep alive? Rather, when Israel would look upward and subject their hearts to their Father in heaven, they were healed, and if not their [flesh] would melt away. A deaf-mute, a lunatic, and a minor cannot cause

> others to fulfill their religious obligation. This is the general principle: One who is not himself obligated in the matter cannot perform it on behalf of others. (Rosh HaShana 3:8)

The mishna teaches us that the miraculous redemption in both cases – Moses lifting his hand in war and the remedy effected by the bronze serpent – did not stem from any magical effect, but rather from an internal religious occurrence. Walfish, in a reading of the literary and philosophical structure of the chapter, points out the importance of this mishna, and especially the significance of its juxtaposition with the previous mishna, which calls for intention when fulfilling the mitzva of shofar:

> The intention of the heart appears explicitly in the Mishna twice – in mishnayot 7 and 8. The literary context reflects a philosophical link between two different aspects of the intention of the heart. The chapter's literary structure shows that the intention of the heart – especially on the spiritual-aggadic level – underpins many of the laws in our chapter, and even contributes to the elaboration of the idea of intention.[1]

To my mind, that is the prism through which we should view our mishna. Like the verses in mishna 3:8, the verse quoted in mishna 3:2 is also taken from the story of a miraculous military victory: the falling of the walls of Jericho: "And it shall be, when they make a long blast with the ram's horn, and when you hear the sound of the horn, all the people shall shout with a great shout; and the wall of the city shall fall down flat, and the people shall go up every man straight before him" (Joshua 6:5). When the Mishna tells of the power of Moses's hands during the battle with Amalek, it both lends an additional level of meaning to the halakhic requirement to subject the heart while the shofar is blown, and explains the victories of his successor, Joshua, as though to say: "Did the sound of the shofar tumble walls? Rather, when Israel would blow the

1. Walfish, *Rosh HaShanah*, 265.

shofar and subject their hearts to their Father in heaven…" The story of the falling of the walls of Jericho is the link between Moses' hands and the shofar blown on Rosh HaShana. On the one hand, it represents a miraculous military victory, but on the other, this victory is effected by blowing the shofar. Thus, the verse in 3:2 fuses the halakhic and aggadic elements of the chapter into a single unit.

Seeing and Hearing

Furthermore, the parallel between the two miracles sheds light on the basic structure of the entire tractate. The first and second chapters of Tractate Rosh HaShana deal with the sanctification of the new month, while the third and fourth are devoted to Rosh HaShana. Thus we encounter a question that many commentators on the Mishna wrestled with: Why does Chapter 3 continue the discussion of the new month in its first mishna, and move on to the shofar for Rosh HaShana only in mishna 2? On the face of it, would it not have made more sense to include mishna 3:1 in Chapter 2 and begin Chapter 3 with 3:2?

In his comprehensive work, Walfish shows that one of the main effects of the tractate's literary structure is to create a link between the two topics it discusses: Rosh Ḥodesh and Rosh HaShana. The decision to open Chapter 3 with a mishna whose topic is the sanctification of the month is part of the same effort.

Walfish suggests[2] that this effort is informed by a connection between the two mediums by which humanity can encounter God: the senses of sight and hearing. A major motif of the sanctification of the new month is the seeing of the moon; the equivalent on Rosh HaShana is hearing the shofar. Our chapter shows us that through seeing and listening, the people of Israel subject their hearts to heaven.

We can extend Walfish's idea and say that the two senses that can effect an encounter with God correspond to two wars in which the people of Israel were victorious: In the battle of Jericho, victory came through the intention of the heart via the sense of hearing, while in the

2. Ibid., 304–6.

battle against Amalek, they won due to intention of the heart via the sense of sight. It is the work of the heart, not magic, that brings victory to the people of Israel against its enemies.

Shofar and Prayer

ראש השנה ד, ה

סֵדֶר בְּרָכוֹת, אוֹמֵר אָבוֹת וּגְבוּרוֹת וּקְדֻשַּׁת הַשֵּׁם, וְכוֹלֵל מַלְכִיּוֹת עִמָּהֶן, וְאֵינוֹ תוֹקֵעַ. קְדֻשַּׁת הַיּוֹם, וְתוֹקֵעַ. זִכְרוֹנוֹת, וְתוֹקֵעַ. שׁוֹפָרוֹת, וְתוֹקֵעַ. וְאוֹמֵר עֲבוֹדָה וְהוֹדָאָה וּבִרְכַּת כֹּהֲנִים, דִּבְרֵי רַבִּי יוֹחָנָן בֶּן נוּרִי. אָמַר לוֹ רַבִּי עֲקִיבָא, אִם אֵינוֹ תוֹקֵעַ לַמַּלְכִיּוֹת, לָמָּה הוּא מַזְכִּיר? אֶלָּא אוֹמֵר אָבוֹת וּגְבוּרוֹת וּקְדֻשַּׁת הַשֵּׁם, וְכוֹלֵל מַלְכֻיּוֹת עִם קְדֻשַּׁת הַיּוֹם, וְתוֹקֵעַ. זִכְרוֹנוֹת, וְתוֹקֵעַ. שׁוֹפָרוֹת, וְתוֹקֵעַ. וְאוֹמֵר עֲבוֹדָה וְהוֹדָאָה וּבִרְכַּת כֹּהֲנִים:

Rosh HaShana 4:5

The order of blessings [in the Musaf *Amida* of Rosh HaShana]: He says "Patriarchs," "Powers," and the "Sanctification of the Name," and includes the "Kingship" verses with them and does not blow [the shofar]; the "Sanctification of the Day" and blows [the shofar]; the "Remembrance" verses and blows [the shofar]; and the "Shofar" verses and blows [the shofar]. Then he says [the blessing of the] "Temple Service," and "Thanksgiving," and the priestly blessing – these are the words of Rabbi Yoḥanan ben Nuri. Rabbi Akiva said to him: If he does not blow the shofar for the "Kingship" verses, why should he say them? Rather, he says: "Patriarchs," "Powers," and the "Sanctification of the Name," and includes the "Kingship" verses with the "Sanctification of the Day" and blows the shofar. Then he says the "Remembrance" verses and blows, and the "Shofar" verses and blows. Then he says the "Temple Service," and "Thanksgiving," and the priestly blessing.

Rabbi Joseph B. Soloveitchik argues that based on this mishna, the blowing of the shofar is a form of prayer, which is why it was included in the Rosh HaShana *Amida*:

> These things must be understood, for what connection is there between the commandment to blow the shofar and uttering the blessings of the [*Amida*] prayer?...And it seems to follow that the commandment to blow the shofar falls under the category of prayer, even though the universal custom is to pray with speech. On Rosh HaShana, which is the Day of Judgment...we pray by blowing the shofar – prayer without [spoken or written] words, for we do not truly know what to ask for.[1]

The idea that blowing the shofar is a form of prayer is congruent with the Talmud's statement that the shofar "brings the remembrance of Israel to their Father in heaven" (Shabbat 131b). However, a close reading of the development of the law in the Mishna can yield an additional, specific reason for this juxtaposition.

Many sources in rabbinic literature consider the blowing of the shofar as a supplement to the system of sacrifices.[2] It seems that the source of this idea is the observation linking the Torah verses about the shofar to those mandating the blowing of trumpets "over your burnt offerings, and over the sacrifices of your peace offerings" (Numbers 10:10). After the destruction of the Temple, prayer began to take the place of the sacrifices.[3] Thus, the Musaf prayer stood for the *musaf* offering and the shofar blasts that accompanied it. The Yerushalmi refines this idea, and says that the ten verses of the "Shofar" blessing correspond to the ten animals that composed the Rosh HaShana Musaf offering: "Ten *shofarot* representing seven male lambs, a bullock, a ram, and a male goat" (Y. Rosh HaShana 4:7). The Yerushalmi further contends that the shofar is blown during Musaf, rather than elsewhere in the service, because the most significant element of the mitzva of Rosh HaShana is Musaf, i.e., the Musaf offering (4:8).

---

1. Joseph Soloveitchik, "Defining the Commandment to Blow the Shofar," *Mesorah* 6 (1991) [Hebrew], 19–20.
2. Gedalyahu Alon, "On Philo's Halakha," in *Jews, Judaism, and the Classical World: Studies in Jewish History in the Times of the Second Temple and Talmud* (Jerusalem: Magnes Press, Hebrew University: 1977), 89–137.
3. See Berakhot 26b.

Thus, we find that the inclusion of shofar blowing in the *Amida* is a reminder of the original role that the shofar played in the system of sacrifices. The original meaning of the juxtaposition of prayer and shofar should be examined in the context of the meaning and role of the sacrifices.[4]

4. It is possible that the sacrifice is considered a gift accompanying the blowing of the shofar that elicits memories of the Jewish people. It is also possible that the sacrifice is essential because it inspires revelation (see Leviticus 9:24) and opens up a channel of communication for the shofar between heaven and earth.

Communal Prayer and Individual Prayer

ראש השנה ד, ט

סֵדֶר תְּקִיעוֹת, שָׁלֹשׁ, שֶׁל שָׁלֹשׁ שָׁלֹשׁ. שִׁעוּר תְּקִיעָה כְּשָׁלֹשׁ תְּרוּעוֹת. שִׁעוּר תְּרוּעָה כְּשָׁלֹשׁ יְבָבוֹת. תָּקַע בָּרִאשׁוֹנָה וּמָשַׁךְ בַּשְּׁנִיָּה כִּשְׁתַּיִם אֵין בְּיָדוֹ אֶלָּא אַחַת. מִי שֶׁבֵּרַךְ וְאַחַר כָּךְ נִתְמַנָּה לוֹ שׁוֹפָר, תּוֹקֵעַ וּמֵרִיעַ וְתוֹקֵעַ שָׁלֹשׁ פְּעָמִים. כְּשֵׁם שֶׁשְּׁלִיחַ צִבּוּר חַיָּב, כָּךְ כָּל יָחִיד וְיָחִיד חַיָּב. רַבָּן גַּמְלִיאֵל אוֹמֵר, שְׁלִיחַ צִבּוּר מוֹצִיא אֶת הָרַבִּים יְדֵי חוֹבָתָן:

Rosh HaShana 4:9

The order of the blasts: three sets of three each. The length of a *tekia* is equal to three *teruot*, and the length of a *terua* is equal to three *yevavot*. If one prolonged the first *tekia* so that it went directly into the second, it counts only as one. One who has blessed [recited the *Amida*] and was then given a shofar, sounds a *tekia-terua-tekia* three times. Just as the communal prayer leader is obligated, so every single individual is obligated. Rabban Gamliel says: The communal prayer leader causes the whole congregation to fulfill their obligation.

In communal prayer, the *Amida* is recited silently by the individual members of the congregation and then out loud by the prayer leader. What is the basis for this repetition? Which of the two prayers is the more decisive? And what is the role of each prayer? These questions touch upon Rabban Gamliel's dispute with the preceding opinion in our mishna. He emphasizes the power of the leader's prayer to obviate the need for an individual's prayer, while the other opinion stresses the obligation of every member of the congregation to pray. The Talmud cites a *baraita* in which each side in this dispute engages with the other side's idea of prayer:

> "Just as the communal prayer leader is obligated, so every single individual, etc." – it has been taught: They said to Rabban Gamliel, "Accepting your view, why does the congregation [first] say the [*Amida*] prayer?" He replied, "So as to give the leader time to prepare his prayer." Rabban Gamliel then said to them, "Accepting your view, why does the leader go down [and stand] before the ark?" They replied, "So as to fulfill the obligation of those who are not familiar [with the prayers]." He said to them, "Just as he fulfills the obligation of those who are not familiar, so he fulfills the obligation of those who are familiar." (Rosh HaShana 34b)

According to Rabban Gamliel, the sole purpose of individual prayer during the communal gathering is to make things easier for the prayer leader. The leader's prayer is decisive for all members of the congregation, and is more than just a solution for those who are unable to pray on their own. This raises the question: In light of the oft-quoted assertion that "it is more meritorious [to fulfill a mitzva] oneself than through one's agent" (Kiddushin 41a), why is the leader's prayer preferable to that of the individual? Rabban Gamliel holds that the leader's prayer has unique character and meaning, as we can see from the talmudic tradition by which "Rabban Gamliel allowed even the people in the fields to have their obligation fulfilled [by the leader]" (Rosh HaShana 35a). The implication is that the leader's prayer is public, to the extent that it represents the entire community – even those who are not present when it is recited. It seems that Rabban Gamliel's approach stems from the idea that the prayers were established as substitutes for the *tamid* offerings,[1] meaning that they are public and recurrent in essence. It is for the same reason that Rabban Gamliel opines that, "Every day a person must pray eighteen [blessings of *Shemoneh Esreh*]" (Berakhot 4:3) – just like the *tamid* offering, which would be sacrificed daily. Finally, just as the *tamid*

1. Berakhot 26b.

was a public offering brought for the entire people, so the leader's prayer fulfills the obligation of even the people in the fields.[2]

By contrast, we recall the lament of Rabban Gamliel's brother-in-law, Rabbi Eliezer the Great: "One who makes his prayer 'set,' his prayer does not constitute 'pleading'" (Berakhot 4:4).[3] Prayer cannot rely solely on the communal aspect, because it must be "pleading" for what the *Amora'im* termed "mercy" (Berakhot 20b, 26a).

The argument can also be made that Rabbi Eliezer's approach stems from his conception as to the source of prayer. Countering the approach that establishes prayer as a substitute for the *tamid*, there is the position by which "The prayers were instituted by the Patriarchs" (Berakhot 26b). The prayers of the patriarchs are individual and personal, and generally focus on requests for mercy. According to this outlook, the prayer of the individual is of paramount importance, which explains the opinion that the role of the prayer leader is merely ex-post-facto – to fulfill the obligation of those who are not familiar.

The halakhic ruling follows the opinion that privileges individual prayer and states that the leader's prayer fulfills the obligation only of those who are not familiar with the prayers.[4] We could, perhaps, conclude that when the entire congregation knows how to pray, there is no need for a prayer leader. Therefore, it is surprising to read Maimonides's opinion, which nevertheless emphasizes the importance of the leader's prayer:

> Communal prayer is always heard. Even when there are transgressors among [the congregation], the Holy One, blessed be He, does not reject the prayers of the many.

---

2. Compare this to the Mishna's statement regarding the Musaf prayer, according to which the term "Musaf" indicates that the source of the prayer is the sacrifice of the same name that was brought while the Temple still stood: "Rabbi Elazar ben Azarya says: The Musaf prayer is said only with the local congregation. The Sages say: Either with or without the congregation. Rabbi Yehuda says in his name: Wherever there is a congregation, an individual is exempt from saying the Musaf prayer" (Berakhot 4:7).
3. See comments above about the relations between Rabbi Eliezer and Rabban Gamliel, in the fourth chapter of Tractate Berakhot.
4. *Mishneh Torah, Hilkhot Tefilla* 8:9, save for Rosh HaShana and Yom Kippur of a Jubilee year, when the prayer leader fulfills everyone's obligation.

> Therefore, a person should include himself in the community and should not pray alone whenever he is able to pray with the community...What is implied by [the term] communal prayer? One [person] prays aloud, and all [the others] listen. (*Mishneh Torah, Hilkhot Tefilla* 8:1, 5)

Maimonides states explicitly that the unique power and quality of communal prayer come through the recitation of the leader on behalf of the entire congregation. It bears mention that Maimonides, despite ruling like the first opinion in the mishna, does not completely rule out Rabban Gamliel's approach.[5] Prayer has two aspects that the individual must strive to bring together: the personal prayer propounded by the first opinion in the mishna, which one can only fulfill alone, and public prayer of the kind favored by Rabban Gamliel, which requires a prayer leader.

Maimonides's ruling is consistent with the approach of the editor of the mishna in Berakhot, in that it seeks to strike a balance between "set" prayer and spontaneous prayer. Indeed, in Berakhot the Mishna's ruling follows Rabban Gamliel, who contends that the individual must pray daily with a fixed formula; yet, the editor of the chapter found ways to actualize Rabbi Eliezer's demand that prayer be founded upon "pleading."

---

5. In his responsa (225), as opposed to in the *Mishneh Torah*, Maimonides explains the need for a prayer leader according to the second opinion as it appears in the *baraita* in the Talmud. It is worth noting in this context that his various books are not always consistent. It is also possible that in his responsa, he chose to provide the explicit reason rather than detail the full complexity of his approach.

Withdrawal of the High Priest Before Yom Kippur

יומא א, א

שִׁבְעַת יָמִים קֹדֶם יוֹם הַכִּפּוּרִים מַפְרִישִׁין כֹּהֵן גָּדוֹל מִבֵּיתוֹ לְלִשְׁכַּת פַּלְהֶדְרִין, וּמַתְקִינִין לוֹ כֹּהֵן אַחֵר תַּחְתָּיו, שֶׁמָּא יֶאֱרַע בּוֹ פְּסוּל. רַבִּי יְהוּדָה אוֹמֵר, אַף אִשָּׁה אַחֶרֶת מַתְקִינִין לוֹ, שֶׁמָּא תָמוּת אִשְׁתּוֹ, שֶׁנֶּאֱמַר (ויקרא טז) וְכִפֶּר בַּעֲדוֹ וּבְעַד בֵּיתוֹ. בֵּיתוֹ, זוֹ אִשְׁתּוֹ. אָמְרוּ לוֹ, אִם כֵּן, אֵין לַדָּבָר סוֹף:

Yoma 1:1

Seven days before Yom Kippur, they remove the high priest from his house to the chamber of the counselors, and they set up another priest to take his place lest something should occur to him to disqualify him [from being able to serve]. Rabbi Yehuda said: They even prepare another wife for him in case his wife should die, as it says, "And he shall make atonement for himself and for his house" (Leviticus 16:6). "His house" – this refers to his wife. They said to him: If so, there would be no end to the matter.

Rite of Passage

> Seven days before Yom Kippur, they remove the high priest from his house to the chamber of the counselors. (Yoma 1:1)

In halakhic midrashim, the high priest's seclusion in preparation for the Yom Kippur rituals is derived from the days of consecration – the seven days during which the Tabernacle and the priests were initiated.

The implication is that every year, before Yom Kippur, we reconstruct the high priest's initiation processes.[1]

Every initiation confers a new status. A period of passage is a common element in initiation ceremonies. During the initiation, the initiate severs himself from his previous existence, and at its conclusion he receives his new status. This process is an apt description of the process that the priest undergoes during the seven days that he is removed from his home. The seclusion period, seven days, is a full unit of time; thus the period of passage is defined as a separate unit. During these seven days the priest resides in the Temple and attends to the rituals, and "his service initiates him" (Yoma 12b): "All seven days he sprinkles the blood, and burns the incense, and cleans lamps, and offers the head and the leg" (Yoma 1:2).

The Mishna emphasizes the priest's separation from his home. This idea permeates the literary structure of the chapter, which follows the process of the priest's passage from his house to God's house. Walfish notes that the word "house" recurs throughout the chapter as a key word. The description of the Yom Kippur ritual begins in Chapter 1 with the priest's withdrawal from his **house** and his wife ("His **house** – this refers to his wife"). He is then handed over to the elders of the court (the Hebrew for "court" is *beit bin*, or "**house** of judgment"), and brought to the **house** of Avtinas, where he is adjured in the name of "the One who caused His name to dwell in this house." The Hebrew root p-r-sh also occurs throughout the high priest's process: First they remove (*mafrishim*) him from his home; then his isolation and loneliness deepen when he withdraws from his colleagues: "He turned aside (*poresh*) and wept, and they turned aside and wept (*porshim*)."

A Wise Man Is Superior to a Priest

> They delivered to him elders from the elders of the court and they read before him [throughout the seven days] from the order of the day. And they say to him, "Sir, high

1. See at length in Israel Knohl and Shlomo Naeh, "Milluim Ve-Kippurim," *Tarbiz* 62 (1992) [Hebrew]: 17–44.

> priest, you read it yourself with your own mouth, lest you have forgotten or lest you have never learned." (Yoma 1:3)

This mishna too can be elucidated via a comparison to the consecration of the Tabernacle. Then, during the days of consecration, Moses taught Aaron all of the sacrificial rites; here, Moses's successors, the elders of the court, impart lessons to Aaron's descendants. This interpretation appears explicitly in a *baraita* quoted by the Talmud:

> And what is mentioned in the section about the consecration? Aaron was removed for seven days and then officiated for one day, and Moses transmitted [instructions] to him throughout the seven days to train him in this service. Also in the future the high priest is to be removed for seven days and to officiate for one day, and two scholars of the disciples of Moses transmitted [instructions] to him throughout the seven days to train him in the service. (Yoma 4a)

The reconstruction of this element of the days of consecration has special significance; when a person gains a new status, his role in the hierarchy must be fully redefined, which means fleshing out his new authority and to whom he is subordinate. Throughout the passages that deal with the consecration of the Tabernacle it is clearly apparent that Moses is above Aaron:[2] Moses is enjoined to initiate Aaron, and Moses is the one who anoints, washes, and dresses Aaron and his sons.[3] The Torah mentions seven times that the details of the consecration of the Tabernacle were carried out "according to all that the Lord commanded Moses,"[4] and the consecration concludes with the following statement: "And Aaron and his sons did all the things which the Lord commanded by the hand of Moses" (Leviticus 8:36).

---

2. Milgrom, *Leviticus*, 1012.
3. Leviticus 8:6–14. There is a well-known story about the coronation of Charlemagne. As the story goes, the pope wanted to place the crown on Charlemagne's head. The latter refused, instead snatching the crown and placing it himself on his head, thus declaring that he was not subordinate to the Church.
4. Milgrom, *Leviticus*, 542.

What is the purpose of emphasizing Moses's superior position over Aaron? Milgrom suggests that the point is to express the superiority of the prophet over the priest. To me it seems that Aaron's subordination to Moses should be understood in light of the Sages' assertion that "a wise man is superior to a prophet" (Bava Batra 12a). In the Sages' eyes, Moses is first and foremost a sage, one who received the Torah and passed it on to subsequent generations.

And just as a wise man is superior to a prophet, he is superior to a priest, as the Mishna asserts in no uncertain terms in the final mishna of Tractate Horayot: "The scholar *mamzer* takes precedence over the ignorant high priest" (3:8).

Mishna 5 elaborates on the relationship between the priest and the wise man. The high priest is described as an agent of the court, who lacks the authority to act on his own and must adhere to the court's instructions:

> The elders of the court handed him over to the elders of the priesthood, and they took him up to the upper chamber of the house of Avtinas. They adjured him and then left. And they said to him [when leaving]: "Sir, high priest, we are agents of the court, and you are our agent and the agent of the court. We adjure you by the One who caused His name to dwell in this house that you do not change anything of what we said to you." He turned aside and wept, and they turned aside and wept. (Yoma 1:5)

While here it is the elders of the priesthood who adjure the high priest, they are subordinate to the courts. Their authority to adjure the priest flows from their position as "agents of the court." Thus the Mishna reiterates the idea that while the high priest is "highest among his brethren," the purpose of the annual ceremony is to remind him that he answers to a higher authority: the Torah sages.

Return to the Garden of Eden

> On the eve of Yom Kippur in the morning they place him at the eastern gate and pass before him oxen, rams, and sheep, so that he may recognize and become familiar with the service. (Yoma 1:3)

During the high priest's days of seclusion and study, he is shown the various animals that are sacrificed and taught to recognize them. The need for this instruction is not immediately clear, for obviously the priest who is "highest among his brethren" should be able to distinguish between the animals. It seems that this ceremony has symbolic significance. As Knohl and Naeh note, "Ostensibly, the high priest cannot distinguish between a sheep and a bullock! What emerges is a picture of an entirely basic education. It seems, therefore, that there exists – alongside the teaching and instruction that are truly required during the seven days – a ceremonial, ritual 'educational' aspect."

Beyond the educational implications of the days of seclusion, we can find a symbolic dimension in the Mishna's description. The Temple often appears as a symbol of the Garden of Eden, with the priests serving as representations of Adam. Thus, for example, Adam's role in the garden was to "serve and keep" (Genesis 2:15) – two words that are juxtaposed elsewhere in the Bible only in the context of the Temple, in describing the roles of the priests and Levites.[5] Furthermore, the connection between the high priest and Adam in the Garden of Eden emerges as early as the story of the days of consecration in the Tabernacle: Aaron and his sons do not dress upon entering the Tent of Meeting; rather, Moses is the one who dresses them (Exodus 29, Leviticus 8). The wording in the verses evokes the story of the dressing of Adam and Eve before their departure from Eden:

5. Numbers 3:7–8, 8:26, 18:5.

"And the Lord God made for Adam and for his wife **garments** of skins, **and clothed them.**" (Genesis 3:21)	"And for Aaron's sons you shall make **garments**.... And you shall **clothe** Aaron your brother with them, and his sons." (Exodus 28:40–41)

Our mishna strengthens this parallel with another common element: the sacrificial animals being passed before the high priest, recalls Adam naming all of the animals in the Garden of Eden: "And out of the ground the Lord God formed every beast of the field, and every fowl of the air; and brought them to the man to see what he would call them; and whatsoever the man would call every living creature, that was to be the name thereof. And the man gave names to all cattle, and to the fowl of the air, and to every beast of the field" (Genesis 2:19–20). "The eastern gate" of the Temple also evokes the Garden of Eden, which was planted "eastward" (v. 8). Similarly, in Mishna 5, the high priest is adjured in the name of God to adhere to what is said to him, which brings to mind the sin of Adam, who did not adhere to God's instruction: "but of the tree of the knowledge of good and evil – you shall not eat of it" (v. 17). This comparison highlights the elemental nature of Yom Kipper, and the manner in which it constitutes a return to the very beginning, every year anew.

We have learned that Yom Kippur transports the individual back to the starting point, to Creation and the Garden of Eden. The high priest learns everything again, is initiated once more, and is consecrated so that he can serve as the high priest for another year. We can understand this need to start anew every year through the prism of the conception of reality espoused by an ancient foundational book: *Sefer Yetzira*[6] divides reality into three parallel dimensions – world, year, and soul, which can be thought of as space, time, and the human. As opposed to space and the human, which are described in practically infinite terms, time is represented with the unit of a single year. Every year is a microcosm, the beginning of an entire world. The big world and the individual (the little world) are reborn every year to receive their purpose.

6. From 3:3 until the end of the book.

The Talmud (Yoma 3b) refers to Yom Kippur as "the first service held in its place." It is given this definition because every year is a new reality, independent of the previous year. Thus, Yom Kippur is always fresh service in a new "place" to which no one has been, and **every year** we repeat the events involved in the consecration of the Tabernacle. Yom Kippur atones by returning the individual to the starting point, to Creation and the Garden of Eden, to a time that preceded the world's defilement by humanity's sin.

The Wife of the High Priest

יומא א, א

שִׁבְעַת יָמִים קֹדֶם יוֹם הַכִּפּוּרִים מַפְרִישִׁין כֹּהֵן גָּדוֹל מִבֵּיתוֹ לְלִשְׁכַּת פַּלְהֶדְרִין, וּמַתְקִינִין לוֹ כֹּהֵן אַחֵר תַּחְתָּיו, שֶׁמָּא יֶאֱרַע בּוֹ פְּסוּל. רַבִּי יְהוּדָה אוֹמֵר, אַף אִשָּׁה אַחֶרֶת מַתְקִינִין לוֹ, שֶׁמָּא תָמוּת אִשְׁתּוֹ, שֶׁנֶּאֱמַר "וְכִפֶּר בַּעֲדוֹ וּבְעַד בֵּיתוֹ". בֵּיתוֹ, זוֹ אִשְׁתּוֹ. אָמְרוּ לוֹ, אִם כֵּן, אֵין לַדָּבָר סוֹף:

Yoma 1:1

Seven days before Yom Kippur, they remove the high priest from his house to the chamber of the counselors, and they set up another priest to take his place lest something should occur to him to disqualify him [from being able to serve]. Rabbi Yehuda said: They even prepare another wife for him in case his wife should die, as it says, "And he shall make atonement for himself and for his house" (Leviticus 16:6). "His house" – this refers to his wife. They said to him: If so, there would be no end to the matter.

The Mishna includes two rulings relating to the high priest's personal life in the lead-up to Yom Kippur: he must be married, and he must withdraw from his wife. On the face of it, the ideas behind these two rulings contradict one another. Is the relationship between husband and wife a portal to the holy or an impediment to encountering it? We can perhaps resolve this tension if we consider the priest's obligation to marry to be a mere technicality, stemming from the verse, "And he shall make atonement for himself and for his house." But Maimonides implies that there is an essential need for the high priest to be married:

> Similarly, all of the other services performed on this day, such as the offering of the daily incense offering and the kindling of the Candelabrum's lamps, are all performed by a married high priest, as it states: "And he shall make atonement for himself and for his house" (Leviticus 16:7). "His house" – this refers to his wife. (*Mishneh Torah, Avodot Yom HaKippurim* 1:2)

It emerges that marriage is intrinsic to the high priest's identity and a condition for his leading the Yom Kippur rituals. Yet, this essential element cannot be expressed on Yom Kippur itself. I wish to interpret the significance of the tension between the obligations to marry and to withdraw based on the outlook of the holy Zohar. According to the Zohar, unmarried people are incomplete. An unmarried priest is impaired, and thus unworthy of offering sacrifices:

> "When a person (*adam*) brings a sacrifice" – excluding one who is unmarried...Only a person who is both male and female is worthy of bringing an offering. (Zohar, *Vayikra* 5b)

Yet, if a person can become complete only through a male-female relationship, why must the high priest withdraw from his wife? According to one explanation, the high priest's withdrawal is derived from Moses's withdrawal before ascending Mount Sinai, which according to the Zohar was not initially intended:

> Rabbi Yitzḥak asked: Why is the *alef* of "*Vayikra*," "He called," small? He replied: Moses was established in wholeness but not totally, for he withdrew from his wife. In books of the ancients they say this in praise; as for us, we have learned: One who would ascend should link himself above and below; then he is complete. (Zohar, *Vayeḥi* 234b)

The Zohar discusses the small *alef* in the word "*Vayikra*" in the verse, "And the Lord called (*Vayikra*) to Moses, and spoke unto him out of the

Tent of Meeting" (Leviticus 1:1). It explains that notwithstanding the ancient books that praise Moses for withdrawing from his wife, he was in fact marred by his actions, an idea hinted at by the small *alef*. Perfection, the ideal spiritual stature, is attained when one has the capacity to remain connected both above and below – to ascend Mount Sinai without relinquishing his family life. Another passage from the Zohar further elucidates this idea:

> He opened, saying, "*Vayikra el Moshe*," "He called to Moses." Here, a small *alef*. Why? Because this "calling" was not consummate…there, consummation of male and female: "Adam, Seth, Enoch." Adam – consummation of male and female. (Zohar, *Vayeḥi* 239a)

In contrast with the small *alef* in "*Vayikra*," which reflects a lack of completeness due to disconnection, there is an outsize *alef* in the name Adam in the beginning of I Chronicles, reflecting the completeness of the male-female bond.

The very idea of a completeness that can be found only in a union of the feminine and the masculine, and the contrast that the Zohar draws between Moses and Adam, who is on a higher spiritual level, is developed by Rabbi Abraham Isaac Kook:

> There is a difference between that light [of Moses's shining prism] and Adam's level of supernal splendor, in that with the shining prism the body retains some of its power, and from the waist down one is still considered a man – this was said of Moses, and it is why he withdrew from his wife. But with the supernal splendor of Adam, all of one's body is uplifted: "You are Godlike beings." (*Shemoneh Kevatzim* 8:8)[1]

Rabbi Moshe Chaim Luzzatto's book *Mishkanei Elyon* (Exalted Towers) is dedicated to describing the Third Temple. He explains that "Adam's

1. See also *Shemoneh Kevatzim* 3:66.

sin degraded the world" and was the sole reason for the fact that Solomon's Temple did not attain the spiritual level that existed just after Creation. The First and Second Temples were incomplete, but the Third will attain prelapsarian heights. In kabbalistic terms, Solomon's Temple was linked to the *sefira* of *Hokhma* (wisdom), while the third is linked to *Keter* (crown or nothingness).

In light of the Zohar and the vision of Rabbi Luzzatto, we can conclude that in the Third Temple, the high priest's connection with the supernal world will not require him to withdraw and disconnect from the physical world, so that he will be able to encounter divine holiness from a place of wholeness – the union of masculine and feminine.

The High Priest on Yom Kippur: A Journey of Personal Growth

יומא א, ו

אִם הָיָה חָכָם, דּוֹרֵשׁ. וְאִם לָאו, תַּלְמִידֵי חֲכָמִים דּוֹרְשִׁין לְפָנָיו. וְאִם רָגִיל לִקְרוֹת, קוֹרֵא. וְאִם לָאו, קוֹרִין לְפָנָיו. וּבַמֶּה קוֹרִין לְפָנָיו. בְּאִיּוֹב וּבְעֶזְרָא וּבְדִבְרֵי הַיָּמִים. זְכַרְיָה בֶּן קְבוּטָל אוֹמֵר, פְּעָמִים הַרְבֵּה קָרִיתִי לְפָנָיו בְּדָנִיֵּאל:

Yoma 1:6

If he was a sage he would expound, and if not, the disciples of the sages would expound before him. If he was familiar with reading [the Scriptures] he would read, and if not they would read before him. From what would they read before him? From Job, Ezra, and Chronicles. Zekharya ben Kevutal says: I have often read before him from Daniel.

יומא א, ז

בִּקֵּשׁ לְהִתְנַמְנֵם, פִּרְחֵי כְהֻנָּה מַכִּין לְפָנָיו בְּאֶצְבַּע צְרָדָה, וְאוֹמְרִים לוֹ, אִישִׁי כֹּהֵן גָּדוֹל, עֲמוֹד וְהָפֵג אַחַת עַל הָרִצְפָּה. וּמַעֲסִיקִין אוֹתוֹ עַד שֶׁיַּגִּיעַ זְמַן הַשְּׁחִיטָה:

Yoma 1:7

If he wished to sleep, young priests would snap their middle finger before him and say: "Sir high priest, stand up and drive the sleep away by standing once on this [cold] floor. They would keep him busy until the time for the slaughtering [of the daily morning offering] would arrive.

The first mishnayot of our chapter describe the high priest's isolation from his home and friends, and his reinitiation. The subsequent mishnayot draw a picture of the high priest that one must admit is not flattering in the least.

Mishna 6 raises the possibility that the priest is not a sage, and is perhaps even unversed in Scripture. Furthermore, the testimony, "I have often read before him," shows us that this is not merely a theoretical possibility. On the great night, the eve of Yom Kippur, which should be filled with anticipation and excitement before the coming day, an entire team is required to ensure that the high priest does not fall asleep. The means at the team's disposal – "snap their middle finger" and "keep him busy" – do not indicate an atmosphere of awe and respect, to put it mildly, toward the priest who is "highest among his brethren."

To a certain extent, the Mishna here reflects the historical reality in the last days of the Second Temple, when high priests were appointed based on money and political connections, and their personal and religious qualifications were often lacking.

Still, perhaps there is another explanation for the Mishna's descriptions. Yom Kippur is a day of repentance, a day on which the individual is expected to change and improve. The high priest personifies this day, and the Mishna wishes to give voice to the dramatic change that he undergoes throughout it, via the rites that he conducts in the Temple. The image of the high priest as a shallow figure forms a backdrop that calls attention to the future change in him. A comparison of the high priest from the beginning of the tractate to the image that is drawn at the conclusion of the day's rites[1] yields two vastly different figures:

> The high priest [then] came to read. If he wished to read in linen garments, he reads, and if not he reads in his own white cloak. The synagogue attendant would take a Torah scroll and give it to the head of the synagogue, and the head of the synagogue gives it to the deputy high priest, and the deputy high priest gives it to the high priest, and the high priest stands and receives it, and reads [the sections beginning], "After the death…" (Leviticus 16:1–34) and, "But on the tenth…" (Leviticus 23:26–32). Then he would roll up the Torah scroll and put it in his bosom and say, "More

1. Chapter 7 ends the chronological description of the day. Chapter 8 is dedicated to various other subjects, such as the five mortifications of the day.

> than what I have read out before you is written here." And "On the tenth…" (Numbers 29:7–11) that is in the book of Numbers he recites by heart. And he recites on it eight benedictions: "For the law," "For the Temple service," "For thanksgiving," "For the forgiveness of sins," and "For the Temple" on its own, and "For Israel" on its own, and "For Jerusalem" on its own, "For the priests" on their own, and "For the rest of the prayer." (Yoma 7:1)
>
> They brought him his own clothes and he put them on. And they would accompany him to his house. And he would make a day of festivity for his friends whenever he came out of the Holy [of Holies] in peace. (Yoma 7:4)

While the first chapter paints a portrait of a passive high priest who is read to by others, in Chapter 7 he reads aloud before the entire nation and even recites passages he has memorized. The literary structure of the two chapters further highlights this contrast. The three sections that the high priest reads or recites – "After the death," "But on the tenth," and "On the tenth" (7:1) – are parallel to the three books that would be read to him: Job, Ezra, and Chronicles (1:6). The high priest's recitation "by heart" of "On the tenth" in Chapter 7 is parallel to the entreaty, "Sir, high priest, you read it yourself with your own mouth" (1:3), which expresses suspicion that the priest is unfamiliar with the verses.[2]

The description of the high priest's Torah reading depicts him as a major spiritual leader of the Jewish people. The ceremony in which the Torah scroll is transferred from one person to another until it reaches the high priest – "The synagogue attendant would take a Torah scroll and give it to the head of the synagogue, and the head of the synagogue gives it to the deputy high priest, and the deputy high priest gives it to the high priest" – emphasizes his place at the top of the hierarchy. And the eight blessings that he recites after reading from the scroll – "For

2. My thanks to Motti Perry and Shuri Hazan for bringing to my attention the contrast between the high priest's reading here and his inability to read in Chapter 1. Perry expounds on this point in "Parallels Converge," 36–38.

the Temple," "For Israel," etc. – reinforce his position as a fountainhead of bounty and blessing.

In the beginning of the tractate, the High Priest is severed from his household – "they remove the high priest from his house" (1:1) – and his colleagues: "He turned aside and wept, and they turned aside and wept" (1:5). He comes full circle at the end of the holy day, when "they would accompany him to his house" and "he would make a day of festivity for his friends." On the eve of Yom Kippur he cries, but at its conclusion he celebrates.

A liturgical poem that is customary to include in Musaf of Yom Kippur describes the state that the high priest attains by the end of the day: "Indeed, so splendorous was the high priest upon his emergence from the Holy of Holies, alive and unharmed…The sight of the high priest was like a star shining on the eastern horizon."

I often feel like Yom Kippur catches me unprepared. The month of Elul has passed, along with the Ten Days of Repentance, and yet I feel as if I am at the beginning of my path. The journey of the high priest inspires me and encourages me to see that even if I start the holy day on the bottom, by its end I may be soaring through the heights.

The Goats and the Gates: Fate and Miracle

יומא ג, ט	**Yoma 3:9**
בָּא לוֹ לְמִזְרַח הָעֲזָרָה, לִצְפוֹן הַמִּזְבֵּחַ, הַסְּגָן מִימִינוֹ וְרֹאשׁ בֵּית אָב מִשְּׂמֹאלוֹ. וְשָׁם שְׁנֵי שְׂעִירִים, וְקַלְפִּי הָיְתָה שָׁם וּבָהּ שְׁנֵי גוֹרָלוֹת. שֶׁל אֶשְׁכְּרוֹעַ הָיוּ, וַעֲשָׂאָן בֶּן גַּמְלָא שֶׁל זָהָב, וְהָיוּ מַזְכִּירִין אוֹתוֹ לְשֶׁבַח:	He [the high priest] then went to the east of the Temple court, to the north of the altar, the deputy high priest at his right and the head of the [priestly] family [ministering that week] at his left. There were two goats, and an urn was there, and in it were two lots. They were of boxwood, and ben Gamla made them of gold, and they would mention his name in praise.

This description opens the story of the lots placed on the goats that were sacrificed on Yom Kippur, one of which was sacrificed as a sin offering and the other sent to Azazel. Curiously, the narrative flow is interrupted by two mishnayot that appear to deal with an entirely different topic:

> Ben Katin made twelve spigots for the laver, for there had been before only two. He also made a mechanism for the laver, in order that its water should not become unfit by remaining overnight. King Monbaz had all the handles of all the vessels used on Yom Kippur made of gold. His mother, Helena, made a golden candelabrum over the opening of the Sanctuary. She also made a golden tablet, on which the portion concerning the suspected adulteress was inscribed.

> For Nicanor miracles happened to his doors. And they were all mentioned for praise.
>
> And these they mentioned to their shame: Those of the house of Garmu did not want to teach anything about the preparation of the showbread. Those of the house of Avtinas did not teach anything about the preparation of the incense. Hugras, a Levite, knew a chapter [concerning] the song but did not want to teach it. Ben Kamtzar did not want teach anyone his art of writing. Concerning the former it is said: "The memory of the righteous shall be for a blessing" (Proverbs 10:7); concerning the others it is said (v. 7): "but the name of the wicked shall rot." (Yoma 3:10–11)

These mishnayot, which cite, both for praise and for scorn, figures who were active in the Temple, must be considered in the context of the end of 3:9: "and ben Gamla made them of gold, and they would mention his name in praise." Still, the length and detail of the ensuing mishnayot are hard to explain, especially since they postpone until the next chapter the rest of the story of the goats and their lots.

It seems that there is an essential link between these two mishnayot and the description of the lots, which led to their juxtaposition. The list of personages cited for praise and scorn can be seen as a parallel to the two lots, one to God and the other to Azazel. The righteous to God: "The memory of the righteous shall be for a blessing," and the wicked to Azazel: "but the name of the wicked shall rot."[1] But the parallel is incomplete, and the difference hints at the major implication: God decides where each of the two goats will go, while human beings, who are responsible for their own fates, decide on their own path on Yom Kippur.

The material that the lots were made of, boxwood, which the Mishna elsewhere states is the color of the children of Israel's skin, also alludes to the two options faced by the individual:[2]

---

1. My thanks to Hovav Yehieli who pointed out to me that the manner in which the Mishna contrasts the righteous and the wicked corresponds to its contrasting of the two goats – one to God and the other to Azazel.
2. My thanks to Motti Perry for bringing my attention to this connection. My contribution

> Rabbi Yishmael says: The children of Israel (may I be atonement for them!) are like boxwood, neither black nor white but of an intermediate shade. (Nega'im 2:1)

That mishna yields another parallel between the fate of the goats and that of the people of Israel. The Mishna in Nega'im hints at two connotations for the word "intermediate." The overt connotation is skin of a shade that is neither black nor white, but rather somewhat dark. However, the context of the mishna – afflictions that are caused by sin, alongside Rabbi Yishmael's readiness to atone for Israel – raises another possibility: The people of Israel are intermediate not only in the color of their skin, but also in terms of their spiritual stature. They are neither righteous not wicked.

Those on this intermediate level have a special connection to Yom Kippur and the two paths that it represents. Like the two goats, they face two possible fates:

> Rabbi Kruspedai said in the name of Rabbi Yoḥanan: Three books are opened [in heaven] on Rosh HaShana, one for the thoroughly wicked, one for the thoroughly righteous, and one for the intermediate. The thoroughly righteous are forthwith inscribed definitively in the book of life; the thoroughly wicked are forthwith inscribed definitively in the book of death; the doom of the intermediate is suspended from Rosh HaShana until Yom Kippur. If they deserve well, they are inscribed in the book of life; if they do not deserve well, they are inscribed in the book of death. (Rosh HaShana 16b)

The Lots and the Miracle of Nicanor

One of the figures praised by the Mishna is Nicanor, for whose doors "miracles happened." The meaning of Nicanor's miracle becomes clear when it is compared to the story of the lots.

---

here is the elaboration on the double meaning of the word "intermediate."

The Bavli notes that one of the mitzvot that is a source of ridicule from gentiles is the commandment to send a goat to Azazel.[3] According to Nahmanides, the reason for this is "because they think that we act as they do," meaning that they think sending the goat, which is thought to stand for a demonic force, to Azazel, proves that Jewish people, too, worships more than one god, the second of whom resides in the desert. But that could not be further from the truth, as Nahmanides explains:

> This then is the reason [for having someone] who casts the lots [on the two goats]. If the priests were to dedicate them only verbally [without casting the lots], saying, "one for the Lord" and "one for Azazel," that would be like worshipping [Azazel] or taking a vow in its name. Rather, the priest set the two goats before the Eternal at the door of the Tent of Meeting, **for both of them were a gift to God, and he gave to His servant** [Azazel] **that portion which came to him from God. It is he [the priest] who cast the lots on them, but it is His hand that apportioned them**, something like that which says: The lot is cast into his lap; but the whole disposing of it is of the Eternal. Even after the casting of the lots, the priest placed the two goats before the Eternal, thus proclaiming that both are His and that by sending one away [to the desert] we intend merely to fulfill God's wish, just as it said: "[And the goat on which the lot fell for Azazel] shall be set alive before the Eternal, to make atonement over him, to send him away..." That is the reason why we do not ourselves do any act of slaughtering [of that goat, as this would imply that it is a proper offering, which requires slaughtering]. (Nahmanides on Leviticus 16:8)

The Jewish people bring the two goats before God, and He, by way of the lots, chooses which will be sent to Azazel. Thus, the very act of giving one of the goats to Azazel, which is effected through God's choice,

3. Yoma 67b.

defines the hierarchy between them, clarifying who is the master and who the servant. The ceremony teaches us that all of the forces in the world, including that of Azazel, are under the dominion of God, King of the universe.

The Tosefta relates the story of Nicanor:

> What was the miracle that happened to [the doors of Nicanor]? They said: When Nicanor was bringing them from Alexandria, a sea wave came over them to drown them. They took one of them and threw it in the sea. They wanted to throw the second one as well, but Nicanor did not let them. He said to them: If you throw the second, throw me in with it. He was grieved until he reached the port of Jaffa. As soon as he reached the port of Jaffa, [the first gate] came up from underneath the boat. Some say a sea monster had swallowed it, and when Nicanor reached the port of Jaffa it spewed it out and threw it up on dry land. (Tosefta Yoma 2:4)

The ship got caught in a storm and was in danger of sinking. The sailors threw one of Nicanor's doors into sea, and he risked his life to save the second door for the Temple. While he survived, he lamented the loss of the first door. But God showed His satisfaction with Nicanor's sacrifice by miraculously saving – along with Nicanor and the door he kept aboard the ship – the first door, which had been thrown into the sea.

The Hebrew word *se'ir* (goat) looks similar to the word *shaar* (gate), and this similarity is reflected here in the content of these elements in the mishna. Like the gates, the goats are meant to stand before God in the Temple. The goat that is sent to Azazel corresponds to the door that was either thrown into the sea[4] or swallowed by a sea monster. Ultimately, we find out, it is God's will directing the course of events and the final fates of both the goats and the gates, whether through miracle or lot, as even that which is ostensibly for Azazel in fact belongs to God.

---

4. The Hebrew word for "throwing" (*hatala*) is also used in the context of casting lots. See Tosefta Bava Batra 3:7.

In the Bavli's telling of the story of the miracle, the similarity to the lots is even more conspicuous:

> Our Rabbis taught: What miracles happened to his doors? It was reported that when Nicanor had gone to fetch doors from Alexandria of Egypt, on his return a gale arose in the sea to drown him. Thereupon they took one of his doors and cast it into the sea **and yet the sea would not stop its rage**. When, thereupon, they prepared to cast the other into the sea, he rose and clung to it, saying: "Cast me in with it!" [They did so, and] the sea immediately stopped its raging.

A close reading of the text reveals that, in casting the doors into the sea, the sailors did not merely seek to lighten the ship's load: "Thereupon they took one of his doors and cast it into the sea and yet the sea would not stop its rage." Rather, by throwing the doors, they sought to appease the sea with a sacrifice. Yet the sea continued to rage. The sailors, however, persisted with their hypothesis and concluded that their gift fell short; therefore, they tried to "sacrifice" the other door as well. Nicanor, in contrast, wanted the door to go to God, so he risked his life to save it. And it was his act, which was directed toward God, rather than toward appeasing the sea, that quieted the sea's rage.[5] The sailors' belief that the sea is an independent force is contrasted here with Nicanor's faith in God's kingship over the world.[6] This understanding of Nicanor's story lends special significance to the assertion in the *Sifra* that the two goats were placed at Nicanor's gates:[7]

---

5. Thus, according to the Bavli there are two miracles: not only was the door returned, but also the storm ceased. Note that the Bavli and Mishna say "miracles," while the Tosefta says "miracle."
6. Alma Cohen Vardi pointed out to me that the gates and the goats evoke the story of Jonah the prophet, which is read during Minḥa on Yom Kippur. Jonah, like Nicanor and his gates, sets sail on a ship that gets caught in a storm. There, as with the ceremony of the goats, the sailors cast lots, and Jonah, whose lot is chosen, is cast into the sea, as are the doors to the gates. Like in the Nicanor story, God miraculously intervenes, saving Jonah from drowning and leading him to shore.
7. The outlook of the *Sifra* differs from that of the Mishna, by which the lots were cast inside the courtyard.

> "And he shall take the two goats" – this teaches us that one is dependent on the other. "Before the Lord at the door of the Tent of Meeting" – he places them at Nicanor's gates, with their rumps pointed eastward and their faces westward. (*Sifra, Aḥarei Mot* 2)

Two Nicanors

In conclusion, we will note that rabbinic literature features two figures named Nicanor. The first is the one whose doors came to adorn the Temple, while the second was made an example of – his body parts came to hang on the gates of Jerusalem, opposite the Temple. In other words, the first was cited for a blessing, to God, and the second, whose name shall rot, to Azazel:

> It has been taught: Nicanor was one of the Greek generals; every day he waved his hand against Judah and Jerusalem and exclaimed, "When shall it fall into my hands that I may trample upon it?" But when the Hasmonean rulers proved victorious and triumphed over him, they cut off his thumbs and his big toes and suspended them from the gates of Jerusalem, as if to say: Of the mouth that spoke arrogantly, of the hands that were waved against Jerusalem, may vengeance be exacted. (Taanit 18b)

To Enter and Exit the Holy of Holies

יומא ה, א

הוֹצִיאוּ לוֹ אֶת הַכַּף וְאֶת הַמַּחְתָּה, וְחָפַן מְלֹא חָפְנָיו וְנָתַן לְתוֹךְ הַכַּף, הַגָּדוֹל לְפִי גָדְלוֹ, וְהַקָּטָן לְפִי קָטְנוֹ, וְכָךְ הָיְתָה מִדָּתָהּ. נָטַל אֶת הַמַּחְתָּה בִּימִינוֹ וְאֶת הַכַּף בִּשְׂמֹאלוֹ.הָיָה מְהַלֵּךְ בַּהֵיכָל, עַד שֶׁמַּגִּיעַ לְבֵין שְׁתֵּי הַפָּרוֹכוֹת הַמַּבְדִּילוֹת בֵּין הַקֹּדֶשׁ וּבֵין קֹדֶשׁ הַקֳּדָשִׁים, וּבֵינֵיהֶן אַמָּה. רַבִּי יוֹסֵי אוֹמֵר, לֹא הָיְתָה שָׁם אֶלָּא פָּרֹכֶת אַחַת בִּלְבָד, שֶׁנֶּאֱמַר "וְהִבְדִּילָה הַפָּרֹכֶת לָכֶם בֵּין הַקֹּדֶשׁ וּבֵין קֹדֶשׁ הַקֳּדָשִׁים". הַחִיצוֹנָה הָיְתָה פְּרוּפָה מִן הַדָּרוֹם, וְהַפְּנִימִית מִן הַצָּפוֹן. מְהַלֵּךְ בֵּינֵיהֶן, עַד שֶׁמַּגִּיעַ לַצָּפוֹן. הִגִּיעַ לַצָּפוֹן, הוֹפֵךְ פָּנָיו לַדָּרוֹם, מְהַלֵּךְ לִשְׂמֹאלוֹ עִם הַפָּרֹכֶת עַד שֶׁהוּא מַגִּיעַ לָאָרוֹן, הִגִּיעַ לָאָרוֹן. נוֹתֵן אֶת הַמַּחְתָּה בֵּין שְׁנֵי הַבַּדִּים. צָבַר אֶת הַקְּטֹרֶת עַל גַּבֵּי גֶחָלִים, וְנִתְמַלֵּא כָל הַבַּיִת

Yoma 5:1

They brought out to him the ladle and the pan, and he took two hands full [of incense] and put it into the ladle, a large [high priest] according to his size, a small one according to his size, and thus was its measure. He took the pan in his right hand and the ladle in his left hand. He walked through the Sanctuary until he came to the place between the two curtains that separated the Holy from the Holy of Holies; between them was [a space of] one cubit. Rabbi Yosei says: There was but one curtain, as it is said: "And the curtain shall serve you as a partition between the Holy and the Holy of Holies" (Exodus 26:33). The outer curtain was looped on the south side and the inner curtain on the north side. He walked along between them until he reached the north side. When he reached the north side he turned round to the south and went on along the curtain, to his left, until he reached the Ark. When he reached the Ark he put the pan of burning coals between the two poles. He heaped up the

כֻּלּוֹ עָשָׁן. יָצָא וּבָא לוֹ בְדֶרֶךְ בֵּית כְּנִיסָתוֹ וּמִתְפַּלֵּל תְּפִלָּה קְצָרָה בַּבַּיִת הַחִיצוֹן, וְלֹא הָיָה מַאֲרִיךְ בִּתְפִלָּתוֹ, שֶׁלֹּא לְהַבְעִית אֶת יִשְׂרָאֵל:

incense upon the coals, and the whole house became full with smoke. He came out by the way he entered, and in the outer house he uttered a short prayer. He did not make the prayer long, so as not to frighten Israel.

This tractate is called "Yoma," or "The Day," a title that highlights the unique significance of Yom Kippur. *Sefer Yetzira* (3:2) divides Creation into three dimensions: world, year, and soul, which can be thought of as place, time, and the human. It is apparent from the rituals of the day that Yom Kippur is the apex of all of these three dimensions. It takes place in the holiest location in the world – the Holy of Holies; on the holiest day of the year – a "Sabbath of solemn rest" (*Shabbat shabbaton*); and the rituals are performed by the high priest. Thus, holiness is manifested in all its glory, and in all three dimensions.

Our mishna describes the high point of the great day, when the priest enters the Holy of Holies. The mishna is placed in the heart of the tractate, with four chapters preceding and four following. Thus, in terms of the literary structure, it too is innermost.[1]

After the priest places the incense on the coals, "the whole house" would fill with smoke. The Mishna here alludes to a verse in the book of Isaiah, "and the house was filled with smoke" (6:4), whose context is God's revelation to Isaiah and dedication of him as a prophet.[2] There are further similarities between our mishna and Isaiah's vision. For example, in the mishna the high priest "walked through the Sanctuary," while in the book of Isaiah, "His train filled the [Sanctuary]" (v. 1). Our mishna describes triple holiness – the curtain serves "as a partition between the Holy [the Sanctuary] and the Holy of Holies [the inner Sanctuary]" – while Isaiah describes hearing the call "Holy, holy, holy" (v. 3). These similarities link our mishna to the chapter in Isaiah, and thus forge a comparison between the high priest's entrance into the Holy of Holies and Isaiah's vision.

1. My friend David Tzuri pointed this out to me.
2. Motti Perry, "Parallels Converge," 46–47.

The Understanding That We Do Not Understand

For me, our mishna is also the heart of the chapter for other, personal reasons. In the summer of 2002, at the Otniel yeshiva, we studied the chapters in Tractate Yoma that discuss the rituals of Yom Kippur. In preparation for the summer session, one of my beloved students, Avi Sabag, studied the topic of the cloud of incense smoke. He explained to his study partner that he thought the high priest needed that cloud of smoke in the Holy of Holies because "our ticket to enter holy places is the understanding that we do not understand" – the cloud is there to obstruct the priest's vision. Several days later we learned that this insight of Avi's had been our preparation for a painful event that drove home the extent to which "we do not understand." Two days before Passover, Avi was murdered by terrorists on the road between Beit Hagai and Otniel, on his way home to his new wife, Dafna.

Shortly thereafter Israel launched Operation Defensive Shield, and I once again found myself engaged in this mishna. Most of my students were called up to join the fighting, and I tried to keep them up to date on our studies by phone. During one conversation, a student expressed sorrow for missing our course on Yoma. I told him about the ending of our mishna: "And in the outer house he uttered a short prayer. He did not make the prayer long, so as not to frighten Israel.[3]" In the most important moment of his life, the high priest faces the Holy of Holies and prays to God. Though his inclination would naturally be to extend that experience of intimacy as long as possible, the high priest knows that the people are waiting outside, worried and impatient, so

3. My brother Rabbi Dani Genack posited that the high priest's consideration for the people's worry rectifies the sin of the Golden Calf, when the Israelites did not know whether some tragedy had befallen Moses on Mount Sinai. Dani's reading of the mishna is part of a comprehensive approach to the essence of Yom Kippur and its connection to the Giving of the Torah. Among the most salient points is the fact that Yom Kippur is the day when the second Tablets were given, and on which the high priest enters the Holy of Holies, where the Tablets lie within the Ark. See Dani Genack, "Notes on Tractate Yoma," in *K'sones Yosef: In Tribute to Our Illustrious Teacher and Friend Rabbi Joseph Wanefsky* (New York: Rabbi Isaac Elchanon Theological Seminary, 2002) [Hebrew], 327–33.

he relinquishes his place in the Sanctuary and emerges. I explained to this soldier that he is like the high priest, going out from a place of holiness – the *beit midrash* – to a place where the people of Israel are distressed and in need of his assistance.

Mortifications and Repentance, Atonement and Purity

יומא ח, א

יוֹם הַכִּפּוּרִים אָסוּר בַּאֲכִילָה וּבִשְׁתִיָּה וּבִרְחִיצָה וּבְסִיכָה וּבִנְעִילַת הַסַּנְדָּל וּבְתַשְׁמִישׁ הַמִּטָּה. וְהַמֶּלֶךְ וְהַכַּלָּה יִרְחֲצוּ אֶת פְּנֵיהֶם. וְהֶחָיָה תִנְעוֹל אֶת הַסַּנְדָּל, דִּבְרֵי רַבִּי אֱלִיעֶזֶר, וַחֲכָמִים אוֹסְרִין:

Yoma 8:1

[On] Yom Kippur it is forbidden to eat, to drink, to wash, to anoint oneself, to put on sandals, or to have intercourse. A king or bride may wash their face, and a woman after childbirth may put on sandals, says Rabbi Eliezer. But the Sages forbid it.

Priest and Community

The first seven chapter of Tractate Yoma focus on one person – the high priest – and his service in one place – the Temple. By directing all of our attention at a single protagonist in a single arena, the Mishna creates a powerful and detailed picture. But this picture does not acknowledge other aspects of Yom Kippur or its spiritual significance. The final chapter balances out the previous emphasis on the priest and the Temple, by discussing topics that are not part of the priest's service. Thus the tractate presents a complete picture of Yom Kippur, with its range of meaning.

The chapter's first mishna details the mortifications that we are required to engage in on Yom Kippur. By practicing self-denial, the entire nation participates in the process of atonement, which is not dependent only on the high priest.

Many explanations have been offered as to the meaning and essence of the mortifications. According to *Pirkei DeRabbi Eliezer,*[1] for example, the mortifications remove one from the corporeal world so that one can ascend to the level of the angels. In other words, by abstaining, each and every Jew – not just the high priest – attains a lofty, holy status on Yom Kippur. In other words, suffering,[2] and especially fasting,[3] turns one into an offering of sorts. According to this idea, just as the high priest brings sacrificial offerings, so other Jews sacrifice themselves by mortifying their bodies.[4]

Action and Repentance

At the center of the high priest's service, as it is described throughout the tractate, is ritual, i.e., action. Chapter 8, in contrast, says that the internal process is a vital prerequisite for atonement:

> The sin offering and the certain-guilt offering effect atonement. Death and Yom Kippur effect atonement together with repentance. Repentance effects atonement for light transgressions: [violation of] positive commandments and negative commandments. And for more severe transgressions, [repentance] suspends [the divine punishment], until Yom Kippur arrives and effects atonement. (Yoma 8:8)
>
> One who says: I shall sin and repent, sin and repent,[5] they do not afford him the opportunity to repent. [If one

---

1. Chapter 45.
2. See *Sifrei* on Deuteronomy, 32.
3. Berakhot 17a.
4. It is noteworthy that the structure of the tractate reflects that of the verses in Leviticus 16:3–28: there is a description first of the high priest's service and then of the mortifications.
5. This is like the assertion, "Tomorrow I'll start a diet," which is indicative of a propensity for self-deception. Here, the attitude is that repentance can always wait another day.

> says]: I shall sin and Yom Kippur will atone for me, Yom Kippur does not effect atonement. (Yoma 8:9)

Conspicuously absent from the paths to atonement listed by the Mishna – sacrifices, repentance, death, and Yom Kippur – is the goat sent to Azazel bearing all of the Jewish people's sins, which is discussed at length in the Torah and Mishna. It is reasonable to assume that when the Mishna says, "Yom Kippur," it is referring to the sacrificial goats along with the rest of the day's offerings, which, when combined with repentance, effect atonement. It follows that according to the Mishna, even the ceremonies of Yom Kippur, like death, do not effect atonement without repentance.[6]

Furthermore, the head of the goat sent to Azazel is adorned with a thread of crimson wool (Yoma 4:2). According to Rabbi Yishmael, when the goat reached the desert, "the thread turned white, as it is written (Isaiah 1:18): 'Though your sins be as scarlet, they shall be as white as snow'" (Yoma 6:8). From the context of the verse quoted, one can learn more about the connection between repentance, sacrifices, and atonement:

> To what purpose is the multitude of your sacrifices to Me? says the Lord; I am full of the burnt offerings of rams, and the fat of fed beasts; and I do not delight in the blood of bullocks, or of lambs, or of he-goats.... Wash you, make you clean, put away the evil of your doings from before My eyes, cease to do evil; learn to do well; seek justice, relieve the oppressed, judge the fatherless, plead for the widow. Come now, and let us reason together, says the Lord; though your sins be as scarlet, they shall be as white

---

6. The Mishna, taken literally, does imply that the sin offering and the certain-guilt offering effect atonement even without repentance. However, it is possible that the explanation lies in the fact that the sin offering, and sometimes the guilt offering as well (for instance, in the case of one who accidentally misappropriated the priests' portions), are brought to atone for unintentional transgressions that do not defile one's soul. Further along we will encounter the opinion of the Tosefta, which says that these sacrifices, too, require repentance.

> as snow; though they be red like crimson, they shall be as wool. (Isaiah 1:11, 16–18)

There is no value to the Temple rituals if they are divorced from moral behavior. God provides atonement for one's sins only when one removes oneself from evil.

The idea that repentance is a prerequisite for atonement is stressed in the Tosefta.[7] It describes the various stages of atonement, which are based in repentance. Only when they are combined with a process of remorse can sacrifices effect atonement for the individual.

So far we have seen only one side of the outlook put forward by the Mishna and Tosefta – an internal process of repentance as a condition for atonement. But the Mishna gives weight to action as well; repentance alone does not suffice, except in trifling matters. Sin is a real, concrete event, which can be dealt with only on a concrete plane, in the reality in which it took place. The individual must pay a price for the transgression – either suffering or death – or wait for the special time provided by God, Yom Kippur.

I believe that one of the most important teachings of Judaism is that there is a constant movement between internal reality and physical reality, and between abstract and concrete; it calls us to action via mitzvot, but also emphasizes the significance of the expression of our heart and spirit when we do act: "let our hearts cleave to Your commandments, and unite our hearts to love and fear Your name."

The Human and the Divine

The third and final topic – of both Chapter 8 and the entire tractate – is repentance and atonement among people. Contrary to the impression that arises from the chapters that discuss the service of the high priest, Yom Kippur is not only about repairing humanity's relationship with God, but also repairing relations between humans:

7. Yoma 4:6–9.

> For transgressions between man and God, Yom Kippur effects atonement, but for transgressions between man and his fellow, Yom Kippur does not effect atonement, until he has pacified his fellow. (Yoma 8:9)

The purpose of the sacrifices is to pacify God.[8] The wording of the Mishna, "until he has pacified his fellow," draws a parallel between the reconciliation of God and a human being, and reconciliation among human beings: Just as one must pacify God to rectify a trespass, so one must pacify one's fellow. The Mishna adds, furthermore, that the requirement to pacify the other cannot be disconnected from the requirement to pacify God, because He too participates in the interpersonal relationship. Even after one has pacified one's fellow, it is God who completes the process of atonement, via the holy day: "Yom Kippur does not effect atonement, until he has pacified his fellow." It follows that interpersonal transgressions are also considered sins before God, and both relationships must be restored.

The Conclusion of the Tractate

Tractate Yoma ends with a statement from Rabbi Akiva:

> Rabbi Akiva said: Happy are you, Israel! Before whom are you purified? And who is it that purifies you? Your Father who is in heaven, as it is said: "And I will sprinkle pure water upon you and you shall be pure" (Ezekiel 36:25). And it further says: "You are the hope (*mikve*) of Israel, the Lord" (Jeremiah 17:13) – just as a *mikve* purifies the impure, so too does the Holy One, blessed be He, purify Israel. (ibid)

The rituals of sprinkling the blood and sending the goat off to the desert pose the danger that people will develop the impression that these are acts of magic with inherent power. Thus, the Mishna concludes our tractate, which is devoted to the service of the high priest, with

8. Leviticus, e.g., 1:3.

the assertion that God alone is the source of purification from sin. It is only He who has the power to redeem the Jewish people from the sins of the past.

Eating in the Sukka Is Like Eating an Offering

סוכה ב, ו

רַבִּי אֱלִיעֶזֶר אוֹמֵר, אַרְבַּע עֶשְׂרֵה סְעוּדוֹת חַיָּב אָדָם לֶאֱכוֹל בַּסֻּכָּה, אַחַת בַּיּוֹם וְאַחַת בַּלַּיְלָה. וַחֲכָמִים אוֹמְרִים, אֵין לַדָּבָר קִצְבָה, חוּץ מִלֵּילֵי יוֹם טוֹב רִאשׁוֹן שֶׁל חַג בִּלְבָד. וְעוֹד אָמַר רַבִּי אֱלִיעֶזֶר, מִי שֶׁלֹּא אָכַל לֵילֵי יוֹם טוֹב הָרִאשׁוֹן, יַשְׁלִים בְּלֵילֵי יוֹם טוֹב הָאַחֲרוֹן. וַחֲכָמִים אוֹמְרִים, אֵין לַדָּבָר תַּשְׁלוּמִין, עַל זֶה נֶאֱמַר (קהלת א), מְעֻוָּת לֹא יוּכַל לִתְקֹן, וְחֶסְרוֹן לֹא יוּכַל לְהִמָּנוֹת:

Sukka 2:6

Rabbi Eliezer says: A person is obligated to eat fourteen meals in the sukka, one on each day and one on each night. But the Sages say: There is no fixed number, except on the first night of the festival alone. Furthermore, Rabbi Eliezer said: If one did not eat in the sukka on the first night of the festival, he may make up for it on the last night of the festival. But the Sages say: There is no compensation for this. And of this it was said (Ecclesiastes 1:15): "That which is crooked cannot be made straight, and that which is lacking cannot be counted."

The second half of the mishna implies a parallel between eating in the sukka and eating sacrifices:

> Furthermore, Rabbi Eliezer said: If one did not eat in the sukka on the first night of the festival, he may make up for it on the last night of the festival. But the Sages say: There is no compensation for this. And of this it was said: "That which is crooked cannot be made straight, and that which is lacking cannot be counted." (Sukka 2:6)

This law, by which, according to Rabbi Eliezer, if one misses a meal on Sukkot one must make it up, recalls the laws of the festival (*ḥagiga*) offerings. There as well, if one does not bring it on the first day of the festival, one can bring it throughout the next seven days, even though the final day is after the festival. The *Rishonim* (on Sukka 26a) noticed this parallel:

> For he opines that it can be made up, just like offerings can be made up, on the first day and even on the final day of Yom Tov. (Rashi)
>
> [One can make up the missed meal] even until the night of the final day of Yom Tov, and all the more so during the festival itself, for he derives it from festival offerings. (Ritva)

The similarity between the style and structure of our mishna and the style and structure of the Mishna in Tractate Ḥagiga supports this idea:

Rabbi Eliezer said: If one did not eat in the sukka on the first night of the festival, he may make up for it on the last night of the festival. But the Sages say: There is no compensation for this. And of this it was said: "That which is crooked cannot be made straight, and that which is lacking cannot be counted." (Sukka 2:6)	If one did not bring one's *ḥagiga* on the first day of the festival [of Sukkot], he may bring it during the whole of the festival, even on the last festival day. If the festival passed and one did not bring the festival offering, one is no longer liable for it. And of this it was said: "That which is crooked cannot be made straight, and that which is lacking cannot be counted" (Ḥagiga 1:6).

Both mishnayot address commandments that are tied to the festival of Sukkot: the first is about eating in the Sukka, while the second discusses the festival offering. How are the two similar? For one, both commandments can be made up, at least according to Rabbi Eliezer. In addition, the length of time during which they can be made up is identical. This is especially noticeable with the mention of the last festival day, Shemini

Atzeret, which is a separate festival. This is deduced by way of a *gezeira shava*, or verbal analogy:

> Rabbi Yoḥanan said in the name of Rabbi Yishmael: [The term] "solemn assembly" (*atzeret*) is used for the seventh day of Passover, and [the term] *atzeret* is used for the eighth day of the festival [of Sukkot]. Just as there it intimates that one can make good, so here it intimates that one can make good. (Ḥagiga 9a)

Though there is no written source for making up a missed Sukkot meal on Shemini Atzeret, it seems that the law was derived by analogy from Ḥagiga: The verse "that which is lacking cannot be counted" in both mishnayot creates a literary link between the two.

But what is at the base of the allowance to make up a meal that one did not eat in the sukka?

In the biblical era and the Second Temple era, the Temple occupied a crucial role, especially during Sukkot. The festival was the time that King Solomon chose to dedicate the Temple. During Sukkot the Temple also played host to special ceremonies, such as the water libation, the placing of the willow branches, and Simḥat Beit HaSho'eva. The pilgrims celebrated the festival in Jerusalem and built sukkot in the shadow of the Temple. Dwelling in the sukka was seen as an essential aspect of the pilgrimage; hence the link between the Temple ritual and the sukka.[1] Perhaps this is the source for the gravity ascribed to the commandments relating to the sukka.

The prevailing opinion among the Sages is that of Rabbi Akiva, by which the sukka symbolizes the clouds of glory that encircled the Israelites in the desert (*Sifra, Emor* 17:11). This comparison deepens the link between the sukka and the Temple, and defines one's sojourn in the sukka as taking place in the shadow of the Divine Presence.

Expressions of the link between the sukka and the Temple exist from as far back as the Second Temple period. The Temple Scroll, part

---

1. See my book, *Water, Creation and Divinity: Sukkot in the Philosophy of Halakha* (Jerusalem: Maggid Books, 2008) [Hebrew], 35–39.

of the trove of Dead Sea Scrolls uncovered in Qumran, states that the elders should reside in sukkot until the Sukkot sacrifice is brought:

> [A] place for sukkot. The [pillars] shall be eight cubits high, and the sukkot shall be made on their [roof] each year at the festival of Sukkot for the elders of the congregation ... who will ascend and dwell there until the sacrificing of the [burnt offering] on the festival of Sukkot each year. (Temple Scroll, 42:12–17)[2]

Based on this source, Jeffrey Rubenstein raises the possibility that the Israelites' dwelling in sukkot corresponds to the priests' sacrificial service.[3] Rabbi Eliezer's approach in the Mishna can be seen as an elaboration of this idea. However, according to Rabbi Eliezer, there is no option to join the Temple rites by placing a sukka in the Temple and dwelling in it while the sacrifices are being brought; rather, to his mind, the very act of eating in the sukka has the status of a sacrifice.

This reading of the Mishna makes clear why the Yerushalmi cites the days of consecration, when the Tabernacle was consecrated, as a source for the scope of the obligation to eat in the sukka:

> What is the reasoning of Rabbi Eliezer [in obligating one to eat fourteen meals in the sukka]? Here, "**You shall dwell** [in booths seven days]" (Leviticus 23:42) is stated, and there it is stated, "And at the door of the Tent of Meeting **you shall dwell** day and night seven days" (8:35). Just as in the case of the dwelling stated there the nights are equated to the days, so too in the case of the dwelling stated here the nights are equated to the days. (Y. Sukka, chap. 2)

Sukka is a unique mitzva because the focus on eating is not about the quality of the fare or about foods that are forbidden. In contrast with

---

2. Available at archive.org.
3. Jeffrey Rubenstein, *The History of Sukkot During the Second Temple and Rabbinic Periods* (Atlanta: Scholars Press, 1995) 66, note 89.

the obligation to consume the *pesaḥ* sacrifice, matza, and bitter herb on Passover, on Sukkot we are enjoined to eat whatever we want, as long as we do so within the consecrated space, thus fulfilling our obligation to dwell in the sukka.

Sitting in My House, the House of the Lord

סוכה ב, ט

כָּל שִׁבְעַת הַיָּמִים אָדָם עוֹשֶׂה סֻכָּתוֹ קֶבַע וּבֵיתוֹ עֲרַאי. יָרְדוּ גְשָׁמִים, מֵאֵימָתַי מֻתָּר לְפַנּוֹת, מִשֶּׁתִּסְרַח הַמִּקְפָּה. מָשְׁלוּ מָשָׁל, לְמָה הַדָּבָר דּוֹמֶה, לְעֶבֶד שֶׁבָּא לִמְזוֹג כּוֹס לְרַבּוֹ, וְשָׁפַךְ לוֹ קִיתוֹן עַל פָּנָיו:

Sukka 2:9

All seven days [of the festival] a person must make the sukka his permanent residence and his house his temporary residence. If rain fell, when may one be permitted to leave [the sukka]? When the porridge becomes spoiled. They made a parable: to what can this be compared? To a servant who comes to fill the cup for his master, and he poured a pitcher over his face.

A Servant Before His Master

In the tractate's second chapter, we encounter a mishna that underlines the sukka's similarity to the Temple:

> If rain fell, when may one be permitted to leave [the sukka]? When the porridge becomes spoiled. They made a parable: to what can this be compared? To a servant who comes to fill the cup for his master, and he poured a pitcher over his face.

The servant who comes before his master represents one who wishes to fulfill the mitzva of dwelling in the sukka. In the analogy, the master, who pours water from the pitcher on the servant's face in response to something the servant does, is likened to God, who pours rain on the head of the person fulfilling the commandment, in response to his dwelling in the sukka. In analogies, there is always the question of what lesson one can learn from the parable. Walfish demonstrates how the analogy fits organically within the structure of our chapter:[1] The chapter opens with the exemption of a slave from the mitzva of dwelling in the sukka, a statement that is reiterated toward the end of the chapter, in mishna 8. The analogy appears in the following mishna, which concludes the two chapters that deal with the laws of sukka. In light of the analogy and its placement in the chapter, we can deduce that one who sits in the sukka is like a servant who comes before God.

The servant-master relationship described in the Mishna recalls various descriptions in the Bible and rabbinic literature of the pilgrimage to the Temple, for example, "Three times in the year all your males shall appear before the face of the Lord God" (Exodus 23:17). The pilgrim presents himself before the Lord like a servant before his master. The intimacy is conveyed by the words "before the face." Our mishna, perhaps alluding to the above verse, also uses the word "face," implying an intimate, face-to-face connection. The analogy of the master and the servant is reiterated by early *Amora'im*, in halakhic and aggadic sources that address the mitzva of festival pilgrimage:

> But as regards slaves, from where do we deduce [their exemption]? Rav Huna said: Scripture says: "before the face of the Lord God." [This means] one who has one lord, excluding one who has another lord. (Ḥagiga 4a)

Thus we find a common thread linking the two mishnayot that we read in Chapter 2 of Tractate Sukka. In 2:6, Rabbi Eliezer describes eating in the sukka as analogous to eating the festival offering. Similarly, the

1. Walfish, Literary Phenomena, 45.

analogy in 2:9, which compares one who eats in the sukka to a servant coming before his master, portrays him as one who comes before God.

My Sukka Is My Home

Alongside the sukka's Temple-like attributes, the existence of the requirement to sleep in the sukka (Sukka 2:1) indicates that it is not entirely a miniature Temple. In the opening of our mishna we learn that over the seven days of the festival, the sukka is considered a person's home:

> All seven days [of the festival] a man must make the sukka his permanent residence and his house his temporary residence. (Sukka 2:9)

This idea is driven home in other instances where the Mishna employs the word "house" in reference to the sukka:

> One who was on a journey and had no lulav to [ritually] take, when he enters his **house** he should take it [even if he is] at his table. (Sukka 3:9)
>
> [T]hey instituted that each man should take [his lulav] **in his own house**. (Sukka 4:4)

According to the Mishna, during Sukkot one must reside in one's sukka rather than in one's house – so why does it use the word "house" to denote a sukka? It seems the reason is that "one's sukka is considered his house throughout the festival."[2]

The Mishna portrays the dual aspects of the sukka: It is both a house where a person dwells and a representation of the perfected home – a place where God dwells:

> Further said Rav Ḥisda: At first, before Israel sinned [against morality], the *Shekhina* abided with each individual [Rashi:

2. Menachem (Harry) Fox, *A Critical Edition of Tractate Succah with Introduction and Notes* (PhD diss., Hebrew University of Jerusalem, 1979) [Hebrew], 109.

> In their homes]; as it is said: "For the Lord your God walks in the midst of your camp" (Deuteronomy 23:15). When they sinned, the *Shekhina* departed from them; as it is said (v. 15): "That He see no impure thing in you and turn away from you." (Sota 3b)

According to Rav Ḥisda, the ideal state was disrupted by sin, so that now the Divine Presence no longer abides in the home. Sukkot can be seen as a reconstruction of this original ideal state, when the Israelites lived in the desert, in the shadow of the clouds of glory.

The yearning to remain in a place where God dwells is echoed in the Psalmist's plea:

> One thing have I asked of the Lord, that will I seek after: **that I may dwell in the house of the Lord all the days of my life**, to behold the graciousness of the Lord, and to visit early in His Temple. For He conceals me **in His sukka** in the day of evil; He hides me in the covert of His tent; He lifts me up upon a rock. (Psalms 27:4–5)

Humanity and God together dwell in the sukka.

The Four Species as Revelation

סוכה ג, ד	**Sukka 3:4**
רַבִּי יִשְׁמָעֵאל אוֹמֵר, שְׁלֹשָׁה הֲדַסִּים וּשְׁתֵּי עֲרָבוֹת, לוּלָב אֶחָד וְאֶתְרוֹג אֶחָד, אֲפִלּוּ שְׁנַיִם קְטוּמִים וְאֶחָד אֵינוֹ קָטוּם. רַבִּי טַרְפוֹן אוֹמֵר, אֲפִלּוּ שְׁלָשְׁתָּן קְטוּמִים. רַבִּי עֲקִיבָא אוֹמֵר, כְּשֵׁם שֶׁלּוּלָב אֶחָד וְאֶתְרוֹג אֶחָד, כָּךְ הֲדַס אֶחָד וַעֲרָבָה אֶחָת:	Rabbi Yishmael says: three hadasim, two aravot, one lulav, and one etrog, even if two [of the hadasim] have their tips broken off and [only] one is whole. Rabbi Tarfon says: even if all three have their tips broken off. Rabbi Akiva says: just as there is one lulav and one etrog, so too only one hadas and one arava.
וּלְקַחְתֶּם לָכֶם בַּיּוֹם הָרִאשׁוֹן פְּרִי עֵץ הָדָר כַּפֹּת תְּמָרִים וַעֲנַף עֵץ עָבֹת וְעַרְבֵי נָחַל וּשְׂמַחְתֶּם לִפְנֵי ה׳ אֱלֹהֵיכֶם שִׁבְעַת יָמִים. (ויקרא כג, מ)	And you shall take for yourselves on the first day the fruit of goodly trees, branches of palm trees, and boughs of thick trees, and willows of the brook, and you shall rejoice before the Lord your God seven days. (Leviticus 23:40)

On Sukkot we are enjoined to take the four species mentioned in the verse above. The Torah does not state explicitly what those species are, but our Sages identify them as an etrog (citron), a lulav (closed palm frond), hadasim (myrtle branches), and aravot (willow branches). As opposed to the case of the commandment to dwell in the sukka, the Torah does not provide a reason for this mitzva. Nevertheless, midrashic and aggadic literature suggest many rationales. In the coming chapters we will see that some of these ideas undergird many details in the definitions of the mitzva.

Rabbi Yishmael, a third-generation *Tanna*, and Rabbi Tarfon, from the second generation, opine that one must take three hadasim. The former further states that there must also be two aravot. In all, according to Rabbi Yishmael, one binds together seven items (one etrog, one lulav, two aravot, and three hadasim), parallel to the seven days of festivity when the mitzva is practiced: "and you shall rejoice before the Lord your God seven days."

Coins from the time of the Great Revolt against the Romans (first century CE) have been found that feature the Four Species, including multiple hadasim and aravot.[1] These coins, along with the opinions of the two *Tanna'im* above, indicate that the custom was to perform this mitzva with multiple aravot and hadasim.

At the end of the mishna, however, Rabbi Akiva disagrees with Rabbi Yishmael and Rabbi Tarfon, and opines that one should only take one of each species. Evidence of his approach can be found on coins from the Bar Kokhba period (second century CE) which depict only a single instance of each species – another sign of the relationship between Rabbi Akiva and Bar Kokhba.[2]

What informs the opinion of Rabbi Akiva, which stands in opposition to the prevailing view in his time? It seems that at bottom, his aggadic outlook is theologically driven:

> Rabbi Akiva says: "The fruit of goodly (*hadar*) trees" – that is the Holy One, blessed be He, of whom it is written, "You are clothed with glory (*hadar*) and majesty" (Psalms 104:1). "Branches of palm trees" – that is the Holy One, blessed be He, of whom it is written, "The righteous shall flourish like the palm tree" (92:13). "And boughs of thick trees" – that is the Holy One, blessed be He, of whom it is written, "and he stood among the myrtle trees" (Zechariah

1. Daniel Sperber, "A Study of the Bar Kokhba Coins," *Sinai* 55:1–2 (1964) [Hebrew], 38.
2. Ibid.

> 1:8). "And willows (*arvei*) of the brook" – that is the Holy One, blessed be He, of whom it is written (Psalms 68:5), "extol Him who rides upon the skies (*aravot*)." (*Pesikta DeRav Kahana* 27:9)

Rabbi Akiva conceives of the Four Species in mystical terms, where each of them represents God. He differs from his predecessors because, for him, the belief in the unity of God requires that there be only one of each species.

Rabbi Akiva's outlook on the Four Species fits well with his outlook on the sukka, which he sees as a representation of the clouds of glory.[3] Revelation is a major motif of Sukkot,[4] which according to Rabbi Akiva is linked not only to the Temple rites, but also to the two commandments that are kept outside the Temple: sukka and the Four Species.

Rabbi Akiva does not specify the religious significance of taking species that represent God. *Raaya Mehemna*, one of the books included in the Zohar, explains the mitzva as a mystical experience – to bring God closer and to rejoice in Him. The suggestion is informed by the understanding that one is enjoined to take the Four Species and rejoice in them. Thus if the species represent God, in fulfilling the commandment, one takes God and rejoices in Him:

> This commandment, to take a lulav on that day and with its other species, is a Mystery that we and our comrades established. Just as the Holy One, blessed be He, took the people of Israel on those days and rejoiced in them, so too the people of Israel take the Holy One, blessed be He, into their portions and rejoice in Him; and that is the Mystery of the lulav and its species – that it is the Mystery of the image of man. (*Raaya Mehemna, Emor* 3, 104a)

---

3. Yakov Nagen, *Sukkot in Rabbinical Thought: Motifs in the Halakha of Sukkot in Talmudic Literature* (PhD diss., Hebrew University of Jerusalem, 2003) [Hebrew], note 17. Throughout the halakhic midrashim, Rabbi Akiva is the one who opines that sukkot symbolize the clouds of glory. It is only in the Talmud that the opinion is attributed to Rabbi Eliezer.
4. Ibid.

The Four Species as a Sacrifice

סוכה ג ה-ו

אֶתְרוֹג הַגָּזוּל וְהַיָּבֵשׁ, פָּסוּל. שֶׁל אֲשֵׁרָה וְשֶׁל עִיר הַנִּדַּחַת, פָּסוּל. שֶׁל עָרְלָה, פָּסוּל. שֶׁל תְּרוּמָה טְמֵאָה, פָּסוּל. שֶׁל תְּרוּמָה טְהוֹרָה לֹא יִטּוֹל. וְאִם נָטַל, כָּשֵׁר. שֶׁל דְּמַאי, בֵּית שַׁמַּאי פּוֹסְלִין, וּבֵית הִלֵּל מַכְשִׁירִין. שֶׁל מַעֲשֵׂר שֵׁנִי בִּירוּשָׁלַיִם, לֹא יִטּוֹל. וְאִם נָטַל, כָּשֵׁר.

עָלְתָה חֲזָזִית עַל רֻבּוֹ, נִטְּלָה פִּטְמָתוֹ, נִקְלַף, נִסְדַּק נִקַּב וְחָסַר כָּל שֶׁהוּא, פָּסוּל. עָלְתָה חֲזָזִית עַל מִעוּטוֹ, נִטַּל עֻקְצוֹ , נִקַּב וְלֹא חָסַר כָּל שֶׁהוּא, כָּשֵׁר. אֶתְרוֹג הַכּוּשִׁי, פָּסוּל. וְהַיָּרוֹק כְּכַרְתִי, רַבִּי מֵאִיר מַכְשִׁיר, וְרַבִּי יְהוּדָה פּוֹסֵל.

Sukka 3:5–6

An etrog which is stolen or withered is invalid. One from an Asherah or a condemned city is invalid. Of *orla* or of impure *teruma*, it is invalid. Of pure *teruma*, he should not take it, but if he did take it, it is valid. Of *demai* (doubtfully tithed): The school of Shammai declared it invalid, and the school of Hillel declares it valid. Of second tithe, it should not be [ritually] taken [even] in Jerusalem, but if he took it, it is valid.

If a rash spread out on a majority of it, or if its *pitom* is removed, if it is peeled, split, or perforated so that any part is missing, it is invalid. If a rash spread out on a lesser part of it, if its stem was missing, or if it is perforated but no part of it is missing, it is valid. An etrog [that is black] as a *kushi* is invalid. An etrog which is green as a leek: Rabbi Meir declares it valid, and Rabbi Yehuda declares it invalid.

A midrash links between the Four Species and the Temple sacrificial rites:

> Rabbi Abbahu, citing Rabbi Elazar, stated: Whoever takes the lulav with its binding and the willow branch with its wreathing is regarded by Scripture as though he had built an altar and offered a sacrifice upon it. For it is said (Psalms 118:27): "Bind the festival with myrtle branches even onto the horns of the altar." (Sukka 45a)

Equating a mitzva to the Temple rites, as is done here regarding the Four Species, is common, and such comparisons are found in relation to many commandments. The purpose, on the face of it, is to contend with the absence of the Temple, and cast the mitzvot as a substitute of equal value to the Temple rites. Though the midrash does not deal with the content of the similarity between the Four Species and the sacrifices, the fact that in the Mishna many details of the laws of the Four Species are structured similarly to the laws of sacrifices reveals a deep-rooted and fundamental statement about the nature of this mitzva.

Blemishes That Invalidate the Four Species

The Mishna notes many blemishes that can invalidate the Four Species – especially the etrog – and many of them are related to the sacrifices. For instance, the Mishna asserts: "An etrog which is stolen or withered is invalid. One from an Asherah… is invalid" (Sukka 3:5). These blemishes that invalidate an etrog – if it is stolen or dry, or it is from an Asherah, i.e., from idol worship – are also cited in the context of the lulav (3:1), hadas (3:2), and arava (3:3), and they correspond to blemishes that invalidate sacrifices:

1. Stolen:

> "His sacrifice" – to exclude that which is stolen. (*Sifra, Vayikra* 5)
>
> The Talmud (Sukka 30a) cites two sources regarding stolen Four Species: "And you have brought that which is stolen, and the lame and the sick" (Malachi 1:13) and "I the Lord hate robbery in burnt offerings" (Isaiah 61:8). Both sources are from the realm of burnt offerings.

2. Dry:

> In consequence of the following blemishes a firstborn animal may be slaughtered…or if [the ear] has become dry. (Bekhorot 6:1)

3. From an Asherah:

> All [animals] forbidden for the altar render [others] unfit, however few there are. [These are the animals forbidden for the altar]:…or that had been worshipped…And what is meant by "has been worshipped"? That which has been used for idolatry. (Temura 6:1)

Those commonalities between the Four Species and burnt offerings relate to the blemishes that all the Four Species share. In addition, there are invalidating elements that are unique to the etrog among the Four Species, and these are also reminiscent of factors that invalidate sacrifices:

4. Split or perforated:

> Etrogim: "If it is…split, or perforated so that any part is missing, it is invalid…or if it is perforated but no part of it is missing, it is valid." (Sukka 3:6)
>
> Sacrifices: "In consequence of the following blemishes a firstborn animal may be slaughtered…if it is slit although there was no loss [of substance]; if it is perforated with a hole as large as a *karshina*" (Bekhorot 6:1).

5. A rash:

> The Mishna writes in Tractate Sukka that an etrog is invalidated "if a rash spread out on a majority of it." The word for "rash," *ḥazazit*, appears elsewhere in the Mishna only in Bekhorot 6:12: "Or [an animal] affected with… *ḥazazit*." *Ḥazazit* is the Aramaic

translation of the word "*yalefet*," a defect that invalidates a sacrifice, as can be seen in Onkelos's translation of Leviticus 22:22.

6. Black:

The color that the Mishna describes as "*kushi*," which invalidates an etrog, also appears as a defect in the context of a priest (but not a sacrificial animal): "A *kushi*... [disqualifies] in human beings but not in animals" (Bekhorot 7:6).

7. *Orla* or of impure *teruma*:

The rationale for invalidating an etrog that is *orla* or of impure *teruma* is based on the fact that these conditions render it forbidden for eating (Sukka 35a). Similarly, animal sacrifices may be brought only from species that are permitted for eating, as we learn from Ezekiel: "And one lamb of the flock, out of two hundred, from the well-watered pastures of Israel, for a meal offering, and for a burnt offering, and for peace offerings, to make atonement for them, said the Lord God" (45:15). The Talmud explains: "'From the [well-watered pastures] of Israel' – that is, from that which is permitted to Israel" (Menaḥot 6a).

Perfect and Blemished

Rabbi Yehuda's reading of the term "the fruit of goodly trees" (*pri etz hadar*) shows that the analogy between the Four Species and the Temple rites is informed by a basic idea regarding the four species:

> Rabbi said: Read not *hadar* but *hadir* (the stable); just as the stable contains large and small [animals], perfect and blemished ones, so also [the etrog has] large and small, perfect and blemished. (Sukka 35a)

Rabbi Yehuda compares the etrog to a pen where livestock are held, and notes that there are perfect etrogim and blemished ones. What is the implication of this surprising comparison? And what sets apart the etrog so that it is said to have fruits "perfect and blemished"? It seems that Rabbi Yehuda's statement hints at the link between the Four Species and the sacrifices. A blemish in the sacrificial animal or in the person bringing the animal invalidates the sacrifice. In contrast, the word "perfect" (*tamim*) denotes a pure, unblemished sacrifice, one that is worthy of being brought before God. The Sages also use these two words in the context of sacrifices.

Noting the phonetic similarity of the words *hadar* and *hadir*, and by applying the terms "perfect and blemished" to the etrog, Rabbi Yehuda treats the etrog as a sacrifice. Just as the Torah refers to blemishes in sacrifices and calls unblemished sacrifices "perfect," so Rabbi Yehuda invokes the blemishes of etrogim and refers to unblemished etrogim as "perfect."

Appeasement

The purpose of the sacrifices is to appease (*leratzot*), or please, God. The Torah emphasizes that God accepts only perfect, unblemished sacrifices:

> That you may be accepted (*lirtzonḥem*), you shall offer a male without blemish.... Whatsoever has a blemish, that you shall not bring, for it shall not be acceptable (*leratzon*) for you. (Leviticus 22:19–20)

Like the sacrifices, the purpose of the Four Species is to appease God. Thus, we find the oldest known statement regarding the purpose of the Four Species, attributed to Rabbi Eliezer the Great:

> It has been taught: When do we [begin to] make mention of rain [in the *Amida*]? Rabbi Eliezer says: From the time of the taking up of the lulav... Seeing as these Four Species are intended only to make intercession (*leratzot*) for water, therefore as these cannot [grow] without water, so [too] the world cannot exist without water. (Taanit 2b)

The Four Species are an offering of sorts that is meant to intercede with God for water. This is the reason that according to Rabbi Eliezer we begin to ask for rain on Sukkot, which is also when we are commanded to take the lulav. The element of appeasement in the Four Species is one more detail linking them to the sacrifices.

The Four Species in Leviticus

What is the source for the parallel between the Four Species and the sacrifices? The link between the Four Species and the Temple is fairly clear; the Torah implies that the mitzva is to be fulfilled at the Temple: "And you shall take for yourselves on the first day the fruit of goodly trees, branches of palm trees, and boughs of thick trees, and willows of the brook, and you shall rejoice before the Lord your God seven days" (Leviticus 23:40). There is also evidence for this powerful link in coins from the times of the Great Revolt and the Bar Kokhba period, which feature depictions of the Four Species and the Temple.

But the connection between the Four Species and the sacrifices is even more complex. I see the source for this connection in the Sages' commentary on the Torah passages on the three pilgrimage festivals. On each of these festivals there is a commandment relating to the harvest: The Omer offering on Passover, the two-loaves offering on Shavuot, and the Four Species on Sukkot.

It seems that the Sages recognized a pattern and concluded that there was a connection between the three mitzvot. Let us examine the verses in Leviticus chapter 23 regarding the three commandments and see what details the Sages filled in regarding the Four Species: all three have the common denominator of an agricultural offering; the offering is brought "before the Lord"; heaving is mentioned explicitly in the context of Passover and Shavuot, and the Sages extrapolate it to Sukkot as well; and appeasement is explicit in the context of Passover, and is extrapolated to both Shavuot and Sukkot.

	Passover	Shavuot	Sukkot
Offering	Omer	Two loaves	Four Species
Type	Agricultural crops	Agricultural crops	Agricultural crops
Destination	"Before the Lord" (v. 11)	"Before the Lord" (v. 20)	"Before the Lord" (v. 40)
Action	"shall heave," "when you heave" (v. 11)	"shall heave," "heave offering" (v. 20)	-----
Result	"as appeasement for you" (*lirtzonḥem*) (v. 11)	-----	-----

Considering the structure of this section, we can understand Rabbi Eliezer's statement to the effect that the purpose of the Four Species is appeasement (*leratzot*), as in the case of the Omer offering. In the Talmud, Tractate Sukka, Rabba further elaborates on the parallel between the Four Species and the offerings of the Omer and two loaves, and states that one must wave the Four Species:

> We have learned elsewhere: As to the two loaves and the two lambs of Shavuot, how does one proceed? [The priest] places the two loaves upon the two lambs and places his hands beneath them and waves them forward and backward, upward and downward, as it is said, "Which is waved and which is heaved"…In connection with this Rabba remarked: And so with the lulav. (Sukka 37b–38a)

Democratizing the Sacrifices

Alongside the similarities between the Four Species and the sacrifices, there is also a significant difference: The sacrifices are brought by the priests in the Temple on behalf of the entire nation, while the mitzva of the Four Species is required of every individual and can be carried out anywhere. A *baraita* (based on the *Sifra*) cites a source for this: "'And you shall take' [implies] that there should be a 'taking' with the hand of each individual" (Sukka 41b). The fact that a midrash is required in order to deduce the individual obligation of the Four Species is evidence that the Sages were aware that expansion of the group charged with performing central commandments was a departure from the previous practice. The *Arukh LaNer* comments there that this is because "one can say that it is similar to bringing communal sacrifices and the water libation, which the court performs on behalf of all of Israel." In this context, the Four Species are like the Sukka, which we proposed is like the Temple.

These two commandments – Sukka and the Four Species – enable the light of the Temple to shine through, even after the children have been exiled from their father's table and the sacrificial service has ended. They come together in the custom – cited in *Shaarei Teshuva* – to wave the lulav inside the sukka.[1] Thus, after the destruction of the Temple, Jews can still experience something of its flavor in their small sukkot, affirming that even when God's house and dwelling is no more, the commandments that he bequeathed us in His Torah, along with the holy objects in our hands, enable an encounter with His light, which fills the entire world. In the end of days this truth will be expanded further, and not only will every Jew be partner to the mitzva, but every single human being: "The king Messiah will come for no other purpose than to teach the nations of the earth [six] precepts, such as those of the sukka, the lulav, and tefillin" (*Midrash Tehillim* 21).

1. *Shaarei Teshuva* on *Shulḥan Arukh, Oraḥ Ḥayim* 652:1.

Nature's Dance

סוכה ג, ט

וְהֵיכָן הָיוּ מְנַעְנְעִין, בְּהוֹדוּ לַה׳ תְּחִלָּה וָסוֹף, וּבְאָנָּא ה׳ הוֹשִׁיעָה נָּא, דִּבְרֵי בֵית הִלֵּל. וּבֵית שַׁמַּאי אוֹמְרִים, אַף בְּאָנָּא ה׳ הַצְלִיחָה נָא. אָמַר רַבִּי עֲקִיבָא, צוֹפֶה הָיִיתִי בְּרַבָּן גַּמְלִיאֵל וּבְרַבִּי יְהוֹשֻׁעַ, שֶׁכָּל הָעָם הָיוּ מְנַעְנְעִים אֶת לוּלְבֵיהֶן, וְהֵן לֹא נִעְנְעוּ אֶלָּא בְּאָנָּא ה׳ הוֹשִׁיעָה נָּא. מִי שֶׁבָּא בַדֶּרֶךְ וְלֹא הָיָה בְיָדוֹ לוּלָב לִטּוֹל, לִכְשֶׁיִּכָּנֵס לְבֵיתוֹ יִטּוֹל עַל שֻׁלְחָנוֹ. לֹא נָטַל שַׁחֲרִית, יִטּוֹל בֵּין הָעַרְבַּיִם, שֶׁכָּל הַיּוֹם כָּשֵׁר לַלּוּלָב:

Sukka 3:9

And where [in the service] do they wave [the lulav]? At "Give thanks to the Lord" (Psalms 118:1) at the beginning and at the end, and at "O Lord, deliver us" (v. 25) – these are the words of the school of Hillel. The school of Shammai says: Also at "O Lord, let us prosper" (v. 25). Rabbi Akiva says: I was watching Rabban Gamliel and Rabbi Yehoshua, and while all the people were waving their lulavim [at "O Lord, let us prosper"] they waved them only at "O Lord, deliver us." One who was on a journey and had no lulav to [ritually] take, when he enters his house he should take it [even if he is] at his table. If he did not take the lulav in the morning, he should take it at any time before dusk, since the whole day is valid for [taking] the lulav.

This mishna relates the obligation to wave the Four Species. The beginning and ending of the chapter indicate that the act of waving is an integral element of the mitzva. The first mishna defines the required length of the lulav based on the ability to wave it: "A lulav that is three handbreadths in length, long enough to wave, is valid" (Sukka 3:1). The final mishna in the chapter defines a child's obligation to take the lulav based on when he is old enough to wave it: "A minor who knows how to wave [the lulav] is obligated [to take] the lulav" (3:15).

What does this waving consist of? Some define it as a heaving motion – "forward and backward, upward and downward" – which is what Rabba says must be done with the Four Species (Sukka 37b). The Ritva, however, rejects this opinion and asserts that heaving is not the same as waving:

> And this is not the case, for if it were so, why would they require that the lulav emerge a handbreadth above the hadas in order to wave it? For any [gap in length], whether large or small, is sufficient for bringing it forward and backward. Rather, it is clearly because one must shake the lulav and entangle it that they required an extra handbreadth to wave it, and to teach us that when one [moves it] forward and backward, upward and downward, one must wave and shake it. (Ritva on Sukka 37b)

All the Palestinian manuscripts of our mishna[1] jibe with the Ritva's interpretation, and feature the word "shake" rather than "wave" in the first clause. The Kaufman Manuscript, for example, states, "while all the people were **shaking** their lulavim, they **waved** them only at "O Lord, deliver us." Shaking is distinguished here from waving by involving strong movement.

What is the source of this definition? The Torah features two verbs in the context of the Four Species:

> And you shall take for yourselves on the first day the fruit of goodly trees, branches of palm trees, and boughs of thick trees, and willows of the brook, and you shall rejoice before the Lord your God seven days. (Leviticus 23:40)

In the Talmud, the verb "take" is cited as a source for the opinion that it is possible to fulfill one's obligation by merely lifting up the Four Species (Sukka 41b–42a). In the previous chapter, we suggested that the act of heaving the lulav is derived from the Omer and the two-loaves

1. As does Maimonides's version of the mishna.

sacrifices based on the structure of the section in the Torah that discusses the festivals. Thus it seems that the heaving action is an elaboration of the commandment to "take."[2] The waving, in contrast, appears to be an application of the demand to "rejoice" on Sukkot. This can be found in midrashim that describe waving the lulav as being like a dance before God:

> I commanded you to take a lulav and wave it before Me, and although you do that, you do not do it to benefit Me, but rather to repay Me. How so? For when I took you out of Egypt, I made the mountains **wave** before you, as [the Torah] states, "The mountains **danced** like rams" (Psalms 114:4). In the future, too, I will do the same for you, as it is written (Isaiah 55:12): "The mountains and the hills shall break forth before you into singing." (*Pesikta DeRav Kahana*, Appendices, B, 457)
>
> While they brought [the Ark of the Covenant] to Jerusalem, ninety thousand elders walked before it, and the priests carried it, and the Levites played music, and all of Israel played, **those who held a lulav**, those who held cymbals and other instruments, as it is written, "And David and all the house of Israel played before the Lord..." (II Samuel 6:5) – **that is the lulav that one waves**. (Numbers Rabba 4:20)

Based on this idea, which sees waving as an expression of rejoicing and dancing before God, the Mishna places the waving of the lulav within the context of the Hallel service. As the Rosh writes:

> The fact that [the lulav] is waved at "O Lord, deliver us" even though it is neither the beginning nor the end of the chapter is based on Scripture, which states, "Then shall the trees of the wood sing for joy..." (I Chronicles 16)

2. "And you shall take the breast of Aaron's ram of consecration, and heave it for a heave offering before the Lord" (Exodus 29:26).

> and subsequently states, "give thanks to the Lord, for He is good." (Rosh, Sukka 3:26)

The midrash that the Rosh relies on is from Leviticus Rabba:

> "And you shall take for yourselves on the first day" (Leviticus 23:40) – this is [the understanding of] that which is written, "The fields exult and everything in them" (Psalms 96:12): "The fields exult" – that is this world, as it is stated, "and it was when they were in the field" (Genesis 4:8). "And everything in them" – these are the creatures, like you say, "The earth is the Lord's and all that it holds, [the world and its inhabitants]" (Psalms 24:1). "Then shall the trees of the forest shout for joy" (I Chronicles 16:33) – Rabbi Aḥa said: [Here it states,] "the forest," [but in Psalms 96:12 above, it states,] "and all the trees of the forest." "The forest" – those are the trees that produce fruit; "all the trees of the forest" – those are the trees that do not produce fruit. (Leviticus Rabba 30:4)

The midrash paints a breathtaking vision of a partnership that brings humanity, nature, and the universe in joy and song before God. It is no accident that this partnership comes to pass on Sukkot, of all times, and by way of the Four Species. In the previous chapter we saw the statement by Rabbi Eliezer (Taanit 2b), by which the Four Species are nourished by water and thus intercede so as to bring water to the entire world, and indeed, water is one of the themes of Sukkot, when the world is judged for water.[3] The Four Species are a collection taken from among the plants that grow in the Land of Israel, and thus represent the entirety of the natural world as it thirsts for water. They constitute a link to the ideal nature of the world. In its discussion of the identity of the Four Species, the *Sifra* identifies the "fruit of goodly trees" with the etrog, saying, "that which the taste of its tree resembles that of its fruit – this is the etrog" (*Sifra, Emor* 16:4). The statement alludes to the story of Creation:

3. Rosh HaShana 1:2.

> Why was the earth spoiled? Rabbi Yehuda son of Rabbi Shalom said: Because it transgressed a commandment. God said, "Let the earth put forth … fruit tree," [intending that] just as the fruit can be eaten, so can the tree be eaten, but the earth did not do so." (Genesis Rabba 5:9)

In contrast with other plants with ritual use in the Temple, such as the first fruits and the Omer, the Four Species are not generally eaten or used for other mundane purposes. They represent a nature whose purpose is not merely to serve humanity, but rather has intrinsic value. This is the profound significance of rectifying the sin of the earth, where not only the fruit has value, but also the tree.

Let us conclude with the words of Rabbi Abraham Isaac Kook on the meaning of Sukkot as the festival of returning to nature:

> During the Feast of Harvest … we draw closer to nature. We sit in the sukka and take hold of a bundle of fresh branches, rejoicing in the water's gladness, in the gladness of the natural perfusion of God's blessing for the universe, which propagates through the bounded circle of nature's iron rules. We, too, pass into humanity's natural element, into its requisite materialism, into the seventy nations that the Lord divided among the heavenly bodies, and all of it we imprint with the holy splendor that transcends all that is natural – His grace and glory into the depths of nature; into the heart of flesh; into the vast corporeality; into coarse, earthly nature. (*Iggerot HaRe'aya*, vol. 3, p. 58)

The Water Libation as the Waters of Eden

Sukka 4:9

How was the water libation [performed]? A golden flask holding three *log* was filled from the Siloam [pool]. When they arrived at the water gate, they sounded a *tekia* [long blast], a *terua* [a staccato sounding] and again a *tekia*. [The priest then] went up the ramp [of the altar] and turned to his left where there were two silver bowls. Rabbi Yehuda says: They were of plaster, [but they looked silver] because their surfaces were darkened from the wine. They each had a hole like a slender snout, one wide and the other narrow, so that both emptied at the same time.

סוכה ד, ט

נִסּוּךְ הַמַּיִם כֵּיצַד, צְלוֹחִית שֶׁל זָהָב מַחֲזֶקֶת שְׁלֹשֶׁת לֻגִּים הָיָה מְמַלֵּא מִן הַשִּׁלוֹחַ. הִגִּיעוּ לְשַׁעַר הַמַּיִם, תָּקְעוּ וְהֵרִיעוּ וְתָקְעוּ. עָלָה בַכֶּבֶשׁ וּפָנָה לִשְׂמֹאלוֹ, שְׁנֵי סְפָלִים שֶׁל כֶּסֶף הָיוּ שָׁם. רַבִּי יְהוּדָה אוֹמֵר, שֶׁל סִיד הָיוּ, אֶלָּא שֶׁהָיוּ מֻשְׁחָרִין פְּנֵיהֶם מִפְּנֵי הַיָּיִן. וּמְנֻקָּבִין כְּמִין שְׁנֵי חֳטָמִין דַּקִּין, אֶחָד מְעֻבֶּה וְאֶחָד דַּק, כְּדֵי שֶׁיְּהוּ שְׁנֵיהֶם כָּלִין בְּבַת אֶחָת:

The Mishna's description of the water libation contains several parallels to the Creation story. Based on these similarities, we will posit that the ritual of pouring water over the altar is a reconstruction of the Creation story as it is told in Genesis, chapter 2. The water libation is essentially a raining onto the altar, which represents the earth. In Genesis we read:

> But there went up a mist from the earth, and watered the whole face of the ground. Then the Lord God formed man of the dust of the ground, and breathed into his nostrils the

> breath of life; and man became a living soul. And the Lord God planted a garden eastward, in Eden, and there He put the man whom He had formed. And out of the ground the Lord God made to grow every tree that is pleasant to the sight and good for food, the tree of life also in the midst of the garden, and the tree of the knowledge of good and evil. And a river went out of Eden to water the garden, and from there it was parted, and became four heads. (Genesis 2:6–10)

"There went up a mist from the earth..."

The water libation consists of two main actions – the water is drawn and then it is poured over the altar. The priests raise the water from the earth, from the underground Gihon spring, like the water vapor whose source is the earth – "there went up a mist from the earth." The waters of the Gihon, which feed the Siloam pool, are imbued with connection to the waters of Creation.

"...and watered the whole face of the ground"

The second part of the libation ceremony consists of pouring the water onto the altar. Raphael Patai suggests that during the ceremony, the altar represents the earth, which thirsts for water.[1] Patai's assertion is supported by the Bible's own description of the altar: "An altar of earth you shall make to Me" (Exodus 20:20), which the Sages interpreted as a requirement for the altar to be connected to the ground or filled with earth.[2] The full import of the suggestion that the altar stands for the earth is found in the idea – alluded to in the Bible – that the altar is a microcosm of the entire land.[3]

1. Raphael Patai, *Man and Land* (Jerusalem: Hebrew University Press, 1942–43) [Hebrew], vol. 2, 154.
2. Mekhilta of Rabbi Yishmael, *Yitro* 11, in the section beginning with, "An altar of earth."
3. See Numbers 35:34–35.

Furthermore, according to the Sages, the altar stands at the exact spot where man was created:

> "Of the ground (*adama*)" – Rabbi Berekhya and Rabbi Ḥelbo said in the name of Shmuel the Elder: He was created from the place of his atonement, as you read, "An altar of earth (*adama*), you shall make to Me." The Holy One said, "Behold, I will create him from the place of his atonement, and may he endure." (Genesis Rabba 14:8)

And that place is the very same place where the first rain fell on the earth and the mist descended to the earth:

> He caused the deep to rise, and filled the clouds with water to moisten the dust, and man was created. It is like a kneader of bread who first pours in water and afterward kneads the dough; similarly here: He first watered the ground, and afterward He formed man. (Rashi, based on Genesis Rabba 14:1)

According to the midrash, the mist went into the creation of mankind. Thus we find that during Creation, the water fell to the earth at the place of the altar. During the water libation, the water that is poured on the altar represents the original mist that watered the ground. Rabbi Eliezer discusses the time when the first rain fell, and according to his opinion, it fell in the same month in which the water libation is performed:

> It has been taught: Rabbi Eliezer says: From where do we know that the world was created in Tishrei? Because it says, "And God said: 'Let the earth put forth grass, herb-yielding seed, and fruit tree'" (Genesis 1:11). Which is the month in which the earth puts forth grass and the trees are full of fruit? You must say that this is Tishrei. That time was the season of rainfall, and the rain came down and the plants sprouted, as it says, "There went up a mist from the earth." (Rosh HaShana 11a).

According to Rabbi Eliezer, the rising of the mist and the ensuing rainfall become repeated every year, in the season when the first mist rose and dropped again as rain upon the earth. From this he learns that the world was created in Tishrei. His emphasis is on the entire month rather than a specific date.

Moreover, the description of the creation of man contains two elements: One is the dust of the ground; the other is the breath of life that God breathes into his nostrils: "Then the Lord God formed man of the dust of the ground, and breathed into his nostrils the breath of life; and man became a living soul" (Genesis 2:7). A third element can be found in the midrashim that emphasize the importance of water, the "mist" that rises from the earth during the creation of man.

The three elements of man's creation – earth, water, and the breath of life – have parallels in the water libation ceremony.

Earth: We discussed above the link between the altar and the earth and saw that the dust used to form man was taken from the site of the altar.

Water: As we have seen, the water libation reprises the first rain in the year of Creation, as well as the mist that is the source of the water used in the creation of man.

Breath: In the book of Jeremiah, the term "living waters" is used as a metaphor for God: "They have forsaken Me, the fountain of living waters" (Jeremiah 2:13), and "they have forsaken the Lord, the fountain of living waters" (17:13). The term "living waters" (*mayim ḥayim*) echoes the term "breath of life" (*nishmat ḥayim*) from the Creation verses. The waters brought to the altar from the Gihon spring imbued it with a spiritual element. Furthermore, the language of Mishna in describing the bowls with which the water was poured – "They had each a hole like a slender **snout**" (Sukka 4:9) – recalls that God "breathed into [man's] **nostrils** the breath of life" when He created him. Breath and water are the basis of human life.

"And out of the ground the Lord God made to grow…"[4]

One of the commandments associated with Sukkot that is described in Chapter 4 is a ritual that involved placing aravot at the sides of the altar and circling the altar seven times. Patai extends the idea[5] that the altar represents the earth to this ritual, where the aravot symbolize the vegetable kingdom, which is waiting for rain.

To my mind, the presence of nature in the ritual symbolizes the yearning not only for rain, but also for the harvest that comes after it falls. For example, the aravot ritual took place only after the water libation. Some sources indicate that the ritual involved not just the aravot, but that participants held in their hands all four of the species as they circled the altar: "Every day they walked round the altar once, but on that day they walked round it seven times… It was stated: Rabbi Elazar stated [that the circuit was made] with the lulav" (Sukka 43b).[6]

There are even more ancient sources for this ritual. The book of Jubilees, which is estimated to have been written in the second century BCE, describes a similar ritual conducted by Abraham, who was said to have circled the altar with the Four Species.[7] The Mishna itself hints at the use of the Four Species during the aravot ritual. After describing the beating of the palm branches, the Mishna says, "Immediately the children undo their lulavim and eat their etrogim" (Sukka 4:7). The conclusion of the aravot ritual also signifies the end of the requirement for the mitzva of the Four Species. Further along, the Mishna relates that once, "a certain man poured out the water over his feet, and all the people pelted him with their etrogim" (4:9). The ritual that reconstructs the action of the water vapor thus contains a rich, variegated representation of the plant kingdom.

4. Genesis 2:9.
5. Patai, *Man and Land* [Hebrew], vol. 2, 169; *Man and Temple in Jewish Myth and Ritual* (New York: Ktav Publishing House, 1967), 37, 170.
6. According to Rabbi Shmuel bar Natan there, the circuit was made with aravot alone.
7. Jubilees 16:31.

The Four Species are a symbol of the renewal of the world, due to their connection to the description of the growth of plants during Creation, a connection that can be traced back to tannaitic literature. Further along, we will see sources that identify the etrog with the trees of Eden, and especially the Tree of Knowledge. The *Sifra*, for example, states, "That which the taste of its tree resembles that of its fruit – this is the etrog" (*Sifra, Emor* 16:4), "like the Tree of Knowledge" (Genesis Rabba 15). The taking of the Four Species symbolizes nature in its pristine state, as it existed immediately after Creation. Thus the Four Species are part of a larger motif of reprising Creation, which we find in the water libation.

"And a river went out of Eden…"

The process of life's development repeats itself every year, step by step, hinting at a parallel recurring process – that of Creation. Every year, during the rainy season, the world is reborn. The process begins in the center of the world, the place of the altar, where the rising and falling of the mist is reprised. From there, sustenance radiates out from God to the rest of the world. The process is analogous to the gradual spread of water into the world. At first rain falls in the Garden of Eden, from which a river emerges, splitting into four heads that bring water to the entire world.[8] The gradual nature of the process is one of the characteristics of Ezekiel's prophecies of the end times, which describe an ever-increasing flow of water. At first the water "trickles forth" (Ezekiel 47:3), but ultimately it becomes "a river that cannot be passed through" (v. 5).

The Mishna in Tractate Rosh HaShana notes the cosmic significance of Sukkot: "At four set times the world is judged… And on Sukkot they are judged in respect to [water] (Rosh HaShana 1:2). The entire world is judged for its water during the festival, and, as we saw above, the water libation is a ritual that precipitates rainfall.

Although it appears that the Sages do not explicitly state that the water libation on the altar is a reenactment of the Creation process, it is certainly implied by sources to the effect that the rain, which falls upon

8. See Taanit 10a.

the world in return for the water libation, corresponds to the rebirth of the world and its Creation anew. Generally speaking, rain takes on cosmic significance in the Sages' worldview. As we saw above in the statement attributed to Rabbi Eliezer, rain returns each year around the same time that the first rain fell. The rain, which causes the wilderness to bloom, harks back to the action of the first rain – a renewed Creation of nature.

This idea is especially apparent in Tractate Taanit: "Rabbi Ḥama bar Ḥanina said: The day when rain falls is as great as the day on which heaven and earth were created" (Taanit 7b), and "... in order to teach you that the day on which rain falls is as great as the day on which heaven and earth were created" (9b). The same idea emerges from the comparisons of rainfall to the Resurrection of the Dead: "Rabbi Abbahu said: The day when rain falls is greater than [the day of] the Resurrection of the Dead" (7a), and "Just as the resurrection of the dead brings life to the world, so rains bring life to the world" (Y. Taanit 1:1). Rain and the resurrection are also juxtaposed by Rabbi Yoḥanan: "Three keys the Holy One, blessed be He, has retained in His own hands and not entrusted to the hand of any messenger, namely, the Key of Rain, the Key of Childbirth, and the Key of the Resurrection of the Dead" (Taanit 2a). Here, in addition to the resurrection and rain, there is the key of childbirth, or of life. All three keys are interconnected: Life, a person's birth, is linked to his resurrection after death, and further along in that chapter of the tractate, rain is compared to childbirth:

> When the heavens are shut up so that neither dew nor rain falls, it is likened to a woman who is in labor but who cannot give birth. This is in keeping with what Reish Lakish said in the name of Bar Kappara: "Withholding" is applied to rain, and "withholding" is applied to a woman ... "Bearing" is applied to a woman, and "bearing" is applied to rain ... "Remembering" is applied to a woman, and "remembering" is applied to rain. (Taanit 8a–b)

Breathing life into man (the microcosm) reenacts childbirth, which corresponds to the rain, which reprises Creation (the macrocosm). The apportioning of rain for the world is determined on Sukkot, and is not only about fulfilling the needs of an individual or community, but rather about renewing all of Creation.[9]

At the time of year when the primordial mist fell back down upon the earth, we perform a ritual that reenacts the falling of the first rain during Creation:

1. The water is brought up from the earth.
2. The water is poured onto the altar, which corresponds to the ground.
3. A rich variety of plant life appears.
4. The water libation precipitates the rain, which brings bounty to the entire world.

Each of the four elements has mythic significance. The water is the water of the Gihon spring, of Siloam, the water of Creation. The altar is the place of the original mist, a microcosm that represents the earth. The flora that grows is related to the trees of the Garden of Eden and the plants of Creation. The rain that falls in response to the water libation represents the Creation of the world anew, similar to the rivers that flow out of Eden.

There is a fundamental difference between the creation of the world by way of mist in the Garden of Eden and the symbolic Creation through the water libation. Original Creation was entirely God's action, while renewed Creation is a cooperative action involving both God and humanity.

The biblical[10] and midrashic[11] descriptions of the construction of the Temple abound with parallels to the Creation story. The Bavli

9. The following statement underlines the religious importance of rain: "Rav Yehuda said: The day when rain falls is as great as the day when the Torah was given … Rabba said: It is even greater than the day when the Torah was given" (Taanit 7a). Since the Giving of the Torah was a religious-spiritual event, the fact that rainfall is compared to it implies that rainfall too has religious and spiritual significance.
10. The list of evidence can be found in Mordechai Breuer, *Pirkei Mo'adot* (Jerusalem: Horev Press, 1986) [Hebrew], 33.
11. See *Midrash Tanḥuma, Pekudei* 2. This motif jibes with what we saw above regarding the conception of the Temple as a restoration of the Garden of Eden, which is a

emphasizes humanity's harnessing of the powers of Creation to build the Temple:

> Rav Yehuda said in the name of Rav: Bezalel knew how to combine the letters by which the heavens and earth were created. It is written here, "And He has filled him with the spirit of God, in wisdom and in understanding, and in knowledge" (Exodus 35), and it is written there, "The Lord by wisdom founded the earth; by understanding He established the heavens (Proverbs 3); and it is also written (Proverbs 3), "By His knowledge the depths were broken up." (Berakhot 55a)

Analysis of the water libation ceremony reveals that the Temple continued to be a focal point of human cosmological activity even after its construction was completed.

The approach that sees Sukkot as coinciding with the time of Creation reflects the view that every year time itself is born anew. A central theme of *Sefer Yetzira* is that Creation can be seen as being composed of three dimensions: world (place), year (time), and soul (humanity).[12] These can be seen as corresponding to earth (world), water (time), and breath (soul). The three dimensions are parallel to one another,[13] so that **the temporal dimension that is parallel to the world is not time as a whole, but is rather composed of units of a year**; the beginning of each year is also the beginning of the world, i.e., Creation; and each year culminates in the end of the world, meaning the end times.

---

perpetual source of water.

12. See *Sefer Yetzira* 3:3.

13. See *Sefer Yetzira* 3:3 through the end of the book.

Simḥat Beit HaSho'eva: The Celebration of the Temple and Its Annual Dedication

סוכה ה, א	Sukka 5:1
הֶחָלִיל חֲמִשָּׁה וְשִׁשָּׁה. זֶהוּ הֶחָלִיל שֶׁל בֵּית הַשּׁוֹאֵבָה, שֶׁאֵינוֹ דוֹחֶה לֹא אֶת הַשַּׁבָּת וְלֹא אֶת יוֹם טוֹב. אָמְרוּ, כָּל מִי שֶׁלֹּא רָאָה שִׂמְחַת בֵּית הַשּׁוֹאֵבָה, לֹא רָאָה שִׂמְחָה מִיָּמָיו:	The flute was for five or six days. This refers to the flute at the Beit HaSho'eva [the place of the water-drawing], which does not override Shabbat or the festival day. They said: He who has not seen the Simḥat Beit HaSho'eva has never seen rejoicing in his life.

The nights of Sukkot were celebrated in the Temple with song and dance. The celebration known in Jewish sources as "Simḥat Beit HaSho'eva" lasted all night, and the Sages said that "He who has not seen the Simḥat Beit HaSho'eva has never seen rejoicing in his life."

The rejoicing was, to my mind, the annual celebration of the Temple – an expression of the peoples' joy over the existence of the House of God and the Divine Presence therein. Simḥat Beit HaSho'eva ceremonies were a stage for the reenactment of events and foundational rituals from the time of the dedication of the First Temple by King David and his son Solomon. These reenactments were a rededication of sorts of the Temple. Simḥat Beit HaSho'eva, which took place on every evening of Sukkot, came to define the character of the entire week as the festival of the Temple. To understand this idea, we will examine the similarities between the tannaitic literature on Simḥat Beit HaSho'eva on the one hand, and the biblical stories of how David brought the Ark of Covenant to Jerusalem and the dedication of the Temple in the days of Solomon, on the other.

The Meaning of the Name

Simḥat Beit HaSho'eva (literally the "Rejoicing of the Water-Drawing House") is generally linked to the drawing of the water during the water-libation ritual. Rashi explains: "Beit HaSho'eva – all of this rejoicing is only over the water libation, as it written, 'Therefore with joy you shall draw water' (Isaiah 12:3)."[1] According to this explanation, Beit HaSho'eva is the place where the water was drawn for the libation ritual. But the claim is hard to accept, because rabbinic texts make no mention of the water libation in its descriptions of Simḥat Beit HaSho'eva.[2] Furthermore, it is hard to understand how the word "house" (*Beit*) would be read in the context of this explanation, as the water for the libation ritual was drawn not from a house but from the Gihon spring.

Sources from the Land of Israel offer a different explanation of the expression:

> Rabbi Yehoshua ben Levi said: Why is it called Beit HaSho'eva? Because from there they would draw (*sho'avin*) the Holy Spirit, as it is said, "Therefore with joy you shall draw water out of the wells of salvation."... Jonah son of Amittai, one of the holiday pilgrims, would enter Simḥat Beit HaSho'eva, and the Holy Spirit would rest upon him. (Y. Sukka 5:1)

1. Sukka 50a, on the phrase "Beit HaSho'eva."
2. Shmuel Safrai, *Pilgrimage in the Time of the Second Temple* (Tel Aviv: Am Hasefer, 1965) [Hebrew], 193.

The Yerushalmi, like the Bavli[3] and Rashi, links Simḥat Beit HaSho'eva to the verse in Isaiah. But unlike them, it reads the verse as an allegory for God's salvation and revelation, which jibes with the Bible's metaphorical treatment of the water:

> Behold, God is my salvation; I will trust, and will not be afraid; for God the Lord is my strength and song; and He has become my salvation. Therefore with joy you shall draw water out of the wells of salvation. And in that day you shall say: Give thanks to the Lord, proclaim His name, declare His doings among the peoples, make mention that His name is exalted. Sing of the Lord; for He has done gloriously; this is made known in all the earth. Cry aloud and shout, you inhabitant of Zion, for the Holy One of Israel is great in your midst. (Isaiah 12:2–6)

What is the place called Beit HaSho'eva, from which the Holy Spirit was drawn? According to the Yerushalmi, it seems that it was the Temple. That was the place where Simḥat Beit HaSho'eva was celebrated with joy that, according to the Yerushalmi, was imbued with the Holy Spirit. This is corroborated by Genesis Rabba (78):

> Another explanation: "**And he looked, and behold! A well in the field**" (Genesis 29:2) – **this refers to Zion**. "And behold! Three flocks of sheep" (v. 2) – this refers to the three pilgrimage festivals. "**Because from that well they would water the flocks**" (v. 2) – **because from there they would draw the Holy Spirit**. "And a huge rock" (v. 2) – this refers to Simḥat Beit HaSho'eva [the celebration of the water drawing]. Rabbi Hoshaya said: Why did they call it the celebration of the water drawing? Because from there they would draw the Holy Spirit. "And all the flocks would gather there" (v. 3) – they would come all the way from Mevo Ḥamat to the stream of Egypt. "And they would

3. Sukka 50b.

> roll the rock off the mouth of the well and water the sheep" (v. 3) – because from there they would draw the Holy Spirit. "And then they would return the rock onto the mouth of the well, to its place" (v. 3) – left to rest for the next pilgrimage festival.

The place from which the Holy Spirit is drawn is thus Zion, which was originally a name for the Temple.[4] According to the Midrash, the drawing of the Holy Spirit took place on all of the three pilgrimage festivals, and thus does not derive from the water libation, which took place only on Sukkot.

This interpretation works because it explains both the use of the word "house" and the fact that the Mishna makes no reference to the water libation in its description of Simḥat Beit HaSho'eva. Still, we cannot overlook the fact that the verse in Isaiah refers to drawing actual water, which invokes the libation ritual. Further along, I will propose that here is indeed a connection between the water libation and Simḥat Beit HaSho'eva, but from the other direction: that Simḥat Beit HaSho'eva is not an expression of joy over the water libation but rather over the Temple. The drawing of the water in Isaiah, which the Sages imbued with allegorical significance, fits into this celebration. The Yerushalmi's interpretation, attributed to Rabbi Yehoshua ben Levi, a first-generation *Amora* from the Land of Israel, can give us perspective on the significance of the ritual in tannaitic literature.

We can thus conclude that the name "Simḥat Beit HaSho'eva" is not only a description of the **place** of celebration but also of its **content** – the people's rejoicing in the Temple, where the Holy Spirit indwells.

---

4. See Nahmanides's paraphrase in his commentary on Genesis 29:2: "…for the well hints at the Temple…'Because from that well they would water the flocks' – for it was from there that they would draw the Holy Spirit" (similar to Rabbenu Bahya's commentary there).

The Biblical Background

The descriptions of the celebration in the Mishna and Tosefta appear to draw on the story of the procession that brought the Ark of the Covenant to the City of David and the story of the dedication of the Temple. These ancient narratives inspired the structure of the Simḥat Beit HaSho'eva ritual and informed its spiritual content. Thus, if we are to understand Simḥat Beit HaSho'eva, we must first review briefly its biblical background.

The Ark of the Covenant was brought to the City of David[5] in the presence of a large crowd, with joyously offered sacrifices and music and song. During the procession, King David expressed his merriment with exhilarating, ecstatic dance in front of the Ark. David said that his willingness to be self-deprecating was the source of his advantage over the House of Saul.

But bringing the Ark to the City of David was only the first step in the process of building the Temple. Indeed, immediately after the arrival of the Ark, David intended to start building the Temple.[6]

The effort to retrace David's jubilation can already be found in the Bible itself, in the story of the dedication of Solomon's Temple.[7] The story of the dedication of Solomon's Temple begins with conveying the Ark, with the king and all of the people on hand,[8] to its "place."[9] This recalls the story of the procession of the Ark under King David. In both stories sacrifices are offered along the way.[10] In addition, during the dedication of the Temple, some of the musical instruments that were used in David's time are again brought out.[11] Further along in the story, Solomon blesses the people, like David in his time,[12] and the event con-

5. II Samuel 6:12–23; I Chronicles 15:25–16:2.
6. II Samuel 7.
7. Sigmund Mowinckel, *The Psalms in Israel's Worship* (Oxford: Basil Blackwell, 1962), 127–130.
8. Compare II Chronicles 5:2–3 to II Samuel 6:15.
9. Compare II Chronicles 5:7 to II Samuel 6:17.
10. Compare II Chronicles 5:6 to II Samuel 6:13.
11. Compare II Chronicles 5:12 to II Samuel 6:5.
12. Compare II Chronicles 6:3- to II Samuel 6:18.

cludes with joy,[13] just as the procession of the Ark to Jerusalem in the time of David was a joyous occasion.[14]

The extensive evocation of elements from the story of the Ark's relocation by David is a sign of the importance of the story of the Temple's dedication by Solomon – told in II Chronicles – as a foundational event conveying the significance of the Temple.

The biblical scholar Sigmund Mowinckel contends that the procession of the Ark in the time of King David was reconstructed not only in the dedication of the Temple, but also annually, with a Temple rededication ritual on Sukkot.[15] His claim is based on the biblical descriptions – not the Sages' descriptions of the Temple celebrations. In fact, he does not connect his idea of the Temple rededication to Simḥat Beit HaSho'eva. As we will see, Simḥat Beit HaSho'eva, as it is described in rabbinic literature, resembles the rededication ritual that Mowinckel expected to find on Sukkot based on his readings of the Bible.

Parallels between Biblical Events and Simḥat Beit HaSho'eva

1. The Dance of the Leaders

> Men of piety and good deeds used to dance before them with lighted torches in their hands, and they would sing songs and praises. (Sukka 5:4)
>
> There is a story of Rabban Shimon ben Gamliel: He was dancing with eight lighted torches, and as he did so none of them fell to the ground. And when he prostrated himself he put his finger on the ground, on the floor, bending himself and kissing it, and then stood upright again. (Tosefta Sukka 4:3)

13. II Chronicles 7:10.
14. II Samuel 6:12. Also see the parallel description in II Chronicles 15:16, 15:25.
15. Mowinckel, *The Psalms in Israel's Worship*, especially 116 and onward.

The Tosefta's description of Rabbi Shimon's behavior is surprising; where is the dignity and majesty of the leader of Israel, the president of the Sanhedrin? It seems that the editors of the Tosefta sought to emphasize his actions, for they recall the behavior of King David, who frolicked and twirled ecstatically before God while the Ark was being transported to Jerusalem.

The Bible plays up the public nature of David's actions: The celebration took place in the presence of "all the house of Israel" (II Samuel 6:15), and David's dance was witnessed by "the handmaids of his servants" (v. 20). This fact, which is underlined in the exchange between David and his wife Michal, the daughter of Saul, highlights David's authentic humility. It shows why he was chosen to be king of Israel and how he was preferable to the offspring of Saul. The descriptions of Simḥat Beit HaSho'eva also emphasize the public aspect. The Tosefta relates how the entire nation, men and women both, would watch the dances:

> Formerly when they were beholding the joy at Simḥat Beit HaSho'eva, the men were beholding it from within the Temple precincts and the women from without. But when the supreme court saw that they behaved in a frivolous manner they erected three balconies in the court, facing the three sides, from which the women might behold the rejoicing at the ceremony. So when they were beholding the rejoicing at the ceremony the sexes were not mixed together. Saints and pious men were dancing before them with torches, and saying words of praise. (Tosefta Sukka 4:1–2)

The identity of the dancers also underlines the connection between Simḥat Beit HaSho'eva and the procession of the Ark to Jerusalem. Indeed, in both cases, it is the leaders who dance. But perhaps the link between the two leaders is even stronger, considering the fact that, according to sources from the Land of Israel, the line of the house of the president (*nasi*) of the Sanhedrin was descended from the House of David.

The comparison between the actions of King David and those of Rabbi Shimon ben Gamliel is hinted at in the Yerushalmi, which juxtaposes the two stories:

> It is said that Rabban Shimon ben Gamliel would dance with eight golden torches, and as he did so none of them would touch the other. And when he would bow down, he would stick his big toe in the ground and bow and immediately stand upright again…It is written, "Then David returned to bless his household, and Michal the daughter of Saul came out to meet him"… She said: Today the honor of Father's house was revealed. It was said that never in their lives did the House of Saul ever show an ankle or a big toe… "And David said to Michal: Before the Lord, who chose me above your father, and above all his house… And I will be yet viler than now, and will be base in my own sight; and with the handmaids of whom you have spoken – with them will I get me honor." For they are not handmaids (*amot*), but rather mothers (*imahot*). And what was her punishment? "And Michal the daughter of Saul had no child until the day of her death." (Y. Sukka 5:4)

It follows that the parallel between Rabbi Shimon and David stems from the idea that Simḥat Beit HaSho'eva, which was a celebration of the Temple and God's presence within it, is parallel to the celebration by David and the people of Israel of the Ark's relocation. David's celebration, which is ostensibly about the Ark, is in fact a rejoicing in the dwelling of the Divine Presence, as the Torah says: "And David arose, and went with all the people that were with him, from Baale-Judah, to bring up from there the Ark of God, upon which the Name is called, even the name of the Lord of hosts, who sits upon the cherubim" (II Samuel 6:2). After the Temple is built, it becomes a home for the Divine Presence, and the festival revelries there serve the same role as David's celebration of the Ark.

As the procession of the Ark to Jerusalem was the first step on the way to building the Temple, the similarity in the content of the two events is no coincidence. It is only natural that the annual celebration of the Temple will mention and commemorate, in various ways, its foundational events and rituals.

2. The Praise of the Pious

> Men of piety (hasidim) and good deeds used to dance before them with lighted torches in their hands, and they would sing songs and praises. (Sukka 5:4)

David and the story of the procession of the Ark to Jerusalem also apparently inform the descriptions in the Mishna. It describes excited public dances "with lighted torches" – just like the procession of the Ark under David. It also notes that praises were said, similar to David's prayer before the Ark after it was deposited in the City of David: "That we may give thanks to Your holy name, that we may triumph in Your praise" (I Chronicles 16:35). But the similarity is epitomized in the figure of the pious man, or "hasid."

In the mishna, the hasidim are the ones who dance and sing praises, but the word "hasid" may also allude to King David. One psalm attributed to David states, "for I am pious (a hasid)" (Psalms 86:2); indeed, the identification of David with the figure of the hasid is a recurring theme in the book of Psalms. The hasidim mentioned in the Mishna, who lived in the end of the Second Temple period, are also reminiscent of the figure of King David, with his spontaneity and joy before God. Shmuel Safrai summarizes his study of the hasidim thus: "The hasidim were unique in their religious outlook and their unmediated sense of connection to the divine … and were seen as 'a household member,' as a personal servant serving the master, not as 'a minister before the king.'"[16]

The descriptions of the Temple dedication also mention "hasidim," who are said to sing and make merry. The psalm about the dedication of the Temple says, "Sing praise to the Lord, O pious ones (*ḥasidim*), and give thanks to His holy name" (Psalms 30:5), as does

16. Shmuel Safrai, *In the Days of the Temple and in the Days of the Mishnah: Studies in the History of Israel* (Jerusalem: Magnes Press, 1994) [Hebrew], 518.

Solomon's prayer during the dedication: "Now therefore arise, O Lord God, into Your resting place, You and the Ark of Your strength; let Your priests, O Lord God, be clothed with salvation, and let Your pious ones (*ḥasidim*) rejoice in good" (II Chronicles 6:41). The equivalent verse in Psalms states: "Arise, O Lord, into Your resting place; You and the Ark of Your strength. Let Your priests be clothed with righteousness, and let Your pious ones (*ḥasidim*) shout for joy" (Psalms 132:8–9).

3. The Leader's Declaration and Blessing

> Hillel the Elder used to say: To the place that my heart loves, there my feet lead me. If you come to My house [says God], I will go to yours. If you do not come to My house, then I will not go to yours. For it is said (Exodus 20:20), "In every place where I cause My name to be mentioned, I will come to you and bless you." (Tosefta Sukka 4:3)

This section appears in the Tosefta before the story of Rabban Shimon ben Gamliel's revelry, which we discussed above. Hillel was Rabban Shimon's great-grandfather, and his behavior serves a similar role as David's – foreshadowing Rabban Shimon's conduct.

The body takes its cues from the emotions. God's invitation to participants of Simḥat Beit HaSho'eva to enter his house, and his promise to visit their house in return, paints a picture of intimacy and closeness between God and the Jewish people in the Temple – and especially during Simḥat Beit HaSho'eva.

Hillel's words recall David's yearning for a house of God, as it emerges from various sources in the book of Psalms. In one of these, David is described, like Hillel, as being led by his legs:

> "I considered my ways and I turned my feet to your testimonies" (Psalms 119:59) – said David to the Holy One, blessed be He, "Master of the universe, on each and every day I would consider and say, 'To this place I am walking, to the home of that one I am walking,' but my feet would bring me to the synagogues and the houses of study. About

> this it is written, '…and I turned my feet to your testimonies.'" (Leviticus Rabba 35)

Further points of similarity between the content of Hillel's words and the story of the dedication of the Temple and the House of David can be found in II Samuel 6–7.

Covenant

Hillel's words express a close relationship with God, one of mutuality: "If you come to My house, I will go to yours" – if you, the believer, come worship Me in My Temple, "I will go to your [house]," meaning My blessing and Presence will dwell within you.

There is a similar reciprocal element in the story of God's promise to David that his son will build the Temple.[17] The word "house" appears more than twenty times in that chapter and serves as a key word.[18] David says, "See now, I dwell in a **house** of cedar, but the Ark of God dwells within curtains" (II Samuel 7:2), and God promises, "the Lord will make you a **house** (v. 11), meaning David will have a dynasty beginning with the ascension of his son to the throne, "and He shall build a **house** for My name (v. 13). Clearly, the mutual relationship between God and David revolves around the concept of a "house," as in the case of Hillel.

Blessing

The Tosefta cites as a source for Hillel's statement the verse "In every place where I cause My name to be mentioned, I will come to you and bless you" (Exodus 20:20). In the context of Hillel's words, we can understand the verse thus: God enters the homes of His believers and bestows upon them His blessing.

David, too, asks God to bless his house: "Now therefore let it please You to bless the house of Your servant, so that it may continue

17. II Samuel 7.
18. Jon Levenson notes this point in *Sinai and Zion* (Minneapolis: Harper One, 1985), 98.

forever before You; for You, O Lord God, have spoken it; and through Your blessing let the house of Your servant be blessed forever" (II Samuel 7:29). Just as the blessing of Simḥat Beit HaSho'eva is extended to all of the pilgrims who come to the Temple, so David blesses the crowd that joins him to celebrate the procession of the Ark.[19] There, too, it is hinted that the blessing has to do with houses:

> And when David had made an end of sacrificing the burnt offering and the peace offerings, he blessed the people in the name of the Lord of hosts. And he dealt among all the people, even among the whole multitude of Israel, both to men and women, to each a cake of bread, and a cake made in a pan, and a sweet cake. So all the people departed each to his house. Then David returned to bless his house. (II Samuel 6:18–20)

The Ark's relocation to Jerusalem marks the beginning of a transformation in God's presence in the world, a process that culminates in the construction of the Temple. As we saw, some elements of that event are reconstructed in the Simḥat Beit HaSho'eva ritual, making it a celebration of sorts of the institution of the Temple. Indeed, the very name of the event, "Simḥat **Beit (house)** HaSho'eva," reinforces the idea that it is, at bottom, a celebration of the Temple as the house of the Lord. This reconstruction expresses a renewal of the relationship between the leaders of the people and God, which led to the construction of the Temple.

4. Instruments

> Men of piety and good deeds used to dance before them with lighted torches in their hands, and they would sing songs and praises. And Levites with innumerable harps, lyres, cymbals, and trumpets, and other musical instruments stood upon the fifteen steps leading down from the

19. II Samuel 6:18. Solomon, too, blesses the entire nation in the story of the dedication of the Temple (I Kings 8:55).

> Court of the Israelites to the Court of the Women, corresponding to the fifteen songs of ascents in Psalms, and it was on these [steps] that the Levites stood with their musical instruments and sang their songs. Two priests stood by the upper gate, which leads down from the Court of the Israelites to the Court of the Women, with two trumpets in their hands. (Sukka 5:4)

Jacob Nahum Epstein[20] and Menachem (Harry) Fox[21] noted the similarity between the Mishna's formulation here and the verses in Chronicles:

> And they set the Ark of God upon a new cart.... And David and all Israel played before God with all their might; even with songs, and with harps, and with lyres, and with timbrels, and with cymbals, and with trumpets. (I Chronicles 13:7–8)

I think that this is no passing allusion; rather, it hints at the reenactment of the celebration of David and the people before God, as they brought the Ark to Jerusalem.

All the musical instruments in the print edition of the Mishna appear in the list of instruments in I Chronicles, in the description of the first attempt to bring the Ark to Jerusalem during the reign of King David, including the "trumpets." This word appears only in the print edition – not in the three manuscripts of the Mishna (Kaufman, Parma, and Cambridge). Fox saw the addition as "a habit of speech, probably due to the influence of I Chronicles 13:8 above or the Mishna below."[22] Still, the link to David's celebration is retained in the manuscript editions of the Mishna as well: "And Levites with innumerable harps, lyres and cymbals." The list of instruments is identical both to the list that appears further along in the story of the Ark's delivery to Jerusalem and to the

20. Jacob Nahum Epstein, *Introduction to the Mishnaic Text* (Jerusalem: Magnes Press, 1964) [Hebrew], 1130–31. Epstein discusses only II Chronicles 15:16, 25:6.

21. Fox, *Succah*, 178.

22. Ibid.

description of the dedication of the Temple in Solomon's day. Here is the story of David:

> And David assembled all Israel at Jerusalem, to bring up the Ark of the Lord to its place, which he had prepared for it.... And the children of the Levites bore the Ark of God upon their shoulders with the bars thereon, as Moses commanded.... And David spoke to the chief of the Levites to appoint their brethren the singers, with instruments of music, lyres and harps and cymbals, sounding aloud and lifting up the voice with joy. (I Chronicles 15:3–16)

Further along, the trumpets are mentioned. As in the ending of the mishna above, they are in the hands of the priests:

> And Berechiah and Elkanah were doorkeepers for the Ark. And Shebaniah, and Joshaphat, and Netanel, and Amasai, and Zechariah, and Benaiah, and Eliezer, the priests, did blow with the trumpets before the Ark of God; and Obed-Edom and Jehiah were doorkeepers for the Ark. (I Chronicles 15:23–24)

The same instruments appear in the description of Solomon's dedication of the Temple:

> Also the Levites...were the singers...with cymbals and lyres and harps...and with them a hundred and twenty priests sounding with trumpets. It came even to pass, when the trumpeters and singers were as one, to make one sound to be heard in praising and thanking the Lord; and when they lifted up their voice with the trumpets and cymbals and instruments... (II Chronicles 5:12–14)

David's instructions to the Levites and priests during the procession of the Ark are perpetuated as part of the Temple ritual, as the story concludes:

> And they brought in the Ark of God, and set it in the midst of the tent.… And he appointed certain of the Levites to minister before the Ark of the Lord, and to celebrate and to thank and praise the Lord, the God of Israel.… With lyres and with harps; and Asaph with cymbals, sounding aloud; and Benaiah and Jahaziel the priests with trumpets continually, before the Ark of the covenant of God. (I Chronicles 16:1–6)

Here too we find all four instruments mentioned in the manuscripts of the Mishna: Levites played the lyres, harps, and cymbals, while priests played trumpets.

5. The Date

Solomon dedicated the Temple on Sukkot, as the Bible says: "And all the men of Israel assembled themselves around King Solomon at the feast, in the month Eitanim, which is the seventh month" (I Kings 8:2). It follows that Sukkot is an appropriate festival for the yearly celebration of the dedication of the Temple.

It is also no accident that Sukkot falls at the end of the biblical year: "And the feast of ingathering, at the end of the year" (Exodus 23:16); "and the feast of ingathering at the turn of the year" (34:22). In the cycle of the year, the end is also the beginning, an ideal time to dedicate the Temple. The Talmud, in explaining the opinion that the world was created in Tishrei, says that Tishrei is the start of the rainy season.[23] Sources in rabbinic literature see rainfall as a recapitulation of Creation.

Considering that sources from the biblical and Second Temple eras, as well as rabbinic literature, consider the Temple a microcosm of the entire world, it is clear why Sukkot, which falls in the month of Creation, is an appropriate time for the dedication of the Temple and the annual celebration and reenactment of this event.

---

23. Rosh HaShana 11a.

The Priests' Procession on Simḥat Beit HaSho'eva

סוכה ה, ד

חֲסִידִים וְאַנְשֵׁי מַעֲשֶׂה הָיוּ מְרַקְּדִים לִפְנֵיהֶם בַּאֲבוּקוֹת שֶׁל אוֹר שֶׁבִּידֵיהֶן, וְאוֹמְרִים לִפְנֵיהֶן דִּבְרֵי שִׁירוֹת וְתִשְׁבָּחוֹת. וְהַלְוִיִּם בְּכִנּוֹרוֹת וּבִנְבָלִים וּבִמְצִלְתַּיִם וּבַחֲצוֹצְרוֹת וּבִכְלֵי שִׁיר בְּלֹא מִסְפָּר, עַל חֲמֵשׁ עֶשְׂרֵה מַעֲלוֹת הַיּוֹרְדוֹת מֵעֶזְרַת יִשְׂרָאֵל לְעֶזְרַת נָשִׁים, כְּנֶגֶד חֲמִשָּׁה עָשָׂר שִׁיר הַמַּעֲלוֹת שֶׁבַּתְּהִלִּים, שֶׁעֲלֵיהֶן לְוִיִּם עוֹמְדִין בִּכְלֵי שִׁיר וְאוֹמְרִים שִׁירָה. וְעָמְדוּ שְׁנֵי כֹהֲנִים בְּשַׁעַר הָעֶלְיוֹן שֶׁיּוֹרֵד מֵעֶזְרַת יִשְׂרָאֵל לְעֶזְרַת נָשִׁים, וּשְׁתֵּי חֲצוֹצְרוֹת בִּידֵיהֶן. קָרָא הַגֶּבֶר, תָּקְעוּ וְהֵרִיעוּ וְתָקְעוּ. הִגִּיעוּ לְמַעֲלָה עֲשִׂירִית, תָּקְעוּ וְהֵרִיעוּ וְתָקְעוּ. הִגִּיעוּ לָעֲזָרָה, תָּקְעוּ וְהֵרִיעוּ וְתָקְעוּ. הָיוּ תוֹקְעִין וְהוֹלְכִין, עַד שֶׁמַּגִּיעִין לְשַׁעַר הַיּוֹצֵא

Sukka 5:4

Men of piety and good deeds used to dance before them with lighted torches in their hands, and they would sing songs and praises. And Levites with innumerable harps, lyres, cymbals, and trumpets, and other musical instruments stood upon the fifteen steps leading down from the Court of the Israelites to the Court of the Women, corresponding to the fifteen songs of ascents in Psalms, and it was on these [steps] that the Levites stood with their musical instruments and sang their songs. Two priests stood by the upper gate, which leads down from the Court of the Israelites to the Court of the Women, with two trumpets in their hands. When the cock crowed they sounded a *tekia* [a drawn-out blast], a *terua* [a staccato sounding], and again a *tekia*. When they reached the tenth step they sounded a *tekia*, a *terua*, and again a *tekia*. When they reached the Court [of the Women] they sounded a *tekia*, a *terua*, and again a *tekia*. They would sound their trumpets and proceed until they reached the gate that leads out to the east. When

מִזְרָח. הִגִּיעוּ לְשַׁעַר הַיּוֹצֵא מִמִּזְרָח, הָפְכוּ פְּנֵיהֶן לַמַּעֲרָב, וְאָמְרוּ, אֲבוֹתֵינוּ שֶׁהָיוּ בַּמָּקוֹם הַזֶּה אֲחוֹרֵיהֶם אֶל הֵיכַל ה' וּפְנֵיהֶם קֵדְמָה, וְהֵמָּה מִשְׁתַּחֲוִים קֵדְמָה לַשָּׁמֶשׁ, וְאָנוּ לְיָהּ עֵינֵינוּ. רַבִּי יְהוּדָה אוֹמֵר, הָיוּ שׁוֹנִין וְאוֹמְרִין, אָנוּ לְיָהּ, וּלְיָהּ עֵינֵינוּ:

they reached the gate that leads out to the east, they turned their faces from east to west and said, "Our fathers who were in this place, their backs were toward the Temple of the Lord, and their faces toward the east, and they worshipped the sun toward the east, but as for us, our eyes are turned to the Lord." Rabbi Yehuda said: They used to repeat [the last words] and say, "We are the Lord's and our eyes are turned to the Lord."

The key to understanding the connection between Simḥat Beit HaSho'eva and the dedication of the Temple is the procession of priests who emerge from the Temple accompanied by trumpets. At the heart of both the story of the Ark and that of the dedication of the Temple lies a procession. The description of Simḥat Beit HaSho'eva also includes a procession, which, like the procession of the Ark, features the blowing of trumpets. However, it appears that the significance of this procession is put into relief only by its connection to a third biblical context mentioned by the Mishna.

The Simḥat Beit HaSho'eva procession contrasts between "Our fathers who were in this place" and worshipped the sun (Ezekiel 8:16) and the participants, who declare that their "eyes are turned to the Lord." In Ezekiel, the sinners turned their backs on the Temple to bow down to the sun. During Simḥat Beit HaSho'eva, the marchers were also facing east, but as a celebratory gesture rather than an expression of abandoning the Temple. That is why they turn their heads to the west and declare, "Our eyes are turned to the Lord."

Additional details reinforce the contrast between the sins of the people and the departure of the Divine Presence in Ezekiel (8:11) on the one hand, and Simḥat Beit HaSho'eva on the other hand. Simḥat Beit HaSho'eva begins at the "upper gate" (Sukka 5:4), while in Ezekiel, "six men came from the way of the upper gate" (9:2) to sack the city. It is possible that the Mishna's mention of the "upper gate" to the Temple courtyard is also an allusion to another prophecy of Ezekiel, which begins with him being brought "to the door of the gate of the inner court that looks toward the north" (8:3) – another of the courtyard's gates.

The people's devotional call, "Our eyes are turned to the Lord," also alludes to Ezekiel, where the wicked elders declare, "The Lord does not **see us**, the Lord has forsaken the land" (8:12). In the face of this declaration, God emphasizes to Ezekiel many times in chapter 8 that He indeed does see the sinners, and that His open eye will not have mercy on them. In contrast, the Simḥat Beit HaSho'eva revelers affirm their devotion to God with the same motif of the eye: "Our eyes are turned to you."

Among the participants in both events are the leaders of the people (Hillel and Rabban Shimon ben Gamliel on the one hand, and the elders of Israel on the other), as well as women; however, in Ezekiel they are all sinners. Another point of contrast is the fact that during Simḥat Beit HaSho'eva Jerusalem is filled with light (Sukka 5:3), whereas in the book of Ezekiel the Temple is filled with the dead, and the city becomes the target of God's fury and is sacked (Ezekiel 9:7–8). Finally, the punishment for the sins described in Ezekiel's prophecy is the departure of the Divine Presence, the opposite of the dwelling of the Divine Presence in the story of the Temple dedication.

There are further points of contrast between Ezekiel's prophecy and the Temple dedication in the days of Solomon. The Temple dedication begins with an assembly of leaders:

> Then Solomon assembled the elders of Israel, and all the heads of the tribes, the princes of the fathers' houses of the children of Israel, to King Solomon in Jerusalem, to bring up the Ark of the covenant of the Lord out of the city of David, which is Zion. (I Kings 8:1)

And in the book of Ezekiel, the abominations are committed by the leaders of the people:

> And there stood before them seventy men of the elders of the house of Israel, and in the midst of them stood Jaazaniah the son of Shaphan.... Then He said to me: "Son of

> man, have you seen what the elders of the house of Israel do in the dark, every man in his chambers of imagery? For they say: The Lord does not see us, the Lord has forsaken the land." (Ezekiel 8:11–12)

The "seventy men of the elders of the house of Israel" allude to the "seventy of the elders of Israel" mentioned in Exodus 24:1–9 and the "seventy men of the elders of Israel" in Numbers 11:16. The allusion sets up a contrast between the heretical elders who deny the Divine Presence and cause it to depart, and the elders of Israel who are rewarded with a revelation of the Divine Presence. The leaders who cause the Divine Presence to depart are also contrasted with the leaders of Israel who bring the Ark to the Temple and cause the Divine Presence to manifest therein. These heretical elders, in contradiction of God's promise that "My eyes and My heart shall be there perpetually" (I Kings 9:3), assert, "The Lord does not see us, the Lord has forsaken the land." Similarly, both the entrance of the Divine Presence into the Temple in the book of Kings and its exit in Ezekiel are described as gradual, a symmetry that underlines the contrast between the two events. The descriptions of the cloud of glory in both events also call attention to this contrast. In the story of the dedication of the Temple, "the cloud filled the house of the Lord" (I Kings 8:10), while the description of the departure of the Divine Presence states that "the cloud filled the inner court" (Ezekiel 10:3), because God's glory was withdrawing from the Temple.

It is clear that the departure of the Divine Presence in Ezekiel is contrasted with its entry into the Temple in the story of the dedication, as well as with the descriptions of Simḥat Beit HaSho'eva. It follows that during Simḥat Beit HaSho'eva, the Divine Presence further indwells in the Temple, as it did in the dedication in Solomon's time.

So far, we have established two sets of allusions that link Simḥat Beit HaSho'eva and the dedication of the Temple: The comparison of the two events and the story of the procession of the Ark in the time of David, and, on the other hand, the contrast with the story of the departure of the Divine Presence in Ezekiel. Now we will examine the invitation of the Divine Presence to dwell in the Temple during the Simḥat Beit HaSho'eva ritual.

The participants in the ritual engage in activities that are diametrically opposed to the actions of the Temple defilers described in Ezekiel, thus rectifying the damage that caused the Divine Presence to depart. But beyond that, they reconstruct the actions of those who first induced the indwelling of the Divine Presence – as these are described in the story of the dedication of the Temple.

Sukka 5:4	II Chronicles 5:11–14	
Two priests stood by the upper gate ... when they reached ... when they reached	And it came to pass, when the priests were come out of the holy place	Movement eastward
And Levites ... stood upon the fifteen steps leading down from the Court of the Israelites to the Court of the Women ... that the Levites stood	Also the Levites ... stood at the east of the altar	The presence of the Levites and where they stand
Two priests ... with two trumpets in their hands ... they sounded a *tekia*, a *terua*, and again a *tekia*	Priests sounding with trumpets	The presence of the Levites and their instruments
And Levites with innumerable harps, lyres, and cymbals	Also the Levites.... with the trumpets and cymbals and instruments[1]	The Levites' instruments

1. See the following verse, "and instruments of music."

Sukka 5:4	II Chronicles 5:11–14	
And they would sing songs and praises	It came even to pass, when the trumpeters and singers were as one, to make one sound to be heard in praising and thanking the Lord…"for He is good, for His mercy endures forever"	Song and praise

The procession of the Ark to Jerusalem began the process of accentuating God's presence in the world, a process that was completed with the construction of the Temple. We have seen that many elements of these events recur in the descriptions of the Simḥat Beit HaSho'eva rituals in the Mishna and Tosefta (as quoted in the previous chapter), highlighting their significance as celebrations of the Temple's dedication.

In the previous chapter, we pointed out two difficulties: the difficulty in seeing Simḥat Beit HaSho'eva as a celebration of water, and, conversely, the hard-to-ignore link between the water libation and Simḥat Beit HaSho'eva, a link that emerges from the correlation of both rituals to Isaiah 12:2–6.[2] We discussed the Yerushalmi's outlook, which links the verses to Simḥat Beit HaSho'eva, and read Isaiah's statements regarding the drawing of the water as a metaphor for divine redemption and God's revelation in the world. Yet, the verse and the Yerushalmi's metaphor do not seem to reduce the requirement to draw actual water during the water libation, so that ultimately the drawing of water from the Gihon spring appears to be a physical manifestation of the spiritual metaphor.

The Simḥat Beit HaSho'eva procession, which precipitates the indwelling of the Divine Presence in the Temple, is an inversion of the story of the departure of the Divine Presence in the book of Ezekiel. The waters of the Gihon spring are "living waters," an expression that is a

2. See Sukka 48b and 50b – the reference to the verses in Isaiah in the context of both rituals.

metaphor for God in the context of the Temple: "Your throne of glory, on high from the beginning, Your place of our Sanctuary, You are the hope of Israel, the Lord! All that forsake You shall be ashamed; those that depart from You shall be written in the earth, because they have forsaken the Lord, the fountain of living waters" (Jeremiah 17:12–13). There a link between the drawing of the water during the water libation and the drawing of the Holy Spirit,[3] to the extent that drawing the water and bringing it to the Temple can be seen as a symbol of drawing the Holy Spirit itself.

3. Menachem (Harry) Fox, "The Joy of the Place of Drawing," *Tarbiz* 55 (1986) [Hebrew]: 197.

The Heroes of Tractate Taanit

תענית ד, א

בִּשְׁלֹשָׁה פְרָקִים בַּשָּׁנָה כֹּהֲנִים נוֹשְׂאִין אֶת כַּפֵּיהֶן אַרְבַּע פְּעָמִים בַּיּוֹם, בַּשַּׁחֲרִית, בַּמּוּסָף וּבַמִּנְחָה וּבִנְעִילַת שְׁעָרִים, בַּתַּעֲנִיּוֹת וּבַמַּעֲמָדוֹת וּבְיוֹם הַכִּפּוּרִים:

Taanit 4:1

On three occasions during the year – on fast days, on *maamadot*, and on Yom Kippur – the priests lift up their hands to bless [the people] four times during the day: at Shaḥarit, at Musaf, at Minḥa and at *Ne'ila*. And these are the three times: During communal fasts and during non-priestly watches [*ma'amadot*] and on Yom Kippur.

Tractate Taanit is mostly concerned with prayers for rain, and includes a series of dates that form the yearly cycle. The tractate begins with the words, "The first day of the festival," meaning the fifteenth of Tishrei, which is, according to Rabbi Eliezer, when we begin to "mention the powers of [bringing] rain" during the *Amida* prayer. Later in the chapter, the Mishna lists dates when the public must fast if rain has yet to fall. The tractate's final chapter, Chapter 4, is concerned with summer, listing the dates when the wood offering would be brought, as well as national days of mourning. The year comes full circle in the final mishna of the tractate, whose topic is Yom Kippur, which occurs in Tishrei, the month that the tractate opened with. Later we will see that all of the dates have something in common.

Chapter 4 opens with a list of the dates on which the priests would bless the people four times in a single day – fast days, "*maamadot*," and Yom Kippur. Since the previous chapters deal with the fast days, the

Mishna does not dwell on them. Rather, it explains what *maamadot* are and concludes with a reference to Yom Kippur. As noted, in between these two topics, the chapter discusses the wood offering and national days of mourning. We will now examine each of these topics on its own and try to uncover a common thread.

Maamadot

> What are the *maamadot*? Since it is said, "Command the children of Israel and say to them: My offering, My food" (Numbers 28:2); now how can a man's offering be offered and he is not present? [Therefore] the former prophets instituted twenty-four guard shifts (*mishmarot*). For each *mishmar* there was a *maamad* [at the Temple] in Jerusalem consisting of priests, Levites, and Israelites. When the time came for the *mishmar* to go up [to Jerusalem], the priests and Levites went up to Jerusalem, and the Israelites of that *mishmar* assembled in their cities and read the story of Creation. (Taanit 4:2)
>
> The men of the *maamad* fasted on four days of that week, from Monday to Thursday; they did not fast on Friday out of respect for Shabbat, or on Sunday in order not to switch from the rest and delight [of Shabbat] to weariness and fasting and [thereby] die. On Sunday [they read], "In the beginning" and, "Let there be a firmament"; on Monday, "Let there be a firmament" and, "Let the waters be gathered together"; on Tuesday, "Let the waters be gathered together" and, "Let there be lights"; on Wednesday, "Let there be lights" and, "Let the waters swarm"; on Thursday, "Let the waters swarm" and, "Let the earth bring forth"; on Friday, "Let the earth bring forth" and, "And the heavens [and the earth] were completed." For a long section two people read and for a short section one person. [This is how they would read] at Shaḥarit and Musaf. And at Minḥa they assemble and read the section by heart, as they recite

> *Shema*. On Friday at Minḥa they did not assemble out of respect for Shabbat. (Taanit 4:3)

The Mishna dedicates an entire tractate to the *tamid* offering, which was brought twice a day. Tractate Tamid describes at length the actions of the priests surrounding the bringing of the offering, as well as some of the roles played by the Levites. Unsurprisingly, the tractate remains silent about the rest of the people of Israel – the vast majority, who are not members of the Levite tribe. But our mishna teaches us that Israelites too (or their proxies)[1] must be on hand when the *tamid* is brought. Furthermore, according to the Tosefta, the presence of the "people," meaning members of the community who do not play active roles in sacrificing the offering, is a condition for bringing it: "Rabbi Shimon ben Elazar said: The priests, Levites, the musical instruments, and **the people** prevent [by their absence] the offering of the sacrifices" (Tosefta Taanit 3:3).

The Mishna's question – "Now how can a man's offering be offered and he is not present?" – expresses a demand to create an affinity and identification between those who bring the sacrifice, i.e., the people of Israel, and the sacrifice. Furthermore, according to the Mishna, beyond being present for the bringing of the sacrifice, the people of the *maamadot* also created a spiritual partnership with the sacrifice and the process by which it is brought. It emerges that they fasted all week long, other than on Shabbat and the days around it, and that through the act of fasting they too became a sacrifice of sorts.[2] Moreover, the expression that the Mishna employs to describe the role of the *maamadot* – "*omed al gabav*" (literally: standing over it) – evokes an image of the one bringing the sacrifice as being part of the sacrifice.

Another special role reserved for the members of the *maamadot* is reading "the story of Creation." According to the Talmud, this halakha expresses the special importance of the *maamadot*, without whose members "heaven and earth could not endure" (Taanit 27b). It follows that, as opposed to the impression that we are left with in Tractate Tamid,

1. Tosefta Taanit 3:2.
2. Berakhot 17a; Zohar, *Mishpatim* 119b.

even an Israelite, who is neither a priest nor a Levite, plays a significant role in bringing the *tamid* sacrifice, as well as in the larger cosmological role of the Temple, which illuminates and nourishes the entire world.

The Wood Offering

> On any day when there is Hallel there is no *maamad* at Shaḥarit; [on a day when] there is a *musaf* offering, there is no [*maamad*] at *Ne'ila*. [On the day of] the wood offering, there is no [*maamad*] at Minḥa – the words of Rabbi Akiva. Ben Azzai said to him: Thus did Rabbi Yehoshua learn: [On a day when] there is a *musaf* offering, there is no [*maamad*] at Minḥa; [on the day of] the wood offering, there is no [*maamad*] at *Ne'ila*. Rabbi Akiva retracted and learned like ben Azzai.
>
> The times of the wood of the priests and the people were nine: On the first of Nisan the family Araḥ of Yehuda. On the twentieth of Tamuz the family of David of Yehuda. On the fifth of Av the family of Parosh of Yehuda. On the seventh of the same month, the family of Yonadav of Rekhav. On the tenth of the same month, the family of Snaah of Binyamin. On the fifteenth of the same month, the family of Zattu of Yehuda, and with them were the priests, and Levites, and all those who were not certain of their tribe, and the family of Gonve Eli, and the family of Kotze Ketizot. On the twentieth of the same month the family of Paḥat Moav of Yehuda. On the twentieth of Elul the family of Adin of Yehuda. On the first of Tevet the family of Parosh of Yehuda [offered] a second time. On the first of Tevet there was no *maamad*, for there was Hallel, Musaf, and the wood festival. (Taanit 4:4–5)

At first glance it seems that the discussion of the wood offering is merely tangential to the rest of the chapter, appearing in the context of a discussion of the *maamadot* that do not take place on the day the wood offering was brought. However, as we have seen before, the associative stream, though seemingly arbitrary, often serves to highlight a deeper idea. In this case, the listing of the dates for the wood offering within the chronology of the rest of the chapter allows us to link the offering to the other topics that the chapter and our tractate discuss. But what, indeed, is the connection between the wood offering and the *maamadot*? The link emerges from the Bavli's description of the history of the wood offering:

> It is reported that when the exiles returned [to the Land of Israel] they found no wood in the [Temple wood] chamber, and the families here mentioned came forward and offered wood of their own. The prophets among them then made it a condition that even if at any time the chamber would be full of wood, they should still continue their offerings, as it is said (Nehemiah 10:35), "And we cast lots – the priests, the Levites, and the people – for the wood offering, to bring it into the house of our God, according to our fathers' houses at times appointed, year by year, to burn upon the altar of the Lord our God, as it is written in the Torah." (Taanit 28a)

Every year, the families that were the first to donate wood to the newly built Second Temple in the days of Ezra and Nehemiah are given the honor of donating the wood for the altar on the same date, year by year. The Tosefta adds that the days on which the wood was brought to the Temple were festive days, on which it was forbidden to mourn or fast (Tosefta Taanit 3:6). The added joy associated with bringing the wood offering is an expression of the partnership of the Israelites – those who are not priests or Levites and do not serve in the Temple – in the sacrifices and other service in the Temple. The families that would bring the wood did not merit to do so because they were rich or part of the nobility, but rather because of their good deeds and their dedication to the Temple. The fact that the wood offering is called that despite it not being offering in the usual sense recalls to mind the same lesson that emerges from the *maamadot* of the *tamid* sacrifice – that the entire nation of Israel participates in bringing the sacrifices.

Petition for Rain

The main subject of the tractate, fasting in times of drought, also emphasizes the role played by the entire nation in an area that is seemingly the exclusive domain of the Temple and priesthood: water. On Sukkot, the priests conduct the water libation ritual over the altar as a unique event – part of a ceremony that asks for rain for the entire world. According to some commentators, the aravot that were brought to the Temple on Sukkot, as well as the seventy bullocks offered, were also part of this petition for rain. In contrast with this approach, which ascribes all of the responsibility for rain to the priests, Tractate Taanit teaches us that the entire nation takes part; the tractate is concerned mostly with fast days and special prayers conducted by the people during a drought, in which the priests and the Temple do not play a special part.

The layperson's contribution to rainfall is given further expression in the Mishna. Although the Mishna tends to keep its storytelling to a minimum, a large portion of our tractate is devoted to the legendary Ḥoni the Circle Maker, whose prayers brought rain in a time of drought. Ḥoni, who has no title – certainly not that of rabbi or priest – is presented as a man of the people. He is not part of the cohort of rabbis, and yet he is closer to God (Taanit 3:8).

Days of Mourning

> There were five events that happened to our ancestors on the seventeenth of Tamuz, and five on the ninth of Av. On the seventeenth of Tamuz the Tablets were shattered, the *tamid* offering was canceled, the [walls] of the city were breached, and Apostomos burned the Torah and placed an idol in the Temple. On the ninth of Av it was decreed that our ancestors should not enter the land, the Temple was destroyed the first and the second time, Beitar was captured, and the city was plowed up. When Av enters, they limit their rejoicing. (Taanit 4:6)

Just as the people are partners in the Temple rites, so they play a part in the mourning over its destruction. The Tosefta promises that the days of fasting and mourning "will in the future become days of joy for Israel… and whoever mourns for it [Jerusalem] in this world will rejoice with it in the World to Come" (Tosefta Taanit 3:13). However, the Mishna also surprises us by revealing that the mourning on those days is not only for the destruction of the Temple and the loss of national independence (which culminated with the sacking of Beitar), but also for the Torah's tragedy – the breaking of the Tablets and the burning of the Torah. The link between the Torah and the Temple recurs at the end of the tractate, this time in an optimistic context:

> Similarly it says, "O maidens of Zion, go forth and gaze upon King Solomon wearing the crown that his mother gave him on his wedding day, on the day of the gladness of his heart" (Song of Songs 3:11). "On his wedding day" – this refers to the Giving of the Torah. "And on the day of the gladness of his heart" – this refers to the building of the Temple, may it be rebuilt speedily in our days, Amen. (Taanit 4:8)

As we will see, balancing out the two days of mourning for the Torah and the Temple are two "days of joy for Israel" that according to the Mishna are more joyful than any other days – Yom Kippur and the fifteenth of Av. Yom Kippur, the culmination of the Temple rites, is also the day on which we received the "second Tablets," as well as the only day of the year in which the high priest enters the Holy of Holies, where the Ark resides with the Tablets inside. In other words, Yom Kippur is the day on which it is revealed that at the heart of the Temple lies the Torah.

The close link between the Torah and the Temple is another expression of the people's belonging to the Temple. Through the study of Torah, which crosses boundaries of class and upbringing, anyone can touch the heart of the Temple. It is for this reason that the Talmud counts Torah study as tantamount to bringing sacrifices,[3] and the Mishna states

---

3. Menaḥot 110a.

that "if a *mamzer* is a scholar and a high priest an ignoramus, the scholar *mamzer* takes precedence over the ignorant high priest" (Horayot 3:8).

Yom Kippur and the Fifteenth of Av

> Rabbi Shimon ben Gamliel said: There were no days of joy in Israel greater than the fifteenth of Av and Yom Kippur. On these days the maidens of Jerusalem would go out in borrowed white garments in order not to shame anyone who had none. All these garments required immersion. The maidens of Jerusalem come out and dance in the vineyards. What would they say? Young man, lift up your eyes and see what you choose for yourself. Do not set your eyes on beauty but set your eyes on the family. "Grace is deceitful, and beauty is vain, but a woman that fears the Lord, she shall be praised" (Proverbs 31:30). And it further says, "Give her of the fruit of her hands; and let her works praise her in the gates" (v. 31). (Taanit 4:8)

Why are these two days so joyous? On the face of it, the rejoicing stems from the dancing of the girls in the vineyards and the families that would follow from their marriages to the young men who saw them. Yet, although this explanation makes sense for the fifteenth of Av, it seems implausible that the Mishna would reduce the unique quality of Yom Kippur – about which the Torah says, "For on this day atonement shall be made for you, to purify you" – to dancing in the vineyards. Still, Pinchas Mandel, based on an analysis of the Mishna's manuscripts, suggests that the section dealing with matchmaking (beginning with, "What would they say?") is a later addition, so that in the original Mishna the dance of the maidens was an *expression,* rather than a *source,* of joy.[4]

We are left with the question of the reason for the special joyousness of these days. As Mandel notes, the fifteenth of Av was the main

4. Pinchas Mandel, "There Were No Days of Joy in Israel Greater Than the Fifteenth of Av and Yom Kippur: On the Final Mishna in Tractate Taanit and Its Evolution," *Teudah* 11 (1996) [Hebrew], 147–78.

day when the wood offering would be brought, with many people from various segments of the nation on hand. According to several traditions, it was also the final day of the year on which the offering was brought.[5] Thus, there is a similarity between that day and Yom Kippur: Both emphasize the people's participation in the Temple – one with the wood offering and the other with the revelation of the Torah in the heart of the Temple. Mandel's conclusion is congruent with the idea that we suggested for the entire chapter: "This yields Rabbi Shimon ben Gamliel's main message, for it was on these two days in particular that the people's – the entire people's – powerful connection to the Temple was especially evident."[6]

The fourth chapter of Tractate Taanit opens with the priests: "On three occasions during the year… the priests lift up their hands to bless four times during the day" – and ends with the people: "There were no days of joy [for] Israel greater than…" Throughout the tractate we see that the focus of the three occasions – fast days, *maamadot,* and Yom Kippur – is not the priests but rather the laity. The people fast on all three occasions, and are active participants in the rituals and meaning of the day. The law regarding the priestly blessing is not intended to teach us about the special role of the priests but rather about the special status of the rest of the people, who receive a myriad of blessings on those days.

In studying Taanit, we are given a glimpse of the true hero of the tractate – the people of Israel, "a kingdom of priests and a holy nation" (Exodus 19:6).

---

5. Ibid., 168.
6. Ibid., 170. See note 92 there about the testimonies of the many participants in the wood offering.

You Shall Dance Before the Lord Your God

Taanit 4:8

Rabbi Shimon ben Gamliel said: There were no days of joy in Israel greater than the fifteenth of Av and Yom Kippur. On these days the maidens of Jerusalem would go out in borrowed white garments in order not to shame anyone who had none. All these garments required immersion. The maidens of Jerusalem come out and dance in the vineyards. What would they say? Young man, lift up your eyes and see what you choose for yourself. Do not set your eyes on beauty but set your eyes on the family. "Grace is deceitful, and beauty is vain, but a woman that fears the Lord, she shall be praised" (Proverbs 31:30). And it further says, "Give her of the fruit of her hands; and let her works praise her in the gates" (v. 31). Similarly it says, "O maidens of Zion, go forth and gaze upon King Solomon wearing the crown that his mother gave him on his wedding day, on the day of the gladness of his heart" (Song of Songs 3:11). "On his wedding day" – this refers to the Giving of the Torah. "And on the day of the

תענית ד, ח

אָמַר רַבָּן שִׁמְעוֹן בֶּן גַּמְלִיאֵל, לֹא הָיוּ יָמִים טוֹבִים לְיִשְׂרָאֵל כַּחֲמִשָּׁה עָשָׂר בְּאָב וּכְיוֹם הַכִּפּוּרִים, שֶׁבָּהֶן בְּנוֹת יְרוּשָׁלַיִם יוֹצְאוֹת בִּכְלֵי לָבָן שְׁאוּלִין, שֶׁלֹּא לְבַיֵּשׁ אֶת מִי שֶׁאֵין לוֹ. כָּל הַכֵּלִים טְעוּנִין טְבִילָה. וּבְנוֹת יְרוּשָׁלַיִם יוֹצְאוֹת וְחוֹלוֹת בַּכְּרָמִים. וּמֶה הָיוּ אוֹמְרוֹת, בָּחוּר, שָׂא נָא עֵינֶיךָ וּרְאֵה, מָה אַתָּה בוֹרֵר לָךְ. אַל תִּתֵּן עֵינֶיךָ בַּנּוֹי, תֵּן עֵינֶיךָ בַּמִּשְׁפָּחָה. (משלי לא) שֶׁקֶר הַחֵן וְהֶבֶל הַיֹּפִי, אִשָּׁה יִרְאַת ה׳ הִיא תִתְהַלָּל וְאוֹמֵר, תְּנוּ לָהּ מִפְּרִי יָדֶיהָ, וִיהַלְלוּהָ בַשְּׁעָרִים מַעֲשֶׂיהָ. וְכֵן הוּא אוֹמֵר (שיר השירים ג) צְאֶינָה וּרְאֶינָה בְּנוֹת צִיּוֹן בַּמֶּלֶךְ שְׁלֹמֹה בַּעֲטָרָה שֶׁעִטְּרָה לּוֹ אִמּוֹ בְּיוֹם חֲתֻנָּתוֹ וּבְיוֹם שִׂמְחַת לִבּוֹ. בְּיוֹם חֲתֻנָּתוֹ, זוֹ מַתַּן תּוֹרָה. וּבְיוֹם שִׂמְחַת

לִבּוֹ, זֶה בִּנְיַן בֵּית הַמִּקְדָּשׁ, שֶׁיִּבָּנֶה בִּמְהֵרָה בְיָמֵינוּ. אָמֵן.	gladness of his heart" – this refers to the building of the Temple; may it be rebuilt speedily in our days, Amen.

Many think of the fifteenth of Av as the festival of love. The source is the story in our mishna about the maidens of Jerusalem who would go dancing in the vineyards on that day to find husbands.

But the rest of that mishna is not as well known. It says that the maidens would dance in the vineyards not only on the fifteenth of Av, but also on Yom Kippur (we will suggest later that Yom Kippur was even more closely associated with dancing than the fifteenth of Av). It is a fact that many have forgotten, perhaps due to the association of the Day of Atonement with immensely powerful and meaningful traditions: fasting, penance, and the priestly service in the Temple. Yet, the Mishna implies that the dancing of the maidens was no less momentous that the day's other events, for it attests to the fact that "There were no days of joy in Israel greater than…Yom Kippur. What was the secret of the dance? And why does it, alone among all the other customs of Yom Kippur, express the special joy of that day?

Yom Kippur is the only day of the year when a person could enter Holy of Holies, the most holy section of the Temple. At the heart of the Holy of Holies was the Ark of the Covenant, atop which stood the two cherubim. On Yom Kippur, the Divine Presence would reveal Itself in a cloud between them. The Talmud tells us that the cherubim were shaped as a male and a female locked in perpetual embrace, so as to equate the love between God and the Jewish people to the intimate bond between man and woman (Yoma 54a). It also relates that the Ark's two staves (the wooden poles attached to its sides) jutted outward from the Holy of Holies and formed two bulges in the curtain like "the two breasts of a woman" (Yoma 54a). The Talmud ties this idea to the verse "My beloved is to me like a bag of myrrh, that lies between my breasts" (Song of Songs 1:13).

The entrance of the high priest, who represents the entire nation, into the Holy of Holies, is likened to the intimate union of two lovers. This union is at the heart of the Song of Songs, which describes the relationship between God and His people in allegorical terms, as the relationship between the beloveds.[1]

These ideas can teach us about the dancing of the maidens of Jerusalem, which, it turns out, was about much more than solving some "*shiddukh* crisis." Let us take a closer look at the story in the mishna. The white garments of the dancers symbolize the white vestments that the high priest wears when he enters the Holy of Holies on Yom Kippur. The halakha quoted in this seemingly aggadic mishna – "all these garments required immersion" – reinforces the link between the dancing of the maidens and the world of the Temple, with its stringent requirements of ritual purity. This law is infused with further significance by the final mishna in Tractate Ḥagiga, which states, "All the vessels that were in the Temple required immersion" (Ḥagiga 3:8).[2]

These insights suggest that the dances are directed toward God; He is the audience. The priest's encounter with God is occasioned by the Temple rituals, while the women come before Him in dance. The dance takes shape first and foremost against the backdrop of Yom Kippur, a day of purity and white clothing. The connection to the fifteenth of Av emerges from the previous chapter, where we learned that on that day the people were included in the Temple rites. The literary structure of the mishna shows us that the emphasis is placed on the Yom Kippur dance. Yom Kippur serves as a kind of preface to a chapter that opens with the days on which the priests bless the people four times, days that include Yom Kippur. Furthermore, as we noted in the previous chapter, Yom Kippur is the terminus of Tractate Taanit's journey through time, which begins with the first day of Sukkot (the fifteenth of Tishrei), traverses the entire year, and culminates on the tenth of Tishrei.

What, then, is the significance of the maidens' dance before God? Further along, the Mishna expounds on the verse from the Song

---

1. One can find a hint of the fact that the Holy of Holies is the arena for the fulfillment of the Song of Songs in the words of Rabbi Akiva, who says that "all the Scriptures are holy, but The Song of Songs is the Holy of Holies" (Yadayim 3:5). The Song of Songs is linked to the life of the Temple. The Zohar (*Teruma* 143a) says that King Solomon recited the Song of Songs upon completing the construction of the Temple.
2. My thanks to Hovav Yehieli for pointing out to me the mishna in Ḥagiga.

of Songs that describes the wedding day as an allegory for the building of the Temple and the Giving of the Torah:

> Similarly it says, "O maidens of Zion, go forth and gaze upon King Solomon wearing the crown that his mother gave him on his wedding day, on the day of the gladness of his heart" (Song of Songs 3:11). "On his wedding day" – this refers to the Giving of the Torah. "And on the day of the gladness of his heart" – this refers to the building of the Temple. (Taanit 4:8)

The dance is the fulfillment of the verse in the Song of Songs about the gladness of the heart and the wedding day, which the Mishna links to the Temple and the Giving of the Torah. What is the significance of this? My friend Amnon Dokov notes that the story of the dancers contains many allusions to the Song of Songs, primarily in the description of the women as "maidens of Jerusalem," a term that appears in the Song of Songs seven times. The location of the dance – the vineyards – is also mentioned many (nine) times in the Song of Songs. In addition, in the Mishna, as in the Songs of Songs (5:15), the potential lovers are referred to as "young men," (*baḥurim*). Based on the fact that in the Song of Songs the maidens of Jerusalem serve as bridesmaids who mediate between the bride and her beloved,[3] Dokov concludes:

> The dances are an enactment and realization of sorts of the verses in the Song of Songs – a feminine awakening on the part of the maidens of Jerusalem aimed at reinvigorating the relationship between the beloved and the bride. It was no coincidence that on the same day that the high priest would enter the Holy of Holies, the maidens of Jerusalem

3. See also the "maidens of Jerusalem" mentioned in the quote from the Song of Songs at the end of the mishna. According to the verse quoted there, they are the bridesmaids who accompany the bride on her wedding day.

> would go out and sing the song of love of the people of Israel for God.[4]

To me it seems that the maidens are not merely "bridesmaids" or "supporting actors," but rather that they represent the [female] beloved of the Song of Songs herself when they present themselves to the young men, bedecked in white. They correspond to the high priest entering the Holy of Holies.[5]

Femininity in Israel

The dance shows us not only that women were active in the Temple ritual, but that the Jewish people is the feminine party in its relationship with God, just as in the Song of Songs. According to Kabbala, the image of the Jewish people as a woman, identified with the *Shekhina,* meaning the feminine side of the divine, is behind the fact that the Jewish calendar is based on the moon, a feminine symbol, rather than on the masculine sun. In the context of standing before God at least, a Jewish person takes the role of a woman.

---

4. The article was published in a newsletter for Otniel yeshiva alumni who serve in the IDF.
5. The Talmud (Taanit 31a) discusses the future dance of the righteous around the Lord in the Garden of Eden. There the righteous are in direct contact with the Holy One, blessed be He, which is proof that the dance of the maidens must not be seen as a mere dance of the bridesmaids, but rather as that of the bride herself. There is no contradiction in the characterization of the maidens as both bridesmaids and as the female beloved herself, for in rituals people often play several roles at once. Thus, for example, during *Kabbalat Shabbat,* and especially in the liturgical song *Lekha Dodi,* the participant serves a dual role. On one hand, he walks toward the Sabbath like a groom greeting his bride, echoing the Midrash that states that the Jewish people and the Sabbath share a marriage vow (Genesis Rabba 11:8). But he also has another role: to bring God to unite with Shabbat. (In *Lekha Dodi* we read, "Your God will rejoice concerning you / As a groom rejoices over a bride.") This image is based on the kabbalistic principle whereby any movement that transpires below, in the human realm, precipitates a parallel movement on high, in the divine realm. Just as on Shabbat the worshipper is both the Sabbath's lover and the one who awakens God's love for her, so the dancing maidens can be both the female beloved and the bridesmaids who awaken God's love for Israel.

A Restorative Experience

The Mishna links the phrase "his wedding day" from the Song of Songs to the Giving of the Torah. According to that interpretation, the Giving of the Torah is the marital contract between God and Israel. However, there is a catch to this pleasing analogy: If the Giving of the Torah is the marriage of God and Israel, then the sin of the Golden Calf is tantamount to a bride committing adultery under her bridal canopy (Song of Songs Rabba 8). This points us toward another level of meaning in the dance of the maidens on Yom Kippur. On the seventeenth of Tamuz, in the aftermath of the sin, Moses breaks the tablets he received on Mount Sinai (Taanit 5:4), but the rectification of that shattering, the receiving of the second tablets, takes place on Yom Kippur. That is why the Talmud describes Yom Kippur as the most joyous day for the Jewish people: "because it is a day of forgiveness and pardon and **on it the second Tablets of the Law were given**" (Taanit 30b).

Now we can truly understand the dance of the maidens. The shattering of the tablets marked a crisis in the relationship between God and the Jewish people, and the giving of the second Tablets is a healing, restorative experience. The dance of the maidens in the vineyards represents the renewed bond between the Lover and His wife, the bride and her Beloved.

Yet, there is even more to the dance. When a horrified Moses witnesses the sin of the Golden Calf, he notes the dancing around the idol: "he saw the calf and the dancing; and Moses' anger waxed hot, and he cast the Tablets out of his hands, and broke them beneath the mount" (Exodus 32:19). The dancing of the maidens before God is the remedy for the dance around the Golden Calf. But there is also special significance to the fact that it was the women who danced in the vineyards. Beyond the fact that women can represent the entire Jewish people as a bride, according to some traditions women refused to participate in the sin of the Golden Calf, thus reserving their right to lead the holy dance (Numbers Rabba 21:10).

Husband and Wife, and the Divine Presence Abides with Them

As the Mishna tells us, the maidens also dance for a more mundane purpose – to find husbands. Yet, the intimacy and love expressed in their dance are on two intertwined planes: in both the relationship between God and Israel and the one between husband and wife. The Song of Songs, too, teaches us about our relation not only to the supernal world, but to this one as well. Rabbi Akiva, who calls the Song of Songs "the Holy of Holies" (Yadayim 3:5), says, "When husband and wife are worthy, the Divine Presence abides with them" (Sota 17a). The image of man and woman is not merely a metaphor for the relationship between God and humanity; indeed, the very encounter with God is achieved by way of interpersonal relationships.

The dance of the maidens on Yom Kippur precipitates the earthly and the supernal love. It bears a lesson about women and femininity in Judaism, as well as about the Jewish people, about God, and about their relationship.

Nature and History

Taanit, Chapters 1 and 4

It took much artistry to shape Tractate Taanit into a single cohesive unit. We noted that the tractate is laid out in chronological order, spanning the entire Jewish calendar, from Sukkot on the fifteenth of Tishrei to Yom Kippur on the tenth. We also saw that the common thread linking the topics of Taanit is the people's partnership in the dialogue with God, especially in the Temple. In addition, a parallel is drawn between the fast days mentioned in Chapter 1 and those mentioned at the end of Chapter 4. The beginning of the tractate concerns itself with fast days that are called due to drought, while the latter section is about fast days prescribed in memory of historical calamities. One message of Tractate Taanit is the connection between these two types of fast days.

Let us compare two sets of fast days, those at the beginning of the year and those at the end. The first fast regarding delayed rainfall is set for the seventeenth of Ḥeshvan (Taanit 1:4), the day when the Flood began (Genesis 7:11). The three weeks of mourning over the destruction of Jerusalem also begin with a fast on the seventeenth day of the month, in this case Tamuz (Taanit 4:6). Both systems of fast days become progressively more stringent, with the second phase beginning on the Rosh Ḥodesh following the first fast day (Taanit 1:5, 4:6). Both systems also include a transition from a short fast, in which one fasts during the day but not at night, to a fast in which one abstains during the night as well, and takes on the mortifications of Yom Kippur (the prohibitions against washing or anointing oneself, wearing leather shoes, or engaging in intercourse). The two sets of fast days teach us that we can also encounter God and His providence within nature and within history.

The book of Deuteronomy states that rain is an expression of the providence of God, who sustains us with water based on our actions:

> But the land that you go over to possess is a land of hills and valleys, and you will drink water as the rain of heaven comes down, a land that the Lord your God cares for; the eyes of the Lord your God are always upon it, from the beginning of the year even until the end of the year. And it shall come to pass, if you shall listen diligently to My commandments.... I will give the rain of your land in its season.... Take heed to yourselves, lest your heart will be deceived.... and the anger of the Lord be kindled against you, and He will shut up the heaven, so that there shall be no rain, and the ground shall not yield its fruit; and you will perish quickly from off the good land that the Lord is giving you. (Deuteronomy 11:11–17)

A dearth of rainfall is a sign of God turning away from His people, which is why, when fasts petitioning for rain are not answered, joy is minimized:

> If these [communal fasts] passed and there was [still] no answer, then they restrict engaging in business, and in building, planting, betrothal, and marriage, and in greeting one another, as if they were people undesirable to God. (Taanit 1:7)

As for calamities, from the days of the Prophets through the Sages, the recurring message was that they are caused by our sins. This paradigm is alluded to in the structure of the Mishna, in the list of calamities that occurred on the seventeenth of Tamuz and in the list of those that took plane on Tisha B'Av. Each of the lists begins with an event that transpired in the desert in reaction to a sin committed by the Israelites, implying that sins also precipitated the other events mentioned in the Mishna. As in cases of drought, on days of mourning over calamities, we "limit our rejoicing" (4:6).

The two main new years are in Tishrei, on the day when the world was created – the new year in terms of nature; and in Nisan, the month when the Israelites went out of Egypt – the new year in terms of history. The dates in the dialogue with God regarding rainfall, in Chapter 1, begin in Tishrei and continue throughout the winter into Nisan. Conversely, the dates relating to history (the wood offering, whose origin relates to events during the Second Temple era) in Chapter 4 begin with Nisan and continue throughout the summer into Tishrei. Nisan, the month of the Exodus, marks the beginning of the Jewish people's history – "this month shall be to you the beginning of all months" (Exodus 12:2) – while Tishrei is the beginning of the year for nature, because it is the month when the world was created.

Judaism recognizes the Lord as the God of nature, who created the world, and the God of history, who brought the Jewish people out of Egypt. Similarly, Shabbat is at once a testimony to Creation and a testimony to the Exodus, as we recite in the evening and daytime Kiddush and prayers. The Torah also teaches us of three pilgrimage festivals, each of which has an agricultural aspect and a historical aspect. Judaism's grand message is the belief in a single God who reveals Himself in nature and in history, thus bringing the two together.

Seeing the Face of God in the Temple and in the Torah

חגיגה א, ח

הֶתֵּר נְדָרִים פּוֹרְחִין בָּאֲוִיר, וְאֵין לָהֶם עַל מַה שֶּׁיִּסְמֹכוּ. הִלְכוֹת שַׁבָּת חֲגִיגוֹת וְהַמְּעִילוֹת, הֲרֵי הֵם כַּהֲרָרִים הַתְּלוּיִין בְּשַׂעֲרָה, שֶׁהֵן מִקְרָא מֻעָט וַהֲלָכוֹת מְרֻבּוֹת, הַדִּינִין וְהָעֲבוֹדוֹת הַטַּהֲרוֹת וְהַטֻּמְאוֹת וַעֲרָיוֹת יֵשׁ לָהֶן עַל מַה שֶּׁיִּסְמֹכוּ. הֵן הֵן גּוּפֵי תוֹרָה.

Ḥagiga 1:8

[The laws concerning] the dissolution of vows hover in the air and have nothing to rest upon. The laws concerning Shabbat, *ḥagigot*, and trespassing are as mountains hanging by a hair, for they have scant scriptural basis but many halakhot. [The laws concerning] civil cases and [Temple] worship, purity and impurity, and the forbidden relations have what to rest upon, and they are the essentials of the Torah. (Ḥagiga 1:8)

חגיגה ב, א

אֵין דּוֹרְשִׁין בַּעֲרָיוֹת בִּשְׁלשָׁה וְלֹא בְּמַעֲשֵׂה בְרֵאשִׁית בִּשְׁנַיִם. וְלֹא בַמֶּרְכָּבָה בְּיָחִיד, אֶלָּא אִם כֵּן הָיָה חָכָם וּמֵבִין מִדַּעְתּוֹ. כָּל הַמִּסְתַּכֵּל בְּאַרְבָּעָה דְבָרִים, רָאוּי לוֹ כְּאִלּוּ לֹא בָּא לָעוֹלָם, מַה לְּמַעְלָה, מַה לְּמַטָּה, מַה

Ḥagiga 2:1

They may not expound upon the subject of forbidden relations in the presence of three. Nor the work of Creation in the presence of two. Nor [the work of] the chariot in the presence of one, unless he is a sage and understands of his own knowledge. Whoever speculates upon four things, it would have been better had he not come into the world: what is above, what is beneath, what came before,

לְפָנִים, וּמַה לְאָחוֹר. וְכָל שֶׁלֹּא חָס עַל כְּבוֹד קוֹנוֹ, רָאוּי לוֹ שֶׁלֹּא בָא לָעוֹלָם.	and what will come after. And whoever takes no thought for the honor of his Creator (*Kono*), it would have been better had he not come into the world. (Ḥagiga 2:1)

Tractate Ḥagiga is devoted to the pilgrimages to the Temple: "Three times in the year all your males shall appear before the face of the Lord God" (Exodus 23:17). Its first half is concerned with *ḥagigot*, the festival sacrifices brought by the pilgrims, the second half with the laws of ritual purity and impurity that stem from the encounter with the holy. Since Ḥagiga 1:8 and 2:1 do not fit into either category, the *Rishonim* discussed why they were placed in the tractate. The Me'iri writes that the sole reason the topics of 1:8 are listed alongside *ḥagigot* is the fact that, like *ḥagigot*, they are not mentioned explicitly in the Torah.

In his groundbreaking paper on wordplay in the Mishna,[1] Avraham Walfish highlights a web of literary connections between Ḥagiga 1:8 and other mishnayot in the tractate. Our mishna writes of the laws of *ḥagiga* that they "have **scant** (*me'at*) scriptural basis but **many** halakhot," while 1:5 says of the offerings of the festival that "He who has **many** people to eat [with him] and **little** (*me'at*) money, brings **many** thanksgiving offerings and **few** (*me'at*) burnt offerings. Also, the expression "have what/nothing to rest upon (*lismokh*)" in our mishna corresponds to the "laying of the hands" (*lismokh*) in 2:2–3. In addition, our mishna's description of the laws of *ḥagigot* as "**mountains** hanging by a hair" allude to the opening of the chapter, which discusses ascending to the Temple **Mount**. Finally, the mishna that opens Chapter 2, which discusses the work of the chariot (*merkava*) corresponds to the first mishna in the tractate: "Whoever is unable to ride (*lirkov*) on his father's shoulders."

Beyond the literary devices pointed out by Walfish, our mishna (1:8) lists major topics and motifs of our tractate, and is thus a key to understanding the tractate as a whole. It discusses the relationship between the Oral Torah and the Written Torah when it comes to the

1. Walfish, "Wordplays," 82–84.

laws of *ḥagigot* – the topic of the first half of the tractate – as well as in relation to "purity and impurity," which is the topic of the second half of the tractate. The mishna opens with the dissolution of vows, corresponding to mishna 4, which discusses vow offerings to fulfill the obligation of the festival. After vows, the mishna mentions the laws of Shabbat, which appear in several other contexts in the tractate (Ḥagiga 2:4, 3:7). The issue of forbidden relations also appears in our mishna as well as in the mishnayot that immediately precede and follow it.

It emerges that the placement of this mishna in Tractate Ḥagiga is no accident. But what exactly is its significance?

Walfish posits that the purpose of our mishna is to set up a parallel between employing the pilgrimage sacrifices as a means of seeing God, and doing so through Torah study. When it comes to the esoteric teachings of the Torah (Ḥagiga 2:1), the message is clear: To experience the work of the chariot is to lay eyes on the supernal realm. The mishna warns of transgressing boundaries: "Whoever speculates [also: gazes upon] upon four things, it would have been better had he not come into the world." The mishna further alludes to seeing "the face of the Lord [also: master] God" by referring to Him as *Kono*, which connotes one's master. Walfish's unique contribution, based on his in-depth comparison between our mishna and 1:5,[2] is that equation of Torah study and seeing God is relevant not only to esoteric teachings, but also to the other realms of the Torah, as they are listed in 1:8. To his mind, what informs this idea is "equating the Oral Torah and the Sages' exegeses to the revelation and the Tablets at Mount Sinai."[3] Below we will further substantiate Walfish's approach.

Two Types of *Semikha*

> Yosei ben Yo'ezer says that [on a festival] the laying of the hands [on the head of a *ḥagiga* sacrifice] may not be performed; Yosei ben Yoḥanan says that it may be performed.

2. Ibid.
3. Ephraim E. Urbach, *The World of the Sages: Collected Essays* (Jerusalem: Magnes, 1988) [Hebrew], 493.

> Yehoshua ben Peraḥya says that it may not be performed; Nittai the Arbelite says that it may be performed. Yehuda ben Tabai says that it may not be performed; Shimon ben Shataḥ says that it may be performed. Shemaya says that it may be performed; Avtalyon says that it may not be performed. Hillel and Menaḥem did not disagree. Menaḥem went out, Shammai entered. Shammai says that it may not be performed. Hillel says that it may be performed. The former [of each] pair were presidents, and the latter were heads of the court. (Ḥagiga 2:2)

Mishna 2:3 cites the dispute between Hillel and Shammai; what need is there, then, for mishna 2:2? What is the point of conveying that the dispute over laying hands (*lismokh*) predates the schools of Shammai and Hillel? The key to the answer is the comparison, mentioned above, between this mishna and 1:8. The mishna in 1:8 uses the term *lismokh* to connote a connection between the law and the biblical text, while here it is employed in the context of the person bringing a sacrifice laying his hands on it.

This connection between the mishnayot teaches us that the real topic of each is not the laws of *ḥagigot* but rather the traditions of the oral law. The message is that despite the gap between the Oral Torah and Written Torah, there are traditions going back generations as to the laws themselves. Thus there is a response to a sage who renounces the Torah (1:7) as well as to those who renounce the Oral Law (2:4).[4]

Yet, this does not explain why tradition is such a major theme of Tractate Ḥagiga. We need to further the develop the idea put forth by Walfish about the wordplay between the various mishnayot.

Mishna 1:8 describes three different degrees to which a law is reliant on the biblical text:

1. The dissolution of vows "have nothing to rest upon."
2. Shabbat, *ḥagigot,* and trespassing are "as mountains hanging by a hair."

4. See Albeck, *Mishna*.

3. Civil cases and [Temple] worship, purity and impurity, and forbidden relations – these laws "have what to rest upon."

Ḥagigot are situated between the two extremes of laws that have something to rest upon and those that do not. The status of *ḥagigot* is also apparent in the fact that there are disputes about them that have yet to be resolved – they are in limbo, midway to full resolution. Thus, one who comes to lay his hands (*lismokh*) on a *ḥagiga* sacrifice corresponds to one who seeks to establish (*lismokh*) the laws of *ḥagigot* in the biblical text.

When it comes to laying hands, there appears to be additional wordplay, this time between the Bible and the Mishna. The five pairs of Sages who discuss the question of laying hands in the Mishna are also mentioned in the first chapter of Tractate Avot, which describes the transmission of the law through the generations, from Sinai to the Sages of the Mishna. It begins with the words, "Moses received the Torah at Sinai and transmitted it to Joshua" (Avot 1:1). The Torah states that this transmission of authority from Moses to Joshua was effected through a literal laying of hands: "And the Lord said to Moses: 'Take Joshua the son of Nun, a man in whom there is spirit, and **lay your hand** upon him'" (Numbers 27:18). Based on this story, the Talmud uses the term "*semikha*" to denote the ceremony at which one receives the title of rabbi, thus joining the line of transmission from Sinai. This ceremony is connected to the biblical story not only lexically (based on the word *samakh*); it also includes an actual laying of hands.

The listing of the five pairs is meant to convey the line of transmission. The two connotations of *semikha* also link up through their physical location: As the Mishna notes, the five pairs, the presidents and heads of the Sanhedrin, sat in the Hall of Hewn Stones, in the Temple. It follows that the word *semikha* is used in three connotations:

1. The *semikha,* or laying of hands, that connects one to the *ḥagiga* sacrifice.
2. The *semikha,* or laying of hands, that connects a Sage to the line of transmission from Sinai.
3. The *semikha,* or reliance, that links halakha to the biblical text.

The structure of the tractate generates a parallel between the various modes of approaching the Holy – both the Temple Mount and Mount Sinai.[5] The laying of hands on a sacrificial animal creates a bond between the one bringing the offering to be sacrificed to God and the offering itself, which fulfills the commandment to see "the face of the Lord." The laying of hands in the context of the line of transmission, and the linking of halakha to the written Torah, connects the individual to the revelation at Sinai.

A Person Is Obligated to Go to Pay His Respects to His Teacher on Festivals

> Rabbi Yitzḥak further said: A person is obligated to go to pay his respects to his teacher on festivals, as it says, "Why do you go to him today? It is neither a New Moon nor a Sabbath" (I Kings 4:23), from which we infer that on a New Moon and Shabbat one ought to go. (Rosh HaShana 16b)

The talmudic source for the obligation to pay respects to one's rabbi talks about Shabbat and the New Moon, but the halakha was ultimately established that this occurs during the three pilgrimage festivals. It seems that the halakha is informed in this case by the literary structure of our tractate, based on which the pilgrimage to the Temple to see God is replaced by a commandment to see one's rabbi.

In Tractate Avot, the rabbi is compared to God: "And [establish] the reverence for your teacher as the reverence of heaven" (Avot 4:12). In addition, the requirement to fear Torah sages is derived from the commandment to fear God (Bava Kama 41b). The requirement to fear the Torah sage, and the connection between the rabbi and the Divine Presence, is reminiscent of the revelation at Mount Sinai. When Moses descends from the Mount, the Torah says, "the skin of his face sent forth beams.... and [the people] were afraid to come near him" (Exodus

5. See the Mishna (1:6–7), which compares a botched *ḥagiga* offering to forbidden relations (which are also included in 2:1) and forsaking the Torah.

34:30–31). According to Rashi, what Moses does to Joshua, "And you shall put of your honor upon him" (Numbers 27:20), bestows upon his disciple that same light that his own face emitted when he descended from Sinai, so that Joshua's face begins to shine.

The Mishna in Avot, which relates the line of transmission going back to Sinai, teaches us that the encounter with Torah is also an encounter with the Holy:

> Rabbi Ḥalafta of Kefar Ḥananya said: When ten sit together and occupy themselves with Torah, the Divine Presence abides among them, as it is said: "God (*Elohim*) stands in the congregation of God (*El*)" (Psalm 82)... How do we know that the same is true even of one? As it is said: "In every place where I cause My name to be mentioned, I will come to you and bless you" (Exodus 20:21). (Avot 3:6)

Rabbinic literature constructs the festival of Shavuot so that it brings together all of the disparate elements of Tractate Ḥagiga. While the Bible mentions only the agricultural aspects of the festival, the Sages infuse it with renewed significance as a celebration of the Giving of the Torah. Thus, the festival experience includes both a pilgrimage to the Temple with the offering of a *ḥagiga* sacrifice, and joy over receiving the Torah. Indeed, the Torah portion read on Shavuot is the revelation at Sinai, and the *haftara* is the vision of the chariot in Ezekiel (Megilla 31a).

When the Temple still stood, God could be approached only via mediation by the prophet or priest. After the Temple was destroyed, the Sages instituted a change in the status of the sage, so that he came to replace the prophet and the priest: "a wise man is superior to a prophet" (Bava Batra 12a), and "the scholar *mamzer* takes precedence over the ignorant high priest" (Horayot 3:8). In the wake of the destruction of the Temple and the cessation of prophecy, the sage is the only one with access to the Holy: "Since the day that the Temple was destroyed, the Holy One, blessed be He, has nothing in this world but the four cubits of halakha alone" (Berakhot 8a).

Traditions and Disputes

חגיגה ב, ב

יוֹסֵי בֶּן יוֹעֶזֶר אוֹמֵר שֶׁלֹּא לִסְמוֹךְ, יוֹסֵי בֶּן יוֹחָנָן אוֹמֵר לִסְמוֹךְ. יְהוֹשֻׁעַ בֶּן פְּרַחְיָה אוֹמֵר שֶׁלֹּא לִסְמוֹךְ, נִתַּאי הָאַרְבֵּלִי אוֹמֵר לִסְמוֹךְ. יְהוּדָה בֶּן טַבַּאי אוֹמֵר שֶׁלֹּא לִסְמוֹךְ, שִׁמְעוֹן בֶּן שָׁטָח אוֹמֵר לִסְמוֹךְ. שְׁמַעְיָה אוֹמֵר לִסְמוֹךְ. אַבְטַלְיוֹן אוֹמֵר שֶׁלֹּא לִסְמוֹךְ. הִלֵּל וּמְנַחֵם לֹא נֶחֱלָקוּ. יָצָא מְנַחֵם, נִכְנַס שַׁמַּאי. שַׁמַּאי אוֹמֵר שֶׁלֹּא לִסְמוֹךְ, הִלֵּל אוֹמֵר לִסְמוֹךְ. הָרִאשׁוֹנִים הָיוּ נְשִׂיאִים, וּשְׁנִיִּים לָהֶם אֲבוֹת בֵּית דִּין.

Ḥagiga 2:2

Yosei ben Yo'ezer says that [on a festival] the laying of the hands [on the head of a sacrifice] may not be performed; Yosei ben Yoḥanan says that it may be performed. Yehoshua ben Peraḥya says that it may not be performed; Nittai the Arbelite says that it may be performed. Yehuda ben Tabai says that it may not be performed; Shimon ben Shataḥ says that it may be performed. Shemaya says that it may be performed; Avtalyon says that it may not be performed. Hillel and Menaḥem did not disagree. Menaḥem went out, Shammai entered. Shammai says that it may not be performed; Hillel says that it may be performed. The former [of each] pair were presidents, and the latter were heads of the court.

The Tosefta in Ḥagiga sees the dispute over the laying of hands as reflecting a failure to transmit the tradition:

> Rabbi Yosei said: At first there was no dispute in Israel… But when the time came that there were many students of Shammai and Hillel who did not serve their rabbis sufficiently, disputes proliferated in Israel, and it was as if there were two Torahs…What was the laying of hands on which they disagreed? The school of Shammai said: They

> do not lay hands on a festival day, and when one brings a peace offering one lays hands on it on the eve of the festival day. The school of Hillel says: One can bring peace offerings and burnt offerings and lay hands on them. (Tosefta Ḥagiga 2:9–10)

The Bavli also contains an opinion that finds fault with Rabbi Yosei ben Yo'ezer, who was a party to the dispute over the laying of hands:

> It has been taught: All the "grape clusters" who arose in Israel from the days of Moses until the death of Yosei ben Yo'ezer of Tzereida were free from all taint (*dofi*). From that time onward some matter of taint was found in them… Rav Yosef said: [The word *dofi* here means] dispute, [i.e., the dispute] relating to "laying on of hands." But does not Yosei ben Yo'ezer himself differ with regard to the law of laying on of hands? When he differed it was in his latter years, when his mental powers declined. (Temura 15b–16a). Rashi explains:
>
> "Dispute (*dofi*) relating to laying of hands" – until Yosef ben Yo'ezer, there was no dispute over laying of hands or over anything else, for the heart had yet to diminish, and [the Talmud] here cites laying of hands because it was the first-ever source of dispute among the Sages. Indeed, from the days of Yosef ben Yo'ezer onward, they [the Sages] were tainted (*dofi*) in the matter of laying hands, for they had a dispute regarding laying hands on a peace offering on a festival day, as [the Talmud in] Ḥagiga (15) says: Shammai says to lay hands and Hillel says not to lay hands.

It seems that the Mishna takes the opposite stance regarding the dispute. The Mishna says that even before the dispute between the schools of Shammai and Hillel regarding laying of hands, each of the pairs in the line of transmission disagreed over something. The message is apparently that there is nothing wrong with dispute; rather than representing an atrophying of tradition, it is an intrinsic part of it. Evidence of this can be found in the story the Mishna relates regarding the fate of the only man who did not challenge the president: "Hillel and Menaḥem did not disagree. Menaḥem went out, Shammai entered." The tradition is, and must remain, composed of many opinions.

This idea appears in Tractate Avot, which is devoted entirely to the line of transmission from Sinai and mentions the five pairs of Sages who appear in our mishna: "Every dispute that is for the sake of Heaven will in the end endure, while one that is not for the sake of Heaven will not endure. Which is a dispute that is for the sake of Heaven? Such was the dispute of Hillel and Shammai. And which is a dispute that is not for the sake of Heaven? Such was the dispute of Koraḥ and all his congregation" (Avot 5:17). That mishna teaches that there is a dispute that is "for the sake of Heaven," and that such a dispute "will in the end endure." This is precisely the message of our mishna: There is a dispute that endures throughout the chain of transmission over the generations. The pairs are mentioned so as to glorify, rather than denounce, the dispute. And in fact, later the Mishna goes so far as to mention Yosei ben Yo'ezer in a positive context: "Yosei ben Yo'ezer was the most pious in the priesthood" (2:7).

Tractate Eiruvin (13b) relates how a heavenly voice declared that in all the disputes between the schools of Shammai and Hillel, both sides "are the words of the living God." Both approaches are expressions of God's will; the disputes do not arise from an error in the transmission of the Torah, but rather from the innate plurality of God's word.[1] I am suggesting that the Mishna is alluding to what the Talmud states overtly. The string of disputes between the houses of Shammai and Hillel stand out in the Mishna. Our tractate opens with three such disputes, and, before arriving at the fourth, teaches us that they are expressions of fidelity to tradition.

Let us revisit the story in Eiruvin: After stating that both sides are "words of the living God," the heavenly voice proclaims that the halakha is in accordance with the school of Hillel. The Talmud says

1. See Rabbi Aviya Hacohen's assertion, quoted earlier in the chapter "Halakha: Law and Life," that the disputes between the schools of Shammai and Hillel stem from differing voices within the Torah itself.

that this was because the members of the school of Hillel "were kindly and modest; they studied their own rulings and those of the school of Shammai, and were even so [humble] as to mention the actions of the school of Shammai before theirs" (Eiruvin 13b). It is possible that the fundamental dispute between the school of Shammai and the school of Hillel was about the very approach to disputes: The school of Shammai holds that it has exclusive claim to the truth, and therefore need not heed contradictory opinions.[2] The school of Hillel believes that there is truth in the approach of the school of Shammai as well, and that other opinions should be studied; therefore, halakha is in accordance with the school of Hillel.

In the previous chapter we learned that a main message of Tractate Ḥagiga centers on the capacity to see God in the tradition of the Oral Torah. At bottom, a dispute is not an expression of a failure to transmit the tradition, but rather an expression of its integrity. Disputes can occur only in the gap between the Written Torah and halakha, as the mishna at the end of Chapter 1 states. We learn that this gap is an intrinsic part of halakha – an idea that is stated explicitly in the Jerusalem Talmud:

> Rabbi Yannai said: If the words of the Torah had been clear-cut, we would be without a leg to stand on ... [Moses] asked God, "Master of the universe, tell me, how shall we know the law?" God answered him, "Side with the many." When the majority is in favor, rule in favor; when the majority is against, rule against, so that the Torah will be interpreted forty-nine faces impure and forty-nine faces pure. (Y. Sanhedrin 4:2)

Even the Torah that Moses received was not cut and dried, but open, containing a plurality of faces and interpretations. The gap between the Written Torah and halakha – the topic of the Mishna at the end of the first chapter of Ḥagiga – is deliberate. It is meant to create space for an

2. As a friend of mine put it, if halakha had been in accordance with the school of Shammai, we would never know the opinions of the school of Hillel.

abundance of interpretations, as we see in the mishna that details the dispute over laying hands.

Halakhic literature – the Mishna and Talmud – is founded on disagreement, with the student delving into all of the opinions, not only those that informed halakhic practice. Often an opinion that is rejected in one context manages to shape halakha in another context. Indeed, the Hebrew word "halakha" is an anagram of the word "*hakhala*," or encompassment. It seems that talmudic literature, whose essence is dispute – and which is generally studied in pairs, a format that invites debate – survived not in spite of these disputes, but rather because of them.

Virgins Marry on Wednesdays

כתובות א, א	**Ketubot 1:1**
בְּתוּלָה נִשֵּׂאת לְיוֹם הָרְבִיעִי, וְאַלְמָנָה לְיוֹם הַחֲמִישִׁי. שֶׁפַּעֲמַיִם בַּשַּׁבָּת בָּתֵּי דִינִין יוֹשְׁבִין בַּעֲיָרוֹת, בַּיּוֹם הַשֵּׁנִי וּבַיּוֹם הַחֲמִישִׁי, שֶׁאִם הָיָה לוֹ טַעֲנַת בְּתוּלִים, הָיָה מַשְׁכִּים לְבֵית דִּין:	A virgin is married on the fourth day [of the week], and a widow on the fifth day, for twice in the week the courts sit in the towns, on the second day [of the week] and on the fifth day; so that if he [the husband] had a claim as to the virginity [of the bride] he could go early [on the morning of the fifth day of the week] to the court.

Tractate Ketubot opens with a list of the days of the week on which one can marry. The Mishna also explains why a presumed virgin should marry on Wednesday: so that if her husband discovers that she is not a virgin, he can go to the courts on the following day to change the sum in the marriage contract (*ketuba*). The *Aḥaronim*[1] note that it appears, based on the discussion in the Yerushalmi, that this reasoning is a later addition to the Mishna. The Yerushalmi ignores that explanation and offers another reason for marrying on Wednesday:

> A virgin is married on the fourth day. Bar Kappara says this is because they are described as a blessing. (Y. Ketubot 1:1)

1. Appears in the *Yafeh Mareh* commentary on the Yerushalmi. See also S. Lieberman, *Tosefta Ki-Fshutah* on Ketubot, 185.

Further along in the debate, when the Yerushalmi proposes that Wednesday is preferred because it is the day before the court convenes, it cites the *Amora* Rabbi Eliezer, rather than the Mishna, as the basis for this suggestion.

I wish to bolster the notion that the courts explanation is not part of the original mishna, while offering another possible rationale for the choice of day. Generally speaking, the Mishna does not explain its rulings. Furthermore, the courts explanation does not explain the beginning of the mishna, as there would be no reason for a virgin not to marry on Sunday (as the courts also convene on Mondays). It also does not explain the permission to marry a widow on Thursday. And in terms of prosody, the Mishna reveals its poetic structure when we remove the explanation:

> A virgin is married on the fourth day [of the week], and a widow on the fifth day. (Ketubot 1:1)
>
> A virgin, her *ketuba* [payment] is two hundred [*zuz*], and a widow a *maneh*. (Ketubot 1:2)

It seems to me that the virginity claim appears in our mishna not to explain the choice of Wednesday, but rather in order to link the chapter's first topic, the wedding day, to the rest of the chapter, which deals with virginity claims.

"So as Not to Uproot the Designation of the Fourth Day"

> So why not let her marry on the first day, and he can go early to the court on the second day? If you wish, say that [one should not marry on Sunday] so as not to uproot the designation of the fourth day. Or if you wish, say this is in keeping with the *baraita* of bar Kappara, for bar Kappara stated that it is because they [Wednesdays] are described as a [day of] blessing. (Y. Ketubot 1:1)[2]

2. The Yerushalmi questions the designation of Wednesday as a day of blessing, which

What, then, is special about Wednesday? Apparently, the debate is not about what sets Wednesday apart, but rather about the importance of setting a common day for weddings. The main role of any ritual, including weddings, is to generate order and structure, and a regular time promotes that goal. Having a set day of the week for weddings can help when choosing a date, and prevent confusion and misunderstandings. This regularity lends the chosen day with a unique quality, turning it into a "day of love" or a "day of weddings," and imbuing it with special content.

The importance of setting a regular time for ceremonies is conveyed elegantly in the book *The Little Prince* by Antoine de Saint-Exupery:

> The next day when the little prince returned, "You must come back at the same hour every day," said the fox. "If, for example, you decide to come at four o'clock in the afternoon, from three o'clock I will begin to feel happy.… But if you come at any odd time, I will never know when to be glad.… We must have rituals."
>
> "What is a ritual?" asked the little prince.
>
> "It is also something no one really thinks about," said the fox. "Rituals make one day different from the other days, or one hour from the other. My hunters have a ritual. Every Thursday they dance with the village girls. So Thursday is the perfect day for me! I can take a walk right up to the vineyards. But if the hunters danced at any odd time, every day would be the same, and I would never get a day off."[3]

The natural need for regularity leads to a custom of holding marriage ceremonies on a certain day of the week. Wednesday becomes the preferred day for several reasons: first, the court gathers on the following day; second, it is a day of blessing; and third, it is in the middle of the

---

underscores the idea that the reasons for choosing specifically Wednesday were post-facto ones.

3. Saint-Exupery, *The Little Prince*, https://www.tbr.fun/the-little-prince-chapter-21/.

week, which makes it easier to plan the event. Since the source of the law is the very need for regularity, the custom continues to take precedence; even if the conditions and rationales are no longer valid, we do not "uproot the designation of the fourth day."

The Vows of the Wicked

נדרים א, א	**Nedarim 1:1**
כָּל כִּנּוּיֵי נְדָרִים כִּנְדָרִים, וַחֲרָמִים כַּחֲרָמִים, וּשְׁבוּעוֹת כִּשְׁבוּעוֹת, וּנְזִירוּת כִּנְזִירוּת. הָאוֹמֵר לַחֲבֵרוֹ, מֻדְּרַנִי מִמָּךְ, מֻפְרְשַׁנִי מִמָּךְ, מְרֻחֲקַנִי מִמָּךְ, שֶׁאֵינִי אוֹכֵל לָךְ, שֶׁאֵינִי טוֹעֵם לָךְ, אָסוּר. מְנֻדֶּה אֲנִי לָךְ, רַבִּי עֲקִיבָא הָיָה חוֹכֵךְ בָּזֶה לְהַחְמִיר כְּנִדְרֵי רְשָׁעִים, נָדַר בְּנָזִיר וּבְקָרְבָּן וּבִשְׁבוּעָה. כְּנִדְרֵי כְשֵׁרִים, לֹא אָמַר כְּלוּם. כְּנִדְבוֹתָם, נָדַר בְּנָזִיר וּבְקָרְבָּן	All the substitutes for vows have the validity of vows. Those [substitutes] for *ḥaramim* have the validity of *ḥaramim*, and those for oaths have the validity of oaths, and those for nazirite [vows] have the validity of nazirite [vows]. If one says to his fellow, "I am forbidden from you by a vow," "I am separated from you," "I am distanced from you," "that I should eat from yours," "that I should taste from yours" – he is prohibited. If he says: "I am banned to you," Rabbi Akiva was inclined to rule stringently. [If one says,] "As the vows of the wicked," he has vowed in respect of being a nazirite, or a sacrifice, or an oath. [If he says,] "As the vows of the fit," he has said nothing. [But if he said,] "As their freewill offerings," he has vowed in respect to naziriteship and a sacrifice.

The opening mishna of Tractate Nedarim teaches that when a person vows to abstain from something and notes that his vow is like "the vows of the wicked," the vow is valid. In contrast, if he defines his vow as "the vows of the fit," "he has said nothing." It is no coincidence that this mishna appears in the beginning of the tractate. It contains a fundamental message regarding vows: only the wicked vow.

This negative outlook on vows is also apparent in the tractate's second mishna:

> One who says, "*konam*," "*konaḥ*," or "*konas*" – these are the substitutes for *korban* (a sacrifice). "*Ḥerek*," "*ḥerekh*," or "*ḥeref*" – these are substitutes for *ḥerem* (excommunication). "*Nazik*," "*naziaḥ*," [*nadiaḥ*] or "*paziaḥ*" – these are substitutes for nazirite vows. "*Shevutah*," "*shekuka*," or one who vows with the word "*mota*" – these are substitutes for [the word] oath (*shevua*). (Nedarim 1:2)

Most of the words listed in the Mishna express disgust, at least regarding nazirite vows and vows of excommunication. The word "*nazik*" comes from the root for "harm," implying that a nazirite is seen as harming himself. "*Nadiaḥ*" implies that the nazirite is banished outside society. "*Paziaḥ*" comes from the word "*paḥaz*," meaning recklessness. "*Ḥeref*" is like "curse," "*ḥerek*" is a thing that creaks, and "*ḥerekh*" sounds like the Hebrew word for scorching.[1] What is the reason for this stark aversion to vows, an aversion that the Talmud goes on to express in statements such as, "Even when one fulfills his vow he is called wicked" (Nedarim 22a) and "He who vows, even though he fulfills it, is designated a sinner" (Nedarim 77b)?

The question becomes even more acute when we examine the biblical approach to vows, which is seemingly quite positive. The heroes of the Bible make vows when they are in trouble and turn to God for help and salvation: "And Jacob vowed a vow, saying, 'If God will be with me.... of all that You shall give me I will surely give a tenth to You'" (Genesis 28:20–22), and later the Lord reveals Himself to Jacob as the same God to whom Jacob vowed (31:13); the Israelites offer a vow to God before their war with Canaan, and He listens to their vow and helps them achieve victory (Numbers 21:2–3); and Hannah vows that if God will give her a son, she will consecrate him as a nazirite and dedicate his entire life to God. In Psalms, on the other hand, vows appear not only

1. Moshe Benovitz, "Substitute Vow Formulas," *Sidra* 12 (1996) [Hebrew], 9.

in the context of petitions, but also divine worship, thanks, and praise (Psalms 61:9, 116:16–18).

Vows and Prayer

The Bavli in Berakhot (26b) offers two opinions as to the source of prayer: According to one, prayer was instituted by the Patriarchs; according to the other, the daily prayers are meant to mirror the *tamid* sacrifices. These opinions reflect two aspects of prayer – supplication and worship. The prayers of the Patriarchs were prayers of supplication, while the *tamid* expressed the ongoing divine service in the Temple. These two aspects can also be found in vows: Some vows request salvation in a time of distress, as we find with Jacob, Hannah, Jonah, and the Israelites during battle; others are vows of divine service and cleaving, as we find in Psalms.

A vow is an intensified prayer, which passes from words into deeds, from the abstract into the concrete. This is why vows often appear in the context of prayers, such as in the case of Hannah. Thus we are faced with a stark question as to the difference between the status of prayer and that of the vow. While prayer remains to this day a pillar of Jewish spiritual life, vows, it would seem, have been diminished to the point of illegitimacy.

Holy Vows and Vows of Abstention

One major difference between vows in biblical times and vows in the time of the Sages is the fact that during the mishnaic era there was no longer a Temple. As a result, the basic form of a vow – bringing a sacrifice to God – was no longer an option. Thus, the most prevalent form of vow was a vow of abstention from something. This type of vow appears as early as the Bible, in *Parashat Matot*: "When a man vows a vow before the Lord, or swears an oath to bind his soul with a bond, he shall not break his word; he shall do according to all that proceeds out of his mouth" (Numbers 30:3).

We find in the Mishna that vows of abstention are also considered positive: "Rabbi Akiva said…vows are a fence to abstinence" (Avot

3:13), distancing one from the item from which he wishes to abstain. Yet, apparently there is a danger in the transition from vowing to dedicate something to God to vowing to abstain from something. The concern turned out to have been justified, and this transition ultimately led to the debasement of vows.

The creation of new prohibitions, as Rabbi Akiva notes in Tractate Avot, can be a means for attaining spiritual goals, but it can also be a weapon of violence and aggression against another. Prohibitions can serve to instill anger. One who wants to hurt another need not even resort to violence or yelling, which are transient actions. Rather, a vow can generate a permanent rift between people.

A vow can also be a means of manipulation in relationships – whether between friends, parents and children, or husband and wife. These possible uses for a vow became publicly known, and were widely deployed, so much so that the Mishna is rife with cases that indicate the widespread use of vows for such purposes.

The vows mentioned in the tractate's first mishna seem far removed from any spiritual practice: "I am forbidden from you by a vow"; "I am separated from you"; "I am distanced from you." Such vows are meant to generate alienation and distance. As such, its purpose is diametrically opposed to the original purpose of vows: to bring people closer to God.

The seventh chapter of Tractate Ketubot features a list of vows by which a man tries to control his wife, but ultimately bring about the dissolution of the marriage: "If a man forbade his wife by vow to have any benefit from him.... from tasting any kind of produce.... that she should not adorn herself with any type of adornment.... that she may not go to her father's house.... from visiting a house of mourning or a house of feasting, he must divorce her and give her the *ketuba* [payment], because he has closed [people's doors] against her" (Ketubot 7:1–5).

The Mishna concerns itself not only with theoretical scenarios but also with case studies: "It happened to one in Beit Ḥoron that his father was forbidden to benefit from him..." (Nedarim 5:6); "And it once happened that a man vowed not to benefit from his wife..." (Nedarim 9:5); "And thus it happened with one who vowed not to benefit from his sister's daughter..." (Nedarim 9:10). That vows serve to push people apart is apparent from one of the possible justifications offered by the Mishna for annulling a vow:

> Rabbi Meir also said: They release [the vow] by using what is written in the Torah, and they say to him, "Had you known that you were violating [the prohibitions]: 'You shall not avenge' (Leviticus 19:18), 'You shall not bear a grudge' (v. 18), 'You shall not hate your kinsfolk in your heart' (v. 17), 'Love your neighbor as yourself' (v. 18), 'Let him live by your side' (25:37), for he might become poor and you would not be able to provide for him, [would you have vowed]?" And should he reply, "Had I known that this is so, I would not have vowed," he is permitted [the vow is absolved]. (Nedarim 9:4)

To my mind, this explanation for the debasement of vows explains not only interpersonal vows, but also many other vows that appear in the Mishna, in which people take upon themselves prohibitions unrelated to their relationships with others. Anger and alienation can be directed not only at other people; we often feel angry at ourselves, and could come to "punish" ourselves. Still, this explanation does not apply to all forms of vows – for instance it does not explain why the Mishna came to see even nazirite vows as being tantamount to "the vows of the wicked." We require further explanation in order to fully grasp the picture of what vows have become.

Nazirite: A Dedication to the Lord

> Shimon HaTzaddik said: I never ate the guilt offering of a nazirite who had become impure (by contact with a dead body), but once. Once a nazirite came to me from the south. His eyes were beautiful, he was very handsome, and his hair was wavy. I said to him: "What prompted you to destroy this beautiful hair [at the end of the nazirite period]?" He answered: "I was a shepherd for my father in my town. Once, while drawing water from the well, I gazed

> upon my reflection and my evil inclination seized hold of me and threatened to snatch me from the world – whereupon I said to it: 'Empty one, why do you vaunt yourself in a world that is not yours, where you are destined to be consigned to worms and maggots? I swear, I shall shear you in the name of Heaven!'" I thereupon arose, and, kissing him on the head, said to him: "May nazirites like you multiply in Israel, doing the will of the Lord! Of such as you it is written, 'A man... if he shall declare to vow the vow of the nazirite to be a nazirite to the Lord.'" (*Sifrei*, Numbers 32)

As the *Sifrei* reads the words "a nazirite to the Lord" (Numbers 6:2), they demand that the nazirite vow be a vow of dedication to divine service, one that cannot be made out of egocentric motives. The story of the nazirite encountered by Shimon HaTzaddik is antithetical to the myth of Narcissus, who, according to Greek mythology, falls in love with himself when he sees his own reflection, and eventually dies of hunger because he is unable to pull himself away. The fact that the story represents the only time that Shimon HaTzaddik, who was the high priest, was willing to partake of the guilt offering of a nazirite, teaches us that nazirite vows taken for pure motives, for the sake of Heaven, were the exception to the rule.

A story is told of a man who would fast all week long except for Shabbat. Rabbi Naftali Zvi of Ropshitz, suspecting the purity of the man's motives, decided to test him. One day, when he saw a child bump into the man, the rabbi scolded the child: "How dare you hurt a man who fasts every Monday and Thursday?" The man was enraged: "What do you mean, every Monday and Thursday? I fast all week long!" Thus the rabbi revealed the man's true motives: His piety was motivated by ego rather than an authentic desire to be close to God.[2]

2. Shlomo Carlebach, *The Heart of Heaven – Passover* (Jerusalem: Self-published, 2005) [Hebrew], 90.

Asceticism as Sin

In the Talmud we encounter a principled objection to the nazirite way of life, based on the worldview of the *Tanna'im*:

> Rabbi Elazar HaKappar in the name of Rabbi said: As it was taught, "And he shall make atonement for him, for he sinned against a soul" (Numbers 6:11). Against which "soul" has he sinned? Indeed, it is because he afflicted himself through abstention from wine. Now, does this not afford an argument from the minor to the major? If one who afflicted himself only in respect to wine is called a sinner, how much more so one who ascetically refrains from everything! (Nedarim 10a)

According to the biblical text, the "sin" appears to be a result of the nazirite's impurity. However, Rabbi Elazar HaKappar says that the nazirite lifestyle is itself a sin. It emerges that there is an objection in principle to vows of abstinence, through which a person takes on additional prohibitions.

The Jewish objection to asceticism is explained by Professor Ephraim Elimelech Urbach:

> The dichotomy of body and mind, flesh and soul, strips the body of all value and casts it as a prison and gravestone for the soul.... [It] was a major rationale for Hellenistic asceticism in its various forms, which sought to liberate the soul from the body and from the corporeality that permeated it, too, in the form of base passions and desires. Christian asceticism, too, was nourished, from its outset, by the flesh-soul dichotomy.... This motif is, however, almost entirely absent from the Sages' accounts of self-denial and the nazirite life. God is the Creator, "and this is the attribute of

the Holy One, blessed be He – that he created the entire world by wisdom."[3]

"He Has Vowed in Respect to Naziriteship and a Sacrifice"

Let us return to our mishna. As opposed to vows (*nedarim*) that are like "the vows of the wicked," in which one "has said nothing," when one says, "As their freewill offerings (*nedava*)," that vow is valid for both being nazirite and bringing a sacrifice. What is the difference between a vow and an offering"? And how can a freewill offering even be possible in the case of a nazirite when on the face of it one can become a nazirite only by taking a vow? The answer seems to be that the word "vow" itself has become a pejorative term that stands for the negative phenomena described above. The word "offering," on the other hand, expresses the possibility that there is yet a vow that emanates from a generous heart and maintains the original purpose of the vow – to connect rather than sever; to open, rather than close, the heart.

3. Ephraim E. Urbach, "Asceticism and Suffering in the Talmudic and Mishnaic Sources," *Yitzchak F. Baer Jubilee Volume on the Occasion of His Seventieth Birthday* (Jerusalem: Historical Society of Israel, 1960) [Hebrew], 48–68.

The Essence of Marriage

גיטין ט, י

בֵּית שַׁמַּאי אוֹמְרִים, לֹא יְגָרֵשׁ אָדָם אֶת אִשְׁתּוֹ אֶלָּא אִם כֵּן מָצָא בָהּ דְּבַר עֶרְוָה, שֶׁנֶּאֱמַר (דברים כד) כִּי מָצָא בָהּ עֶרְוַת דָּבָר. וּבֵית הִלֵּל אוֹמְרִים, אֲפִלּוּ הִקְדִּיחָה תַבְשִׁילוֹ, שֶׁנֶּאֱמַר כִּי מָצָא בָהּ עֶרְוַת דָּבָר. רַבִּי עֲקִיבָא אוֹמֵר, אֲפִלּוּ מָצָא אַחֶרֶת נָאָה הֵימֶנָּה, שֶׁנֶּאֱמַר וְהָיָה אִם לֹא תִמְצָא חֵן בְּעֵינָיו:

Gittin 9:10

The school of Shammai says: A man should not divorce his wife unless he has found her guilty of some unseemly conduct, as it says, "Because he has found some unseemly thing in her" (Deuteronomy 24:1) The school of Hillel says [that he may divorce her] even if she merely has burnt his dish, since it says, "Because he has found some unseemly thing in her." Rabbi Akiva says, [he may divorce her] even if he finds another woman more beautiful than she is, as it says, "it comes to pass, if she finds no favor in his eyes" (v. 1).

The final mishna in Tractate Gittin discusses the cases and conditions under which a couple break up. The dissolving of a marriage is not to be taken lightly, which is why the Sages say a reason is required. The Mishna presents three opinions on the matter, and it seems they reflect varying conceptions of the essence of wedlock.

The School of Shammai: Marriage as Imperative

The first commandment to Adam and Eve was, "Be fruitful and multiply, and replenish the earth" (Genesis 1:28). Based on this verse, many sources from the Second Temple era posited that procreation was the primary purpose of the relationship between husband and wife.[1] This outlook also appears in another mishna in our tractate, when the Sages of the school of Shammai explain why they are loath to abide a situation in which one is prevented from marrying: "But wasn't the world made only to be populated?" (Gittin 4:5)[2] In a different context (Berakhot 1:3) we saw the tendency of the school of Shammai to see the performance of the mitzvot as the pinnacle of holiness. The conception of marriage as a means for procreation is an extension of the view that human existence is a means for the performance of mitzvot.

An implication of limiting the meaning of the institution of marriage to a commandment is to minimize the range of legitimate reasons for the dissolution of a marriage. Matrimony, according to the school of Shammai, should be geared toward religious objectives in the area of intimate relations, so that only a religious transgression in that area – "uncovered her shame (*erva*)"[3] – can be grounds for divorce. This is the case both as a matter of principle and as a halakhic consequence; an adulteress is forbidden from having relations with her husband, so that the couple is prevented from fulfilling the commandment to procreate.

The School of Hillel: Marriage as Life

The school of Hillel permits divorce "even if she merely has burnt his dish." The implication is that any damage to a couple's shared life – not just their intimate relations – is grounds for divorce. Of course, the image of a burnt dish is an example, a symbol for the problems that can arise in a marriage. But it is not a random image: The Hebrew word for "burnt," "*hikdiḥa*," comes from the root k-d-ḥ, which in the Bible connotes anger, and the school of Hillel employs it in order to hint at the range of problems that arise in the home:

1. Adiel Schremer, *Male and Female He Created Them: Jewish Marriage in Late Second Temple, Mishnah and Talmud Periods* (Jerusalem: The Zalman Shazar Center for Jewish History, 2003) [Hebrew], 304. These sources include *Tanna'im* and Josephus.
2. My thanks to Aviad Yehieli, who brought this to my attention.
3. According to the Kaufmann Manuscript this is what the Mishna says, rather than "found her guilty of some unseemly conduct (*ervat davar*)".

> "For a fire is kindled (*kadḥa*) in My nostril, and burns into the depths of the netherworld, and devours the earth with its produce, and sets ablaze the foundations of the mountains." (Deuteronomy 32:22)
>
> And elsewhere:
>
> And I will make you to pass with your enemies into a land that you know not; for a fire is kindled (*kadḥa*) in My nostril, which shall burn upon you. (Jeremiah 15:14)

The link between God's wrath and marital strife casts the rift between the partners as a "cosmic" disaster; not merely an ending, a missed opportunity to fulfill a commandment, but the death of a complete organism – the family unit.

For the school of Hillel, the connection between husband and wife is not reduced to intimate relations and procreation, but rather includes the entirety of their relationship: "Enjoy life with the wife whom you love" (Ecclesiastes 9:9). The marital relationship is about "life" – not some achievement or specific goal, but rather the shared life itself. As we have seen,[4] the schools of Shammai and Hillel have a fundamental disagreement over whether meaning is to be found only in the context of mitzvot, as the school of Shammai posits, or rather in life itself, which is the opinion of the school of Hillel. This dispute is also reflected here. According to the school of Shammai it is only through the performance of mitzvot that one can attain religious and spiritual meaning, while the school of Hillel strives to inject holiness into mundane existence.

Rabbi Akiva: Love

Unlike the schools of Shammai and Hillel, who permit divorce only in negative contexts, Rabbi Akiva says that even if on the face of it "everything is fine" between husband and wife other than diminished attraction, there are grounds for divorce. It is noteworthy that in using the word "beautiful," Rabbi Akiva does not mean only physical beauty. The

4. In the chapter discussing Berakhot 1:3.

Talmud quotes him as saying: "Who is wealthy?... He who has a wife [beautiful] in deeds" (Shabbat 25b).

Rabbi Akiva's opinion in our mishna stems from his belief in the sanctity of the love between husband and wife as the foundation of marriage. Here is what he says about the Song of Songs: "The whole world is not worth the day on which the Song of Songs was given to Israel; for all the writings are holy, but the Song of Songs is the Holy of Holies" (Yadayim 3:5). It seems his statement does not relate only to the allegorical meaning of the Song of Songs – as a parable of the love between God and Israel – but also to the text's overt meaning, as a love story between husband and wife. To him, that love is itself the Holy of Holies and is anchored in supernal love: "Rabbi Akiva expounded: When husband and wife are worthy, the Divine Presence abides with them" (Sota 17a). For Rabbi Akiva, love is the goal; therefore, divorce becomes a possibility even for couples that function in general but are no longer attracted to each other. The Yerushalmi (Kiddushin 1:1) offers the opinion that only Jewish couples are allowed to divorce – and not gentiles – as natural law would dictate that after a man and woman become "one flesh" (Genesis 2:24) by marital union this bond is irreversible. It is only because in Judaism the marital bond is so demanding that there is divine dispensation to dissolve the marriage when the high expectation are not met. The Yerushalmi's statement there that "God only mentioned His name in the context of divorce with regard to Israel" hints at Rabbi Akiva's outlook, by which God brings His presence to the marital relationship.

The Creation of Man and Woman

The source for the varying approaches of the *Tanna'im* to marriage can be found in the different emphases placed by the story of the creation of Adam and Eve:

Marriage as commandment: "And God said to them, 'Be fruitful, and multiply, and replenish the earth'" (Genesis 1:28);

Marriage as shared life: "And the Lord God said: 'It is not good that the man should be alone'" (Genesis 2:19);

And marriage as love ("love" in Hebrew has the same numerical value as "one"): "Therefore a man shall leave his father and his mother, and cleave to his wife, and they shall be one flesh" (Genesis 2:24).

Finally, it is crucial that the allowance of divorce, and the existence of circumstances that call for the dissolution of a marriage, not erode our understanding of the price that comes with it. It is in this spirit that the Talmud ends Tractate Gittin:

> Rabbi Elazar said: If a man divorces his first wife, even the altar sheds tears, as it says (Malachi 2), "And this as well you do: You cover the altar of the Lord with tears, with weeping and with sighing, because He no longer regards your offering, nor does he receive it with good will from your hand. Yet you say, 'Why?' Because the Lord has been a witness between you and the wife of your youth, whom you have treated with treachery, though she is your companion and the wife of your covenant." (Gittin 90b)

The Revelation of Elijah in Tractate Kiddushin

Kiddushin 1:7

All obligations of the son upon the father, men are obligated, but women are exempt. But all obligations of the father upon the son, both men and women are obligated. All positive, time-bound commandments, men are obligated, and women are exempt. But all positive non-time-bound commandments, both men and women are obligated. And all negative commandments, whether time-bound or not time-bound, both men and women are obligated, except for the prohibition against rounding [the corners of the head], and the prohibition against marring [the corner of the beard], and the prohibition [for a priest] to become impure through contact with the dead.

קידושין א, ז

כָּל מִצְוֹת הָאָב עַל הַבֵּן, הָאֲנָשִׁים חַיָּבִים וְהַנָּשִׁים פְּטוּרוֹת. וְכָל מִצְוֹת הַבֵּן עַל הָאָב, אֶחָד אֲנָשִׁים וְאֶחָד נָשִׁים חַיָּבִין. וְכָל מִצְוַת עֲשֵׂה שֶׁהַזְּמָן גְּרָמָהּ, אֲנָשִׁים חַיָּבִין וְהַנָּשִׁים פְּטוּרוֹת. וְכָל מִצְוַת עֲשֵׂה שֶׁלֹּא הַזְּמָן גְּרָמָהּ, אֶחָד אֲנָשִׁים וְאֶחָד נָשִׁים חַיָּבִין. וְכָל מִצְוָה בְּלֹא תַעֲשֶׂה בֵּין שֶׁהַזְּמָן גְּרָמָהּ וּבֵין שֶׁלֹּא הַזְּמָן גְּרָמָהּ, אֶחָד אֲנָשִׁים וְאֶחָד נָשִׁים חַיָּבִין, חוּץ מִבַּל תַּשְׁחִית וּמִבַּל תַּקִּיף וּמִבַּל תִּטַּמֵּא לַמֵּתִים:

A Sage or a Prophet

The well-known mishna above from Kiddushin discusses two types of commandments with significance in the context of the family: All obligations of the son upon the father, men are obligated, but women are exempt. But all obligations of the father upon the son…" It seems that the formulation for these categories can be found in the closing verse of the Bible's Prophets section, which describes the prophet Elijah's future mission:

> Behold, I will send you Elijah the prophet before the coming of the great and terrible day of the Lord. And he shall turn the heart of the fathers upon the sons, and the heart of the sons upon their fathers; lest I come and smite the land with utter destruction. (Malachi 3:23–24)

The two sources are concerned with the relationship between fathers and sons, and both express the mutuality of that relationship by reversing the opening sentence ("of the son upon the father" to "of the father upon the son," and "of the fathers upon the sons" to "of the sons upon their fathers"). Furthermore, in the Mishna, as in the biblical verse, the relation between the fathers and sons is described with the word "upon."[1]

Malachi 3:24	Kiddushin 1:7
And he shall turn the heart	All obligations
of the fathers	of the father
upon	upon
the sons	the son
and the heart	[and] obligations
of the sons	of the son
upon	upon
their fathers	the father

1. Further along, we will discuss the significance of the word "upon" in this context.

What is the significance of the similarity between the mishna and the verse? What can we learn from the intertextual link between the two sources?

The verse describes a state of alienation between fathers and sons. Elijah, when he arrives, will bring fathers and sons closer together and restore the relationship. The major difference between the two sources is that while the biblical verse discusses "turning the heart," the mishna talks about the "obligations" that lie between father and son. On the face of it, this is a major difference. However, the content of these commandments, as they are delineated in the Tosefta, yields a fresh perspective on the connection between the two sources:

> What is an obligation of the son upon the father? Feeding, giving drink, clothing, anointing, taking out and bringing in, washing his face, hands, and legs.... What is an obligation of the father upon the son? To circumcise him, redeem him [if he is a firstborn], to teach him Torah, to teach him a trade, and to marry him to a wife. Some say: Also [to teach him] to swim in the river. (Tosefta Kiddushin 1:8)

The commandments defining the mutual obligations are a realization of the vision of reconciliation between fathers and sons. The son's obligations express his role and status as a son – honoring his father and caring for him – while the father fulfills his role by observing five commandments that contain all of the necessary elements to ensure the son's material survival and religious development. One side of the coin is that the son is raised to become the next link in the generational chain: He is initiated into the covenant through circumcision, and he studies the Torah in order to lead a religious lifestyle. On the other side of the coin, in order to ensure the son's material survival, the father must teach him a profession and find him a wife – so that he can earn a livelihood and build a family of his own.[2] We see here a mutual system: The son's

2. My friend Amnon Dokov pointed out to me that the obligation "to marry him to a wife" closes one circle of life and opens another one – when the son himself becomes a father.

mission is to honor his father and care for his needs, while the father's responsibility is to prepare his son for life.

In his essay "A Sage Is Preferable to a Prophet,"[3] Rabbi Abraham Isaac Kook compares the figure of the prophet, the possessor of sweeping vision, to the sage, a man of details. It seems that we can employ his distinction in order to describe the passage from the Bible to the Mishna on this topic: While Malachi's prophecy presents a general vision of intimacy between fathers and sons, the Mishna lays down a concrete and detailed method for characterizing and shaping that relationship.

The continuation of the line of succession from father to son, as part of the covenant between God and the Jewish people, also relates to the Jewish people's presence on its land:

> Therefore you shall lay these My words in your heart.... And you shall teach them to your children, talking of them when you sit in your house, and when you walk by the way, and when you lie down, and when you rise up.... that your days may be multiplied, and the days of your children, upon the land that the Lord swore to your fathers to give them, as the days of the heavens above the earth. (Deuteronomy 11:18–21)

Returning to the father's obligations toward the son in the above Tosefta, we see that those commandments relate to both the chain of tradition and the perpetuation of the covenant, both of which enable the close relationship between God and the Jewish people. Circumcision, the first commandment in the Torah, brings the son into the Jewish people's covenant with God.[4] When the father teaches his son Torah, he channels the "Torah of Moses" and transmits the tradition and covenant to future generations. The redemption of the son also brings him into the chain of

---

3. *Orot HaKodesh* 120–21.
4. As we noted, Elijah is the one sent to reunite the hearts of the fathers and sons, and indeed there is a tradition according to which he shows up at every circumcision. See the *Pesikta DeRav Kahana* (Mandelbaum edition) 28:4, in the section beginning with "*Ten ḥelek*"; and *Pirkei DeRabbi Eliezer* 20.

tradition, by instilling the historic consciousness that comes with recalling the Jewish people's foundational event – the Exodus from Egypt.[5]

It seems that conveying the tradition and raising the son are not one-sided actions. The father gives to the son, who in turn honors his father. It takes two sides to carry on the Jewish tradition – together father and son constitute a single link in the mighty chain of generations.

Inheriting the Land

Like the transmission of tradition from father to son, our verse – "And he shall turn the heart of the fathers upon the sons, and the heart of the sons upon their fathers" – relates to the Jewish people's return to the Land of Israel. The verse concludes, "lest I come and smite the land with utter destruction," meaning that a failure to carry out Elijah's mission to bring fathers and sons together will cause the failure of the covenant of Mount Horeb, the covenant of the land.

> Similarly, the Mishna in Kiddushin, right after listing the commandments that divide men from women, and those that are required by father and sons, notes the connection between observance and the land:
>
> Anyone who performs one commandment is rewarded, his days are prolonged, and he inherits the land. But anyone who does not perform one commandment is not rewarded, his days are not prolonged, and he does not inherit the land. (Kiddushin 1:10)

According to the Mishna, each commandment has an effect on the relationship between the individual and the land. The Mishna, according to which the inheritance of the land depends on adherence to the commandments, is based on the verses that appear directly following the Ten Commandments in the book of Deuteronomy:

5. See Exodus 13:14–15.

> But as for you, stand here by Me, and I will speak to you **all the commandment**, and the statutes, and the ordinances, which you shall teach them, **that they may do them in the land that I give them to possess it.**… You shall walk in all the way that the Lord your God has commanded you, so that you may live, **and so that it may be well with you, and so that you may prolong your days in the land that you shall possess.** (Deuteronomy 5:27–29)

If the Israelites are to live a life of abundance on the land, they must fulfill their end of the covenant by following the statutes and ordinances. Conversely, if the heart of the sons is not turned upon their fathers, and the fathers do not fulfill their obligations toward their sons, they will suffer the calamity that Malachi describes at the end of the verse: "…lest I come and smite the land with utter destruction." In the words of the Mishna, "he who does not perform one commandment is not rewarded, his days are not prolonged, and he does not inherit the land."

The Mishna continues in a similar vein:

> One who is familiar with Bible, Mishna, and the ways of the land will not easily sin, as it is said, "And a threefold cord is not quickly broken" (Ecclesiastes 4:12). But one who is not familiar with Bible, Mishna, and the ways of the land does not belong to civilization. (Kiddushin 1:10)

Rabbi Walfish[6] notes that "Bible, Mishna, and the ways of the land" are among the obligations of the father upon the son (based on the Tosefta's elaboration), so that this mishna is thematically linked to 1:7. Based on our proposal above, we can say that the connection between the two mishnayot lies in the observation that a father's failure to live up to his obligations toward his son is in effect a failure to turn the heart of the fathers upon the sons. According to the verse in Malachi, this failure results in the smiting of the land, while the Mishna says that one who fails "does not belong to civilization." It follows that the two sections in

6. Walfish, *Rosh HaShanah*, 45–46.

the second half of our chapter are parallel to the two parts of the verse in Malachi.

The Jewish Tradition Is Maintained Thanks to the Parent-Child Relationship

I once heard Rabbi Jonathan Sacks tell of two ancient nations that sought eternity and found it. The Egyptians immortalized themselves by building magnificent monuments to withstand the winds of time – the pyramids, which stand to this day throughout the desert. The Israelites, too, found their way to eternity, but via a different approach. In Moses's first address to the children of Israel, even before the Exodus is completed, he entreats his flock to tell their children and their children's children what they have seen. Since then, every generation has carried out Moses's will, and the Jewish tradition is thus maintained through the living bond between parents and children. Ultimately, Egypt's eternity is perpetuated in death, while the Jewish eternity is via life.

The Mishna's Interpretation and That of the *Rishonim*

The word "upon" (*al*), which appears twice in the verse in Malachi – "And he shall turn the heart of the fathers upon the sons, and the heart of the sons upon their fathers" – is used in the sense of "to." Thus, the verse describes the intimacy between fathers and sons that will be generated when their hearts will return each to the other. However, some commentators diverge from that interpretation, which seems to be the one favored by the Mishna, and read the verse in the broader context of the chapter. To them, the verse, like the rest of the chapter, is part of a narrative regarding the Jewish people's return to God, as is discussed in the preceding chapters: Return to Me and I will return to you, says the Lord of hosts (Malachi 3:7). That was the reason the commentators tended to see the verse about turning the hearts of the fathers as a type of response to the beginning of the chapter, which describes a return of the Jewish people to God rather than a reunification of the fathers and the sons.

However, I wish to propose another possibility: Based on the Mishna, we can posit an interpretation of the verse in Malachi that retains the straightforward reading of the verse while allowing us to understand its broader context in the chapter. First, we must note that the coming together of the fathers and the sons is what ultimately facilitates the coming together of the Jewish people and God. The answer to the question, "How shall we return?" (Malachi 3:7) is:

> Remember the law of Moses My servant, which I commanded to him in Horeb for all of Israel, even statutes and ordinances. (Malachi 3:22)

To remember that "which I commanded to him in Horeb" is to recall the covenant between God and the Israelites, which they uphold by adhering to the commandments (Deuteronomy 5:2–3). Based on our proposal, the Mishna sees in the "turning of the heart" between the fathers and the sons an intimacy that also has an imperative aspect, a shift that shows the way to repentance – back to God. The intimacy expressed through the commandments is, among other things, a remembrance, a tradition passed from father to son and the upholding of the covenant made at Sinai – a covenant that enables the Jewish people's return to their God.

Acquisition and Obligation

קידושין א, ו

כָּל הַנַּעֲשָׂה דָמִים בְּאַחֵר, כֵּיוָן שֶׁזָּכָה זֶה, נִתְחַיֵּב בַּחֲלִיפָיו. כֵּיצַד, הֶחֱלִיף שׁוֹר בְּפָרָה אוֹ חֲמוֹר בְּשׁוֹר, כֵּיוָן שֶׁזָּכָה זֶה, נִתְחַיֵּב בַּחֲלִיפָיו. רְשׁוּת הַגָּבוֹהַּ, בְּכֶסֶף. וּרְשׁוּת הַהֶדְיוֹט, בַּחֲזָקָה. אֲמִירָתוֹ לַגָּבוֹהַּ, כִּמְסִירָתוֹ לַהֶדְיוֹט:

Kiddushin 1:6

Whatever can be used as payment for another object, as soon as this one takes possession [of the object], the other one assumes liability for what is given in exchange. How so? If one exchanges an ox for a cow, or a donkey for an ox, as soon as this one takes possession, the other one assumes liability for what is given in exchange. The Sanctuary's title to property [is acquired] by money; the title of an ordinary person to property by *ḥazaka*. Dedication to the Sanctuary is equal to delivery to an ordinary person.

The first chapter of Tractate Kiddushin in the Mishna can be divided into two parts: The first part (mishnayot 1–6) is about acquisition, while the second part (mishnayot 7–10) is about obligation in mitzvot. Although a casual reading may yield the impression that the two parts of the chapter were "stitched together," Rabbi Walfish has established a connection between them, in terms of both theme and literary form.

He claims that the editor of the chapter uses mishna 6 as a "transitional mishna" to link the two parts together. While the mishna's theme places it in the first half of the chapter, it opens with the word "all" (*kol*)[1] – just like the mishnayot of the second half, which deal with commandments. In addition, it favors the term "*nitḥayev*" (translated here as "assumes liability"), which is prevalent in the second half of the chapter, over the term "*kana*" (or "acquired"), which pervades the first half.[2] Walfish further points at several instances of wordplay linking the two parts of the chapter together:[3]

1. The **death** of the husband/his brother (the *yavam*)/master (1:1–2); "the prohibition to become impure through contact with **the dead**" (1:7); "his days are prolonged" (1:10).
2. "A woman is acquired in **three ways**" (1:1); "and a **threefold** cord... and the **ways** of the land (1:10).
3. "Money, deed, or possession (*ḥazaka*)" (1:3, 1:5); "the title of an ordinary person to property by possession" (1:6); "one who holds (*hamaḥazik*) to all three" (1:10).

According to Walfish, the link between the "acquisition section" and the "commandment section" is the link between the family unit and performing mitzvot, including the settlement of the land:

> The halakhic acquisition, of a woman or of land, underlies the inheritance at the end of the chapter.... One can say that the term "inheritance" ("*naḥala*," which also connotes a tract of land) merges one's familial status and financial situation.... The acquisition of a wife in the acquisition section establishes the family unit that appears at the outset of the commandment section, in which the father is enjoined to prepare his son to take his place in society, both spiritually and financially, and to carry on the family by acquiring a wife of his own. Thus, when one adheres to

1. Walfish, Literary Phenomena, 40.
2. Ibid., 43, see footnote 36 there.
3. Ibid., 46.

> these commandments fully, he prolongs his own days and those of his family, and they inherit the land.[4]

In this chapter we will develop this interpretation, both in relation to the chapter's literary structure and in terms of the implication of the juxtaposition of its two sections. The assertion that there is an intentional link between the two parts of the chapter is supported by several parallels between them. For example, the first section (1:1–5) lists ten things that can be acquired: a wife, a *yevama*, a Hebrew slave, a Hebrew maidservant, a slave "whose ear is bored," a Canaanite slave, a large animal, a small animal, a property that has security, and a property that does not have security.

We find in the second section of the chapter (1:7–10) ten statements that begin with the word "*kol*" (translated as "all," "anyone," or "every"). These statements can be divided into two – five dealing with the differences in the obligations of men and women (1:7), and five regarding the land (1:9–10).

It seems that the "transitional mishna" (1:6) has an important role in establishing the connection between the two parts of the chapter: It is concerned with transactions, and links together the two parts in terms of its style while thematically echoing the message of the entire chapter:

> Whatever can be used as payment for another object, as soon as this one takes possession [of the object], the other one assumes liability for what is given in exchange. How so? If one exchanges an ox for a cow, or a donkey for an ox, as soon as this one takes possession, the other one assumes liability for what is given in exchange. The Sanctuary's title to property [is acquired] by money; the title of an ordinary person to property by *ḥazaka*. Dedication to the Sanctuary is equal to delivery to an ordinary person. (Kiddushin 1:6)

4. Walfish, *Literary Phenomena*, 59. He also notes there that the chapter is structured after the verse "Moreover, Ruth the Moabitess, the wife of Mahlon, I have acquired to be my wife, to raise up the name of the dead upon his inheritance."

We noted above that our mishna uses the term "*nit'ḥayev*" (translated here as "assumes liability") instead of "*kana*" (or "acquired"), which is used repeatedly in 1:1–5. It seems that the substitution is deliberate. In 1:5 we read, "[Property] that does not have security is acquired only by being drawn [to the purchaser]," meaning that to take ownership of goods and chattels, which do not have security, one must hold them physically in one's hand. For this reason, mishna 4, which relates to the ways in which one can acquire animals, emphasizes the need for a physical action in order to transfer ownership. The idea that acquisition is physical is bolstered by the principle elucidated at the end of 1:6: "the title of an ordinary person to property by *ḥazaka*," meaning that one can assume ownership of something only through concrete action.

It appears that the root of the issue is the idea that ownership is concrete and does not rely solely on an abstract legal relationship. A person can be considered the owner of an object only if he has physically held it. Acquisition constitutes transfer of ownership, so that it makes sense that the transfer would be effected by passing the property from hand to hand (or by pulling it, or raising it up, and so forth) – a gesture signifying that from now on the buyer owns that property. This also explains why payment on its own is not enough to take ownership: the transfer of funds is not an expression of *ḥazaka* over the property.

In light of these insights, let us reexamine what type of ownership transfer would not require physical action. As we noted, the mishna does not employ the language of acquisition to describe barter, but rather uses the term "assumes liability." The implication is that although the first party in the transaction takes ownership of an object through a regular acquisition, i.e., applying physical action to the object, the second party receives only a commitment and not ownership, as no action has been performed by him on the object he seeks to acquire.[5]

Again, when we take another look at the placing of our mishna within the chapter, we find that it forms the link between the two parts of the chapter, between acquisitions and commandments. **The affinity**

5. Thus it is clear why a woman cannot be acquired through an exchange: The basis of the relationship between husband and wife is manifested in their concrete, physical connection, so that a mere commitment is insufficient to create a bond.

between the two parts of the chapter expresses the idea that a person's property generates a responsibility to fulfill the mitzvot.

The connection between responsibility and ownership is also apparent in the shared topics addressed by both the first and the second sections of the chapter. The part that deals with acquisitions opens with acquiring a wife, while the section that focuses on commandments opens with the commandments of fathers and sons, which derive from the acquisition of a wife and starting a family. In the middle of the section on acquisitions we read about the ways in which an animal is acquired (1:4), while the middle of the second section contains an elaboration of the commandments having to do with animals that are brought as sacrifices (1:8). Ending both sections are discussions of issues related to the land: mishna 5 is devoted to the acquisition of land, while mishna 9 is about commandments that derive from it.

It follows that the chapter has a cyclical structure, from the world of acquisitions to the world of commandments (acquisitions generate a responsibility regarding the commandments), and from the world of commandments to the world of acquisitions (adherence to the commandments ensures that the land will be inherited): "Anyone who performs one commandment is rewarded, his days are prolonged, and he inherits the land. But anyone who does not perform one commandment is not rewarded, his days are not prolonged, and he does not inherit the land" (Kiddushin 1:10).

Our chapter's two sections constitute twin aspects of the covenant between God and the Jewish people, establishing the reciprocative link between inheritance and commandments, as summed up by mishna 10. Thus we return to the central topic of the previous chapter – the mission of Elijah the Prophet, the Angel of the Covenant, to reunite the hearts of fathers and sons.

The Structure of the Second Half of the Chapter

In the context of the structure of the chapter it is noteworthy that there are ten mishnayot. Furthermore, as we saw, the second half of the chapter includes a list of ten items, just like the first half. In fact, this list is made up of two similarly structured sub-lists. Each of those lists includes five items; they consist of a principle and its opposite, another principle and its opposite, and a fifth principle. This structure provides further evidence of deliberate literary editing:

	1:7–8	1:9–10
Principle	**All** obligations of the son upon the father, men are obligated, but women are exempt.	**Every** commandment that is dependent on the land is practiced only in the land [of Israel].
Its opposite	**All** obligations of the father upon the son, both men and women are obligated.	**Every** commandment that is not dependent on the land is practiced both in and outside the land.
Principle	**All** positive, time-bound commandments, men are obligated and women are exempt.	**Anyone** who performs one commandment is rewarded, his days are prolonged, and he inherits the land.
Its opposite	**All** positive, non-time-bound commandments, both men and women are obligated.	**Anyone** who does not perform one commandment is not rewarded, his days are not prolonged, and he does not inherit the land.
Principle	**All** negative commandments, whether time-bound or not time-bound, both men and women are obligated.	**Anyone** who is not familiar with Bible, Mishna, and the ways of the land does not belong to civilization.

Ox or Mr. Ox?

בבא קמא א, א

אַרְבָּעָה אֲבוֹת נְזִיקִים, הַשּׁוֹר וְהַבּוֹר וְהַמַּבְעֶה וְהַהֶבְעֵר לֹא הֲרֵי הַשּׁוֹר כַּהֲרֵי הַמַּבְעֶה, וְלֹא הֲרֵי הַמַּבְעֶה כַּהֲרֵי הַשּׁוֹר. וְלֹא זֶה וָזֶה, שֶׁיֵּשׁ בָּהֶן רוּחַ חַיִּים, כַּהֲרֵי הָאֵשׁ שֶׁאֵין בּוֹ רוּחַ חַיִּים. וְלֹא זֶה וָזֶה, שֶׁדַּרְכָּן לֵילֵךְ וּלְהַזִּיק, כַּהֲרֵי הַבּוֹר שֶׁאֵין דַּרְכּוֹ לֵילֵךְ וּלְהַזִּיק. הַצַּד הַשָּׁוֶה שֶׁבָּהֶן, שֶׁדַּרְכָּן לְהַזִּיק וּשְׁמִירָתָן עָלֶיךָ. וּכְשֶׁהִזִּיק, חָב הַמַּזִּיק לְשַׁלֵּם תַּשְׁלוּמֵי נֶזֶק בְּמֵיטַב הָאָרֶץ.

Bava Kama 1:1

There are four primary causes of injury: the ox, and the pit, and the crop-destroying beast, and fire. [The distinctive feature of] the ox is not like [that of] the crop-destroying beast, nor is [the distinctive feature of] either of these, which are alive, like [that of] fire, which is not alive; nor is [the distinctive feature of] any of these, whose way it is to go forth and do injury, like [that of] the pit, whose way it is not to go forth and do injury. What they have in common is that it is their way to do injury and that you are responsible for watching over them; and if one of them caused injury, whoever [is responsible] for the injury must make restitution [to the damaged party] with the best of his land.

Tractate Bava Kama opens with four types of damage, which are called primary causes of injury: oxen, pits, crop-destroying beasts, and fire. Rashi explains the order of the list: "They are ordered in the Mishna in the same order in which they appear in the *parasha* [*Mishpatim*], for the first section discusses an ox, the second a pit."[1]

1. Rashi on Bava Kama 2:1, in the section beginning with the words "the ox and the pit."

Rashi's statement is surprising in light of the fact that the section about a pit – "And if a man shall open a pit" (Exodus 21:33) – precedes the section that discusses an ox that causes damage: "And when one man's ox should hurt another's" (v. 35). Rashi, in saying that the "first section" addresses the ox, was probably alluding to verse 28: "And when an ox should gore a man or a woman to death." However, that verse is not about an ox that causes damage but rather one that kills a person. It follows that the Mishna uses the word "ox" to refer to two separate cases that seemingly belong in two separate legal categories: manslaughter and property damage. The Me'iri makes this case explicitly, writing: "The ox: both an ox that causes damage to a man, about which [the Torah] says, 'And when [an ox] should gore'... and an ox that damages another ox, about which [the Torah] says, 'And when [one man's ox] should hurt another's.'"

The equation of a killer ox to an ox that damages is a motif of Tractate Bava Kama. When an ox injures or kills a person, the Torah uses the word "gore" (*yigaḥ*), but when an ox injures an animal it employs the term "hurt" (*yigof*). The Mishna, on the other hand, always uses "gore" – even when the victim is another ox.[2]

The structure of the tractate supports the comparison. Throughout Bava Kama, the Mishna elaborates on each of the four primary causes of injury listed in our mishna. The section of the tractate dealing with the definition of "the ox" (3:8 through 5:4) combines the laws of a killer ox with those of an ox that damages. In some cases, a single mishna transitions from one topic to another without warning:

> [If] an ox of a person of sound senses gored the ox of a deaf-mute, an insane person, or a minor, [its owner] is obligated. [If] an ox of a deaf-mute, an insane person, or a minor gored the ox of a person of sound senses, [its owner] is exempt... An ox from the stadium is not liable to be put to death, as it says, "When [it] should gore" (Exodus 21:28), and not "When others cause it to gore." (Bava Kama 4:4)

2. Bava Kama 4:1, 3–4; 5:1. My thanks to my friend Rabbi Meir Lichtenstein for pointing this out to me.

This mishna opens with an ox that gores another ox and concludes with an ox that kills a man. The next few mishnayot are about a killer ox, but 4:9 revisits the subject of an ox that causes damage. While we may assume the editor deliberately blended the two categories in the Mishna, what is the message he sought to convey?

Whenever two categories are merged, the question is which of them defines the other. The use of the word "gore," from the verses dealing with a killer ox, in the context of an ox that merely causes damage – as well as the choice to put "the ox" before "the pit" in the mishna above, as we have seen – shows us that the Mishna is seeking to define the laws of an ox that damages in light of the laws of a killer ox. The Torah verses on killer oxen can help us unearth the significance of this comparison.

Punishment of a Killer Ox

> And when an ox should gore a man or a woman to death, the ox shall surely be stoned, and its flesh shall not be eaten, but the owner of the ox is exempt. But if the ox was wont to gore in times past, and its owner has been warned but he has not kept it in, and it has killed a man or a woman, the ox shall be stoned, and its owner shall also be put to death. (Exodus 21:28–29)

The sentence for a killer ox is death by stoning. Some Torah commentators[3] consider this law a realization of the demand in *Parashat Noaḥ*: "And surely your blood of your lives I will require; at the hand of every beast I will require it; and at the hand of man, even at the hand of every man's brother, will I require the life of man" (Genesis 9:5). In the demand for the blood of the slain no distinction is made between a human who kills a human and an animal that kills a human – both are liable. Based on the verses above, from Exodus, the purpose of killing the ox is not to punish its owner, for the Torah states that "the owner of the ox is exempt." Nor is the purpose solely to prevent more damage, for the

---

3. Nahmanides on Genesis 9:5.

specific instruction is to stone the ox – the insistence on killing it in a certain way implies that the ox is being punished.

The Mishna contains further evidence that the ox is killed as a punishment:

> The ox that is stoned [is judged] by twenty-three, as it says, "The ox shall be stoned, and its owner shall also be put to death" (Exodus 21:29) – as is the death of the owner, so too is the death of the ox. (Sanhedrin 1:4)

We have seen that, legally speaking, a killer ox falls into the same category as a human murderer. Another similarity lies in the fact that both humans and oxen are exempt if they kill involuntarily:

> If an ox was rubbing itself against a wall and it fell on a person; or if it intended to kill an animal and it killed a man; or if it intended to kill a gentile and it killed an Israelite; or if it intended to kill an untimely birth and it killed a viable infant, it is exempt [from death by stoning]. (Bava Kama 4:6)

Another killer ox that is exempt from execution is a fighting bull:

> An ox from the stadium is not liable to be put to death, as it says, "When [it] should gore" (Exodus 21:28), and not "When others cause it to gore." (Bava Kama 4:4)

The stadium ox is an ox that has been trained to kill. One would think that, if the putting to death of an ox had to do with preventing future damage, the stadium ox would be the first to be killed, because it is the most dangerous. And yet, it is exempt. Because the nature of this ox is to kill, it does not have moral liability, just like a "captured infant" (a Jew who is raised without a religious education). According to Rav (Bava Kama 40b), because it was forced to become a killer, the stadium ox is also not precluded from being offered as a sacrifice – unlike other oxen that have killed.

The ox's similarity to a person is also evident in the severity with which the act of killing is treated. The Mekhilta of Rabbi Yishmael rules that no use can be made of the carcass of an ox that was stoned to death – via an a fortiori argument from a similar law regarding the decapitated calf (see Deuteronomy 21):

> If a decapitated calf, which does not defile the land and does not drive away the Divine Presence, is forbidden from [human] enjoyment, should not a stoned ox, which does defile the land and drive away the Divine Presence, be forbidden from [human] enjoyment? (Mekhilta of Rabbi Yishmael, *Masekhta DeNezikin, Mishpatim* 10)

The Mekhilta too compares killer oxen to human murderers, of whom it is said that they defile the earth.

The Ox's Responsibility for Itself

It is often thought that a person's responsibility for damage caused by his property is a criminal liability stemming from the fact that he was not careful with his property. However, this perspective is challenged in the case of a so-called "harmless" ox (an ox is given three strikes before it is considered "dangerous") that gores another ox: One would think that if "the owner of the ox is exempt" when it kills a man, and is considered negligent only if the ox has gored in the past, the case would be the same with an ox that merely causes damage. Why, then, does the Torah require payment in the case of an ox that injures another ox?

It seems that the Mishna's answer to the question lies in its equation of the killer ox to the ox that damages. On a basic level, it is not the owner of the ox who is liable, but rather the ox itself. When an ox is a murderer it must be put to death, and when it causes damage it must pay. The ox itself is considered a legal person, so that he is no longer just any old ox, but rather Mr. Ox. But the question remains: What does it mean for the ox to "pay"? Do oxen possess property?

The answer is, to me, the strongest proof for the assertion that the ox has legal personality, for indeed, in the case of a harmless ox that gores another ox, it is the goring ox that pays rather than its owner! Thus we can explain one of the most surprising laws regarding a harmless ox: It can pay damages only "from its own body" (Bava Kama 1:4), meaning that the compensation to the injured party cannot exceed the value of the attacking ox. In addition, as opposed to other types of damage, for which the owner must pay "with the best of his land" (1:1), here the payment itself is made with the body of the attacking ox, as the verse shows: "And when one man's ox should hurt another's, so that it dies, they shall sell the live ox and divide the price of it, and the dead they also shall divide" (Exodus 21:35).

It seems that the underlying logic here is the same as in the case of a killer ox, which is also punished for its actions. The stoning of a killer ox is equivalent to the payment of damages in the case of an ox that damages. The owner is not the party responsible for the damages caused by the ox, so the ox itself assumes liability and the damages are collected from its body. This idea – that the ox is liable rather than the owner – appears explicitly in the name of the *Tanna* Rabbi Shimon:

> In case of injury [an ox caused] unintentionally, Rabbi Yehuda says there is liability to pay [damages], but Rabbi Shimon says there is no liability to pay. What is the reason of Rabbi Yehuda? He derives [the law of damages] from that of *kofer*: Just as for *kofer* there is liability even where there was no intention [to kill], so also for damages for injuries there is liability even where there was no intention [to injure]. Rabbi Shimon, on the other hand, derived [the law of damages] from that of the killing of the ox: Just as the stoning of the ox is not required where there was no intention [to kill], so also damages are not required where there was no intention [to injure]. But why should Rabbi Yehuda not also derive [the ruling in this case] from [the law applying to the] killing [of the ox]? It is proper to derive [a ruling regarding] payment from [another ruling regarding] payment, but it is not proper to derive [a ruling regarding] payment from [a ruling regarding] killing. Why then should Rabbi Shimon not also derive [the ruling in

> this case] from [the law applying to] *kofer*? It is proper to derive a liability regarding the ox from another liability that similarly concerns the ox, thus excluding *kofer*, which is a liability that concerns only the owner. (Bava Kama 44b)

According to Rabbi Shimon, an ox that damages is liable only when it intended to cause damage. The Talmud asks: Why not compare the requirement to pay damages to the payment of *kofer*, the ransom paid by the owner of the ox to the family of a person killed by his ox even if the killing was inadvertent. The Talmud answers, "It is proper to derive a liability regarding the ox from another liability that similarly concerns the ox, thus excluding *kofer*, which is a liability that concerns only the owner." This means that the Talmud's working premise is that payments for damage caused by the ox, as opposed to *kofer* payments, are considered the responsibility of the ox, not the owner.

The World of Oxen

On the one hand, unlike a human being, an ox cannot be saddled with full responsibility for its actions. On the other hand, as we have shown, an ox is considered to possess a certain degree of choice. It seems that the ox's liability is for actions in which it is clear it has done wrong. Thus, we must try to understand the ox's perspective on reality.

The "crop-destroying beast," also known as "tooth," the third of the four primary causes of injury in the Mishna, is an ox that causes damage while eating. One cannot consider that a crime on the part of the ox, whose nature is to feed, and whose feeding one must not hinder: "You shall not muzzle an ox when it is treading out the grain" (Deuteronomy 25:4). The act of feeding is considered damaging only when the field and the grain do not belong to the ox's owner. In the Torah the passage describing "tooth" damage appears directly after laws regarding theft by a person, which is also considered injurious to another's ownership rather than to the stolen object itself. The ox cannot be saddled with liability for stealing or changing ownership, which is why the responsibility for its actions lies with its owner.

We have seen that "horn" damage (an ox that gores another ox) is defined by intentionality – the ox must purposefully engage in an action that damages others. This turns the action into a moral wrong and makes the ox liable for paying damages. Elsewhere in the Talmud we again encounter this treatment of "horn" damages as a sin of sorts on the animal's part. When the Talmud seeks to prove that an animal can be thought to have an evil element, it cites "horn" and the damage that derives from it:

> Rabbi Naḥman bar Rabbi Ḥisda expounded: What is meant by the text, "Then the Lord God formed (*vayitzer*) man" (Genesis 2:7)? [The word *vayitzer*] is written] with two [letters] *yod*, to show that God created two inclinations, one good and the other evil. Rabbi Naḥman bar Yitzḥak demurred. According to this, he said, animals, of which *vayitzer* is not written, should have no evil inclination, yet we see that they injure and bite and kick. (Berakhot 61a)

This quote from Berakhot can help us explain the difference between "horn" and "tooth" damage when it comes to the basis for payment. When an animal causes damage with its tooth, meaning by feeding, the damages are paid by the owner, who did not prevent his animal from causing damage. We do not blame the animal, because we cannot demand that it refrain from eating. The owner is solely responsible for the damage, because only in the human world does the animal's action constitute damage, and the owner is charged with watching his animal. But when the animal intentionally causes damage, it is itself perceived as having done wrong.

The demand that animals be considered responsible for their actions, which sees them as beings with drives and wants, can lead to them being punished in certain situations. However, there is another side to that coin: The demand for responsibility means that they are not created as objects, but rather as creations worthy of respect.

Thus, we find that the requirement to rest on Shabbat extends to animals as well (Exodus 23:12), that it is forbidden to cook a kid in its mother's milk (v. 19), and that it is forbidden to sacrifice an animal younger than seven days old – so that it can spend that time with its mother (22:29). Furthermore, we are enjoined to leave the fruits of the Sabbatical year for beasts of the field (23:11). The Talmud also forbids causing suffering to animals (Bava Metzia 32b). The moral treatment of animals does not only saddle them with responsibility but also grants them rights.

Human Dignity Is God's Dignity

Bava Kama 8:6

If a man boxed the ear of his fellow, he must pay him a *sela*. Rabbi Yehuda says in the name of Rabbi Yosei the Galilean: A *maneh*. If he slapped him he must pay two hundred *zuz*. If with the back of his hand, he must pay him four hundred *zuz*. If he tore at his ear, plucked out his hair, spat at him and his spit touched him, or pulled his cloak from off him, or loosed a woman's hair in the street, he must pay four hundred *zuz*. This is the general rule: All is in accordance with the person's dignity. Rabbi Akiva said: Even the poor in Israel are regarded as free people who have lost their possessions, for they are the children of Abraham, Isaac, and Jacob. It once happened that a man unloosed a woman's hair in the street, and she came before Rabbi Akiva, and he sentenced him to pay her four hundred *zuz*. He said, "Rabbi, give me time." And he gave him time. He caught her standing at the entrance to her courtyard, and he broke a jug of oil worth one *issar* in front of her. She unloosed her hair and scooped up the oil

בבא קמא ח, ו

הַתּוֹקֵעַ לַחֲבֵירוֹ, נוֹתֵן לוֹ סֶלַע. רַבִּי יְהוּדָה אוֹמֵר מִשּׁוּם רַבִּי יוֹסֵי הַגְּלִילִי, מָנֶה. סְטָרוֹ נוֹתֵן לוֹ מָאתַיִם זוּז. לְאַחַר יָדוֹ, נוֹתֵן לוֹ אַרְבַּע מֵאוֹת זוּז. צָרַם בְּאָזְנוֹ, תָּלַשׁ בִּשְׂעָרוֹ רָקַק וְהִגִּיעַ בּוֹ רֻקּוֹ הֶעֱבִיר טַלִּיתוֹ מִמֶּנּוּ, פָּרַע רֹאשׁ הָאִשָּׁה בַּשּׁוּק, נוֹתֵן אַרְבַּע מֵאוֹת זוּז. זֶה הַכְּלָל הַכֹּל לְפִי כְבוֹדוֹ. אָמַר רַבִּי עֲקִיבָא, אֲפִילוּ עֲנִיִּים שֶׁבְּיִשְׂרָאֵל, רוֹאִין אוֹתָם כְּאִלּוּ הֵם בְּנֵי חוֹרִין שֶׁיָּרְדוּ מִנִּכְסֵיהֶם, שֶׁהֵם בְּנֵי אַבְרָהָם יִצְחָק וְיַעֲקֹב. וּמַעֲשֶׂה בְּאֶחָד שֶׁפָּרַע רֹאשׁ הָאִשָּׁה בַּשּׁוּק, בָּאת לִפְנֵי רַבִּי עֲקִיבָא, וְחִיְּבוֹ לִתֵּן לָהּ אַרְבַּע מֵאוֹת זוּז. אָמַר לוֹ רַבִּי תֶּן לִי זְמָן. וְנָתַן לוֹ זְמָן שְׁמָרָהּ עוֹמֶדֶת עַל פֶּתַח חֲצֵרָהּ וְשָׁבַר אֶת הַכַּד בְּפָנֶיהָ, וּבוֹ כְּאִיסַר שֶׁמֶן. גִּלְּתָה אֶת רֹאשָׁהּ, וְהָיְתָה מְטַפַּחַת וּמַנַּחַת יָדָהּ עַל

in her hand and laid her hand on her head. He had set up witnesses against her, and he came before Rabbi Akiva and said to him, "Rabbi, should I give one such as this four hundred *zuz*?" He answered, "You have said nothing, for if a man injures himself, even though he has no right to do so, he is not liable. But others who injure him are liable. And if a man cuts down his own saplings, even though he has no right to do so, he is not liable. But if others cut them down, they are liable."

רֹאשָׁהּ. הֶעֱמִיד עָלֶיהָ עֵדִים, וּבָא לִפְנֵי רַבִּי עֲקִיבָא, אָמַר לוֹ רַבִּי, לָזוֹ אֲנִי נוֹתֵן אַרְבַּע מֵאוֹת זוּז. אָמַר לוֹ לֹא אָמַרְתָּ כְּלוּם. שֶׁהַחוֹבֵל בְּעַצְמוֹ, אַף עַל פִּי שֶׁאֵינוֹ רַשַּׁאי פָּטוּר. אֲחֵרִים שֶׁחָבְלוּ בוֹ חַיָּבִין. וְהַקּוֹצֵץ נְטִיעוֹתָיו, אַף עַל פִּי שֶׁאֵינוֹ רַשַּׁאי פָּטוּר. אֲחֵרִים שֶׁקָּצְצוּ אֶת נְטִיעוֹתָיו, חַיָּיבִים:

There are five types of compensation that one who injures another is required to pay. One of these is for the injured party's shame. The demand for financial redress is evidence of the idea that harm to another person's feelings or social status is considered a real injury. Toward the end, the mishna explicitly states that a person who demeans himself is fully considered to have "injured himself." The Mishna here expresses an idea of a human being as a single essence incorporating both body and mind. The importance of a person's emotional state is also apparent in the astronomical sum that Rabbi Akiva awards as damages for shame – four hundred *zuz*, the equivalent of two years' salary at the time, and twice the sum on a woman's *ketuba*.

The Mishna relates the case of a woman who is willing to reveal her hair in order to ensure that an amount of oil worth one *issar* – a paltry amount – does not go to waste. Rabbi Akiva rules that even though it is apparent that the woman does not care about her honor, if another person unlooses her hair, he must pay her the full amount in damages for her shame. His opinion is surprising, because one could say that people who do not care about their own honor feel no shame, so that if someone else tries to shame them they should not be eligible for damages. It seems that Rabbi Akiva's outlook is informed by his basic idea of the essence of humanity, which was created in God's image:

> He used to say: Beloved is man, for he was created in the image [of God]. Especially beloved is he for it was made

> known to him that he had been created in the image [of God], as it is said (Genesis 9:6): "for in the image of God He made man." (Avot 3:14)

According to this point of view, when someone injures a human being it is as if they "injure" God. That is why people are not allowed to injure themselves. The following passage from the Tosefta can help elucidate this idea:

> And just as one is liable for damage to the other, so he is liable for self-inflicted damage ... If he pulls out his own hair or tears his own clothes ... **he is exempt from the laws of man but liable under the laws of heaven**, for it is stated (see Genesis 9:5): "And surely the blood of your lives, from your lives I will demand." (Tosefta Bava Kama 9:31)

The prohibition against harming oneself is derived from a verse (Genesis 9:5) that deals with murder. The following verse provides the explanation: "Whoever sheds man's blood, by man shall his blood be shed, for in the image of God He made man" (v. 6). The severity of the crime of harming another human being is derived from the fact that the injured party was created in the image of God, which is why it is God Himself who demands punishment: "the blood of your lives, from your lives I will demand." Applying these principles to the issue of shame, we conclude that when a person humiliates another it is as though they are humiliating God Himself, in whose image humanity was created.[1] Thus, a person who humiliates a woman in the market must pay damages for the very act of injuring a person created in the image of God, not as compensation for the damaged party's subjective feelings.[2] As we will see below,

1. Rabbi Walfish noted the parallel between the examples of wounds to the human body in the opening of our chapter (8:1) and the list (in Bekhorot 5:5) of blemishes that render an animal unfit to be offered as a sacrifice. He opines that "there is a hint here ... that someone who wounds his fellow does not only injure his body and his capacity to work, but also mars his holiness as a member of 'a kingdom of priests, and a holy nation.'" Walfish, "Literary Considerations," 49–52.
2. See the remarkable commentary of *Tosefot Yom Tov* (on Avot 3:11): "For there is no

linking the damages to God's image does not detract from man's honor. On the contrary, rather than divert attention from the injured party to God, it enhances the individual's honor.

In this context, Maimonides's words regarding the prohibition against compromising with murderers – even with the consent of the victim's family – are illuminating:

> The court is enjoined not to accept ransom from the murderer to save him from execution. Even if he gave all the money in the world, and even if the blood redeemer was willing to forgive him, he should be executed. The rationale is that the soul of the victim is not the property of the blood redeemer, but the property of the Holy One, blessed be He. (*Mishneh Torah, Hilkhot Rotze'aḥ*, 1:4)[3]

The first part of our mishna presents Rabbi Akiva's outlook, by which damages are paid to the injured party due to that party's intrinsic value:

> If he tore at his ear, plucked out his hair, spat at him and his spit touched him, or pulled his cloak from off him, or loosed a woman's hair in the street, he must pay four hundred *zuz*. This is the general rule: All is in accordance with the person's dignity. Rabbi Akiva said: Even the poor in Israel are regarded as free people who have lost their possessions, for they are the children of Abraham, Isaac, and Jacob.

---

greater heretic than one who humiliates his fellow in public. And to me it seems that he is considered to have despised an aspect of the Lord ('*devar Hashem*,' usually translated as 'the word of the Lord,' based on Numbers 15:31), for humanity was created in God's image, and he is an aspect of the Lord." My thanks to Aharon Topper for drawing my attention to this passage.

3. In Shakespeare's play *The Merchant of Venice*, Shylock demands "a pound of flesh" in order to forgive an unpaid loan. Rabbi Shlomo Zevin shows that a contract demanding part of the body as payment is contrary to Jewish law, because people are not considered the owners of their own bodies. Zevin, *In the Light of the Law* (Beit El: Beit El Library, 1977) [Hebrew], 310–38.

Unlike the Tosefta's approach, as well as his own statement in Avot, which emphasizes the fact that *humanity* was created in God's image, here Rabbi Akiva states that it is the woman's *Jewish* identity that merits significant compensation in a case of humiliation.[4] It seems that according to Rabbi Akiva, Jewishness is another layer in an outlook that ascribes intrinsic value to human beings. Further along in the Mishna in Avot, Rabbi Akiva addresses God's special love toward humanity, which was made in His image, as well as the unique status of Israel, who, in addition to being cast in God's image, are considered His actual children:

> Beloved are Israel, since they are called children of the Omnipresent. Especially beloved are they as it is revealed to them that they are called children of the Omnipresent, as it says (Deuteronomy 14:1), "You are children of the Lord your God." (Avot 3:14)

Cutting Down Saplings

The mishna concludes with a prohibition against cutting down trees: "And if a man cuts down his own saplings, even though he has no right to do so, he is not liable. But if others cut them down, they are liable." The placement of this passage is surprising, because it seems to deviate from the main topic of our mishna – human injury.

The passage hints at the spiritual underpinning of our mishna. The term "cutting down saplings" (*mekatzetz benetiot*) has two meanings: At face value, it refers to a prohibition against damaging trees, but it is also employed to refer to the sin of Elisha b. Avuya. Unlike Rabbi Akiva, who entered "the garden" (referring to the depths of Jewish mysticism) and emerged unscathed, Elisha's journey led him to "cut down saplings" (Ḥagiga 14b). Elisha concluded that there are "two authorities" in the universe, meaning that there are powers operating in the world apart from God and independent of His will. That is the meaning of "cutting down saplings": instead of recognizing that the trees are connected to

4. Among the students of Rabbi Akiva there is a saying that "All of Israel are the children of kings," which they imbue with halakhic significance (see Shabbat 14:4).

the ground and draw from their roots (meaning God), Elisha "cut them" off from God and saw them as independent authorities. Elisha's error is like the error of the man who loosed the woman's hair in the street; that man considered only a concrete question – was the woman hurt or not? He was unaware of the spiritual implications of his actions. When Rabbi Akiva deemed him liable, he did so because people are not authorities unto themselves, and thus cannot be the "owners" of their honor. People are made in God's image, and God is inside of them, so that any injury to an individual is an affront to God.

A *baraita* expands on the dialogue between Rabbi Akiva and the man who loosed the woman's hair in the street. His last statement alludes to there being a profound mystery underlying our chapter:

> Rabbi Akiva said to him, "You have dived into the depths and have brought up a pottery shard in your hand." (Bava Kama 91a)

If Two People Are Grasping a Cloak

בבא מציעא א, א

שְׁנַיִם אוֹחֲזִין בְּטַלִּית, זֶה אוֹמֵר אֲנִי מְצָאתִיהָ וְזֶה אוֹמֵר אֲנִי מְצָאתִיהָ, זֶה אוֹמֵר כֻּלָּהּ שֶׁלִּי וְזֶה אוֹמֵר כֻּלָּהּ שֶׁלִּי, זֶה יִשָּׁבַע שֶׁאֵין לוֹ בָהּ פָּחוֹת מֵחֶצְיָהּ, וְזֶה יִשָּׁבַע שֶׁאֵין לוֹ בָהּ פָּחוֹת מֵחֶצְיָהּ, וְיַחֲלֹקוּ.

Bava Metzia 1:1

If two people are grasping a cloak: One says, "I found it," and the other says, "I found it"; or one says, "It's all mine," and the other says, "It's all mine." One swears that he doesn't own less than half of the cloak, and the other swears that he doesn't own less than half of the cloak, and they split the cloak

The opening mishna of Tractate Bava Metzia is among the most famous in the entire Mishna. For thousands of years, the sages have been engaged in the basic questions that it raises: the rationales for splitting, the rationales for swearing, and the connection between the two. We will attempt to provide an answer to these questions based on an examination of the structure of the mishna.

"Two people are grasping a cloak"

The mishna opens with a scenario: two people are grasping a single cloak. The beginning of the sentence does not give away the fact that there is a problem, for the cloak could conceivably belong to both parties. We, the outside observers, do not see a person taking another's property. The Bavli expresses this idea: "When we see a person holding a garment we presume that it is his, and we are in the position of witnesses who can testify that each claimant is entitled to the half he is holding" (Bava Metzia 3a).

"One says, 'It's all mine,' and the other says, 'It's all mine'"

As soon as the two parties grasping the cloak open their mouths and begin to voice their claims, the harmony collapses and we discover that we are faced with a head-on conflict – neither is willing to make room for the other.

"They each swear that they don't own less than half of the cloak"

As we have seen, the root of the problem is not the mutual grasping, but rather the fact that each party claims exclusive ownership of the cloak. Therefore, the Mishna suggests that they state their claims anew, in a manner that diminishes the gap between them to the extent possible. Each is expected to swear in a manner that does not contradict his initial statement while also not conflicting with the other party's claim. Thus the tension of this difficult conflict is reduced, and we can begin to approach a solution.

"And they split the cloak"

Now, when the conflict has been defanged, we can return to the reality that existed before the conflicting claims were lodged, in which both parties grasping the cloak are its rightful owners, and based on that situation – in which no conflict is apparent – rule regarding a split.

This idea is also conveyed by the structure of the mishna. The mishna consists of two styles: One is used to describe the case and the final ruling, and the other to describe the claims and argument.

(1) If two people are grasping a cloak

(2) **One** says, "I found it" **and the other** says, "I found it"; or

(3) **one** says, "It's all mine," **and the other** says, "It's all mine."

(4) **One** swears that he doesn't own less than half of the cloak, **and the other** swears that he doesn't own less than half of the cloak,

(5) and they split the cloak.

Lines 2 and 3 above are phrased in terms bespeaking confrontation and argument. From the formulation of the fourth section, we can deduce that swearing is mandated not in an attempt to resolve the basic issue of "two people grasping a cloak" by way of a manipulation that will lead one of the sides to confess. Rather, its goal is to resolve the difference between the claims and reestablish the basic situation, meaning shared ownership. That is why the two do not swear that the entire cloak is their property, but only half. Shared ownership, which is expressed by splitting the cloak, is the *goal* of the swearing. It is not merely an unintended side effect of a failed attempt to adjudicate.

In contrast with the middle sections, which are concerned with confrontation and division, the final section appears as a brief statement: "and they split the cloak" (in the original Hebrew it is a single word), just like the opening section, "If two people are grasping a cloak." The stylistic similarity enables us to see line 5 as a direct continuation of the opening sentence: "If two people are grasping a cloak…they split the cloak." Style-wise, one could claim that the split, which is a concrete action, is a response to a situation in which "two people are grasping," while the swearing, which is a speech act, is a response to the verbal claim, "It's all mine."

The link between the opening and the conclusion of the mishna, and the idea that the act of swearing is designed to neutralize the claims, exposes the similarity of the Mishna and the Tosefta, which states: "If two people are grasping a cloak, one takes what is in his grip and the other takes what is in his grip" (Tosefta Bava Metzia 1:1).

Because the Tosefta is not concerned with claims, it does not make a connection between the splitting of the cloak and the swearing. From the fact that the Tosefta derives the law from whatever is in each party's "grip," it is clear that its basic assumption is that each party is owner of whatever he is "gripping." This understanding – that the grip of both claimants on the object is the basis for how it is split – also arises from the final mishna in Tractate Bava Kama, which directly precedes our mishna:

> Shreds of wool that the laundryman pulls out belong to him, but those that the wool comber pull out belong to the householder. If the laundryman pulled out three threads, they belong to him, but if more than this they belong to the householder... If the tailor left over thread sufficient to sew with or a piece of cloth three fingerbreadths by three fingerbreadths, these belong to the householder. (Bava Kama 10:10)

The two mishnayot share several elements that bind them together, including similar words in the original Hebrew, such as those for "cloak" (*tallit*) and "piece of cloth" (*matlit*). The mishna in Bava Kama is occupied with the question of ownership over objects that remain in the hands of an artisan. Here there is no question of claims and there is no need to swear. The division of the objects is not a result of any doubt as to the identity of the owners, which is clear. The link between the two mishnayot further elucidates that our mishna leaves room for a simple split in the case of property that both parties are grasping, with no need for conflict. The division of the property is not due to doubt but rather to the fact that each party has a right to half.

Neighbors and Partners

Bava Batra, chapter 1

The first chapter of Tractate Bava Batra is concerned with relationships between neighbors. Thus it contends with the question of responsibilities shared by neighbors and offers solutions to questions of ownership that might arise from living side by side. The basic principle that arises from the Mishna is that living next to someone else can yield a relationship that makes us partners of sorts with our neighbors. This outlook makes dealing with issues that arise from relationships with our neighbors inherently different from dealing with issues that arise with strangers.[1]

Mishnayot 1:1–2

> If two partners wish to make a partition in a courtyard they build the wall in the middle. In a place where the custom is to build of unshaped stones, or of hewn stones, or of half-bricks, or of whole bricks, so they should build it – everything according to local custom. [If the wall is made of] unshaped stones, this one supplies [from his property] three handbreadths, and that one supplies [from his property] three handbreadths. [If the wall is made of] hewn stones this one supplies [from his property] one and a half handbreadths, and that one supplies [from his property] one and a half handbreadths. [If the wall is made

1. This chapter was studied and written in collaboration with my friend Baruch Siach.

> of] half-bricks this one supplies [from his property] two handbreadths, and that one supplies [from his property] two handbreadths. [If the wall is made of] whole bricks this one supplies [from his property] one and a half handbreadths, and that one supplies [from his property] one and a half handbreadths. Therefore if the wall falls, the place and the stones belong to them both.
>
> The same is true of a garden: In a place where the custom is to build a fence, they can obligate him to do so. However, in a valley, where it is not customary to build a fence, they cannot obligate him to do so. But if he wants to [build a fence] he must gather into his own portion and build, and he puts a finishing on the outside of the wall. Therefore if the wall falls, the place and the stones belong to him. If they acted with each other's consent, they should build the wall in the middle and put a finishing on both sides. Therefore if the wall falls, the place and the stones belong to them both. (1:1–2)

In the case of a structure located between two privately owned tracts of land, naturally there is a question of ownership over the structure, which may have been built long ago. Our mishna contends with this question according to the various scenarios. The mishna can be divided into three sections, where each case uses the word "therefore" to denote the law:

		Case description	Instruction	The law
The requirement is to build		If two partners wish to make a partition in a courtyard (or in a garden)	They build the wall in the middle	**Therefore** if the wall falls, the place and the stones belong to them both

		Case description	Instruction	The law
There is no requirement to build	One party built	However, in a valley, where it is not customary to build a fence, they cannot obligate him to do so	But if he wants to [build a fence] he must gather into his own portion and build, and he puts a finishing on the outside of the wall	**Therefore** if the wall falls, the place and the stones belong to him
	Both parties built	If they acted [in a valley] with mutual consent	They should build the wall in the middle and put a finishing on both sides	**Therefore** if the wall falls, the place and the stones belong to them both

The basic cases can be divided into two or three: A case in which the neighbors had to construct a partition, and a case in which building the partition was not mandatory. In the latter case, the Mishna distinguishes between a case in which one of the neighbors builds the partition on his own, unilaterally, and a case in which the two make a joint decision to build it. For each of those cases, the Mishna presents instructions on how to build the fence so as to contend with the ownership questions that may come up.

According to this division, our mishna carries on the debate from the final chapter of the previous tractate, Bava Metzia ("A House and an Upper Room"). The first mishna of that chapter presents the case of the collapse of a house with two floors, each of which belongs to someone else, and discusses who has ownership of the debris left by the collapse.

Clarification Versus Prevention

In the beginning of Bava Metzia we also find a mishna similar to ours – the debate over two people claiming ownership of a single cloak. There too the Mishna contends with questions of uncertain ownership. However, the difference between the two mishnayot enables us to appreciate what sets our mishna apart:

> If two people are grasping a cloak: One says, "I found it," and the other says, "I found it"; or one says, "It's all mine," and the other says, "It's all mine." One swears that he doesn't own less than half of the cloak, and the other swears that he doesn't own less than half of the cloak, and they split the cloak. (Bava Metzia 1:1)

Our mishna strives to eliminate all doubt – and by extension the very prospect of conflict between the two parties – from the outset, by determining what is the correct conduct between neighbors. The mishna's statement is directed primarily toward the neighbors rather than toward the court. In Bava Metzia, by contrast, the conflict is between two strangers; when there is no way of determining the nature of the relationship between the parties, the court must get involved. Further driving home the distinction is the fact that in Bava Metzia "one swears … and the other swears … and they split," whereas here there is no effort on the part of the court to make a determination; there is only a declaration: "the place and the stones belong to them both."

The Requirement to Build a Partition

The Mishna could be understood as implying that neighbors are required to build a partition between their properties. What is the source of that requirement? The Mishna says that in the case of a garden, the requirement stems from custom, implying that in the case of a courtyard the requirement does not depend on custom. The Bavli (Bava Batra 2b) brings an approach that explains this requirement based on the idea of "overlooking," or damage caused by sight.

Another approach would see the novelty in our mishna in the fact that the residents of the courtyard are not strangers to one another, but rather neighbors. Thus, they share common responsibilities relating to their shared space. Further along we will expound on this idea of neighborly relations.

Mishna 1:3

> If a man's land surrounded his fellow's land on three sides, and he fenced it on the first and the second and the third sides, they do not obligate him [to share in the costs]. Rabbi Yosei says: If he rose and built a fence on the fourth side, they obligate him to share in all of the costs.

If we are to understand the words of Rabbi Yosei, we must first figure out whether he is discussing the one who is doing the fencing or the one who is being fenced in. There are several indicators that he was talking about the fenced-in party: The use of the verb "rose" indicates that it is someone other than the person the first half of the mishna was referring to. In addition, the next mishna also features the expression "they obligate him to share in all of the costs," referring to a person who derives benefit from building a wall that rests on another wall; this person corresponds to the fenced-in party from our mishna. The parallel between our mishna and the case of someone who builds a wall that is supported by another wall is reinforced by the chapter's literary structure, as we will see below.

Laws of Neighbors

Why is the fenced-in party obligated to pay his share in all four walls? The talmudic dictum by which "If one derives a benefit and the other does not sustain loss, [the former] is exempt" (based on Bava Kama 20a) seems to imply that in our case – where the fenced-in party is deriving benefit from the fence, while the party building the fence does not lose through the other's benefit – the fenced-in party should be exempt.

It seems that the difference between our mishna and a scenario where "one derives a benefit and the other does not sustain loss" is that the latter is relevant only among strangers. Our mishna relies on the assumption that being neighbors generates a relationship with a quality of partnership. This partnership means that each neighbor is required to shoulder part of any necessary burden. However, not everything is considered a necessary burden, so that one cannot force his neighbor to financially participate in every project. In our case, that project is a fence in a valley, which, in contrast to a fence in a courtyard or a garden, is not mandatory, so that if one party builds a fence, his neighbor is not required to share the expense. It appears the reason for this is that, because it is not an essential project, the neighbor is within his rights saying it is of no use to him. However, when the neighbor makes use of the fence builder's work, that activates the basic premise by which neighbors are partners, and they must both share in the expenses.

The Literary Structures of the Mishnayot

The laws in the mishnayot relating to mandated expenses rely on three simple principles:

1. One can force one's neighbor to share in expenses arising from their adjacent homes if they are considered essential (mishna 1: in a courtyard the neighbor must share the expense of building a partition).
2. A neighbor cannot be forced to share in expenses that are not considered essential (mishna 2: in a valley the neighbor is not required to share the expense of building a partition).
3. If, despite initially not being required to pay, the neighbor reveals that he is pleased with the addition, he must share the expense (mishna 3: by revealing his opinion, the neighbor becomes liable to share the expense).

These three principles are explicated by Maimonides, in his discussion of partners in a courtyard and a city:

> When a courtyard is jointly owned by partners, each one may compel the other to build a gatekeeper's room, a door, and any other element that is sorely needed for a courtyard or anything that is customary for the local people to build. He cannot compel him with regard to other matters – paintings, and designs, and the like. If one of the partners in the courtyard made such an addition on his own initiative, and then another demonstrated that he appreciated what his colleague did, he is held responsible for his share in the entire project and must pay his portion of the costs. (*Mishneh Torah, Hilkhot Shekhenim* 5:1)

The law by which a neighbor can be compelled to share the expense of something that is either sorely needed or customary recalls the Mishna's discussion of a partition in a courtyard (1:1) or garden (1:2). The other matters, which the neighbor cannot be compelled to participate in, are equivalent to the partition in a valley (1:2), but if he reveals his positive opinion of them (as in 1:3), "he is held responsible for his share in the entire project."

Mishna 1:4

> If the wall of a courtyard fell down they obligate each of the partners to help in building it up to a height of four cubits. [Each partner] is presumed to have paid [his share] unless the other brings proof that he has not paid. [If the fence was built] four cubits or higher, they do not obligate him [to help in building it]. If [the one who did not contribute] built another wall near it, even if he did not put a roof upon it, they obligate him to share in all of the costs. He is presumed not to have paid [his share] unless he brings proof that he has.

Mishna 1:4 proves that the three principles we enumerated above are the foundation for the Mishna's entire discussion. Our mishna reiterates those principles in the order in which they appear in 1:1–3. The wall itself (up to a height of four cubits) is considered essential, which is why "they obligate each of the partners." Any height above four cubits is not considered essential, so "they do not obligate him." However, if the partner revealed through his actions, by building another wall near it, that he is pleased with the extra height, he becomes liable.

	Mishnayot 1:1–3	Mishna 1:4
They obligate	If two partners wish to make a partition in a courtyard they build the wall in the middle… Therefore if the wall falls, the place and the stones belong to them both. The same is true of a garden: In a place where the custom is to build a fence, **they can obligate him to do so.**	If the wall of a courtyard fell down **they obligate each of the partners** to help in building it up to a height of four cubits. [Each partner] is presumed to have paid [his share] unless the other brings proof that he has not paid.
They do not obligate	However, in a valley, where it is not customary to build a fence, **they cannot obligate him to do so.**	[If the fence was built] four cubits or higher, **they do not obligate** him [to help in building it].
If…they obligate	If a man's land surrounded his fellow's land on three sides, and he fenced it on the first and the second and the third sides, they do not obligate him [to share in the costs]. Rabbi Yosei says: **If** he rose and built a fence on the fourth side, **they obligate him to share in all of the costs.**	**If** [the one who did not contribute] built another wall near it, even if he did not put a roof upon it, **they obligate him to share in all of the costs.** He is presumed not to have paid [his share] unless he brings proof that he has.

As we noted, the mishnayot are also concerned with the question of who owns the shared property, ex post facto. In this context, too, we can divide the mishnayot into three, with 1:4 parallel to 1:1–2:

	1:1–2	1:4
They obligate	If two partners wish to make a partition in a courtyard they build the wall in the middle… **Therefore** if the wall falls, the place and the stones belong to them both.	If the wall of a courtyard fell down they obligate each of the partners to help in building it up to a height of four cubits. [Each partner] **is presumed** to have paid [his share] unless the other brings proof that he has not paid.
They do not obligate	However, in a valley, where it is not customary to build a fence, they cannot obligate him to do so… **Therefore** if the wall falls, the place and the stones belong to him.	[If the fence was built] four cubits or higher, they do not obligate him [to help in building it].
If…they obligate	If they acted with each other's consent, they should build the wall in the middle…Therefore if the wall falls, the place and the stones belong to them both.	If [the one who did not contribute] built another wall near it…they obligate him to share in all of the costs. **He is presumed** not to have paid [his share] unless he brings proof that he has.

There is a common thread to all of the laws in these mishnayot, both in terms of the obligation to pay and in terms of the question of ownership: they are determined by the principles of the laws of neighbors. These principles are different from those generally employed to adjudicate cases of disputed property, as is apparent from the mishnayot in Bava Kama and Bava Batra. Here there is an effort to reduce doubt by determining in advance the financial rights and responsibilities of the neighbors.

We encountered in the first four mishnayot of the chapter a comprehensive presentation of the financial relationship among neighbors. The goal of this relationship, which is based on principles of partnership and mutual responsibility, is to forestall situations of doubt that would require arbitrary and artificial solutions.

Mishna 1:5

> They compel [a partner in a courtyard to contribute to] the building of a gatehouse and a door for the courtyard. Rabban Shimon ben Gamliel says: Not all courtyards are fit for a gatehouse. They compel [a resident of the town to contribute to] the building of a wall for the town, and double doors, and a bolt. Rabban Shimon ben Gamliel says: Not every town is fit for a wall. How long must a man dwell in a town to count as one of the men of the town? Twelve months. If he has purchased a dwelling place he immediately counts as one of the men of the town.

Our mishna details the payments that residents of a town and owners of properties adjacent to a courtyard can be compelled to make to cover the costs of construction that is to everyone's benefit. The mishna can be seen to embody the idea underlying the entire chapter: Just like neighbors, residents of a town and owners of properties adjacent to a courtyard are partners to one another, and share mutual responsibilities.

Mishna 1:6

> They do not divide a courtyard until there are four cubits for this [partner] and four cubits for that [partner]. Nor [do they divide up] a field until it has nine *kav* for this [partner] and nine *kav* for that [partner]; Rabbi Yehuda says: Until it has nine half-*kav* for this [partner] and nine half-*kav* for that [partner]. Nor [do they divide up] a garden

> until it has a half-*kav* for this [partner] and a half-*kav* for that [partner]; Rabbi Akiva says: A quarter-*kav*. Nor [do they divide up] an eating hall, a watchtower, a dovecote, a cloak, a bathhouse, or an olive press until there is sufficient for this [partner] and for that [partner]. This is the general rule: Whatever can be divided and still be called by the same name, they divide; otherwise they do not divide. When is this so? When they do not both wish [to divide the property]. However, if both wish they can divide it even if it is smaller. And with regard to the sacred books, they may not be divided even if both are willing.

Our mishna goes beyond the scope of the previous mishnayot. While the chapter up to this point is concerned with the construction of partitions, our mishna is about the dissolving of partnerships. It is noteworthy that this mishna, the final mishna of the chapter, is similar to the opening mishna. Linguistically, we see that the chapter begins with the words "If two partners wish," and concludes with "if both wish." In terms of its content, the chapter opens with partners, even though the law also applies to neighbors who are not partners per se, and concludes with actual partners. The opening and ending mention similar types of property: the chapter opens with a courtyard, garden, and valley, and concludes with a courtyard, field, and garden. Furthermore, the final mishna employs legal reasoning similar to that employed in 1:1–2, which deals with the construction of a partition: In the first case, one side can be compelled to share the expense if that is what the other side wants; in the next case there is no option to compel; and in the final case, both sides can share the expense if they wish to do so.

This parallel, in addition to indicating a similar legal logic, also highlights the resemblance of the partition question to the business partnership question. From the opening and closing mishnayot of our chapter we can glean the purpose of the editor: to combine the various topics in the chapter. The chapter opens with neighbors, continues with neighbors who are also partners – for instance if they share a courtyard or live in the same city – and concludes with partners who are not necessarily neighbors. Its purpose is to establish the financial relationship between next-door neighbors, neighbors who share a courtyard, and residents of a town based on the model of a partnership, which is the topic of the final mishna in this chapter.

The Dispute over Damages Between Neighbors

בבא בתרא ב, י

מַרְחִיקִין אֶת הַמִּשְׁרָה[1] מִן הַיָּרָק[2] וְאֶת הַכְּרֵישִׁין מִן הַבְּצָלִים, וְאֶת הַחַרְדָּל מִן הַדְּבוֹרִים. רַבִּי יוֹסֵי מַתִּיר בַּחַרְדָּל:

Bava Batra 2:10

A pool for soaking flax must be distanced from vegetables, and leeks from onions, and mustard plant from bees. Rabbi Yosei permits mustard plant.

All neighbors, be they private people, municipalities, or even neighboring countries, experience tensions over borders. Even when the borders are mapped out and a matter of consensus, there are actions that one party can take within their own property that can cause damage to a neighbor. It is these cases that our mishna is concerned about, not cases in which one party purposely sets out to harm the other. A formula must be found that will solve such problems and establish values that can determine which side will prevail or whether compromise is possible.

Generally speaking, there are two diametrically opposed outlooks that such values can be founded upon:

1. The first outlook, whose main proponent is Rabbi Yosei, favors a great deal of freedom of action to each side, with minimal limits, even if such action sometimes comes at the expense of a neighbor. This is not about anarchy, in the vein of "every man did what was right in his own eyes" (Judges

21:25), but rather about minimizing legal intervention as much as possible.

2. The second point of view claims, in contrast, that the system must be founded upon consideration for the other and care for his well-being. Although it is clear that, taken to the extreme, this approach can prevent practically all human action, it remains the guiding principle.

Interpreting the Mishna

Our mishna is concerned with cases in which a person is required to conduct various activities at a distance from a neighbor's property. In the first two cases Rabbi Yosei seemingly agrees that there is need to keep a distance, but on the third he diverges and opines that there is no need to keep a distance. The major difference between the third case and the first two is that it does not entail any encroachment on the neighbor's property. With a soaking pool, the concern is that the water will spill into the neighbor's yard and damage his vegetables, and with leeks there is fear that they will affect the growth or flavor of the neighbor's onions. But in the case of a mustard plant, the potential problem is merely that the neighbors' bees will fly to the mustard and be sickened by it. According to Rabbi Yosei, such indirect damage, which does not entail encroachment on the neighbor's property, is not forbidden.

What is novel about our mishna is the opinion of the first *Tanna*, which limits a person's freedom to act in his own property lest his neighbor, who was the first to plant crops, sustain damage.

The Tree and the Cistern

> A tree may not be grown within twenty-five cubits of a cistern, or within fifty cubits if it is a carob or a sycamore, whether it is higher or on the same level. If the cistern was there first the tree shall be cut down and compensation given. If the tree was there first it shall not be cut down. If it is in doubt which was there first, the tree shall not be

> cut down. Rabbi Yosei says: Even if the cistern was there before the tree it should not be cut down, since this one dug within his own domain and the other planted within his own domain. (2:11)

This mishna, too, is concerned with establishing rights to the land based on precedence – "If the cistern was there first" or "If the tree was there first." Here, too, Rabbi Yosei dissents, in this case explicitly, based on his outlook that favors freedom of action: "this one dug within his own domain and the other planted within his own domain." However, in this case it is a radical claim: Whereas in the previous mishna Rabbi Yosei gave permission for people to do as they please within their properties, when the consequences of their actions do not go beyond the physical boundaries of those properties (the mustard seed is planted on one's property, and that is also where the bees are damaged), in our mishna, the tree, which is planted within one's property, affects a cistern on the neighbor's land. Of course Rabbi Yosei does not permit all such actions, as we saw in the previous mishna.

Emerging from these mishnayot are the two opposing paradigms regarding the desirable relationship between neighbors: The first, anonymous *Tanna* in our mishna, by favoring the party that acted first, attempts to balance out the interests of both neighbors and find a compromise that will address those interests. Rabbi Yosei, in contrast, asserts that the best way to avert tension is to allow extensive leeway to both sides – as long as each acts only within their land.

Rabbi Yosei's opinion should not be taken as an indication that he does not value the obligation to be considerate of the other. Rather, when one party is limited – even if the purpose is to prevent damage to the other party – they are being disadvantaged. As the Tosefta states in its explication of the mishna, "Just as you have done within your [land], so I have done within my [land]."

The expression "Just as you have done within your [land], so I have done within my [land]" recalls a mishna in Tractate Avot:

> There are four types of character in human beings: One that says, "Mine is mine, and yours is yours" – this is a

> commonplace type. And some say this is a Sodom-type of character. [One that says,] "Mine is yours and yours is mine" is an unlearned person. [One that says,] "Mine is yours and yours is yours" is a pious person. [One that says,] "Mine is mine, and yours is mine" is a wicked person.

We can see an allusion to the dispute between Rabbi Yosei and the first *Tanna*: Is one who says, "What's mine is mine, and I will do as I please in my land" reminiscent of Sodom or just a commonplace character? It seems that Rabbi Yosei's approach stems from the idea that compensation ordered by a court does not depend on absolute definitions of permissible and prohibited behavior. Rather, damage is the result of going beyond the bounds of one's property and usage rights.

A Court of Truth

סנהדרין א, א-ג

דִּינֵי מָמוֹנוֹת, בִּשְׁלֹשָׁה. גְּזֵלוֹת וַחֲבָלוֹת, בִּשְׁלֹשָׁה. נֶזֶק וַחֲצִי נֶזֶק, תַּשְׁלוּמֵי כֶפֶל וְתַשְׁלוּמֵי אַרְבָּעָה וַחֲמִשָּׁה, בִּשְׁלֹשָׁה. הָאוֹנֵס וְהַמְפַתֶּה וְהַמּוֹצִיא שֵׁם רַע, בִּשְׁלֹשָׁה, דִּבְרֵי רַבִּי מֵאִיר. וַחֲכָמִים אוֹמְרִים, מוֹצִיא שֵׁם רַע, בְּעֶשְׂרִים וּשְׁלֹשָׁה, מִפְּנֵי שֶׁיֵּשׁ בּוֹ דִּינֵי נְפָשׁוֹת.

מַכּוֹת, בִּשְׁלֹשָׁה. מִשּׁוּם רַבִּי יִשְׁמָעֵאל אָמְרוּ, בְּעֶשְׂרִים וּשְׁלֹשָׁה. עִבּוּר הַחֹדֶשׁ, בִּשְׁלֹשָׁה. עִבּוּר הַשָּׁנָה, בִּשְׁלֹשָׁה, דִּבְרֵי רַבִּי מֵאִיר. רַבָּן שִׁמְעוֹן בֶּן גַּמְלִיאֵל אוֹמֵר, בִּשְׁלֹשָׁה מַתְחִילִין, וּבַחֲמִשָּׁה נוֹשְׂאִין וְנוֹתְנִין, וְגוֹמְרִין בְּשִׁבְעָה. וְאִם גָּמְרוּ בִשְׁלֹשָׁה, מְעֻבֶּרֶת.

סְמִיכַת זְקֵנִים וַעֲרִיפַת עֶגְלָה, בִּשְׁלֹשָׁה, דִּבְרֵי רַבִּי שִׁמְעוֹן. וְרַבִּי יְהוּדָה אוֹמֵר, בַּחֲמִשָּׁה.

Sanhedrin 1:1–3

Cases concerning property [are decided] by three. Cases concerning robbery or personal injury, by three. Claims for full damages or half-damages, twofold restitution, or fourfold or fivefold restitution, by three. Claims against a rapist, a seducer, and one who defames [a virgin are decided] by three, according to Rabbi Meir. The Sages say: "One who defames [a virgin is decided] by twenty-three, for there may arise from it a capital case.

[Cases concerning offenses punishable by] beating [are decided] by three. They said in the name of Rabbi Yishmael: Twenty-three. The intercalation of the month and intercalation of the year [are decided] by three, according to Rabbi Meir. Rabban Shimon ben Gamliel says: The matter is begun by three, discussed by five, and decided upon by seven. But if they decided upon it with three, the intercalation is valid.

The laying on of the elders' hands and the decapitation of the calf [are decided upon] by three, according to Rabbi Shimon; but Rabbi Yehuda says: By five. The rites of *ḥalitza* and "refusal" [are performed] before three. The fruit of fourth year plantings and second tithe whose value is not known [are redeemed] before three. Items dedicated to the Temple [are redeemed] before three. Vows of valuation to be redeemed with movable property [are evaluated] before three; Rabbi Yehuda says: One must be a priest. [Vows of valuation to be redeemed] with land [are evaluated] before nine and a priest. And similarly [for the valuation] of a man.

הַחֲלִיצָה וְהַמֵּאוּנִין בִּשְׁלֹשָׁה. נֶטַע רְבָעִי וּמַעֲשֵׂר שֵׁנִי שֶׁאֵין דָּמָיו יְדוּעִין, בִּשְׁלֹשָׁה. הַהֶקְדֵּשׁוֹת, בִּשְׁלֹשָׁה. הָעֲרָכִין הַמִּטַּלְטְלִין, בִּשְׁלֹשָׁה. רַבִּי יְהוּדָה אוֹמֵר, אֶחָד מֵהֶן כֹּהֵן. וְהַקַּרְקָעוֹת, תִּשְׁעָה וְכֹהֵן. וְאָדָם, כַּיּוֹצֵא בָהֶן.

Tractate Sanhedrin opens with a description of three types of courts: a court of three, which deals mostly with financial issues (1:1–3); a court of twenty-three (called a small Sanhedrin), which is concerned with capital cases (1:4); and a court of seventy-one (called a Great Sanhedrin), whose purview is national and public interest cases (1:5).

The Mishna cites a source for the fact that the small Sanhedrin is composed of twenty-three judges and the Great Sanhedrin of seventy-one (1:6), but, surprisingly, not for the fact that a basic court features a panel of three. However, elsewhere in the tractate the Mishna addresses the formation of a court of three:

> Cases concerning property [are decided] by three [judges]. This [litigant] chooses one, and that [litigant] chooses one, and then the two of them choose another, according to Rabbi Meir. But the Sages say: The two judges choose the other judge. (Sanhedrin 3:1)

The Mishna repeats the opening sentence, "Cases concerning property [are decided] by three," and explains how that panel is formed. There must be one judge for each of the litigants, and a third to decide between them. Still, this law provides only a partial explanation for the source of the three-judge court, as a panel of three also convenes to decide cases that do not involve two litigants – for example to intercalate the month and induct elders. In addition, the mishna above does not describe a fixed panel, but rather an ad hoc court that is convened according to the needs of the litigants. In contrast, the Mishna in Tractate Rosh HaShana indicates the existence of a fixed court of three that is not convened on a case-by-case basis, but is rather considered the successor of Moses's court:

> As it says, "Then Moses and Aaron, Nadav and Avihu, and seventy of the elders of Israel went up" (Exodus 24:9). Why were the names of the elders not mentioned? To teach that every group of three that has acted as a court over Israel, behold it is like the court of Moses.
>
> What, then, is the source for the court of three?[1]

Three Above and Three Below

The Yerushalmi offers a parable about the idea that panels of three judges exist not only on the physical plane, but that the supernal court also features such a panel:

> Rabbi Yehuda ben Pazi said: Even the Holy One, blessed be He, does not judge alone, for it is said, "and all the host of heaven standing by Him on His right hand and on his left" – these tip the scales to acquit and those tip the scales to convict. (Y. Sanhedrin 1:1)

The parable teaches that justice has three facets: the evidence in favor, the evidence against, and the decision. Thus is it clear why the symbol for justice is a balance scale, with a pan on each side and a fulcrum in between, to balance them.

1. There are other sources that deduce from the biblical text the requirement for a three-judge court. Our objective here, however, is to arrive at the rationale for such a panel, and understand its significance.

Three in the World and Three in Humanity

Sefer Yetzira, one of the most ancient kabbalistic books, has a passage that corresponds to the passage in the Yerushalmi:

The Three Mothers are *Alef, Mem, Shin* / Their foundation is a pan of merit, a pan of liability / And the tongue of decree deciding between them. (*Sefer Yetzira* 2:1)

According to *Sefer Yetzira*, the world was created through the powers of letters. Three letters are considered the "mothers" of language: *alef*, *mem*, and *shin*. These letters symbolize the primordial elements of the cosmos (3:4): *Alef* represents air (*avir*), *mem* water (*mayim*), and *shin* fire (*esh*).

The mishna in *Sefer Yetzira* employs terminology from the legal world – merit, liability, and decree. But the fact that it identifies that tripartite structure with the elements of the world shows us that it is a far more fundamental structure, one representing the cosmos itself, which is founded on a dialectic of two opposing forces – merit and liability, water and fire, the *mem* and the *shin* – and the force that balances them out: the decree, the air, and the *alef*.

This idea informs the entirety of *Sefer Yetzira*. For example, based on the understanding that humanity was created in God's image and that "In my flesh I will see God" (Job 19:26), *Sefer Yetzira* sees parallels between God and humanity not only in terms of spirit but also in terms of the body. Thus the foundation of three emerges:

> Ten *sefirot* of Nothingness / In the number of ten fingers / Five opposite five / With a singular covenant / Precisely in the middle / In the circumcision of the tongue / And in the circumcision of the membrum. (*Sefer Yetzira* 1:3)

A person's ten fingers are equivalent to the ten divine *sefirot*. Just as the *sefirot* are divided into two groups, each of which stands at an opposite pole (1:5), so a person's hands "oppose" each other. Thus the two hands are parallel to the pans of merit and liability, and together are equivalent to "the **tongue** of decree deciding between them." Furthermore, the human body manifests the individual covenant "in the circumcision of the **tongue** and in the circumcision of the membrum."

A court – both above and below – is composed of three judges, because three is a foundation not only of the world of jurisprudence, but also of the entire earthly and supernal reality.

Love Peace, and Truth

In another ancient kabbalistic work, *The Bahir*, each of the elements heaven, peace, and truth encompass seeming opposites:

> Why is **heaven** called *shamayim*? This teaches that God kneaded fire and water, and combined them together. From this He made the "beginning of His word." It is thus written (Psalms 119:160), "The beginning of Your word is **truth**." It is therefore called *shamayim* – *sham mayim* (there is water) – *esh mayim* (fire and water). He said to them: This is the meaning of the verse, "He makes **peace** in His heights" (Job 25:2). He placed peace and love between them. May He also place peace and love among us. (*Sefer Bahir*, 59)

Heaven encompasses fire and water, and is identified with both peace and truth, as *Sefer Bahir* states explicitly elsewhere: "Truth is nothing other than peace" (*Sefer Bahir*, 75). Truth is in the middle, encompassing the angel Michael, who is associated with water, and the angel Gabriel, who is identified with fire: "In the middle is truth. This is Uriel" (*Sefer Bahir*, 108).

The deep insight that emerges from this is that reality is complex, and one must conciliate its conflicting elements, which is why the triad is so fundamental. This harmonization brings not only peace to the warring sides, but also reveals the truth. Because every aspect of reality contains an element of truth, the more we are able to encompass all of these facets and find a balance between them, the larger truth will grow.

The idea of truth as a composite of everything can be found in Reish Lakish's delightful comment on the Hebrew word for truth, *emet*, which appears further along in the Yerushalmi quoted above. "*Emet*" is composed of three letters: *alef*, the first letter of the Hebrew alphabet; *mem*, which is in the middle; and *tav*, which is last. Those three letters can be seen as parallel to the structure of the three-judge court: Two extremes – like the pan of merit and the pan of liability – and the *mem*, which decides between them.

This idea, which we encountered in both *Sefer Yetzira* and *Sefer Bahir*, underlies one of the basic premises of Kabbala, by which there are three "lines" in God's relation to reality – right, left and middle. For example, on the right side there is the *sefira* of *Ḥesed* (lovingkindness), on the left is *Gevura* (discipline or judgment), and in between, uniting them, is *Tiferet* (splendor or beauty), which is identified with truth.[2]

The World Is Founded on Three Elements

The triadic structure is the basis for the meaning of the concepts justice, truth, and peace, that each reflects an encompassment of opposing elements and values.[3] The Yerushalmi cites an opinion that the ideal is not to arrive at a judgment but rather to strive for a compromise that will incorporate all sides of the case. Because reality is complex, the solution should also be complex, and include justice, truth, and peace. The value of justice must contain both the value of truth and the value of peace. The decision should be a genuine reflection that ultimate truth is good, while also leading to peace between the opposing parties:

> Rabbi Yehoshua ben Korḥa says: Settlement by arbitration is a meritorious act, for it is written, "Truth, justice, and peace." Where there is truth there is no peaceful judgment, and where there is peace there is no true judgment. But what is that kind of truth that contains a peaceful judgment? We must say: Arbitration. (Y. Sanhedrin 1:1)

2. Hegelian dialectic presents a similar idea of three elements: thesis, antithesis, and synthesis.
3. The triadic structure in *Sefer Yetzira* is made up of the letters *alef-mem-shin*. It is interesting to note that these same letters form an acronym for the three elements: truth (*Emet*), justice (*Mishpat*) and peace (*Shalom*). My thanks to Aviad Yehieli, who brought this to my attention.

We will conclude with a mishna from Avot that teaches that these three matters are also the elements upon which the world is founded:

> Rabban Shimon ben Gamliel used to say: On three things does the world stand: On justice, on truth, and on peace, as it is said (Zechariah 8:16): "Execute the judgment of truth and peace in your gates." (Avot 1:18)

King and Judge

Sanhedrin, chapter 2

The opening chapters of Tractate Sanhedrin are concerned with judges and courts. The first delineates the three types of panels, distinguished by number of judges: three, twenty-three, and seventy-one. From the third chapter onward, the Mishna discusses the laws governing the legal system and trial procedures. The opening mishna of that chapter is a type of commentary on Sanhedrin 1:1: "This [litigant] chooses one and that [litigant] chooses one, and then the two of them choose another" (Sanhedrin 3:1).

Thus it is surprising to discover that wedged in between these two chapters, which complement each other, is a chapter that mostly discusses the laws of kings. On the face of it, this is because 2:1 and 2:2 are concerned with the status of the High Priest and the king as judges and defendants. But this does not explain why a single law regarding the question of a king serving as a judge should generate an entire chapter dedicated to the laws of kings.

A Leader Is a Judge, a Judge Is a Leader

I contend that the key to the answer lies in an idea that emerges even as early as the Bible, which sees a powerful connection between the king and the judge. According to the Torah, the judge does not merely fulfill an administrative role; he is also a public leader – at least one of the public's leaders. Thus, when Moses selects judges, the Torah says, "And Moses chose able men out of all Israel, and made them **heads over the people, rulers of thousands, rulers of hundreds, rulers of fifties,**

and rulers of tens. And they judged the people at all seasons: The hard causes they brought to Moses, but every small matter they judged themselves" (Exodus 18:25–26).

The same idea is at the heart of the book of Judges: The judges are not content to engage in theoretical discussions; they also lead the people through their battles and tribulations. A king, too, possesses this dual role. While the lion's share of his job is to govern and lead, he is also required to sit in judgment of the people. This we see in the people's request of Samuel to appoint for them a king:

> And they said to him: 'Behold, you are old, and your sons walk not in your ways; now make us a king to judge us like all the nations." (I Samuel 8:5)

In a similar vein, when Absalom begins to subvert his father's rule, he takes on the role of judge, as an alternative to King David:

> And it was so, that when any man had a suit that should come to the king for judgment.... And Absalom said: "Oh that I were made judge in the land, so that every man who had any suit or cause might come to me, and I would do him justice!".... And on this manner Absalom did to all Israel that came to the king for judgment; so Absalom stole the hearts of the men of Israel." (I Samuel 15:2–6)

Absalom's brother Solomon, when he is named king, asks God to grant him the ability to judge the people correctly:

> "And now, O Lord my God, You have made Your servant king instead of David my father, and I am but a little child; I know not how to go out or come in. And Your servant is in the midst of Your people, which You have chosen, a great people that cannot be numbered nor counted for multitude. Give Your servant therefore an understanding heart to judge Your people, so that I may discern between good and evil, for who is able to judge this, Your great people?" (I Kings 3:7–9)

The ability to impose internal order and justice among the people is an inherent aspect of leadership and its responsibility to the public, which is why a king must also be a judge. On the other hand, in order for a judge to have the power to implement his edicts and rulings, he must possess authority; thus a judge must also be a leader. Furthermore, if a judge is to have the moral authority to rule as to who is righteous and who wicked, he must be directly acquainted with the people – not only as abstract case studies, but as real people. A judge must also know that he bears responsibility toward the people, and that his judgments must reflect a commitment not only to formal law, but also toward the litigants and defendants themselves.

The link between Chapter 1, which is concerned with judges, and Chapter 2, which is about kings, is a statement on the essence of both these roles and figures, and the relationship between them. For the editors of the Mishna, it was not enough to juxtapose the chapters, and they generated an analogy as well:

> And how many should there be in a city that it may be fit to have a Sanhedrin? One hundred and twenty. Rabbi Neḥemya says: Two hundred and thirty, corresponding to [a Sanhedrin of twenty-three judges,] chiefs of [at least] groups of ten. (Sanhedrin 1:6)
>
> None may ride his horse, and none may sit on his throne, and none may make use of his scepter. No one may see him when his hair is being cut, or when he is naked, or when he is in the bathhouse, for it says, "You shall set a king upon yourself" (Deuteronomy 17:15) – that his awe should be upon you. (Sanhedrin 2:5)

Just as the king's awe must be upon the people (*tzibbur*), so too must the judge's awe be upon the people. Consequently, a judge must be appointed over at least ten people, the smallest group that constitutes a quorum (*tzibbur*). The connection between the king and the judge issues from the source of their authority – God, "the King of Judgment."

A Singular Wonder

סנהדרין ד, ה

כֵּיצַד מְאַיְּמִין עַל עֵדֵי נְפָשׁוֹת, הָיוּ מַכְנִיסִין אוֹתָן וּמְאַיְּמִין עֲלֵיהֶן. שֶׁמָּא תֹאמְרוּ מֵאֹמֶד, וּמִשְּׁמוּעָה, עֵד מִפִּי עֵד וּמִפִּי אָדָם נֶאֱמָן שָׁמַעְנוּ, אוֹ שֶׁמָּא אִי אַתֶּם יוֹדְעִין שֶׁסּוֹפֵנוּ לִבְדּוֹק אֶתְכֶם בִּדְרִישָׁה וּבַחֲקִירָה.

הֱווּ יוֹדְעִין שֶׁלֹּא כְדִינֵי מָמוֹנוֹת דִּינֵי נְפָשׁוֹת. דִּינֵי מָמוֹנוֹת, אָדָם נוֹתֵן מָמוֹן וּמִתְכַּפֵּר לוֹ. דִּינֵי נְפָשׁוֹת, דָּמוֹ וְדַם זַרְעִיּוֹתָיו תְּלוּיִין בּוֹ עַד סוֹף הָעוֹלָם, שֶׁכֵּן מָצִינוּ בְקַיִן שֶׁהָרַג אֶת אָחִיו, שֶׁנֶּאֱמַר (בראשית ד) דְּמֵי אָחִיךָ צֹעֲקִים, אֵינוֹ אוֹמֵר דַּם אָחִיךָ אֶלָּא דְּמֵי אָחִיךָ, דָּמוֹ וְדַם זַרְעִיּוֹתָיו. דָּבָר אַחֵר, דְּמֵי אָחִיךָ, שֶׁהָיָה דָמוֹ מֻשְׁלָךְ עַל הָעֵצִים וְעַל הָאֲבָנִים. לְפִיכָךְ נִבְרָא אָדָם יְחִידִי, לְלַמֶּדְךָ שֶׁכָּל הַמְאַבֵּד נֶפֶשׁ אַחַת , מַעֲלֶה עָלָיו הַכָּתוּב כְּאִלּוּ

Sanhedrin 4:5

How did they admonish witnesses in capital cases? They brought them in and admonished them, [saying], "Perhaps you will say something that is only a supposition, or hearsay, or secondhand, or even from a trustworthy man. Or perhaps you do not know that we shall check you with examination and inquiry?

Know, moreover, that capital cases are not like non-capital cases: In non-capital cases a man may pay money and so make atonement, but in capital cases the witness is answerable for the blood of him [that is wrongfully condemned] and the blood of his descendants [that should have been born to him] to the end of the world. For so have we found it with Cain, who murdered his brother, for it says, "The bloods of your brother cry out" (Genesis 4:10). It does not say, "The blood of your brother," but rather "The bloods of your brother," meaning his blood and the blood of his descendants. Another saying is, "The bloods of your brother" – that his blood was cast over trees and stones. Therefore but a single person was created in the world, to teach that if any man has caused a single life to perish,[1] he is deemed by Scripture as if he had caused a whole world to perish; and anyone who saves a single soul from Israel, he is deemed by Scripture as if he had saved a whole world. Again [but a single person was created] for the sake of peace among humankind, that one should not say to another, "My father was greater than your father." Again, [but a single person was created,] against the heretics, so they should not say, "There are many ruling powers in heaven." Again [but a single person was created] to proclaim the greatness of the Holy One, blessed be He; for humans stamp many coins with one seal and they are all like one another, but the King of kings, the Holy One, blessed be He, has stamped every human with the seal of the first man, yet not one of them are like another. Therefore everyone must say, "For my sake was the world created." And if perhaps you [witnesses] would say, "Why should we be involved with this trouble?" was it not said, "He, being a witness, whether he has seen or known, [if he does not speak it, then he shall bear his iniquity] (Leviticus 5:1). And if perhaps you [witnesses] would say, "Why should we be guilty of the blood of this man?" was it not said, "When the wicked perish there is rejoicing?" (Proverbs 11:10)

אִבֵּד עוֹלָם מָלֵא. וְכָל הַמְקַיֵּם נֶפֶשׁ אַחַת מִיִּשְׂרָאֵל, מַעֲלֶה עָלָיו הַכָּתוּב כְּאִלּוּ קִיֵּם עוֹלָם מָלֵא. וּמִפְּנֵי שְׁלוֹם הַבְּרִיּוֹת, שֶׁלֹּא יֹאמַר אָדָם לַחֲבֵרוֹ אַבָּא גָדוֹל מֵאָבִיךָ וְשֶׁלֹּא יְהוּ מִינִין אוֹמְרִים, הַרְבֵּה רְשׁוּיוֹת בַּשָּׁמָיִם. וּלְהַגִּיד גְּדֻלָּתוֹ שֶׁל הַקָּדוֹשׁ בָּרוּךְ הוּא, שֶׁאָדָם טוֹבֵעַ כַּמָּה מַטְבְּעוֹת בְּחוֹתָם אֶחָד וְכֻלָּן דּוֹמִין זֶה לָזֶה, וּמֶלֶךְ מַלְכֵי הַמְּלָכִים הַקָּדוֹשׁ בָּרוּךְ הוּא טָבַע כָּל אָדָם בְּחוֹתָמוֹ שֶׁל אָדָם הָרִאשׁוֹן וְאֵין אֶחָד מֵהֶן דּוֹמֶה לַחֲבֵרוֹ. לְפִיכָךְ כָּל אֶחָד וְאֶחָד חַיָּב לוֹמַר, בִּשְׁבִילִי נִבְרָא הָעוֹלָם. וְשֶׁמָּא תֹאמְרוּ מַה לָּנוּ וְלַצָּרָה הַזֹּאת, וַהֲלֹא כְבָר נֶאֱמַר (ויקרא ה) וְהוּא עֵד אוֹ רָאָה אוֹ יָדָע אִם לוֹא יַגִּיד וְגוֹמֵר. וְשֶׁמָּא תֹאמְרוּ מַה לָּנוּ לָחוּב בְּדָמוֹ שֶׁל זֶה, וַהֲלֹא כְבָר נֶאֱמַר (משלי יא) וּבַאֲבֹד רְשָׁעִים רִנָּה.

1. There are print editions of the Mishna that add the words "of Israel," but that is not the case in any of the manuscripts of the Mishna or the Yerushalmi. It is likely that version was unknown to some of the Rishonim, including Rashi, Rabbeinu Ḥananel, and Maimonides.

One of the messages of Judaism to the world is its idea of the essence of a human being. The Mishna relates that the Sanhedrin would warn the witnesses in capital cases to avoid any mistake in their testimony, so that an innocent person would not be put to death on their account. The aversion to murder in the Bible is explained as stemming from the sanctity of every human life created in the image of God: "Whoever sheds man's blood, by man shall his blood be shed, for in the image of God He made man" (Genesis 9:6).

However, the Mishna chooses an alternative avenue for explaining the importance of human life. It does not admonish the witnesses only because human beings are created in God's image, but rather offers another point of view that has to do with an individual's inherent worth. The Mishna's in-depth discussion of the implications of the creation of a single person acquaints us with three additional, complementary elements of an individual's essence. First and foremost, based on the notion that man was created alone, the Mishna deduces that humanity is all descended from a single human. Thus, a killer's responsibility toward the person he killed extends also to the children of the victim. Every individual is an entire world, and to lose a human being is to lose an entire world.

Further along in the mishna there are two statements with opposite implications:

> "...for the sake of peace among humankind, that one should not say to another, 'My father was greater than your father.'"

The fact that all of humanity share a common ancestor negates racism and generates peace and amity. These may prompt some to seek to efface the differences between human beings, as in John Lennon's famous song "Imagine":

> Imagine there's no countries
> It isn't hard to do
> Nothing to kill or die for
> And no religion, too

> Imagine all the people
> Living life in peace, you
> You may say I am a dreamer
> But I'm not the only one
> I hope someday you'll join us
> And the world will be as one.

The power of the song comes from the power of the dream, and the depth of our yearning to return to the beginning of the world, to a natural, pristine reality that preceded all mistakes and strife. As the Mishna notes, we all share a single father, were birthed by a single mother. Our Mishna, however, contains not only the root of Lennon's vision, but also its negation:

> Again [but a single person was created] to proclaim the greatness of the Holy One, blessed be He; for humans stamp many coins with one seal and they are all like one another, but the King of kings, the Holy One, blessed be He, has stamped every human with the seal of the first man, yet not one of them are like another. Therefore everyone must say, "For my sake was the world created."

The greatness of God is synonymous with the greatness of humanity. Peace is the common element of all humanity, but if unity means uniformity – "many coins with one seal and they are all like one another" – then the individual loses his worth. Judaism's unique contribution is the attempt to generate uniqueness through unity. It is only by recognizing the inimitability of every individual that a person can say, "For my sake was the world created." The first message of the mishna is that each person is an entire world because of his potential offspring; it concludes with the idea that every individual is an entire world unto themselves.

Woman as the Priestess of Life: The Deeper Meaning of *Nidda* Impurity[1]

שבועות ב, ג-ד

נִטְמָא בָעֲזָרָה וְנֶעֶלְמָה מִמֶּנּוּ טֻמְאָה, וְזָכוּר אֶת הַמִּקְדָּשׁ,[1] נֶעְלַם מִמֶּנּוּ מִקְדָּשׁ וְזָכוּר לַטֻּמְאָה, נֶעְלַם מִמֶּנּוּ זֶה וָזֶה, וְהִשְׁתַּחֲוָה אוֹ שֶׁשָּׁהָה בִּכְדֵי הִשְׁתַּחֲוָאָה, בָּא לוֹ בָּאֲרֻכָּה,[2] חַיָּב. בַּקְּצָרָה, פָּטוּר. זוֹ הִיא מִצְוַת עֲשֵׂה שֶׁבַּמִּקְדָּשׁ שֶׁאֵין חַיָּבִין עָלֶיהָ.

וְאֵיזוֹ הִיא מִצְוַת עֲשֵׂה שֶׁבַּנִּדָּה שֶׁחַיָּבִין עָלֶיהָ, הָיָה מְשַׁמֵּשׁ עִם הַטְּהוֹרָה וְאָמְרָה לוֹ נִטְמֵאתִי וּפֵרַשׁ

Shevuot 2:3–4

If he became impure while in the Temple court [and was aware of it], and then forgot that he was impure, though he remembered that he was in the Temple;[2] [or] he forgot that he was in the Temple, though he remembered that he was impure; [or,] he forgot both; and he prostrated himself, or waited [in the Temple] the time it takes to prostrate; [or] went out the long way,[3] he is liable. [If he went out] the shorter way, he is not liable. This is the positive precept concerning the Temple for which they [the court] are not liable.

And which is the positive precept concerning a menstruating woman (*nidda*) for which they are liable? [This:] if one cohabited with a [ritually] pure woman, and she said to him: "I have become impure," and

1. I thank my friend Shmuel Polachek for his notes on this chapter.
2. Meaning, if the person is aware of being in the Temple but has forgotten that he is impure.
3. Exits the Temple via the long way rather than the short way.

מִיָּד, חַיָּב, מִפְּנֵי שֶׁיְּצִיאָתוֹ הֲנָאָה לוֹ כְּבִיאָתוֹ.	he withdrew immediately, he is liable, because his withdrawal is as pleasant to him as his entry.

Surprisingly, the Mishna in Shevuot juxtaposes impurity laws related to two very different arenas: the Temple and menstrual impurity:

> [If he] went out the long way, he is liable. [If he went out] the shorter way, he is not liable. **This is the positive precept concerning the Temple** for which they [the court] are not liable.
>
> And which is the positive precept concerning a menstruating woman (*nidda*) for which they are liable?... Because his withdrawal is as pleasant to him as his entry.

What is the purpose of this juxtaposition, in which the Mishna even uses the same root, *bet-alef*, to describe exiting the Temple and withdrawing during intercourse? We can find a similar juxtaposition elsewhere in the Mishna:

> [The court] is not obligated [to bring a sacrifice] for the transgression of a positive or a negative commandment relating to the **Temple**; nor [does anyone] bring a sliding-scale guilt offering for the transgression of a positive or a negative commandment relating to the **Temple**. But they are liable for the transgression of a positive or a negative commandment relating to a menstruating woman; and [individuals] bring a sliding-scale guilt offering for the transgression of a positive or negative commandment relating to a menstruating woman. (Horayot 2:4)

The Mishna is saying that if a court hands down an incorrect ruling concerning the laws of the Temple, the judges are not required to bring an offering to atone for their mistake. However, if they erred in a ruling regarding the laws of *nidda*, they must bring an offering. The Talmud (Horayot 8b) explains that, in fact, the judges are liable not only in cases of errors regarding *nidda*, but rather in the case of any forbidden action that if committed inadvertently would require a sin offering. This addition further sharpens the question: Why did the Mishna choose to liken a *nidda* to the Temple? What is the connection?

Almost all of the laws of ritual purity and impurity, which constitute about one-quarter of the Mishna, concern the Temple, as "sensitivity" to impurity, and the need to keep a distance from it, can exist only in a place of holiness: "And you shall not defile the land that you inhabit, in the midst of which I dwell; for I the Lord dwell in the midst of the children of Israel" (Numbers 35:34). The only area outside the Temple where there is sensitivity to purity and impurity is the relationship between men and women. That is why in this day and age as well, despite the absence of the Temple, these laws of purity and impurity persist. The similarity drawn between conjugal life and the Temple teaches us that the sensitivity to impurity does not stem from a negative view of the relationship between husband and wife, but is rather an expression of its holiness and importance. As Rabbi Akiva, one of the preeminent *Tanna'im*, puts it, "When husband and wife are worthy, the Divine Presence abides with them" (Sota 17a). This is also apparent in the comparison to other cases where ritual immersion is required: The only people required by law to immerse are priests entering the Temple and married women after their menstrual cycle.

The Creation of Life and Holiness

Yet, we must ask: Why does menstrual blood render a woman impure? Furthermore, if ritual immersion is indeed an expression of holiness in the life of a married couple, why is the woman alone obligated to immerse, and not the man? The answer to these questions lies in the understanding of the essence of holiness. In Judaism, impurity is linked to death. A corpse is considered the primary source of defilement (*avi avot hatuma*), and every other source of impurity is associated with death or lessening of life. Holiness, on the other hand, is associated with life, and anything that increases life and vitality is holy.

Every month, a woman's body prepares to create a child, and menstrual blood is an expression of that opportunity being missed, of an egg going unfertilized, of a month devoid of new life. *Nidda* impurity does not stem from a primitive taboo, from fear, but from the recognition that menstruation is an expression of a lessening of life. This is evidenced by the fact that after childbirth, there is a period where the blood that comes out of the womb does not defile the woman; rather, because it is an expression of the creation of life, not its lessening, it is called "the blood of purification" (Leviticus 12:4–5).

Purity and impurity stand in opposition to each other, which is why places that are suffused with holiness require extreme caution as to ritual impurity. The idea that menstrual blood causes impurity is linked to the assumption that, during the rest of the month, the life-creating process within the woman's body is holy.

A Cycle of Light

The halakhic system imbues biological reality with religious meaning. But those two systems are also related to a third – the cosmological cycle. There is a well-known parallel between women and the moon, both in terms of the cyclical process and in terms of its approximate length – thirty days. The lunar phase reaches its full state in the middle of the month, two weeks before the end of the cycle, just like a woman's cycle. This affinity is also noted in halakha; for instance in the thirteenth-century book *Or Zarua*:[4]

> Women who choose to refrain from work on the first day of the month are engaging in a worthy and virtuous custom.... Know that every month, the woman renews herself, immerses and returns to her husband, and is dear to him as on their wedding day. Just as the moon renews every first of the month.... That is why the first of the month is a festival for women.

4. *Or Zarua, Hilkhot Rosh Ḥodesh* 454.

A man's body, in contrast, is devoid of cyclicality. He is unable to foster new life within himself and thus cannot be a source of *nidda* impurity.[5] That is why the determination of the period of time when the couple is forbidden from intimate contact is based on the woman. The prohibition against having relations begins with the process taking place inside the women's body, while the couple's return to one another is the culmination of a process of the woman contemplating her body during the seven clean days and immersing in the *mikve*.

One could say that the difference between women and men is analogous to the difference between priests and laypeople. The priest, because he is required to cleave to holiness, is more sensitive to impurity. Women, it follows, are the priestesses of life.

---

5. Seminal emissions, which cause a man to become impure and which are also a lessening of life, are happenstance, rather than something the body prepares for.

Love of Humanity in Tractate Avot

In his preface to the Song of Songs,[1] Rabbi Abraham Isaac Kook distills Rabbi Akiva's life into three loves: At first, when he was merely "Akiva," a humble shepherd, he was blessed to love a woman – Rachel, the daughter of Kalba Savua. Later in his life, when he was a renowned Sage, he ascribed vital importance to love of humanity: "Love your neighbor as yourself – that is a fundamental principle of the Torah" (*Sifra, Kedoshim* 2). Finally, at death's door, while the Romans were torturing him with metal combs, Rabbi Akiva arrived at the pinnacle of divine love, fulfilling with his own soul the teaching, "'And you shall love the Lord your God... with all your soul' – even if He takes your soul" (Berakhot 9:5).[2]

Rabbi Akiva knew that the three loves are intertwined, which is why he says that the carnal love described in the Song of Songs is an allegory for the love between God and the Jewish people: "The whole world is not worth the day on which the Song of Songs was given to Israel, for all the writings are holy, but the Song of Songs is the Holy of Holies" (Yadayim 3:5).

Rav Kook describes how Rabbi Akiva attained love on the human plane and only afterward in the divine realm. In contrast with this order, which seems logical, Tractate Avot presents the traits and attributes

1. *Olat Re'iya*, vol. 2, p. 4.
2. According to the Talmud, there are three sins that one must not commit even on pain of death: murder, incest, and idolatry. These three sins correspond to the three loves of Rabbi Akiva: love of humanity, love of his wife, and love of God, respectively.

required to attain the Torah in the opposite order – first "love God" and only then "love one's fellow creatures" (Avot 6:6). Love of God, which in the life story of Rabbi Akiva seems like the ultimate result and goal, here becomes a cause and source. Soon we will see, based on a reading of Rabbi Akiva's outlook, that, philosophically speaking, love of God is indeed at the root of love for humanity.

As for interpersonal love, Rabbi Akiva's stance is well known: "Love your neighbor as yourself – that is a fundamental principle of the Torah" (*Sifra Kedoshim* 2). The question arises: How can a maxim that refers only to the interpersonal realm be considered the fundamental principle of a Torah that is equally focused on the relationship between God and humanity? The answer lies in the reason Rabbi Akiva himself supplies for the importance of loving others: "He would say: **Beloved is man, for he was created in the image [of God]**. Especially beloved is he, for it was made known to him that he had been created in the image [of God], as it is said (Genesis 9:6): "for in the image of God He made man" (Avot 3:14). The great love for the other stems from man's divine dimension, for the fact that people are created in God's image. Therefore, just as one must love God, one must also love every human being created in His image – which is why love of God can be actualized by loving other people. In other words, what stands behind Rabbi Akiva's fundamental principle is the connection between human and divine, also formulated by Rav Kook in the opening sentence of his book *To the Perplexed of the Generation*: "That humanity was created in God's image is the fundamental principle of the Torah." This principle seemingly eluded Rabbi Akiva's early students, who died because they did not show respect to one another (Yevamot 62b). Perhaps it was that tragic episode that drove Rabbi Akiva to develop this idea.

The Root of Love

If we examine the concept of love, we can understand that its source is on high. True love, which is unconditional (Avot 5:16), does not exist in uncultured nature. Relationships between animals are generated by biological instinct. In the human world, by contrast, we believe that there is a love that springs from a higher source: "This love exists above us; it cannot be apprehended by eyes of flesh" ("*Malḥuyot*" by Etti Ankri). The Zohar (*Teruma* 146b) notes the similarity between the four letters of the name of God (the Tetragrammaton – *yod-heh-vav-heh*) and the four letters of the word *ahava* (love) – *alef-heh-bet-heh*. It teaches that the root of human love is supernal, in the image of God embedded in humanity.

"When husband and wife are worthy, the Divine Presence abides with them; when they are not worthy, fire consumes them" (Sota 17a). The Hebrew words for "man/husband" (*ish*) and "woman/wife" (*isha*) share two letters in common – *alef* and *shin*, spelling *esh*, fire. But *ish* also contains a *yod*, and *isha* contains a *heh*; together these two letters yield "*Yah*," a name of God. The union between husband and wife reflects a union of the letters *yod* and *heh*, so that through their union they complete God's name.

It follows that Rabbi Akiva's idea of the Song of Songs as the Holy of Holies refers not only to its allegorical meaning, to the conception of romantic love as a metaphor for the love between the Jewish people and God, but also to its overt meaning. To him, love between husband and wife is tantamount to the Holy of Holies; it is rooted in supernal love and issues from it.

The link between love of God and romantic love is also apparent in the fact that the Hebrew for "one" (*eḥad*) and "love" (*ahava*) have the same numerical value. That God is one is the central tenet of Jewish belief: "Hear (*Shema*), O Israel: the Lord our God, the Lord is one" (Deuteronomy 6:4). And in the human realm, love can be encapsulated as the yearning to be "one" with the other: "and they shall be one flesh" (Genesis 2:24). This definition of love sheds new light on the story of Rabbi Akiva's death by torture while he recited *Shema*, until his soul departed his body as he uttered the word "one."

Unconditional Love

We will conclude with the opposite of love: hatred. The Sages say the Second Temple was destroyed due to the sin of senseless hatred.[3] This statement is an expression not only of the severity of the sin, but also

3. Yoma 9b.

of the fact that the Temple is a place of love, and will be rebuilt out of love. This is alluded to in the classic story about the Temple having been built in a place where a great show of love occurred between two brothers. The purpose of the Temple is to unite all of the Jewish people, and then for the Jewish people to unite with God: "Rav Katina said: Whenever Israel made a pilgrimage for the festival, the curtain would be removed for them, and the Cherubim were shown to them, whose bodies were intertwisted with one another, and they would be thus addressed: Look! You are beloved before God as the love between man and woman" (Yoma 54a).

The Sages, who saw baseless hatred as the cause of the Temple's destruction, teach that consummation of the love between the Jewish people and God depends on there being love within the Jewish people, among individual people. In light of this, we can understand the plea[4] for the Third Temple to be built only out of a place of unconditional love.

4. Based on the words of Rav Kook. See *Orot HaKodesh* 3:324.

A Person Is Defined by Giving

אבות ה, י

אַרְבַּע מִדּוֹת בָּאָדָם.
הָאוֹמֵר שֶׁלִּי שֶׁלִּי וְשֶׁלְּךָ
שֶׁלָּךְ, זוֹ מִדָּה בֵּינוֹנִית. וְיֵשׁ
אוֹמְרִים, זוֹ מִדַּת סְדוֹם.
שֶׁלִּי שֶׁלָּךְ וְשֶׁלְּךָ שֶׁלִּי, עַם
הָאָרֶץ. שֶׁלִּי שֶׁלָּךְ וְשֶׁלְּךָ
שֶׁלָּךְ, חָסִיד. שֶׁלִּי שֶׁלִּי
וְשֶׁלְּךָ שֶׁלִּי, רָשָׁע.

Avot 5:10

There are four types of character in human beings: One that says, "Mine is mine, and yours is yours" – this is a commonplace type; and some say this is a Sodom-type of character. [One that says,] "Mine is yours, and yours is mine" is an unlearned person. [One that says,] "Mine is yours, and yours is yours" is a pious person. [One that says,] "Mine is mine, and yours is mine" is a wicked person.

The fifth chapter of Tractate Avot includes a sequence of mishnayot, each of which defines four types of characters in different realms: four kinds of temperaments, four types of disciples, four types of charity givers, four types among those who frequent the study house, and four types among those who sit before the Sages. It is noteworthy, then, how fundamental the above mishna is: As opposed to the other definitions, which present various human traits, our mishna sets out to define "types of *human beings*" [emphasis mine]. It is a statement about the essence of what it means to be human. As does the philosophy of Karl Marx, the Mishna sees the question of an individual's relation to property as an expression of something intrinsic in their identity. However, as opposed to Marx's communist outlook, the Mishna does not idealize the abolition of all property rights; that, it says, is the mindset of an unlearned person. On the other hand, neither does the Mishna sanctify ownership, and even cites an opinion that to say "Mine is mine, and yours is yours" is the hallmark of a "Sodom-type of character." What, then, is the meaning and significance of the pious person's complex approach to ownership? And why is it that approach that defines the essence of a person?

To my mind, the key to the secret of the mishna lies in a song that every Israeli child learns in preschool: "So said Rabbi Akiva, so said Rabbi Akiva, love your neighbor as yourself. Mine is yours, yours is yours, mine is yours, yours is yours – that is a fundamental principle of the Torah." The manner in which the song links between Rabbi Akiva's maxim and the Mishna imbues both with fresh meaning. According to the song, in order to love one's neighbor as oneself, one must adopt a code of conduct that tempers the giving encapsulated in "mine is yours" with respect for the other's property rights: "Yours is yours." But this interpretation raises a question: One would expect, if one is to love "as oneself," that one would also treat oneself as one's neighbor, meaning that if one respects the other's right to property, the same attitude should extend to one's own property. And if one forfeits one's property, shouldn't that same treatment be extended to the other's property, in keeping with the communist ideal, which the Mishna dismisses as the approach of an "unlearned person"?

In the previous chapter we asked how "love your neighbor" can be a "fundamental principle of the Torah" while omitting the human relationship to God. Our answer there relied on the connection between Rabbi Akiva's fundamental principle on love and his statement in Avot that "Beloved is man for he was created in the image [of God]" (3:14), and concluded that giving to another human being is also an act of generosity toward God. Rabbi Yehuda Ashlag offers another answer to this question, one that is also founded upon the connection between the human and the divine.[1]

The basic thing we know about God is that He gives without expecting to receive anything in return. Rabbi Ashlag considers such altruistic giving to be the foundation for "love your neighbor as yourself" – that is, unconditional love (Avot 5:16). He derives this idea from

1. His approach is laid out throughout his book, *Gift of the Bible.*

the term "as yourself" (*kamokha*); a capacity to love another as one loves himself indicates that there is no room for ego in the relationship, that there is no personal agenda. In such a state of giving, one takes on a Godly aspect. The connection between the human and the divine, according to Rabbi Ashlag, is what makes loving others the fundamental principle of the Torah. The two answers complete each other: In our proposal, the link between loving others and God is based on the idea that God is in the other; in Rabbi Ashlag's proposal, the link is established through the divine within oneself.

Let us return to our mishna. Rabbi Ashlag's idea explains the importance of the "mine is yours, and yours is yours" type. From within that outlook, the pious person's giving is not predicated on receiving anything in return. One relinquishes one's ownership for the other's benefit without any compensation, which is why one continues to rigorously uphold the other's property rights.

Thus it is clear why the Mishna discusses "types of human beings." Humanity was cast in God's image; the more Godlike a person, the more human. God gives with no strings attached, and the measure of humanity is the capacity to give with no expectation of reward.

The association of "love your neighbor" to our mishna shows us that in order to fulfill the mitzva to love the other it is not enough to feel love in one's heart; love must be expressed in concrete reality. Beyond that, the association shows that "love your neighbor" does not refer only to the weak and needy, as in 5:13 ("four types of charity givers"), but rather extends to one's approach to each and every human being.

Compelled Not to Act in the Manner of Sodom

We find in the mishna an opinion whereby the type of "mine is mine, and yours is yours" is indicative of "a Sodom-type of character." Considering that the denizens of Sodom were considered the height of evil, are we to understand that this character is worse than a wicked person? It seems that the wicked person in our mishna is a run-of-the-mill crook, who uses the idea of property to his own advantage. By contrast, the outlook of Sodom can become an ideology, justifying the behavior of an entire society that sanctifies alienation.

The antidote to Sodom is the patriarch Abraham. *Parashat Vayera* exalts Abraham's concern for the other, demonstrated through his hospitality, his prayers for Sodom, and the reason for which he is chosen – "For I have known him, to the end that he may command his children and his household after him, that they may keep the way of the Lord, to do righteousness and justice" (Genesis 18:19).

Abraham is chosen for his capacity to emulate God, and thus actualize his divine image by giving to the other, with righteousness and justice. In light of the mishna in Avot, we could perhaps explain those twin attributes thus: "justice" expresses respect for the other's property rights, or "your is yours"; "righteousness" is the capacity to give up one's own ownership for the sake of the other, or "mine is yours."

The Talmud accepts the opinion that "mine is mine and yours is yours" is characteristic of the Sodom type, and thus concludes that "a man can be compelled not to act after the manner of Sodom" (Bava Batra 12a). This means that a court has the power to force someone to relinquish ownership in favor of another when the first party does not incur any financial damage from doing so. This moral principle was accepted by the judiciary of the State of Israel, a clear example of the influence of Jewish values on the judicial world.

My Beloved Knocks

תמיד א, ב

מִי שֶׁהוּא רוֹצֶה לִתְרוֹם אֶת הַמִּזְבֵּחַ, מַשְׁכִּים וְטוֹבֵל עַד שֶׁלֹּא יָבוֹא הַמְּמֻנֶּה. וְכִי בְאֵיזוֹ שָׁעָה הַמְּמֻנֶּה בָא, לֹא כָל הָעִתִּים שָׁווֹת, פְּעָמִים שֶׁהוּא בָא מִקְּרִיאַת הַגֶּבֶר, אוֹ סָמוּךְ לוֹ מִלְּפָנָיו אוֹ מִלְּאַחֲרָיו. הַמְּמֻנֶּה בָא וְדוֹפֵק עֲלֵיהֶם, וְהֵם פָּתְחוּ לוֹ. אָמַר לָהֶן, מִי שֶׁטָּבַל יָבוֹא וְיָפִיס. הֵפִיסוּ, זָכָה מִי שֶׁזָּכָה:

Tamid 1:2

Anyone who desired to remove the ashes from the altar used to rise early and bathe before the superintendent came. At what time did the superintendent come? He did not always come at the same time; sometimes he came just at cock-crow, sometimes a little before or a little after. The superintendent would come and knock, and they would open for him, and he would say to them, let all who have bathed come and draw lots. So they drew lots, and whoever merited, merited.

In his *Commentary on the Mishna*, Maimonides writes of Tractate Tamid that there "is no talk in it about the way of wisdom or about the forbidden and the permitted. Rather, **it is a story** that speaks to how they would offer the daily (*tamid*) sacrifice, in order to do so perpetually."[1]

The narrative style of Tractate Tamid diverges from the halakhic and legal style of most of the Mishna's tractates. It contains few disputes, and it rarely mentions the names of any *Tanna'im*. Furthermore, the Bavli, uncharacteristically, notes that several details of the Mishna's story are not historical fact but rather "exaggeration" and "hyperbole."[2]

1. Maimonides, *Commentary on the Mishna*, Introduction, 15:80.
2. Tamid 29a.

The tractate is also unique in its lyrical style,[3] which in a number of places includes rhymes.[4]

It is my contention that any examination of the tractate, and especially of its philosophical underpinnings and literary structure, must consider its intertextual link to the Song of Songs. This is especially true of the connection to the fifth chapter of the Song of Songs, which relates the story of the woman who awaits her beloved in her room in the dead of night and, in a tragic turn of events, squanders the opportunity due to her laziness. Tractate Tamid presents the Temple rites as a rectification of that story – the actualization of the meeting between the woman and her beloved.

The body of rabbinic literature in various places treats the Temple as the site for the rendezvous of the lovers of the Song of Songs. A striking example of this idea can be found in the Bavli:

> Thus was it also taught: "And the ends of the staves were seen." One might have assumed that they did not protrude from their place. To teach us [the fact], Scripture says: "And the staves were so long." One might have assumed that they tore the curtain and showed forth; to teach us [the fact], Scripture says: "They could not be seen without." How then? They pressed forth and protruded as the two breasts of a woman, as it is said: "My beloved is to me like a bag of myrrh, that lies between my breasts" (Song of Songs 1). Rav Katina said: Whenever Israel made a pilgrimage for the festival, the curtain would be removed for them, and the Cherubim were shown to them, whose bodies were intertwisted with one another, and they would be thus addressed: Look! You are beloved before God as the love between man and woman. (Yoma 54a)

3. See Epstein, *Introduction to Tannaitic literature* (Jerusalem: Magnes Press, 1957) [Hebrew].
4. See, for example, the meter of 1:3.

The Mishna similarly hints:

> Similarly it says, "O maidens of Zion, go forth and gaze upon King Solomon wearing the crown that his mother gave him on his wedding day, on the day of the gladness of his heart" (Song of Songs 3:11). "On his wedding day" – this refers to the Giving of the Torah. "And on the day of the gladness of his heart" – this refers to the building of the Temple; may it be rebuilt speedily in our days, Amen. (Taanit 4:8)

In this context, we must mention the words of Rabbi Akiva, who, in order to drive home the exaltedness of the Song of Songs, employs an image of the Temple – "Holy of Holies" – to describe it:

> Rabbi Akiva said: Far be it! No man in Israel disputed regarding the Song of Songs [saying] that it does not defile the hands. For the whole world is not worth the day on which the Song of Songs was given to Israel; for all the writings are holy, but the Song of Songs is the Holy of Holies (Yadayim 3:5).

The Arrival of the Superintendent

The second mishna of Tractate Tamid describes the morning routine in the Temple, which begins with the rising of the priests who wish to take part in the first rite of the day: removing the ashes from the altar. Most of the mishna is occupied with identifying the arrival time of the "superintendent," the officer who governs the Temple operations. This piece of information generates much interest. The Mishna, which is known for its laconic phrasing, devotes fully twenty words (in the original Hebrew) to its explanation of the superintendent's time of arrival. The information is presented by way of a question and answer: "At what time did the superintendent come?" But before an answer is given, the Mishna prefaces it with a statement that amplifies the tension and uncertainty: "He did not always come at the same time." Even the answer is ambiguous, as if time is not a constant: "Sometimes he came just at cock-crow, sometimes a little before or a little after." Ultimately, all of the possibilities are tied to a single event – the crowing of the rooster. What is the significance of the interest surrounding the arrival of the superintendent? Why does the Mishna generate such drama?

It seems that these questions can be tied into the link, described above, to the story in the Song of Songs of the woman waiting for her beloved:

> I sleep, but my heart wakes. Hark, my beloved knocks! "Open to me, my sister, my love, my dove, my undefiled, for my head is filled with dew, my locks with the drops of the night." I have taken off my coat; how shall I put it on? I have washed my feet; how shall I defile them? My beloved put in his hand by the hole of the door, and my heart was moved for him. I rose up to open to my beloved, and my hands dropped with myrrh, and my fingers with flowing myrrh, upon the handles of the bar. I opened to my beloved, but my beloved had turned away, and was gone. My soul failed me when he spoke. I sought him, but I could not find him; I called him, but he gave me no answer. (Song of Songs 5:2–6)

The woman lies in bed awaiting her meeting: "I sleep, but my heart wakes." Then she hears a sound: "Hark, my beloved **knocks**!" The beloved has arrived, and calls out to her in terms of endearment: "**Open** to me, my sister, my love, my dove, my undefiled." But the woman is overcome with lethargy; she does not want to rise from her bed, to dress and defile her feet. By the time she comes to the door the hour has passed and she can no longer find her beloved.

The Mishna also relates a story of an encounter – between the priests and the superintendent. The priests would sleep in the courtyard, and the superintendent would arrive and call them out. But here, unlike the Song of Songs, the meeting takes place – the priests rise in advance and prepare for the arrival of the superintendent. When he arrives he does not have to wait for them outside the locked door: "The superintendent would come and **knock**, and they would **open** for him."[5]

Hence the lengthy description of the coming of the superintendent: the Mishna intends to imbue his arrival, which is essentially a given, with mystery. In this way the Mishna generates tension and enhances the link to the story of the encounter in Song of Songs, where the woman awaits her beloved without knowing when he will arrive.

The opening mishna of Tractate Tamid further enhances the contrast between the two encounter stories:

> And the elders of the clan [serving in the Temple] used to sleep there, with the keys of the Temple courtyard in their hands. The priestly initiates used to place their bedding on the ground. They did not sleep in their sacred garments, but they used to take them off [and fold them] and place them under their heads and cover themselves with their own ordinary clothes.

Two things prevent the woman of the Song of Songs from rising and opening the door for her beloved: "I have **taken off** my coat; how shall I put it on?" and "I have washed my feet; how shall I defile them?" Like her, the priests have undressed: "They did not sleep in their sacred garments, but they used to **take them off.**" Their rising also involves bathing, as we see in 1:2. However, unlike the woman, they would rise "before the superintendent came," and when he knocked, they would open immediately.

The slumber of the priests in 1:1 is one of excitement and anticipation, "with the keys of the Temple courtyard in their hands." Even as they sleep their attention does not waver from the hour at which they are to open the courtyard.

5. The only instance of the word "knock" (*dofek*) is in the Song of Songs, and its only appearance in the Mishna with a similar connotation is in our mishna. The two other appearances of *dofek* in the Mishna (Nazir 7:3 and Ohalot 2:4) are not as a verb, as in the Song of Songs, but as a noun, describing a rock against which rests the rolling stone sealing the entrance to a burial cave.

The story of the woman in the Song of Songs continues. After her beloved "turned away, and was gone," she goes out to search for him and pays the price of her laziness:

> The watchmen that go about the city found me, they smote me, they wounded me; the keepers of the walls took away my mantle from me. (Song of Songs 5:7)

This story is the inspiration for a mishna in Tractate Middot that tells of the punishment meted out to those who are idle in safeguarding the Temple:

> The officer of the Temple Mount used to go round to every watch, with lighted torches before him, and if any watcher did not rise [at his approach] and say to him, "Shalom to you, officer of the Temple Mount," it was obvious that he was asleep. Then he used to beat him with his rod. And he had permission to burn his clothes. And the others would say: "What is the noise in the courtyard? It is the cry of a Levite who is being beaten and whose clothes are being burned, because he was asleep at his watch." Rabbi Eliezer ben Yaakov said: Once they found my mother's brother asleep, and they burnt his clothes. (Middot 1:2)

The Temple Mount officer recalls the watchmen who roam the city in the Song of Songs – he makes the rounds and drops in on watches charged with guarding the Temple to make sure that they are doing their jobs. The penalty of a watcher caught sleeping at his post is reminiscent of the punishment suffered by the woman who idled and slept: The guard is beaten and his clothes are burned, like the woman, who is beaten and whose mantle is taken away. Tractate Tamid, in keeping with its link to the Song of Songs, also invokes the guards who circle the city: The priests, after one is chosen to remove the ashes from the altar, circumambulate the Temple walls:

> He took the key and opened the small door, and went from the fire chamber into the Temple courtyard, and the priests went in after him carrying two lighted torches. They divided into two groups, one of which went along the portico to the east, while the other went along it to the west. They went along inspecting until they came to the place where the griddlecakes were made. There the two groups met and said, "Is all well (shalom)?" "All is well (shalom)!" They then appointed they that made the griddlecakes to make griddlecakes. (Tamid 1:3)

One group of priests turned right, and the other turned left. Together, the two groups completed a circuit of the outside of the Sanctuary, "going along and inspecting," like the guards who "go about the city" and find the woman. Like the story of the woman who walks around looking for her beloved after opening the door, here too there is an inspection following the opening of the door; but whereas in the Song of Songs the woman is beaten at the end of the inspection, here the inspection concludes with "all is well."

The Time of Singing Is Come, and the Voice of the Turtledove Is Heard

תמיד א, ד

מִי שֶׁזָּכָה לִתְרוֹם אֶת הַמִּזְבֵּחַ, הוּא יִתְרוֹם אֶת הַמִּזְבֵּחַ, אוֹמְרִין לוֹ, הִזָּהֵר שֶׁמָּא תִגַּע בַּכֶּלִי, עַד שֶׁתְּקַדֵּשׁ יָדֶיךָ וְרַגְלֶיךָ מִן הַכִּיּוֹר, וַהֲרֵי הַמַּחְתָּה נְתוּנָה בַּמִּקְצוֹעַ בֵּין הַכֶּבֶשׁ לַמִּזְבֵּחַ בְּמַעֲרָבוֹ שֶׁל כֶּבֶשׁ. אֵין אָדָם נִכְנָס עִמּוֹ, וְלֹא נֵר בְּיָדוֹ, אֶלָּא מְהַלֵּךְ לְאוֹר הַמַּעֲרָכָה. לֹא הָיוּ רוֹאִין אוֹתוֹ, וְלֹא שׁוֹמְעִין אֶת קוֹלוֹ עַד שֶׁשּׁוֹמְעִין קוֹל הָעֵץ שֶׁעָשָׂה בֶן קָטִין מוּכְנִי לַכִּיּוֹר, וְהֵן אוֹמְרִים הִגִּיעַ. קִדֵּשׁ יָדָיו וְרַגְלָיו מִן הַכִּיּוֹר, נָטַל מַחְתַּת הַכֶּסֶף וְעָלָה לְרֹאשׁ הַמִּזְבֵּחַ, וּפִנָּה אֶת הַגֶּחָלִים הֵילָךְ וְהֵילָךְ וְחָתָה מִן הַמְאֻכָּלוֹת הַפְּנִימִיּוֹת, וְיָרַד. הִגִּיעַ לָרִצְפָּה, וְהָפַךְ פָּנָיו לַצָּפוֹן, הָלַךְ לְמִזְרָחוֹ שֶׁל כֶּבֶשׁ כְּעֶשֶׂר אַמּוֹת. צָבַר אֶת

Tamid 1:4

The one who merited to clear the ashes would get ready to clear the ashes. They said to him, "Be careful not to touch any vessel until you have washed your hands and feet from the laver. See, the fire-pan is in the corner between the ramp and the altar on the west of the ramp." No one entered with him, nor did he carry any light. Rather, he walked by the light of the altar fire. No one saw him or heard a sound from him until they heard the noise of the wooden wheel that Ben Katin made for hauling up the laver, when they said, "The time has come." He washed his hands and feet from the laver, then took the silver fire-pan and went up to the top of the altar and cleared away the cinders on either side and scooped up the ashes in the center. He then descended, and when he reached the floor he turned his face to the north and went along the east side of the ramp for about ten cubits, and he

then made a heap of the cinders on the floor three handbreadths away from the ramp, in the place where they used to put the crop of the birds, and the ashes from the inner altar, and the ash from the Candelabrum.	הַגֶּחָלִים עַל גַּבֵּי הָרִצְפָּה רָחוֹק מִן הַכֶּבֶשׁ שְׁלֹשָׁה טְפָחִים, מְקוֹם שֶׁנּוֹתְנִין מֻרְאוֹת הָעוֹף וְדִשּׁוּן מִזְבֵּחַ הַפְּנִימִי וְהַמְּנוֹרָה:

To "clear the ashes" meant to clean the altar of the remains of the previous day's offerings so as to prepare it for the work of the new day. On the face of it, one might think of clearing the ashes as menial work, tantamount to collecting the Temple's garbage, but that is not how the Mishna conceived of it. Instead we have a story steeped with drama and mystery: the priest's solitary walk – "No one entered with him," "No one saw him"; the warning as he embarks, as if on a dangerous quest – "They said to him, 'Be careful not to touch any vessel'"; and the tense listening for the sounds that he makes as he walks, culminating in the sense of relief as he arrives at the laver, "when they said, 'The time has come.'"[1]

It is noteworthy in this context that during earlier periods in the Temple, it was not a single, predetermined priest who cleared the ashes, but rather, "he who came first... won the privilege" (Yoma 2:1). The drawing of the lots for the role was instituted only after the original system led to an injury (2:2). Indeed, historically speaking, the solitariness of the priest who cleared the ashes was no more than an unintended consequence of the lots system. And yet, the Mishna chose to describe the clearing of the ashes as a solitary act that a priest engaged in under a cloak of not only mystery, but also intimacy. This intimacy is hinted at in the Mishna's allusions to verses in the Song of Songs:

> The flowers appear on the earth; **the time** of singing **is come**, and **the sound** of the turtledove **is heard** in our land. The fig tree puts forth its green figs, and the vines in blossom give forth their fragrance. Arise, my love, my fair

1. The ceremonial aspect of the work of the priest who clears the ashes is also apparent in the typological number of stages in that work – ten. My thanks to Amnon Dokov for pointing this out.

> one, **and come away**. O my dove, who is **in the clefts** of the rock, in the covert of the cliff, **let me see your countenance, let me hear your voice,** for sweet is your voice, and your countenance is comely. (Song of Songs 2:12–14)

Many words describing the priests waiting for their colleague to return from clearing the ashes seem to be drawn from the Song of Songs 2:12 ("is come," "the sound," "is heard") and 2:14 ("let me see…let me hear your voice"): "No one **saw** him or **heard** a **sound** from him until they **heard** the **sound** of the wooden wheel…when they said, '**The time has come.**'" Further similarity to the Song of Songs can be found in the description of the clearing of the ashes: "[He] went up to the top of the altar and cleared away the cinders on either side (*heilakh v'heilakh*)," which is reminiscent of "Rise up, my love, my fair one, and come away (*ulekhi lakh*)" (Song of Songs 2:10).

The series of allusions casts the clearing of the ashes as a rendezvous in the vein of the Song of Songs – from rectifying the missed chance caused by the woman's laziness to reconstructing her beloved's springtime call to her. In addition to the analogy drawn between the Song of Songs and the clearing of the ashes, there is an internal parallel between the clearing of the ashes and the Mishna's description of the twice-daily incense offering. Furthermore, on Yom Kippur incense would be brought into the Holy of Holies, requiring the high priest to enter the Temple's inner sanctum. The comparisons brought below refer to both types of incense offerings.

First, like the clearing of the ashes, during which "no one entered with him," the incense was also offered in solitude. The Torah says of the Yom Kippur incense offering that "there shall be no man in the Tent of Meeting when he goes in to make atonement in the holy place, until he comes out" (Leviticus 16:17, while the priest who brings the daily incense offering cannot do so until "everyone left" [Tamid 6:3]).

Second, both the priest bringing the incense and the one clearing the ashes would be warned before beginning their tasks: The former would be told, "Be careful not to begin immediately in front of you or else you may burn yourself," (Tamid 6:3) while the latter was warned,

"Be careful not to touch any vessel until you have washed your hands and feet from the laver" (1:4).

Another similarity between clearing ashes and bringing incense is the action itself – in both cases, the priest must take embers from the altar. Furthermore, in describing this action (which in the case of the daily incense offering is not the responsibility of the priest offering the incense), the Mishna repeats itself almost word for word. Regarding the clearing of the ashes, it says:

> [He] took the silver fire-pan and went up to the top of the altar and cleared away the cinders on either side and scooped up the ashes in the center. He then descended. (Tamid 1:4)

And regarding the incense:

> [He] took the silver fire-pan and went up to the top of the altar and cleared away the cinders on either side and scooped up. He then descended. (Tamid 5:5)

The comparison between the two tasks has a surprising implication that completes the link to the meetings in the Song of Songs. Bringing the incense is the "pinnacle" of the Temple rites – it takes place daily inside the Temple and on Yom Kippur inside the Holy of Holies. Bringing the incense is a rite that a priest cannot be chosen for more than once in a lifetime.[2] For the Sages it is the key to the revelation of the Divine Presence. Thus, to compare it to the clearing of the ashes is to imbue a mundane act tantamount to "taking out the garbage" with the quality of the most intimate rite, which establishes the link between the human and the divine.

Ultimately, the figure of the priest who clears the ashes is constructed in the Mishna by way of a double intertextual link – the Song of Songs on one hand, and the bringing of the incense on the other. These

2. See Tamid 5:2.

two literary contexts, separately and combined, cast the clearing of the ashes as an intimate encounter with the sacred.[3]

The Mishna makes a crucial point about divine service. The pinnacle of the relationship with God, the consummation of the love and intimacy described in the Song of Songs, is attained by way of clearing the ashes, a mundane action seemingly tantamount to taking out the garbage. That such significance is attached to such a "trivial" action shows us that more important than external actions and the rituals they entail is the feeling that underlies them, and that "the Holy One, blessed be He, requires the heart" (Sanhedrin 106b). In my view, this path to actualizing the vision of love in the Song of Songs holds true for the relationship between husband and wife as well. To pay attention to the small details in life and the needs of one's partner is to show love – the smaller the details, the greater the love.

---

3. The lot drawn for the clearing of the ashes is the first lot of the day. It is noteworthy that the third lot also alludes to the Song of Songs: Compare "new and old, come and draw lots to see who shall take up the limbs from the ramp to the altar" (Tamid 5:2) to "new and old, which I have laid up for you, O my beloved" (Song of Songs 7:14). And see Braverman, "Biblical Calques in the Mishnah," *Netuim* 10 (2003) [Hebrew]: 12.

As an Apple Tree Among the Trees of the Wood

תמיד ב, ב

הֵחֵלּוּ מַעֲלִין בָּאֵפֶר עַל גַּבֵּי הַתַּפּוּחַ. וְתַפּוּחַ הָיָה בְאֶמְצַע הַמִּזְבֵּחַ, פְּעָמִים עָלָיו כִּשְׁלֹשׁ מֵאוֹת כּוֹר. וּבָרְגָלִים לֹא הָיוּ מְדַשְּׁנִין אוֹתוֹ, מִפְּנֵי שֶׁהוּא נוֹי לַמִּזְבֵּחַ. מִיָּמָיו לֹא נִתְעַצֵּל הַכֹּהֵן מִלְּהוֹצִיא אֶת הַדֶּשֶׁן:

Tamid 2:2

They then began to throw the ashes on to the heap (*tapuaḥ*). This heap was in the middle of the altar, and sometimes there was as much as three hundred *kor* on it. On festivals they did not use to clear away the ash, because it was reckoned an ornament to the altar. It never happened that the priest was neglectful in taking out the ashes.

"As an apple tree (*tapuaḥ*)"

It is apparent that this mishna employs literary devices to glorify the altar. The Babylonian *Amora'im* list the story of the heap in the middle of the altar among the places where the Sages use hyperbole:

> "They made the beast for the daily offering drink from a gold cup." Rabba said: This is an exaggeration. Rabbi Ammi said: ... The Sages used hyperbole in the cases we have just mentioned – the heap, and giving the sacrificial beast to drink from a gold cup. (Tamid 29a)

The *Amora'im* acknowledge the narrative character of the tractate. The massive size of the ash heap is not a legal point or historic fact, but rather an exaggeration meant to embellish the venue and the occasion, as befits a good story. The mishna also cites a typological number – "three hundred *kor*" – the same figure to appear, again in hyperbolic contexts, further along in the dispute:

> Samuel said: In three places the Sages used the language of hyperbole: namely, in connection with the heap, the vine, and the veil… [The exaggeration in the case of] the heap is as stated. In the case of the vine it is as has been taught: A gold vine used to stand at the door of the Sanctuary… Rabbi Elazar son of Rabbi Tzadok said: On one occasion three hundred priests were commissioned to clear it. The case of the veil, as has been taught: We have learned: Rabbi Shimon ben Gamliel says: The thickness of the veil was a handbreadth… and it took three hundred priests to immerse it. (Tamid 29a)

The mishna itself announces its intention to glorify the altar by stating that the heap was considered "an ornament to the altar." I believe that it is not only the heap resting atop the altar that gives it glory; the choice of the Hebrew word *tapuaḥ* (apple or apple tree) to describe the heap is also meant to lend the altar beauty. Aside from the purely aesthetic aspect, this appears to be another allusion to the Song of Songs, where the woman likens her beloved to an apple tree: "As an apple tree among the trees of the wood, so is my beloved among the sons" (Song of Songs 2:3).

The Temple altar is where heaven and earth meet. The connection is established and maintained through the sacrificial offerings as well as via other means, including the ash heap, which symbolizes the beloved. Based on the Sages' allegorical reading of the Song of Songs, which sees the beloved as God, the ash heap, too, represents the Lord, as Rashi says:

> "As an apple tree" – when an apple tree is among trees that do not bear fruit, it is more precious than all of them, for its fruit is good both in taste and in fragrance. "So is my beloved among the sons" – among the young men. The

> allegory is: So is the Holy One, blessed be He, superior to all the gods. Therefore, "in His shade I delighted and sat." (Rashi on Song of Songs 2:3)

Thus, the likening of the top of the altar to an apple tree alludes to and deepens the role of the altar in the relationship between God and the Jewish people. This is also how the Zohar interpreted the image of the apple tree: "Rabbi Elazar opened, saying, 'As an apple tree among the trees of the wood etc.' 'As an apple tree' – that is the Holy One, blessed be He" (Zohar, *Lekh Lekha* 85a).

It is also worth noting that Rabbi Yoḥanan (Sukka 49a) highlights the idea of the altar as the meeting point of lovers: "The drainpipes built into the altar and extending beneath it were created from the six days of Creation, as it is stated: '[How beautiful are your steps in sandals, O prince's daughter!] The hidden of your thighs are like the links of a chain, the work of the hands of a skilled workman' (Song of Songs 7:2)." The Gemara interprets the verse homiletically: "'The hidden of your thighs' – these are the drainpipes that are concealed within the altar."

In the Song of Songs the apple tree serves a dual role – as one of the woman's images for her beloved, as we have seen, and as the meeting place for the beloved and the woman:

> Who is this that comes up from the wilderness, leaning upon her beloved? Under the apple tree I awakened you; there your mother was in travail with you; there she was in travail and brought you forth. (Song of Songs 8:5)

Here too the Mishna offers an opportunity for rectifying the missed encounter in the Song of Songs – by suggesting the altar as a place for the woman and her beloved to meet.[1] The idea expressed here is similar to the idea that appears in the Midrash, to the effect that the sacrifices were

1. Another allusion to the story in the Song of Songs is the statement in the mishna that "It never happened that the priest was neglectful in taking out the ashes." One wonders why such an assertion needs to be made – are we to assume that ordinarily the priests tend to neglect their holy duties? And even if there were a Temple task

an actualization of the missed meeting of the woman and her beloved: "'Let my beloved come into his garden' – that is the Divine Presence; 'and eat his precious fruits' – those are the burnt offerings" (*Seder Olam Rabba* 7). Later in the chapter we will revisit the claim that the ash heap indeed represents the beloved.

"Among the trees of the wood"

> They then began to take up the logs to place onto the fire. Were all kinds of wood valid for the fire? Yes! All kinds of wood were valid for the fire except vine and olive wood. But what they mostly used were boughs of fig trees and of nut trees and of oil trees. (Tamid 2:3)
>
> He then arranged a large pile on the east side of the altar, with its open side on the east, while the inner ends of the [selected] logs touched the ash heap. Spaces were left between the logs in which they kindled the brushwood. (Tamid 2:4)

Once again we encounter a mishna constructed in the form of a question and an answer: "Were all kinds of wood valid for the fire? Yes! All kinds of wood were valid for the fire except vine and olive wood." Once again, special interest is generated, in this case around the question of the choice of wood. Almost all of the types of wood cited by the Mishna appear in the Song of Songs: The vine – "to see whether the vine budded" (6:11); the fig – "The fig-tree put forth its green figs" (2:13); and the nut – "I went down into the garden of nuts" (6:11). The nut is also unique in that this is its only mention in the Bible.

The ash heap (*tapuaḥ*) of the altar, like the apple tree (*tapuaḥ*) of the Song of Songs, is surrounded by trees – "As an apple tree among the trees of the wood, so is my beloved among the sons."

---

that few priests were enthusiastic about, is that something the Mishna would wish to teach us? But seen in light of the link to the Song of Songs, it is clear: the Mishna is ruling out the kind of lethargy that precipitated the woman's downfall.

My Beloved Put in His Hand by the Hole of the Door

תמיד ג, ו

מִי שֶׁזָּכָה בְדִשּׁוּן מִזְבֵּחַ הַפְּנִימִי וְהַמְּנוֹרָה הָיוּ מַקְדִּימִין, וְאַרְבָּעָה כֵלִים בְּיָדָם, הַטֶּנִי וְהַכּוּז וּשְׁתֵּי מַפְתְּחוֹת. הַטֶּנִי דוֹמֶה לְתַרְקָב גָּדוֹל שֶׁל זָהָב, מַחֲזִיק קַבַּיִן וָחֵצִי, וְהַכּוּז דּוֹמֶה לְקִתּוֹן גָּדוֹל שֶׁל זָהָב. וּשְׁתֵּי מַפְתְּחוֹת, אֶחָד יוֹרֵד לְאַמַּת הַשֶּׁחִי, וְאֶחָד פּוֹתֵחַ כֵּיוָן:

Tamid 3:6–7

Those who had won the right to clear the ashes from the inner altar and from the Candelabrum would go first, with four vessels in their hands: the *teni*, the *kuz*, and two keys. The *teni* resembled a large *tarkav* of gold and held two and a half *kav*. The *kuz* resembled a large gold pitcher. And two keys: One of the two keys would reach down to the "*amah* of the armpit" and the other opens immediately.

בָּא לוֹ לְפִשְׁפָּשׁ הַצְּפוֹנִי. וּשְׁנֵי פִשְׁפָּשִׁין הָיוּ לוֹ לְשַׁעַר הַגָּדוֹל, אֶחָד בַּצָּפוֹן וְאֶחָד בַּדָּרוֹם. שֶׁבַּדָּרוֹם לֹא נִכְנַס בּוֹ אָדָם מֵעוֹלָם, וְעָלָיו הוּא מְפוֹרָשׁ עַל יְדֵי יְחֶזְקֵאל (יחזקאל מד), וַיֹּאמֶר אֵלַי ה', הַשַּׁעַר הַזֶּה סָגוּר יִהְיֶה לֹא יִפָּתֵחַ וְאִישׁ לֹא יָבֹא בוֹ כִּי ה' אֱלֹקֵי יִשְׂרָאֵל בָּא בוֹ וְהָיָה סָגוּר. נָטַל אֶת

He then came to the small opening on the north. The great gate had two small openings, one on the north and one on the south. No one ever went in by the opening on the south, about which it is stated explicitly in Ezekiel, "And the Lord said to me, 'This gate shall be closed; it shall not be opened, and no man shall enter by it, for the Lord God of Israel has entered by it" (Ezekiel 44:2). He took the key and opened the small opening, and

הַמַּפְתֵּחַ וּפָתַח אֶת הַפִּשְׁפָּשׁ, נִכְנַס לַתָּא, וּמִן הַתָּא אֶל הַהֵיכָל, עַד שֶׁהוּא מַגִּיעַ לְשַׁעַר הַגָּדוֹל. הִגִּיעַ לְשַׁעַר הַגָּדוֹל הֶעֱבִיר אֶת הַנֶּגֶר וְאֶת הַפּוֹתְחוֹת וּפְתָחוֹ. לֹא הָיָה שׁוֹחֵט הַשּׁוֹחֵט, עַד שֶׁשּׁוֹמֵעַ קוֹל שַׁעַר הַגָּדוֹל שֶׁנִּפְתַּח:

went into the cell, and from the cell to the Sanctuary, until he reached the great gate. When he reached the great gate he drew back the bolt and the latches and opened it. The slaughterer did not slaughter until he heard the sound of the great gate being opened.

After the *tamid* sacrifice was taken from the chamber of lambs, the priest would arrive to open the Sanctuary, marking the end of the preparation stage and the beginning of the day's rites.

In order to open the Sanctuary, the priest would "reach down to the '*amah* of the armpit,'" meaning insert his entire arm, all the way to the armpit, through a hole in the door, and he would unlock the first lock. Then he would use a second key that apparently would unlock the door from the inside. This image resurfaces the memory of the missed encounter between the beloved knocking on the door from the outside and the woman who does not open it in time: "My beloved put in his hand by the hole of the door" (Song of Songs 5:4).

However, in this reenacted rendezvous the roles are reversed. If previously the Mishna cast the priest in the role of the woman awaiting her beloved, here the priest stands for the beloved, who has come to open the door, on the other side of which is God, representing the woman. It is noteworthy that the Songs of Songs is itself rife with similar role reversals.

It seems that our chapter draws its imagery from two scenes in the Songs of Songs: the missed encounter between the woman and the beloved in Chapter 5, which we discussed above, and the entrance into the king's chambers in Chapter 1, which is likened here to the priest's entrance into the Sanctuary. In its opening chapter, the Song of Songs reads, "**Draw me**, we will run **after you**; the king has brought me into his chambers" (1:4), which the previous mishna alludes to:

> The priest who had won the right to slaughter the *tamid* **draws it** with him to the slaughterhouse, and those who

> had won the right to bring the limbs up followed **after him**. (Tamid 3:5)

So far we have been discussing the encounter between the priest and God. Here we come upon another motif – the sacrifice offered to God represents the woman. On the face of it, this is an extraordinary assertion, but the truth is that it is far from unusual for sacrifices in the Temple to stand in for people.[1] Furthermore, the phrasing of mishna 3:4 in our tractate anthropomorphizes the sacrifice: "They gave the animal for the daily sacrifice a drink from a cup of gold." Just as the sacrifice is drawn to the king, its slaughter is timed to coincide with the hour when the king's doors are opened.

We can detect in the description of the *tamid* sacrifice traces of two contrasting and complementary images: that of the priest as the beloved, trying to open the door to the woman, and, in contrast, that of the *tamid* sacrifice as the woman, drawn into the chambers of the king. God is both the woman and the beloved: He is the object of the beloved's desire, standing at the door, and He is the Beloved, the king, to whose chambers the woman runs.

It is important to note that the dwelling of the Divine Presence in the Sanctuary is especially pronounced in this description. The southern gate (small opening) is closed – "No one ever went in by [that opening]" – but in contrast to the beloved, whose entry is prevented by the closed door, here the shuttered gate does not prevent God from entering and dwelling in the Sanctuary. On the contrary, the closed opening, as we learn from the verse in Ezekiel, is itself evidence of God's entry and dwelling. Thus, we can understand why the Mishna devotes so many words to describing the role of the southern opening, which has no direct connection to the *tamid* sacrifice.

---

1. See the Binding of Isaac: "And Abraham went and took the ram, and offered him up for a burnt offering instead of his son" (Genesis 22:13). And see, too, Mishna Tamid 4:1: "They would not tie up the lamb but rather they would bind its legs together (*me'akkedin*)." This alludes to the idea that the *tamid* is a reenactment of the Binding of (*akeidat*) Isaac.

In the Song of Songs, for the woman, the door is opened in a time of crisis – but then she discovers that her beloved is gone. With the *tamid*, on the other hand, the gate is opened for an encounter – "The slaughterer did not slaughter till he heard the sound of the great gate being opened."

Toward the end of Tractate Tamid there is a prayer: "This was the order of the regular daily sacrifice for the service of the house of our Lord. May it be His will that it be rebuilt speedily in our days, Amen" (7:3). Our tractate perpetuates the powerful religious feelings toward the Temple. It lends literary expression to the idea that the Temple service was not mere empty ritual, but rather a framework for consummating the burning love and passion between the human and the divine.

> For all the writings are holy but the Song of Songs is the Holy of Holies. (Yadayim 3:5)

Revealing the Heart

תמיד ד, ב-ג

לֹא הָיָה שׁוֹבֵר בּוֹ אֶת הָרֶגֶל, אֶלָּא נוֹקְבוֹ מִתּוֹךְ עַרְכּוּבוֹ וְתוֹלֶה בּוֹ. הָיָה מַפְשִׁיט וְיוֹרֵד עַד שֶׁהוּא מַגִּיעַ לֶחָזֶה. הִגִּיעַ לֶחָזֶה, חָתַךְ אֶת הָרֹאשׁ וּנְתָנוֹ לְמִי שֶׁזָּכָה בּוֹ. חָתַךְ אֶת הַכְּרָעַיִם וּנְתָנָן לְמִי שֶׁזָּכָה בָהֶן. מֵרַק אֶת הַהֶפְשֵׁט. קָרַע אֶת הַלֵּב וְהוֹצִיא אֶת דָּמוֹ. חָתַךְ אֶת הַיָּדַיִם וּנְתָנָן לְמִי שֶׁזָּכָה בָהֶן. עָלָה לְרֶגֶל הַיְמָנִית, חֲתָכָהּ וּנְתָנָהּ לְמִי שֶׁזָּכָה בָהּ, וּשְׁתֵּי בֵיצִים עִמָּהּ. קְרָעוֹ, וְנִמְצָא כֻלּוֹ גָּלוּי לְפָנָיו. נָטַל אֶת הַפֶּדֶר וּנְתָנוֹ עַל בֵּית שְׁחִיטַת הָרֹאשׁ מִלְמַעְלָן. נָטַל אֶת הַקְּרָבַיִם וּנְתָנָן לְמִי שֶׁזָּכָה בָהֶם לַהֲדִיחָן. וְהַכֶּרֶס מְדִיחִין אוֹתָהּ בְּבֵית מְדִיחִין כָּל צָרְכָּהּ. וְהַקְּרָבַיִם מְדִיחִין אוֹתָן שְׁלֹשָׁה פְעָמִים בִּמְעוּטָהּ, עַל שֻׁלְחָנוֹת שֶׁל שַׁיִשׁ שֶׁבֵּין הָעַמּוּדִים:

Tamid 4:2–3

He did not break the hind leg, but he made a hole in it at the [knee] joint and suspended it from there. He then began to flay it until he came to the breast. When he came to the breast he cut off the head and gave it to the one who merited [bringing it onto the ramp]. He then cut off the hind legs [up to the knees] and gave them to the one who merited [bringing them onto the ramp]. He then finished the flaying. He tore out the heart and squeezed out the blood in it. He then cut off the forelegs and gave them to the one who merited [bringing them onto the ramp]. He then went back up to the right hind leg and cut it off and gave it to the one who merited [to bring it onto the ramp], and the two testicles with it. He then tore it [the remaining carcass] open so that it was all exposed before him. He took the fat and put it on top of the place where the head had been severed. He took the innards and gave them to the one who had merited washing them. The stomach was washed very thoroughly in the washing chamber, while the entrails were washed at least three times on marble tables that stood between the pillars.

נָטַל אֶת הַסַּכִּין וְהִפְרִישׁ אֶת הָרֵיאָה מִן הַכָּבֵד, וְאֶצְבַּע הַכָּבֵד מִן הַכָּבֵד, וְלֹא הָיָה מְזִיזָהּ מִמְּקוֹמָהּ. נָקַב אֶת הֶחָזֶה וּנְתָנוֹ לְמִי שֶׁזָּכָה בוֹ. עָלָה לְדֹפֶן הַיְמָנִית, הָיָה חוֹתֵךְ וְיוֹרֵד עַד הַשִּׁדְרָה, וְלֹא הָיָה נוֹגֵעַ בַּשִּׁדְרָה, עַד שֶׁהוּא מַגִּיעַ לִשְׁתֵּי צְלָעוֹת רַכּוֹת. חֲתָכָהּ וּנְתָנָהּ לְמִי שֶׁזָּכָה בָהּ, וְהַכָּבֵד תְּלוּיָה בָהּ. בָּא לוֹ לַגֵּרָה, וְהִנִּיחַ בָּהּ שְׁתֵּי צְלָעוֹת מִכָּאן וּשְׁתֵּי צְלָעוֹת מִכָּאן.

חֲתָכָהּ וּנְתָנָהּ לְמִי שֶׁזָּכָה בָהּ, וְהַקָּנֶה וְהַלֵּב וְהָרֵיאָה תְּלוּיִים בָּהּ. בָּא לוֹ לְדֹפֶן הַשְּׂמָאלִית, וְהִנִּיחַ בָּהּ שְׁתֵּי צְלָעוֹת רַכּוֹת מִלְמַעְלָן וּשְׁתֵּי צְלָעוֹת רַכּוֹת מִלְּמַטָּן. וְכָךְ הָיָה מַנִּיחַ בַּחֲבֶרְתָּהּ. נִמְצָא מַנִּיחַ בִּשְׁתֵּיהֶן שְׁתַּיִם שְׁתַּיִם מִלְמַעְלָן וּשְׁתַּיִם שְׁתַּיִם מִלְּמַטָּן. חֲתָכָהּ וּנְתָנָהּ לְמִי שֶׁזָּכָה בָהּ, וְהַשִּׁדְרָה עִמָּהּ, וְהַטְּחוֹל תָּלוּי בָּהּ, וְהִיא הָיְתָה גְדוֹלָה, אֶלָּא שֶׁל יָמִין קוֹרִין גְּדוֹלָה, שֶׁהַכָּבֵד תְּלוּיָה בָהּ.

בָּא לוֹ לָעֹקֶץ, חוֹתְכוֹ וּנְתָנוֹ לְמִי שֶׁזָּכָה בוֹ, וְאַלְיָה וְאֶצְבַּע הַכָּבֵד וּשְׁתֵּי כְלָיוֹת עִמּוֹ. נָטַל רֶגֶל הַשְּׂמָאלִית וּנְתָנָהּ לְמִי שֶׁזָּכָה בָהּ. נִמְצְאוּ כֻלָּן עוֹמְדִין בַּשּׁוּרָה וְהָאֵבָרִים בְּיָדָם.

הָרִאשׁוֹן, בָּרֹאשׁ וּבָרֶגֶל. הָרֹאשׁ בִּימִינוֹ, וְחָטְמוֹ כְּלַפֵּי

He then took a knife and separated the lung from the liver and the finger of the liver from the liver, but he did not remove it from its place. He cut out the breast and gave it to the one who had merited [bringing it onto the ramp]. He came up to the right flank and cut into it, and went down as far as the spine, without touching the spine, until he came to the place between two small ribs. He cut it off and gave it to the one who had merited [bringing it onto the ramp], with the liver attached to it.

He then came to the neck, and he left two ribs on each side of it, cut it off and gave it to the one who had merited [bringing it onto the ramp], with the windpipe and the heart and the lung attached to it. He then came to the left flank, in which he left the two thin ribs above and two thin ribs below; and he had done similarly with the other flank. Thus he left two on each side above and two on each side below. He cut it off and gave it to the one who had merited [bringing it onto the ramp], and the spine with it and the spleen attached to it. This was really the largest piece, but the right flank was called the largest, because the liver was attached to it. He then came to the tailbone, which he cut off, and he gave it to the one who had merited [bringing it onto the ramp], along with the tail, the finger of the liver, and the two kidneys. He then took the left hind leg and cut it off and gave it to the one who had merited [bringing it onto the ramp]. Thus they were all standing in a row with the limbs in their hands. The first had the head and the [right] hind leg. The head was in his right hand with its

זְרוֹעוֹ, וְקַרְנָיו בֵּין אֶצְבְּעוֹתָיו, וּבֵית שְׁחִיטָתוֹ מִלְמַעְלָן, וְהַפֶּדֶר נָתוּן עָלֶיהָ. וְהָרֶגֶל שֶׁל יָמִין בִּשְׂמֹאלוֹ, וּבֵית עוֹרוֹ לַחוּץ. הַשֵּׁנִי, בִּשְׁתֵּי יָדַיִם. שֶׁל יָמִין בִּימִינוֹ, שֶׁל שְׂמֹאל בִּשְׂמֹאלוֹ, וּבֵית עוֹרָן לַחוּץ. הַשְּׁלִישִׁי, בָּעֹקֶץ וּבָרֶגֶל. הָעֹקֶץ בִּימִינוֹ, וְהָאַלְיָה מְדַלְדֶּלֶת בֵּין אֶצְבְּעוֹתָיו, וְאֶצְבַּע הַכָּבֵד וּשְׁתֵּי הַכְּלָיוֹת עִמּוֹ, הָרֶגֶל שֶׁל שְׂמֹאל בִּשְׂמֹאלוֹ, וּבֵית עוֹרוֹ לַחוּץ. הָרְבִיעִי, בֶּחָזֶה וּבַגֵּרָה. הֶחָזֶה בִּימִינוֹ, וְהַגֵּרָה בִּשְׂמֹאלוֹ, וְצַלְעוֹתֶיהָ בֵּין אֶצְבְּעוֹתָיו. הַחֲמִישִׁי, בִּשְׁתֵּי דְפָנוֹת. שֶׁל יָמִין בִּימִינוֹ, וְשֶׁל שְׂמֹאל בִּשְׂמֹאלוֹ, וּבֵית עוֹרָן לַחוּץ. הַשִּׁשִּׁי, בַּקְּרָבַיִם הַנְּתוּנִין בְּבָזָךְ וּכְרָעַיִם עַל גַּבֵּיהֶם מִלְמַעְלָה. הַשְּׁבִיעִי, בַּסֹּלֶת. הַשְּׁמִינִי, בַּחֲבִתִּין. הַתְּשִׁיעִי, בַּיַּיִן. הָלְכוּ וּנְתָנוּם מֵחֲצִי הַכֶּבֶשׁ וּלְמַטָּה בְּמַעֲרָבוֹ, וּמְלָחוּם. וְיָרְדוּ וּבָאוּ לָהֶם לְלִשְׁכַּת הַגָּזִית, לִקְרוֹת אֶת שְׁמַע:

nose toward his arm, its horns between his fingers, and the place where it was severed turned upward with the fat covering it. The right hind leg was in his left hand with the place where the flaying began turned away from him. The second had the two forelegs, the right hind leg in his right hand and the left in his left hand, the place where the flaying began turned away from him. The third had the tailbone and the other hind leg, the tailbone in his right hand with the tail hanging between his fingers and the finger of the liver and the two kidneys with it, and the left hind leg in his left hand with the place where the flaying began turned away from him. The fourth had the breast and the neck, the breast in his right hand and the neck in his left hand, its ribs being between two of his fingers. The fifth had the two flanks, the right one in his right hand, and the left one in his left hand, with the place where the flaying began turned away from him. The sixth had the innards on a platter with the knees on top of them. The seventh had the fine flour. The eighth had the griddle cakes. The ninth had the wine. They went and placed them on the lower half of the ramp on its western side, and salted them (see Leviticus 2:13). They then came down and went to the Chamber of Hewn Stone to recite *Shema*.

These mishnayot describe the butchering of the slaughtered animal. One could think they are distastefully graphic, playing up a grim reality of the Temple as an "abattoir," but the atmosphere that emerges is of an entirely different order. The language of the Mishna is steeped in imagery invoking a journey or procession: "Until he came to… when he came to... He then went back up... He came up... and went down... until he came to... He then came to... He then came to... He then came to..."[1] The language suggests that beyond the external level of the realities of the Temple service there is the internal spiritual dimension. Furthermore, the phrase "and [he] gave it to the one who had **merited**" recurs eleven times in these mishnayot. The style expresses the idea that there is nothing distasteful here, but rather a special privilege.

In previous chapters we saw how the Mishna shapes an analogy between the sacrifice offered to God and the image of the woman in the Song of Songs. Based on these insights we can perceive another aspect of the anthropomorphizing of the sacrificial animal. Tractate Tamid has seven chapters, which places the fourth chapter in the middle – the heart of the tractate. And the second of the chapter's three mishnayot is 4:2, the heart of the chapter. And indeed, at the heart of the tractate, in 4:2, we encounter the heart: "He tore out the heart and squeezed out the blood in it."[2] The lamb, which represents a human being, ascends to heaven pure, its heart torn – seemingly a symbolic realization of the verse "And tear your heart, and not your garments, and turn to the Lord your God" (Joel 2:13).

Later the mishna says, "He then tore it [the remaining carcass] open so that it was all exposed before him." Why does the mishna need to note that the entire lamb was exposed before the priest who butchered the carcass? It seems that this emphasis is meant to highlight the manner in which the sacrifice signifies standing before God. In rabbinic literature, the expression "all exposed before Him" denotes God's omniscience, how He searches the innermost parts of the belly:

> But what if not **everything is exposed before Him**? Indeed, the verse already states (Psalms 78:36–37), "But they beguiled Him with their mouth, and lied to Him with their tongue. For their heart was not steadfast with

1. Compare to the Mishna's description of the high priest's entry into the Holy of Holies; the language of the entry lends an aura of a spiritual experience (Yoma 5:1–4).
2. There is also special significance to the middle mishna (5:1) of Tractate Yoma, for it tells of the tractate's main occurrence – the priest's entry into the Holy of Holies.

> Him, nor were they faithful in His covenant." (Tosefta Bava Kama 7:9)

When a sacrifice is offered, metaphorical ideas like "torn heart" and "all exposed" are made flesh, and the sacrifice is imbued with symbolic meaning.

The first mishna in our chapter hints at another spiritual symbol: "They would not tie up the lamb but rather they would bind its legs together (*me'akkedin*)." The choice of the word *me'akkedin* alludes to the idea that sacrificing the *tamid* reenacts the Binding of (*akeidat*) Isaac.[3] This insight ties into traditions that the altar stood in the spot where the Binding of Isaac took place.[4] The link to the Binding of Isaac also emerges from the words of Abraham in the following midrash, which is rife with expressions that appear in our chapter:

> **It is exposed and known before You** that at the time You said to me, "Take your son, your only one," **it was in my heart** to reply against You. (Leviticus Rabba 29)
>
> Abraham, aware of the extent of God's knowledge, asks of Him:
>
> So, just as I could have replied against You, but I suppressed my desire and did not argue with You…so too, when the children of Isaac come into transgressions and bad deeds, keep in mind for them the binding of Isaac their father, and rise from the seat of judgment to the seat of mercy and be filled with mercy for them. (Leviticus Rabba 29)

May it come to pass that by virtue of the sacrifices, Abraham's prayer for mercy will be answered.

3. This is also how the Talmud relates to this mishna in a *baraita*: "The foreleg and the hind leg [tied together] like the binding of Isaac the son of Abraham" (Tamid 31b).
4. *Mishneh Torah, Hilkhot Beit HaBeḥira* 2:1–2.

Bibliography

Albeck, Hanoch. *Mishna*. Tel Aviv: Dvir, 1952 [Hebrew].

Alon, Gedalyahu. "On Philo's Halakha." In *Jews, Judaism, and the Classical World: Studies in Jewish History in the Times of the Second Temple and Talmud*. Jerusalem: Magnes Press, Hebrew University: 1977.

Benovitz, Moshe. "Substitute Vow Formulas." *Sidra* 12 (1996) [Hebrew].

Brand, Yitzhak. "With Trumpets and Sound of the Horn Shout Before the King, the Lord." *Daf Kesher: A Newsletter for the Students of Har Etzion* 300 (1991) [Hebrew].

Braverman, Nathan. "Biblical Calques in the Mishna." *Netuim* 10 (2003) [Hebrew]: 9–17.

Breuer, Mordechai. *Pirkei Mo'adot*. Jerusalem: Horev Press, 1986 [Hebrew].

Carlebach, Shlomo. *The Heart of Heaven – Passover*. Jerusalem: Self-published, 2008 [Hebrew].

Epstein Jacob Nahum. *Introduction to Tannaitic Literature*. Jerusalem: Magnes Press, 1957 [Hebrew].

Epstein Jacob Nahum. *Introduction to the Mishnaic Text*. Jerusalem: Magnes Press, 1964 [Hebrew].

Fleischer, Ezra. "On the Beginnings of Obligatory Jewish Prayer." *Tarbiz* 59 (1990) [Hebrew].

Fox, Menachem (Harry). "The Joy of the Place of Drawing." *Tarbiz* 55 (1986) [Hebrew].

Fox, Menachem (Harry). *A Critical Edition of Tractate Succah with Introduction and Notes*. PhD diss., Hebrew University of Jerusalem, 1979 [Hebrew].

Genack, Dani. "Notes on Tractate Yoma." In *K'sones Yosef: In Tribute to Our Illustrious Teacher and Friend Rabbi Joseph Wanefsky*.

New York: Rabbi Isaac Elchanon Theological Seminary, 2002 [Hebrew].

Goldberg, Avraham. *Commentary to the Mishna: Shabbat*. New York: Jewish Theological Seminary of America, 1976 [Hebrew].

Goldschmidt, Daniel. *The Goldschmidt Passover Haggadah*. Jerusalem: Bialik Press, 1960 [Hebrew].

Hacohen, Aviya. *Appearing Before the Lord: Essays on Tractate Ḥagiga*. Ein Tzurim: Mishlavim, 2016 [Hebrew].

Kaplan, Aryeh. *Jewish Meditation: A Practical Guide*. New York: Schocken Books, 1985.

Kaplan, Aryeh. *Meditation and Kabbalah*. Boston: Weiser Books, 1986.

Kaplan, Aryeh. *Sefer Yetzirah: The Book of Creation*. Boston: Weiser Books, 1997.

Knohl, Israel, and Shlomo Naeh. "Milluim Ve-Kippurim." *Tarbiz* 62 (1992) [Hebrew].

Knohl, Israel. "A Parasha Concerned with Accepting the Kingdom of Heaven." *Tarbiz* 53 (1984) [Hebrew].

Kook, Rabbi Zvi Yehuda. *Lenetivot Israel*. Beit El: Me'avnei Hamakom, 2002.

Levenson, Jon. *Sinai and Zion*. Minneapolis: Harper One, 1985.

Luzzatto, Moshe Chaim. "Mishkanei Elyon" (Exalted Towers). In *Ginzei HaRamḥal*. Bnei Brak, 1984 [Hebrew].

Mandel, Pinchas. "There Were No Days of Joy in Israel Greater Than the Fifteenth of Av and Yom Kippur: On the Final Mishna in Tractate Taanit and Its Evolution." *Teudah* 11 (1996) [Hebrew].

Milgrom, Jacob. *Leviticus 1–16*. New York: Doubleday, 1991.

Mowinckel, Sigmund. *The Psalms in Israel's Worship*. Oxford: Basil Blackwell, 1962.

Naeh, Shlomo. "Creates the Fruit of Lips: A Phenomenological Study of Prayer According to Mishnah Berakhot 4:3, 5:5." *Tarbiz* 63 (1994) [Hebrew].

Nagen, Yakov. *Sukkot in Rabbinical Thought: Motifs in the Halakha of Sukkot in Talmudic Literature*. PhD diss., Hebrew University of Jerusalem, 2003 [Hebrew].

Nagen, Yakov. *Water, Creation, and Divinity: Sukkot in the Philosophy of Halakha*. Jerusalem: Maggid Books, 2008 [Hebrew].

Patai, Raphael. *Man and Land*. Jerusalem: Hebrew University Press, 1942–43 [Hebrew].

Patai, Raphael. *Man and Temple in Jewish Myth and Ritual*. New York: Ktav Publishing House, 1967.

Perry, Motti. "Parallels Converge: Notes on the Literary Structure of Mishna Yoma." *Netuim* 13 (2005) [Hebrew].

Pines, Shlomo, trans. *The Guide of the Perplexed*. Chicago: University of Chicago Press, 1974.

Rosenberg, Shimon Gershon (Shagar). *They Love You Unto Death*. Efrat: Bina L'Itim, 2004 [Hebrew].

Rosenson, Yisrael. "Aggadic Elements in Mishnayot Tractate Berakhot." *Netuim* 2 (1994) [Hebrew].

Rosset, Ehud. "On Mishnah Instruction Using the Method of In-Depth Analysis – Berakhot 9:2 and Megillah 4:2." *Netuim* 1 (1994) [Hebrew].

Rubenstein, Jeffrey. *The History of Sukkot During the Second Temple and Rabbinic Periods*. Atlanta: Scholars Press, 1995.

Safrai, Shmuel. *In the Days of the Temple and in the Days of the Mishnah: Studies in the History of Israel*. Jerusalem: Magnes Press, 1994 [Hebrew].

Safrai, Shmuel. *Pilgrimage in the Time of the Second Temple*. Tel Aviv: Am Hasefer, 1965 [Hebrew].

Saint-Exupery, Antoine de. *The Little Prince*. https://www.tbr.fun/the-little-prince-chapter-1.

Schremer, Adiel. *Male and Female He Created Them: Jewish Marriage in Late Second Temple, Mishnah and Talmud Periods*. Jerusalem: The Zalman Shazar Center for Jewish History, 2003 [Hebrew].

Sharf, Erel. "An Omer is the Tenth Part of an Ephah." *Alon Shvut* 147 (1996) [Hebrew].

Shaviv, Yehuda. "Why Did Tractate Shabbat Open with the Laws of Transferring." In *Batzir Aviezer*. Alon Shvut: Zomet, 1990 [Hebrew].

Soloveitchik, Joseph. "Defining the Commandment to Blow the Shofar." *Mesorah* 6 (1991) [Hebrew].

Sperber, Daniel. "A Study of the Bar Kokhba Coins." *Sinai* 55:1–2 (1964) [Hebrew].

Tabory, Joseph. *The Passover Ritual Throughout the Generations.* Tel Aviv: Hakibbutz Hameuchad, 2002 [Hebrew].

Urbach, Ephraim E. "Asceticism and Suffering in the Talmudic and Mishnaic Sources." In Yitzchak F. Baer Jubilee Volume on the Occasion of His Seventieth Birthday. Jerusalem: Historical Society of Israel, 1960 [Hebrew].

Urbach, Ephraim E. "Review of 'Passover Haggadah,' by Daniel Goldschmidt." *Kiryat Sefer* 36, no. 2 (March 1961) [Hebrew]: 143–150.

Urbach, Ephraim E. *The World of the Sages: Collected Essays.* Jerusalem: Magnes Press, 1988 [Hebrew].

Urbach, Ephraim E. *The Sages: Their Concepts and Beliefs.* Jerusalem: Magnes Press, 1975.

Walfish, Avraham. "Literary Considerations in the Redaction of the Mishnah and Their Meanings." *Netuim* 1 (1994) [Hebrew].

Walfish, Avraham. "Response: To S. Naeh, 'Creates the Fruit of Lips.'" *Tarbiz* 65 (1996) [Hebrew].

Walfish, Avraham. "Teaching the Mishnah as a Literary Text." In *Teaching Classical Rabbinic Texts: Studies in Jewish Education.* Vol. 8. Jerusalem: Magnes Press, 2003.

Walfish, Avraham. "Wordplays in Mishnah." *Netuim* 2 (1995) [Hebrew].

Walfish, Avraham. *Literary Phenomena in Mishnah and their Redactorial and Conceptual Meaning.* Master's thesis, Hebrew University of Jerusalem, 1994 [Hebrew].

Walfish, Avraham. *The Literary Method of Redaction in Mishnah based on Tractate Rosh HaShanah.* PhD diss., Hebrew University of Jerusalem, 2001 [Hebrew].

Yuval, Israel. "The Haggadah of Passover and Easter." *Tarbiz* 65 (1996) [Hebrew].

Zakovitch, Yair. *Through the Looking Glass: Reflection Stories in the Bible.* Tel Aviv: Hakibbutz Hameuchad, 1995 [Hebrew].

Zevin, Shlomo. *In the Light of the Law.* Beit El: Beit El Library 1977 [Hebrew].

Zlotnick, Dov. *The Iron Pillar Mishnah: Redaction, Form and Intent.* Jerusalem: Bialik Institute, 1988.

Index to Mishnayot by Letter of Hebrew Alphabet

It is customary to learn mishnayot during the week of mourning after a death, in memory of the departed, where the opening letter of each mishna spells out the Hebrew name of the departed. Note that not all of the mishnayot appear in the book in their entirety. Also, the book does not include mishnayot beginning with the letters ג, ט, צ; these can be found as follows: ג – Pe'ah 5:1; ט – Yoma 4:1; צ – Moed Katan 1:4.

Acknowledgments

Were our mouth as full of song as the sea, and our tongue as full of joyous song as its multitude of waves... we still could not thank You sufficiently, Lord our God and God of our ancestors.

– *Nishmat Kol Ḥai*

I wish to thank my students at Otniel Yeshiva for the ideas that came up during our studies together and which enriched this book. Special thanks go to the yeshiva's heads, Rabbis Benni Kalmanzon and Re'em Hacohen, and to our Director, Ronen Katz, for a *beit midrash* steeped in the light of Torah and an atmosphere of creativity and freedom.

My gratitude extends to my Rebbe, Rabbi Shmuel Nacham, who taught me that the essential element in the study of Torah are the questions we ask. I devote my life to the study and teaching of Torah because of him. Thank you also to my teacher Rabbi Avraham Walfish, who developed and taught me new methodologies for the study of Mishna.

I am grateful to the team of talented people at Maggid Books. At every stage they have given their input with warmth and dedication, professionalism and marvelous advice. In particular I thank the publisher Matthew Miller; my dear friend, chairman of the editorial board Rabbi Reuven Ziegler and the marketing director Yehudit Singer-Freud.

Thank you to Elie Leshem, who produced a superb translation and succeeded in the daunting task of making a work of rabbinical literature lively and readable in English without sacrificing detail. And to Ilana Sobel, the copy editor, whose professionalism, sensitivity, and fine-tuning gave the book the voice for which I had hoped. Each of you transformed the process of putting out a book from being merely a means to an end to a partnership of joint creativity and vision. Thank you also Yehudit Cohen for the beautiful cover, Estie Dishon for a layout that is pleasing to the eye, and Faigy Badian for her precise proofreading.

I am grateful to my dear friends, Raanan and Nicole Agus and Shimon and Rachel Laufer, who, together with the Targum Shlishi foundation and its director, Aryeh Rubin, supported publication of this book. Finally, I thank my uncle and aunt, Gershon and Ayala Barnett. The support of their foundation has freed me to devote time to writing.

A partner in this book, as in all of my life, has been my wife, Michal. The roots of this book – including love for all human beings and a fusion of Torah and faith with intellectual breadth, openness, and curiosity – were instilled in me by my parents, Azriel and Ahuva Genack. I dedicate this book to them, with love and appreciation.

Yakov Nagen